Propositions for Studio Inquiry

Artwork Scholarship: International Perspectives in Education

Series editors: Anita Sinner and Rita L. Irwin

Print ISSN: 2632-7872 | **Online ISSN:** 2632-9182

The aim of Artwork Scholarship is to invite debate on, and provide an essential resource for transnational scholars engaged in creative research involving visual, literary, and performative arts. Approaches may include arts-based, practice-based, a/r/tography, artistic, research creation, and more, and explore pedagogical and experimental perspectives, reflective and evaluative assessments, methodological deliberations, and ethical issues and concerns in relation to a host of topic areas in education.

In this series:

Artful Methods for Systemic Change: Slow Scholarship in Action, edited by Michelle Ludecke and Geraldine Burke (2027)

Propositions for Studio Inquiry: A Journey Into Artists' Studios, by Alison Shields (2026)

Arts Education in Ireland: From Pedagogy to Practice, edited by Dervil Jordan and Jane O'Hanlon (2025)

The Being of Relation, by Erin Manning (2025)

Modelling International Collaborations in Art Education, by Peter Sramek, Giselle Mira-Diaz and Charisse Fung (2025)

Dissens and Sensibility: Why Art Matters, by Lisbet Skregelid (2024)

Art Education in Canadian Museums: Practices in Action, edited by Anita Sinner, Patricia Osler and Boyd White (2024)

Propositions for Museum Education: International Art Educators in Conversation, edited by Anita Sinner, Patricia Osler and Boyd White (2024)

Walking in Art Education: Ecopedagogical and A/r/tographical Encounters, edited by Nicole Rallis, Ken Morimoto, Michele Sorensen, Valerie Triggs and Rita L. Irwin (2024)

Art, Sustainability and Learning Communities: Call to Action, edited by Raphael Vella and Victoria Pavlou (2024)

A/r/tography: Essential Readings and Conversations, edited by Rita L. Irwin, Alexandra Lasczik, Anita Sinner and Valerie Triggs (2024)

Community Arts Education: Transversal Global Perspectives, edited by Ching-Chiu Lin, Anita Sinner and Rita L. Irwin (2023)

Constructions of the Real: Intersections of Documentary-Based Film Practice and Theory, edited by Christine Rogers, Kim Munro, Liz Burke and Catherine Gough-Brady (2023)

Living Histories: Global Conversations in Art Education, co-edited by Dustin Garnet and Anita Sinner (2022)

Propositions for Studio Inquiry

A Journey Into Artists' Studios

Alison Shields

intellect
Bristol, UK / Chicago, USA

First published in the UK in 2026 by
Intellect, The Mill, Parnall Road, Fishponds, Bristol, BS16 3JG, UK

First published in the USA in 2026 by
Intellect, The University of Chicago Press, 1427 E. 60th Street,
Chicago, IL 60637, USA

EU GPSR Authorised Representative
LOGOS EUROPE, 9 rue Nicolas Poussin, 17000, LA ROCHELLE, France
E-mail: Contact@logoseurope.eu

A catalogue record for this book is available from the British Library.

Copy editor: MPS Limited
Cover designer: Natalie Thomas
Cover image: Leah Rosenberg's Studio, 2014, Vermont Studio Centre.
Frontispiece: Drawings by Miles (left) and Skye (right).
Production manager: Debora Nicosia
Typesetter: MPS Limited

Hardback ISBN 978-1-83595-279-5
Paperback ISBN 978-1-83595-280-1
ePDF ISBN 978-1-83595-282-5
ePUB ISBN 978-1-83595-281-8

Printed and bound by CMP

To find out about all our publications, please visit our website.
There you can subscribe to our e-newsletter, browse or download our current catalogue and buy any titles that are in print.

www.intellectbooks.com

This is a peer-reviewed publication.

I dedicate this book to my nieces and nephew, Olive, Tallulah, Paisley, Cadence, Skye, and Miles who constantly show me the value of art education. I have always loved artmaking with them as they share their playful, creative, and insightful ways that they see the world through art. They are my inspiration and their artworks hung on my 'inspiration wall' in my studio continually impact my own paintings.

The following drawings by Miles (left) and Skye (right) were from an evening we sat together drawing the sunset over the cacti in Palm Springs.

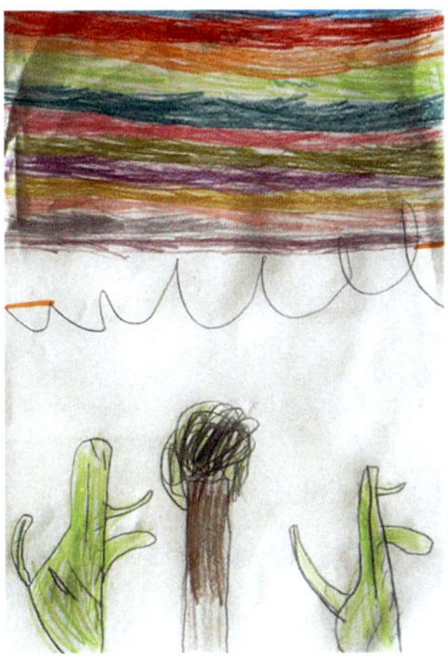

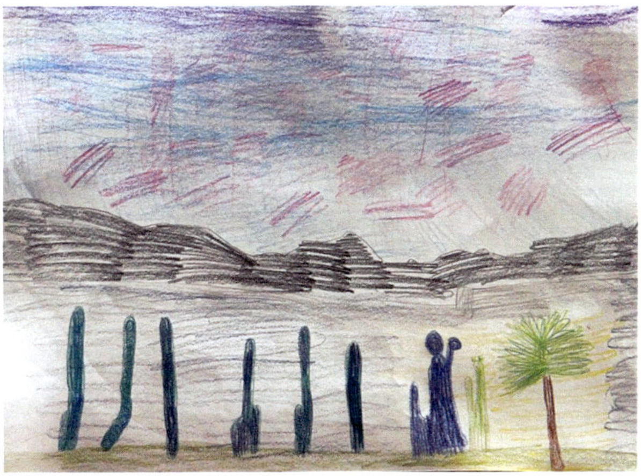

Contents

Figures

Acknowledgements

I would like to thank the artists who I met along my journey for inviting me into their studios and engaging in thoughtful, creative and meaningful conversations about painting. Each conversation led me in new directions and toward new insights and has transformed my understandings of painting. I would like to thank my mentor Rita Irwin who guided me throughout my doctoral work and in the years that have followed, and continues to inspire me as an artist educator. And I'd like to thank Landon Mackenzie for her generosity and support. Our conversations and studio visits continue to inspire my love of painting. Finally, I would like to acknowledge the Social Science and Humanities Research Council of Canada for the support that allowed me to pursue this research through the Joseph-Armand Bombardier Canada Graduate Scholarship without which this research would not have been possible. And I'd like to acknowledge the University of Victoria who have supported me through this research and development of this book.

Introduction: Remain Curious (Studio as Mystery)

The studio is a space and a condition wherein creative play and progressive thinking yield propositions for reflecting on who we are – individually and collectively – and where we might go next.

(Wainwright, 2010, p. ix)

Studio as a Never-Ending Painting

What happens in a studio? How is a studio a way of thinking? These are the questions I often ask myself as I retreat to my studio. My last studio, in Victoria, British Columbia, on the traditional land of the Lək̓ʷəŋən and W̱SÁNEĆ Peoples, was part of an artist studio collective called The Ministry of Casual Living. It was an open-concept space with dividing walls, housing approximately fifteen artists. While I spent much of my time alone in the large space, I was always surrounded by objects and imagery in the studios alongside my own, evidence of the presence of other artists and of artistic practices (Figures I.1–I.4). These objects and imagery, while often nonsensical to others, seemed integral to these artists' practices. In the studio next to me, a hand-made green stuffed creature hung above an orb-like object, appearing to watch over me. In another space, a sign saying 'Don't Miss Anything' that was written on the concrete wall long before I had moved to the building, suddenly disappeared one day. Chairs signified the possibility of a staged meeting. And a dead plant sat in the sink with a sign for the rest of the studio inhabitants. As an artist and art educator, I have always been interested in understanding artistic processes and the drive behind artmaking. Each of these images forms a clue to this mystery. As the site of artistic practices, the studio is the set on which the mystery is played out. I am drawn to these curious objects that somehow transform an old run-down building into something else. These spaces become places where anything can happen. They are spaces of possibility. Within these communal studios, I've often felt like I was part of a community, one that spread around the building, and outward towards the city and across the

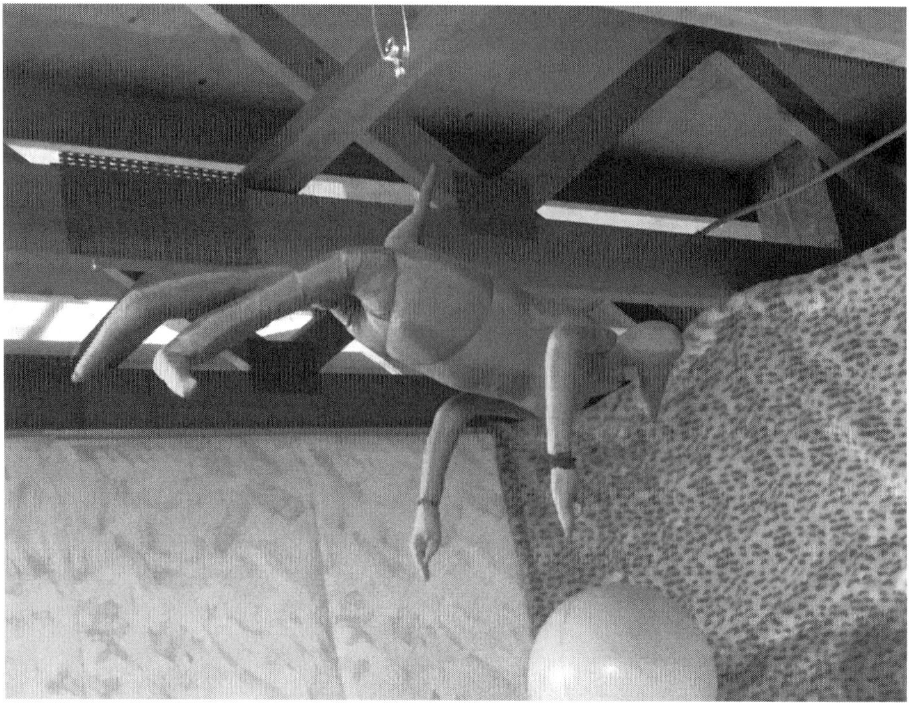

FIGURE I.1: Ministry of Casual Living Artist-Run-Centre, Victoria, BC, 2020.

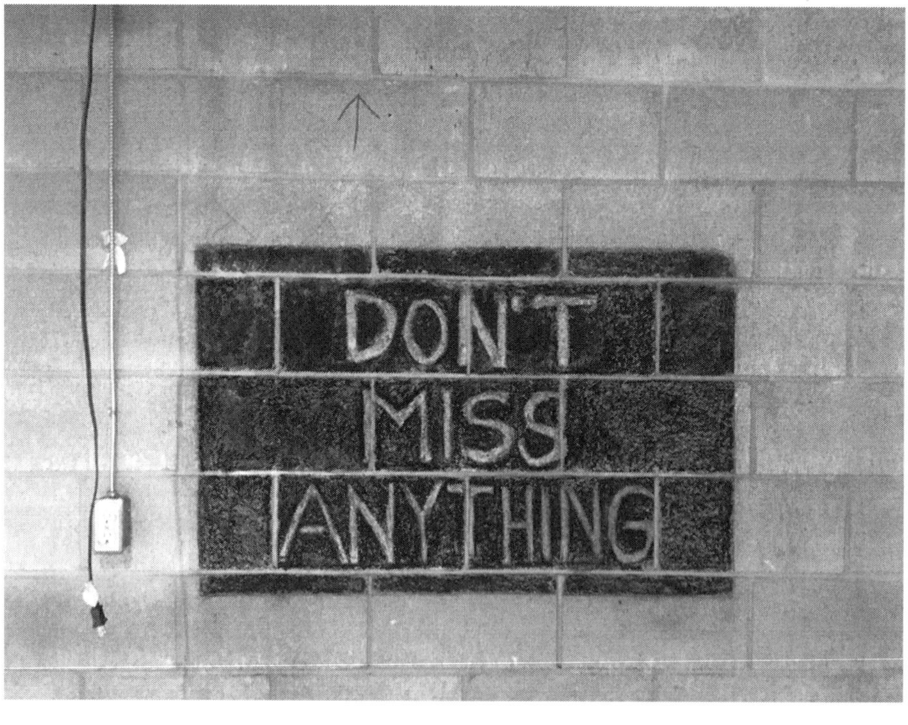

FIGURE I.2: Ministry of Casual Living Artist-Run-Centre, Victoria, BC, 2020.

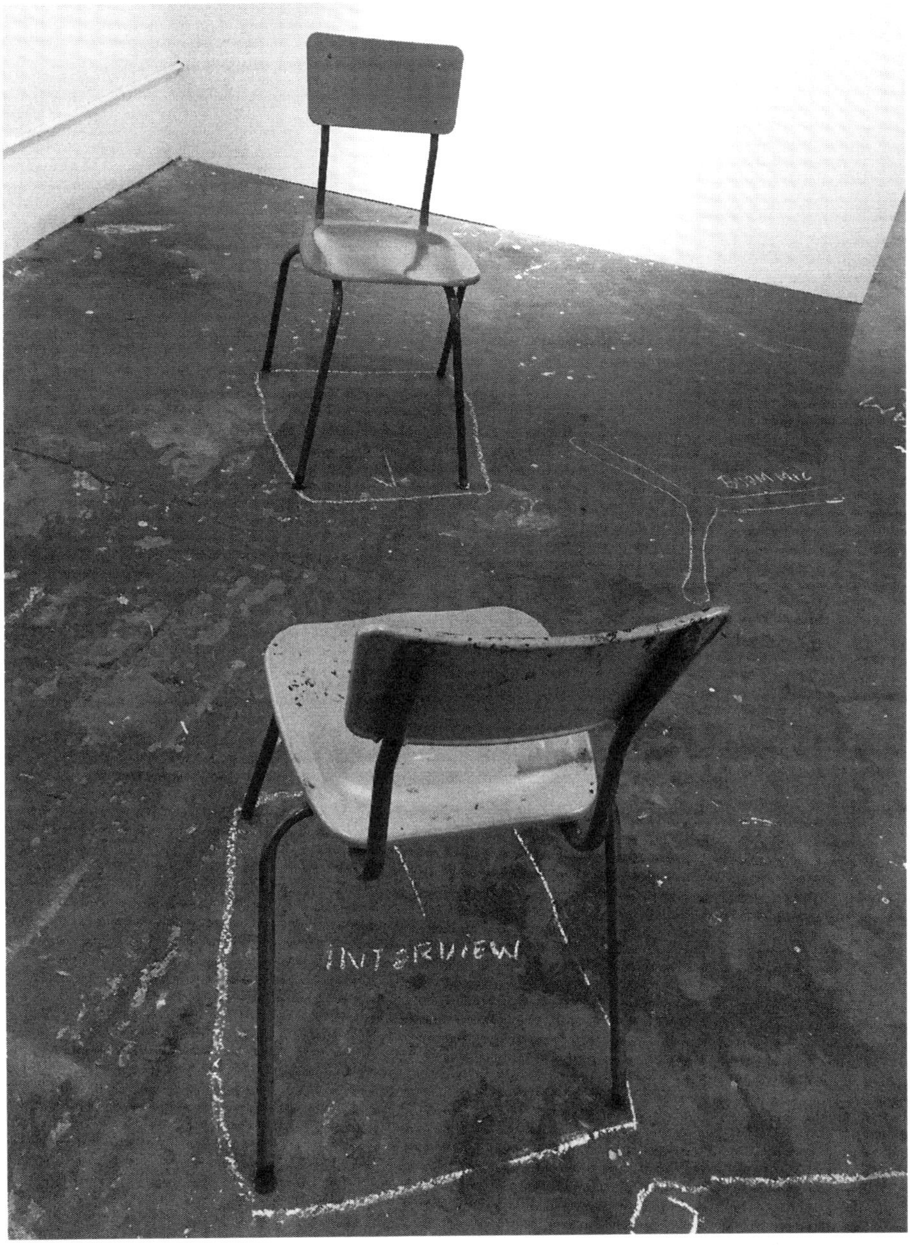

FIGURE I.3: Ministry of Casual Living Artist-Run-Centre, Victoria, BC, 2020.

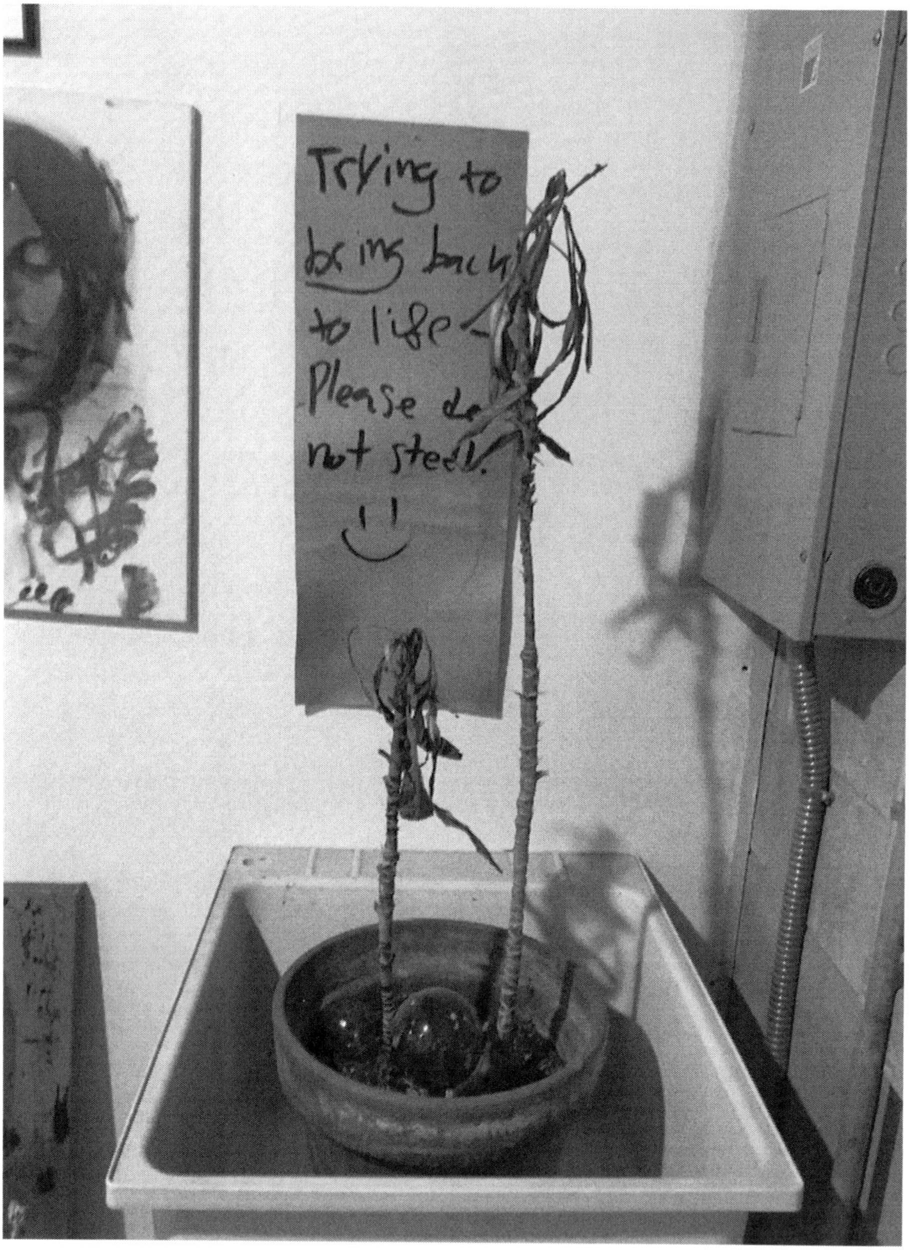

FIGURE I.4: Ministry of Casual Living Artist-Run-Centre, Victoria, BC, 2020.

country. As I work within my current studio, I reflect on a journey I performed years earlier, travelling across Canada, visiting artists in their studios. I take solace in this invisible web of relations that I could imagine after having visited studios across the country, finding connections between the seemingly isolated practices.

Throughout the summers of 2014–16, I indulged my fascination with artists' studios as I embarked on a research trip from Victoria, British Columbia, to St. John's, Newfoundland visiting painters in their studios. Throughout the studio visits, artists described a studio as a stage, a playground, a garden, a laboratory, a waiting room, a puzzle, a cabinet of curiosities, a pressure cooker, a collage, a garden, and a brain. Vancouver-based artist, Fiona Ackerman, described a studio as a 'Heterotopia', a workplace and an anti-workplace, the real and the imaginary coexisting. And in Montreal, Quebec, David Elliott described a painting as a believable parallel universe. In Kamloops, British Columbia, Andrea Kastner said that the studio is full of wormholes and portals; an art studio has the capacity to take us on travels into multiple spaces. For her, time doesn't function in a linear way, and you might get trapped in a wormhole and shoot backwards or forward, or things may happen that you have no control over.

This research emerged from my experience as an artist and art educator. I began my love of art studios as a high school student. At school, I recognized that in the art room, time, and space functioned differently. This space of learning was not one of linear or progressive lessons. It was a space where learning happened in every direction. It was a space where learning happened through our bodies encountering materials. It was a space where the in-between conversations that occurred alongside artmaking created a community unlike any other class. This love of the studio continued through my undergraduate and graduate work as we talked late into the night in the studio as we worked, and into my career as an artist where upon moving to a new city, finding a studio becomes the first priority. The smells, the histories, and in-process artworks fill me up with a feeling of potential.

Within my studio practice throughout the past two decades, I have sought out a space of *not knowing, uncertainty,* and *emergence* through the development of both physical and metaphorical never-ending paintings. Originally conceived to examine the infinite potentials of abstract painting through allowing the paintings to continually evolve over time, the paintings began through developing an elaborate system of tracing, painting, and re-painting as a self-generating mechanism through which they would transform. I compared the paintings to organisms evolving and reproducing or geological land formations changing through time, in both cases changing in relation to what came before. While conceptually based in the language of abstraction, I came to realize that this need for change came from not wanting the painting process to end and an ongoing curiosity and excitement about what it might become. My interest in the concept of a 'never-ending painting' continued throughout the years that followed, although it morphed into other ways of working and reworking the painting, from whiting out and then scraping/wiping away, to eventually cutting up and reconfiguring pieces from various paintings together. This desire for incompletion remained. Or perhaps it was a resistance towards completion.

This desire and/or resistance weaves into how I understand learning, teaching, thinking, and researching. Learning for me is like that never-ending painting that emerges through the process, while always drawing from what came before it. As I engaged with the hows and whys of artmaking within my own practice, I reflected on my interest in the never-ending painting, this desire to 'stay in the painting process'. I began to ask myself *why I make art*, recognizing that I was driven by my desire to follow curiosities, surprise, and newness that, for me, happened in the studio. At the same time, this answer did not seem adequate. There had to be more to this question.

Studio Visit as Encounter

Within a few weeks, I was in my car, driving across Canada, interviewing artists in their studios. Through these visits, I listened to their stories, their artistic processes, and their investigations, and explored the studios as I continued to find more answers and clues to this ongoing mystery: *What happens in a studio? And, how is a studio a way of thinking?* This book is a story of these encounters and the lessons that I learned along the way as I explore the intimate spaces of the studio, the materiality of the space, the artistic processes that emerge therein, and the communities that connect artists across this vast country.

Through this research, I explore studio practice as a particular kind of thinking and being, one that is material-based, in process, messy, unpredictable, and affective. Through the lens of a 'studio visit' as both a research methodology and artistic practice, I draw from the visits and interviews with these artists to examine how a studio is a way of learning and thinking with materials. As the past several years have seen a move towards online education and increasingly digital ways of living, I recognize what is lost when the materiality of the studio and the ecosystem that is created within is not recognized. Within this virtual world, I miss the materiality of the studio and the learning that happens within, alongside, and through art in a studio classroom. In a time when acquiring studio space in cities and educational settings is increasingly challenging, and online and technology-based learning platforms are becoming more prevalent, I believe that it is ever more urgent to examine the significance of artmaking practices that involve handling materials, and by extension to examine the material spaces necessarily at the core of those processes. Further, through the examination of the messy processes inherent to studio practices, I propose that studios may stand as radical counterpoints to an increasingly digitized world. I celebrate the particularities and situatedness of studios through their relational and material quality.

During a visit with Monica Tap in Toronto in 2014, I asked her why she makes art. She said: '*Painting was the one thing I didn't know if I could do. I keep doing it because it's still hard. It still seems interesting. It hasn't revealed itself yet. So, why do I continue? Because I remain curious.*' I similarly attend to research through this lens of curiosity. As an artist and educator, I embrace curiosity as a way of engaging with pedagogy as an affective and relational process (Coats, 2023). Through this lens of curiosity, I believe in the power of art to transform us as individuals and society. I am comfortable (or prefer) existing in a space of ambiguity, uncertainty, and complexity that often seems at odds with many research methods and educational institutions. I am comfortable with my faith in the impact of art while recognizing the danger of trying to quantify it. I acknowledge that a single conversation can cause a huge shift in thinking or a trickle effect across waves of thoughts and actions. I recognize that being within the space of art for a moment can cause a material impact on our body.

Thus, rather than considering art as simply an object and a studio as simply a room with four walls and a door, I view the studio as an encounter. Similarly, as a research methodology, I view the studio visit as a particular type of interview, one that is material-based, practice-led, emergent, and conversational. An encounter is a dialogue, an interaction that challenges our ways of thinking and being in the world (O'Sullivan, 2006). I engaged with each studio visit as an encounter, a series of conversations through which emerged new insights and propositions into studio practice. I attend to this research and data analysis through the theoretical lens of new materialism for its 'embodied, affective, relational understanding of the research process' (Hickey-Moody & Page, 2015, p. 1). Within new materialist theories, '[b]odies and things are not as separate as we were once taught, and their interrelationship is vital to how we come to know ourselves as human and interact with our environments' (Hickey-Moody & Page, 2015, p. 2). Intra-action, the process by which bodies encounter each other and generate movement and change (Barad, 2007), highlights how matter and bodies are entangled. According to Hickey-Moody and Page (2015):

> A materialist ontology, concerned with matter and the processes of matter, and intra-action between human and non-human things and worlds, recognizes the intertwining of all phenomena – human, non-human, social, physical, material, and immaterial.
>
> (p. 4)

Within this framework, I view a studio visit as a new materialist methodology, one that recognizes my own subjectivities within research as well as my encounters with the places and materials of artmaking. And the studio, as both the site and the subject of this research, is recognized for its role within an ecology of making. Further, new materialist theories embrace the role of the body, messiness, unpredictability, and indeterminacy at the core of artistic practice and pedagogy.

Studio as Proposition

To focus on possibilities and potentials rather than conclusions, and generativity rather than closure, the studio is presented through a series of propositions. The propositions are offerings for ways of thinking about artistic practice, each drawn from a quote from an artist during a studio visit. I ground my understanding of propositions through the work of Sarah Truman and Stephanie Springgay (2016) who examine how walking produces propositions rather than conclusions and allows subjects to move through space in an unpredictable way. They suggest that propositions drawn from walking are both actual and speculative as 'a hybrid of movement and *lure for feeling* that can *pave the way along which the world advances into novelty*' (p. 260). Thus, propositions are a pedagogical tool that allows for the emergence of thought, learning, thinking, and being. Rather than defining what learning *is*, it opens up to what learning *can be* and invites an openness to surprise. Erin Manning (2016a) similarly uses propositions as a way of addressing qualities specific to art practice as research. These propositions include (amongst others): 'Create new forms of knowledge'; 'Be speculatively pragmatic'; 'Invent beyond technique'; 'Dwell in the transversal'; 'Create alter-economies of value' (pp. 133–37). Propositions are pedagogical invitations for stimulating conversation about the qualities and potentials of thinking through making in a way that is generative. It is my intention that, rather than direct us to what art making *is*, propositions provoke us to think about what it *could be* to each of us in different ways. Each chapter is titled as a proposition drawn from a comment made in conversation with an artist with whom I visited. These propositions are purposefully ambiguous, to be taken up by readers in their own way.

This book is structured in four sections, each one examining studio practice from a particular lens. It is meant to guide readers to view the interconnection between place, process, and materials within studio practice and to highlight how they come together to foster a unique space for learning that is open-ended, personal, intimate, exploratory, material, and embodied. The introduction of each section addresses that particular lens for a studio followed by more detailed propositions through a discussion of a selection of artists visited. Each section is concluded through a broader discussion of pedagogy and the role of studio-based learning within education. In order to keep the authenticity of the studio visits and foreground the voices of the artists, direct quotes from the interviews are interwoven throughout the book. They are emphasized in italics. A complete list of the artists discussed, including dates and locations of each studio visit is included at the end of the book.

In the first section, 'Studio as Place', I discuss the studio as a pedagogical space. I draw from Ellsworth (2005) who examines architectural and artistic spaces as a form of speculative pedagogy to affirm the role of the body, affect, and subjectivity within pedagogical spaces and to provoke us to imagine what is possible as pedagogy. Within this section, I discuss the methodology of the studio visit as a form of mapping as I situate myself in relation with other artists across the country. I examine a studio as part of an ecosystem (Harris, 2021) and propose that studios exist and thrive as a part of an ever-changing ecosystem. Lastly, I propose that by virtue of the making process, a studio may become a portal that transports us elsewhere.

In the second section, 'Studio as Process', I examine the process of artmaking through discussing how the studio is the site of an event (Manning, 2016b). Drawing from artistic researcher Barbara Bolt (2004, 2007, 2013), I examine artmaking as a 'performative practice', one that generates experience rather than represents. Through a new materialist lens, art practice is emergent and responsive to our experiences in the world and is generative and iterative. Lastly, through the materiality of the studio, I discuss the significance of 'not knowing' within art practice and pedagogy (Fisher & Fortnum, 2013).

In the third section, 'Studio as Material Thinking', I examine the material and embodied qualities of artmaking through Springgay's (2022) discussion of 'feltness', which recognizes the intimate and relational qualities of artmaking and pedagogy. I begin this section by addressing the role of the body in art practice and assert the need to move away from binaries between thinking and feeling, and value the affective process of learning. Next, I explore studio practice as a messy process, one where the materials may disrupt a desire for control and certainty and examine how materials push us to lean into uncertainty and potentiality. Lastly, I consider how a studio as a collage may be taken up as a process of artmaking as well as a metaphor for studio inquiry.

In the final section, 'Studio as Dialogue with the World', I situate studio practice in relation to and in response to the world. Firstly, I examine artmaking as unlearning (Dunne, 2016; Atkinson, 2013) as a way of re-examining how we know what we know. I discuss how through its material quality, a studio may resist traditional understandings of learning. Next, I examine the ways that artmaking invites us to imagine differently. And lastly, I examine how artmaking provokes us to understand our relationship to the world. I propose that through examining the in-process quality of a studio, we shift away from an emphasis on product and instead on the doing of art through treating artmaking as an ongoing encounter and a 'never-ending exploration of what it might mean to exist in and with the world' (Biesta, 2018, p. 17).

At the core of this book is an examination of the processes of artmaking. And in its truest form, a studio is a space of process, one that is ripe with mess, uncertainty, and materials. It is a place where the messiness of the process generates emergent possibilities and where the bodily experience of artmaking may produce affective experiences and relations. For Biesta (2018), education is not a product, 'but a human being with an altered outlook' (p. 13). To view the studio as a space of process is to embrace the 'not knowing' of artmaking and pedagogy and an openness to learning through making. This book is for artist educators seeking to delve deeper into thinking about studio pedagogies, and for undergraduate and graduate students seeking to examine their studio practice. And it is for artistic researchers examining studio-based inquiry and research as a way of understanding themselves and their place in academia and the world through art practice.

Artists' Studios: A Glimpse

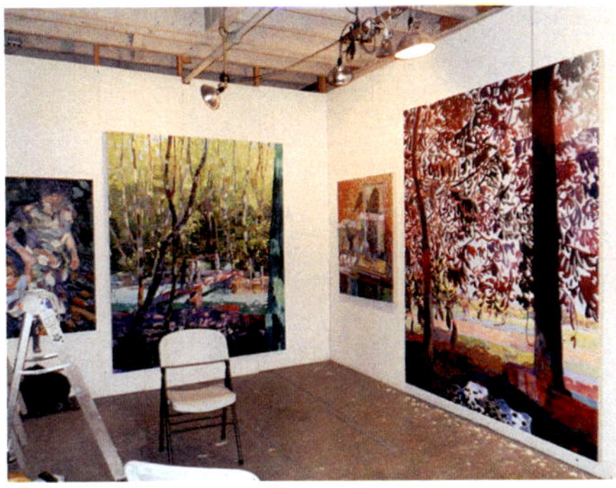

Ben Reeves' Studio, Vancouver, BC, 2014.

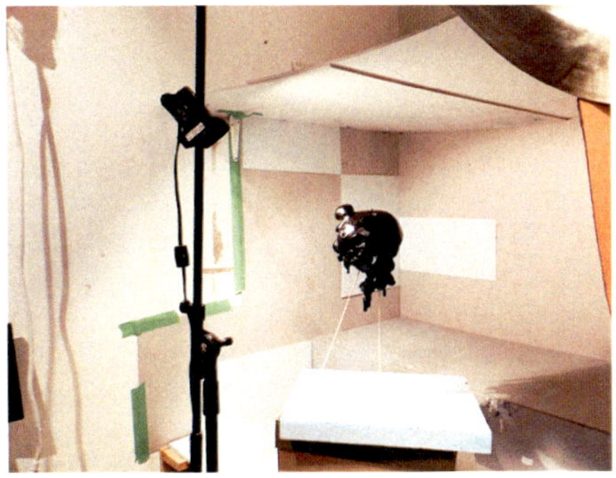

Adam Gunn's Studio, Halifax, NS, 2014.

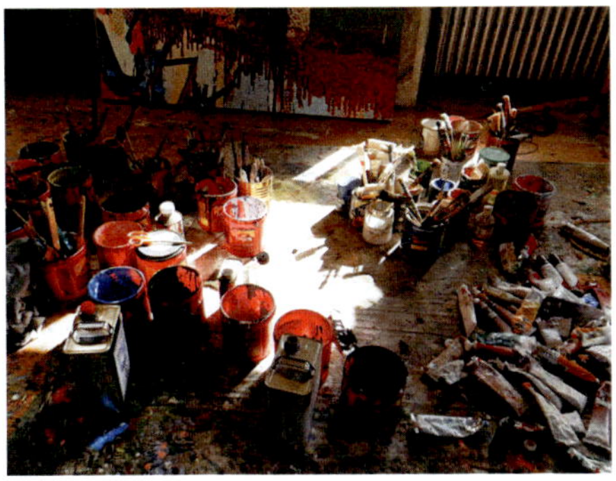

John Kissicks' Studio, Elora, ON, 2014.

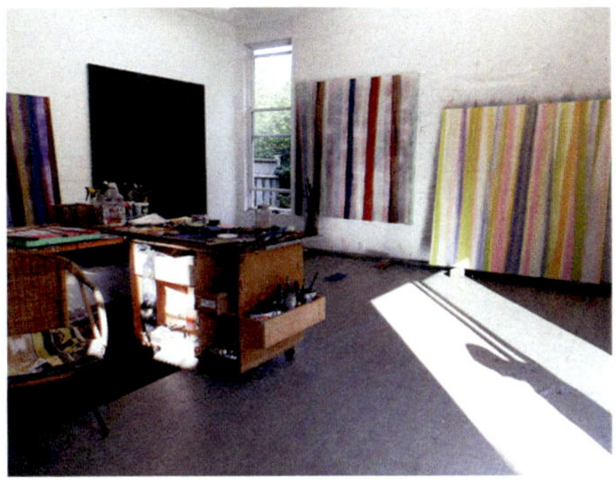

David Blatherwick's Studio, Elora, ON, 2014.

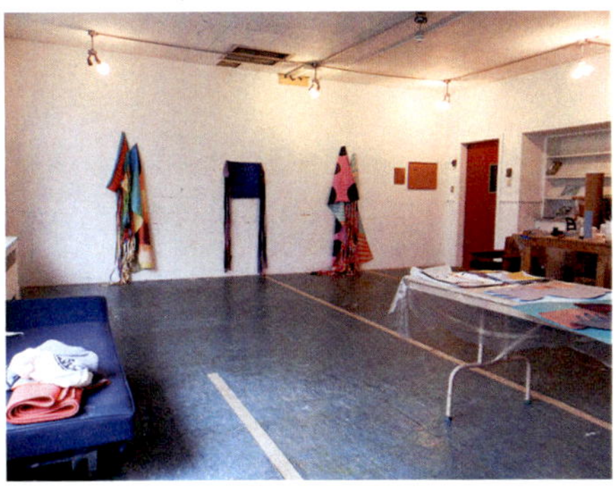

Ashleigh Bartlett's Studio, Toronto, ON, 2015.

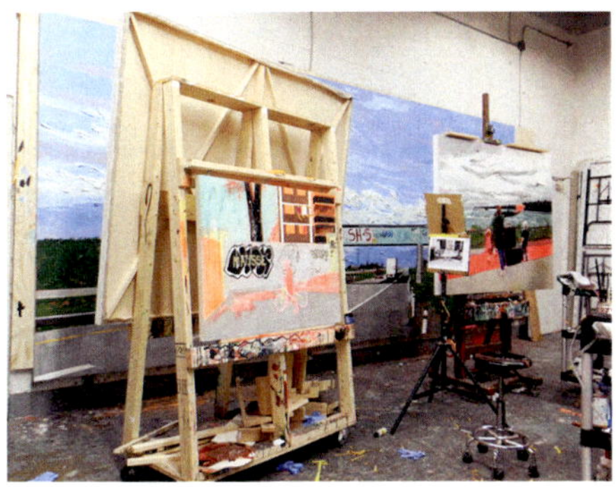

Kim Dorland's Studio, Toronto, ON, 2014.

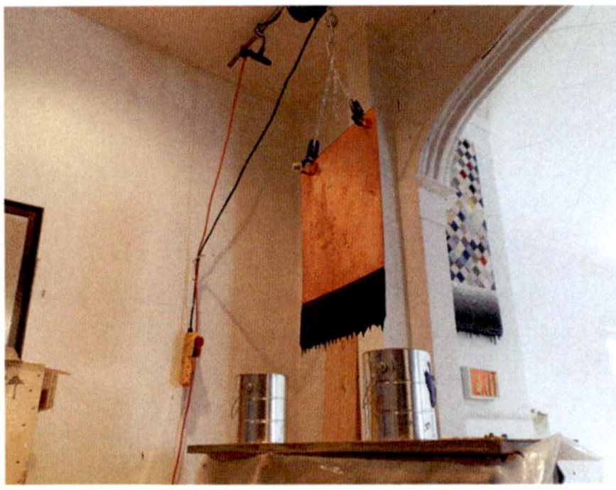

Sean Weisgerber's Studio, Saskatchewan, SK, 2014.

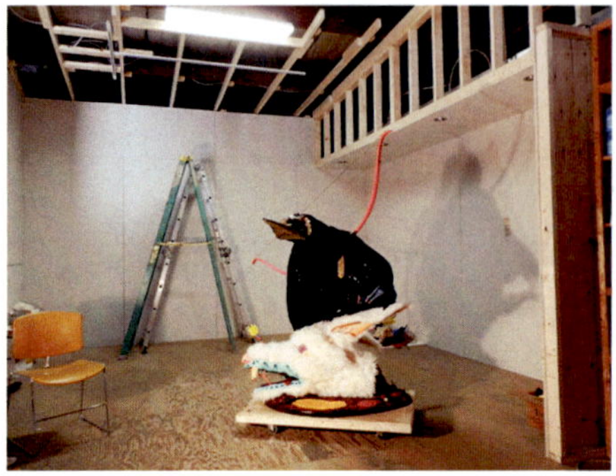

DaveandJenn's Studio, Calgary, AB, 2014.

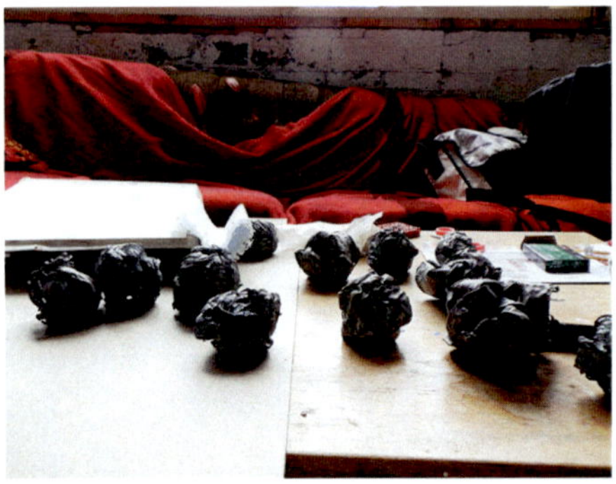

Pearl Van Geest's Studio, Guelph, ON, 2014.

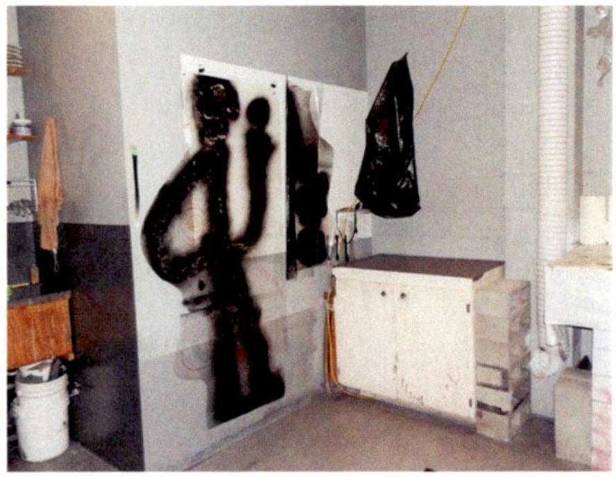

Ryan Peter's Studio, Vancouver, BC, 2015.

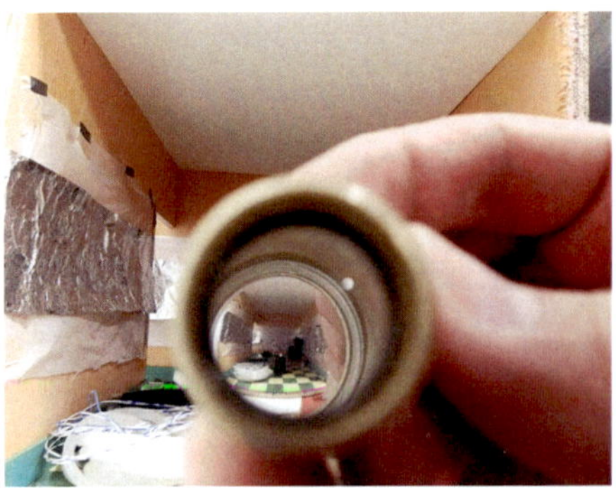

Ian August's Studio, Winnipeg, MN, 2014.

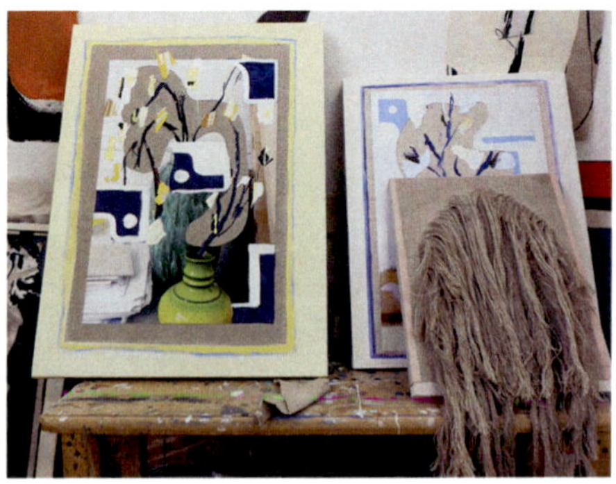

Sarah Cale's Studio, Toronto, ON, 2015.

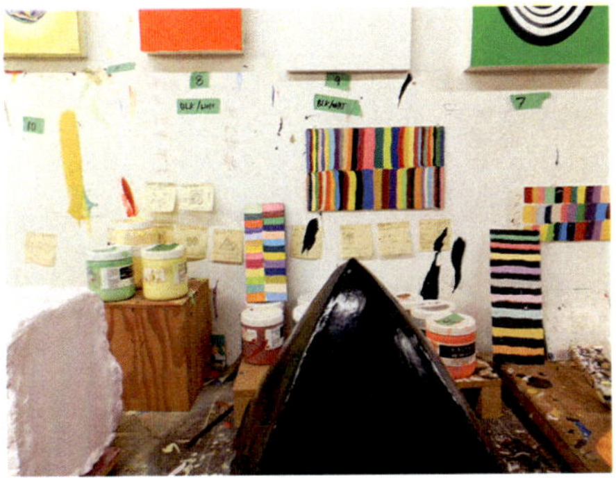

Jeremy Hof's Studio, Vancouver, BC, 2015.

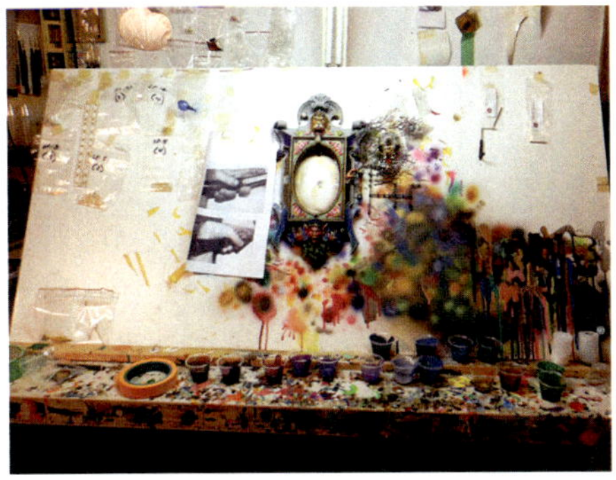

Chris Millar's Studio, Calgary, AB, 2014.

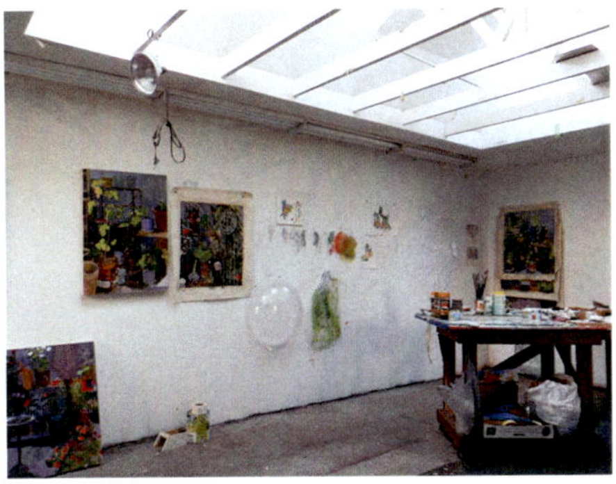

Sara Hartland-Rowe's Studio, Halifax, NS, 2015.

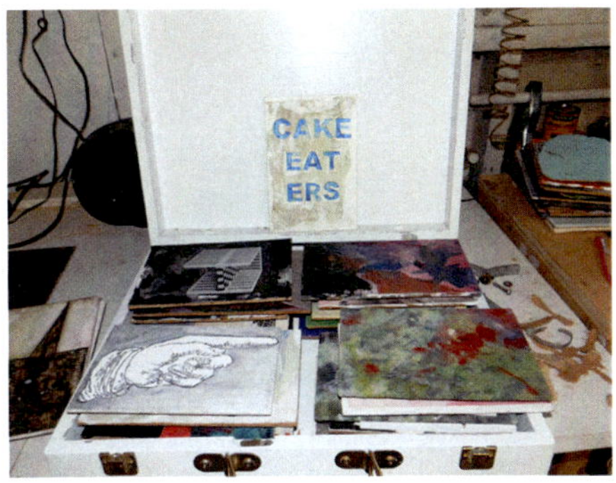

Jordy Hamilton's Studio, Vancouver, BC, 2014.

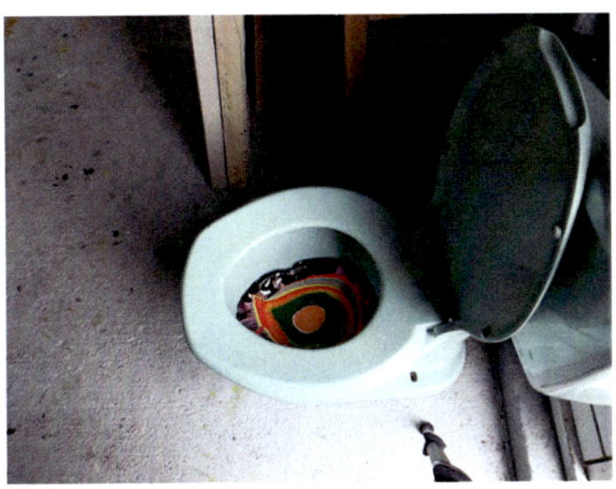

Sara Robichaud's Studio, Nanaimo, BC, 2015.

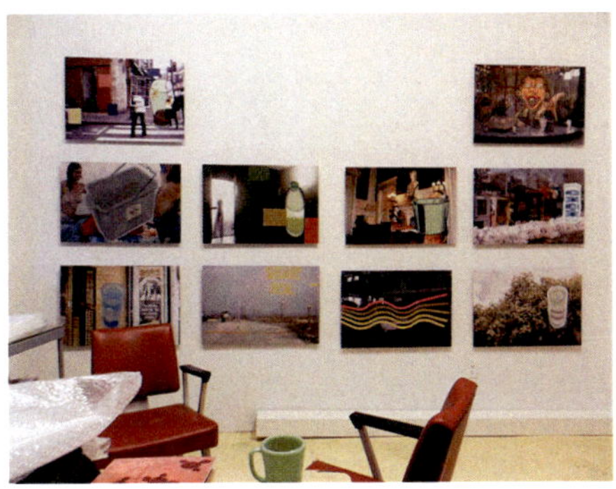

John Armstrong's Studio, Toronto, ON, 2015.

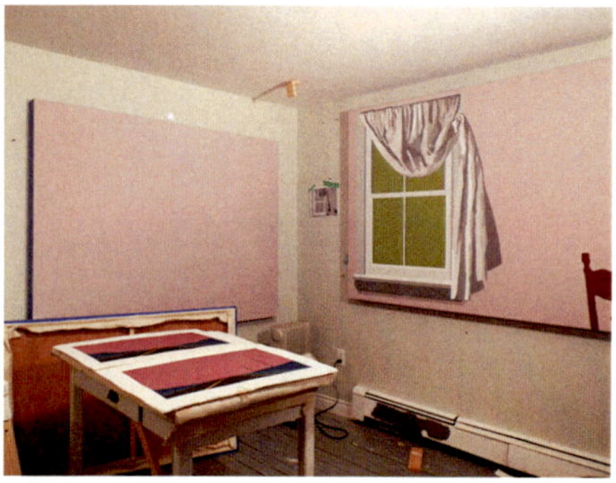

Kym Greeley's Studio, St. John's, NL, 2015.

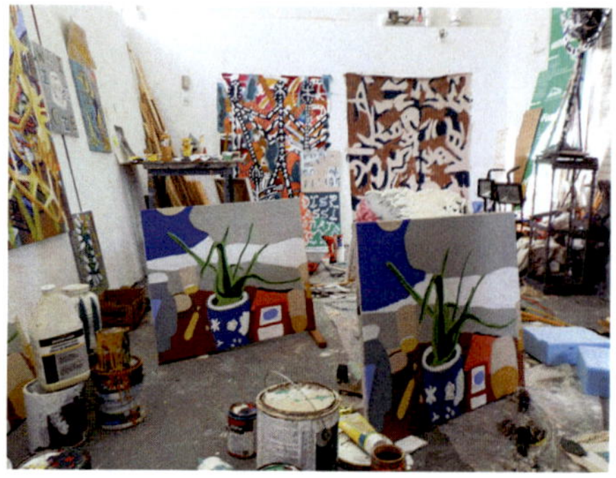

Patrick Cruz' Studio, Guelph, ON, 2015.

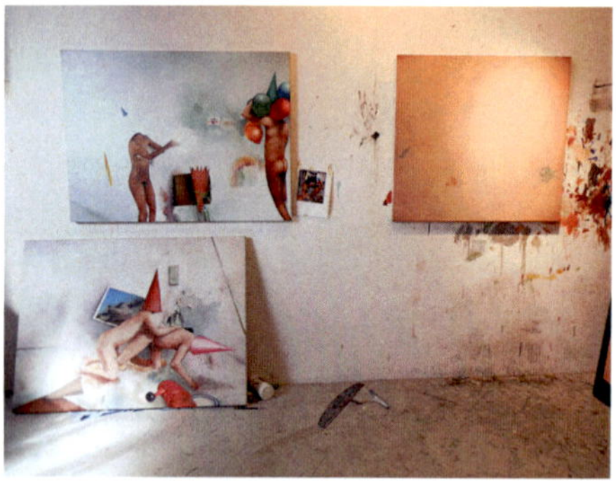

Alexis Lavoie's Studio, Montreal, QC, 2015.

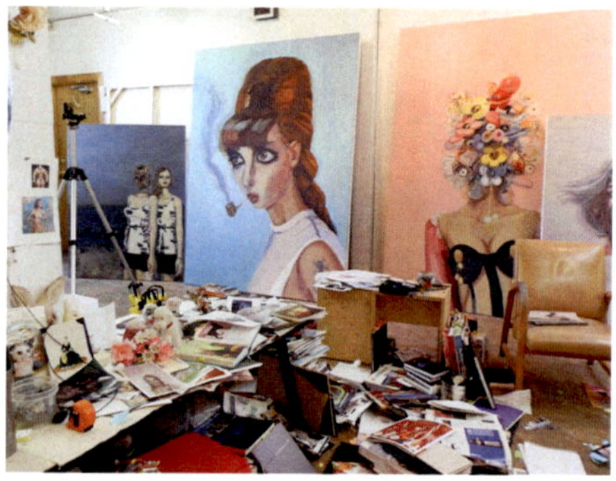

Janet Werner's Studio, Montreal, QC, 2015.

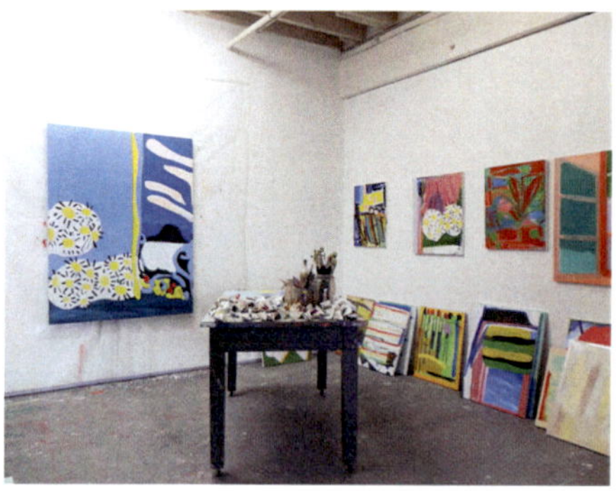

Elizabeth McIntosh's Studio, Vancouver, BC, 2015.

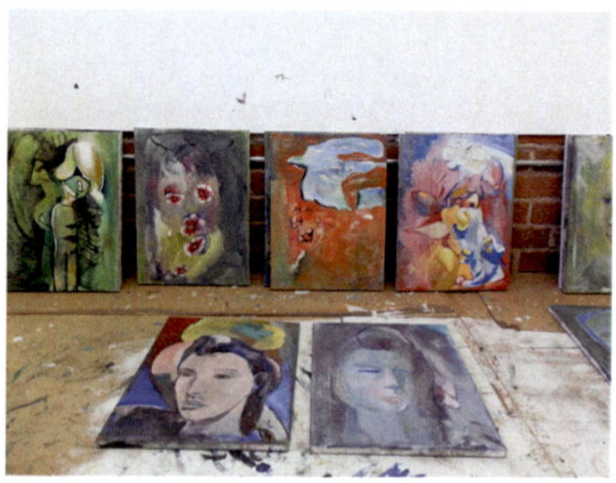

Katie Lyle's Studio, Toronto, ON, 2015.

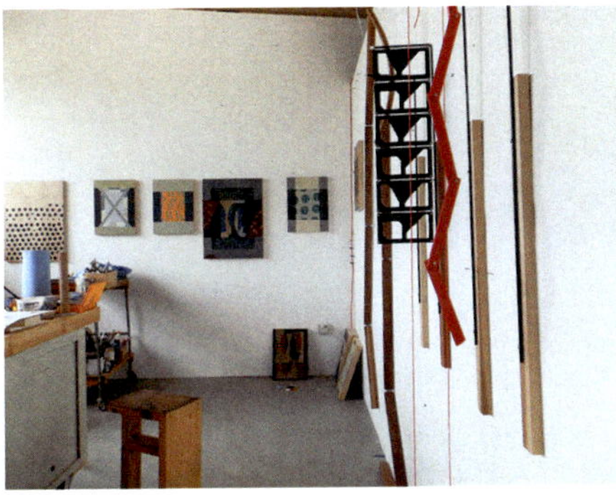

Van Maltese's Studio, Toronto, ON, 2014.

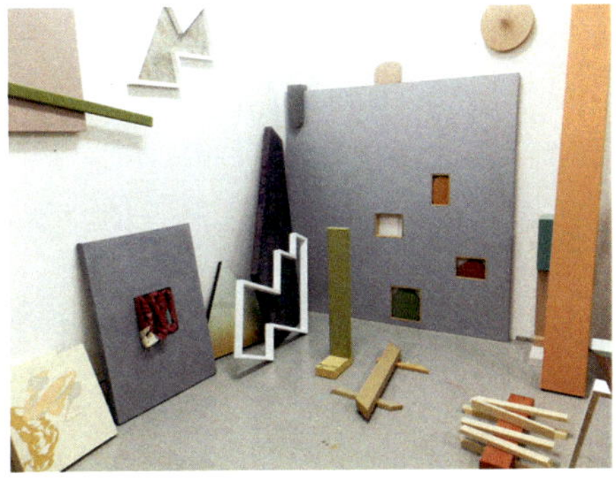

Robert Taite's Studio, Winnipeg, MN, 2015.

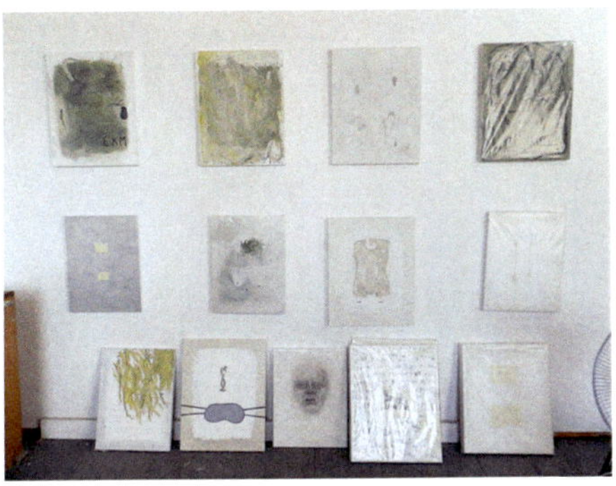

Erica Mendritzki's Studio, Winnipeg, MN, 2015.

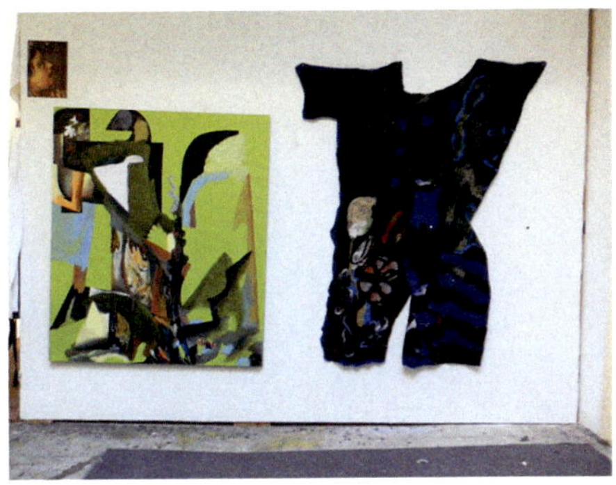

Rebecca Brewer's Studio, Vancouver, BC, 2015.

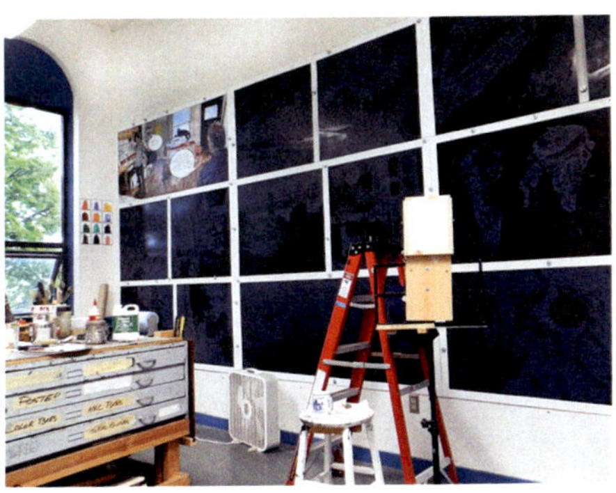

Mathew Reichertz' Studio, Halifax, NS, 2014.

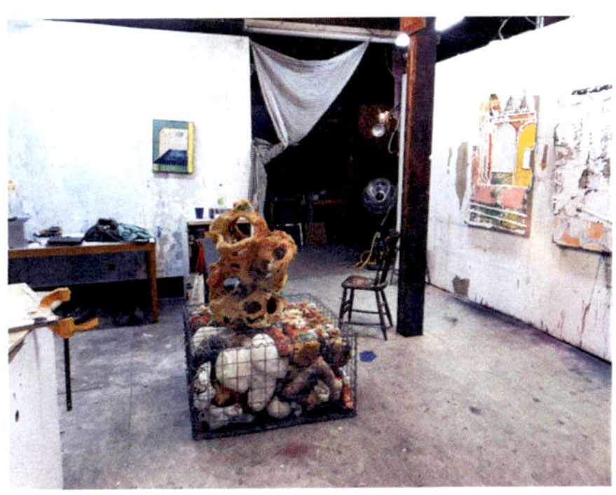

James Gardner's Studio, Toronto, ON, 2015.

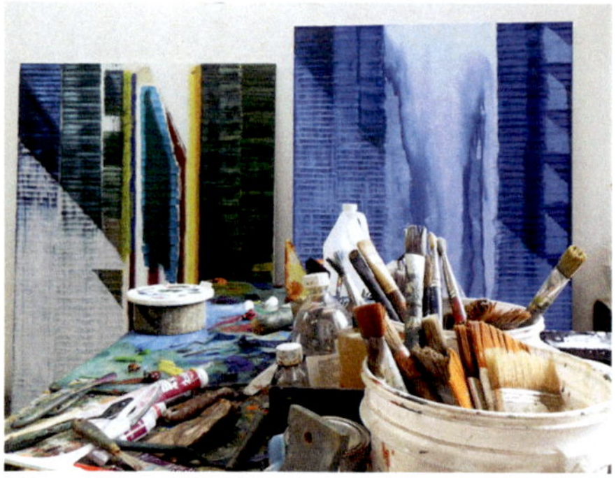

Dil Hidebrand's Studio, Montreal, QC, 2015.

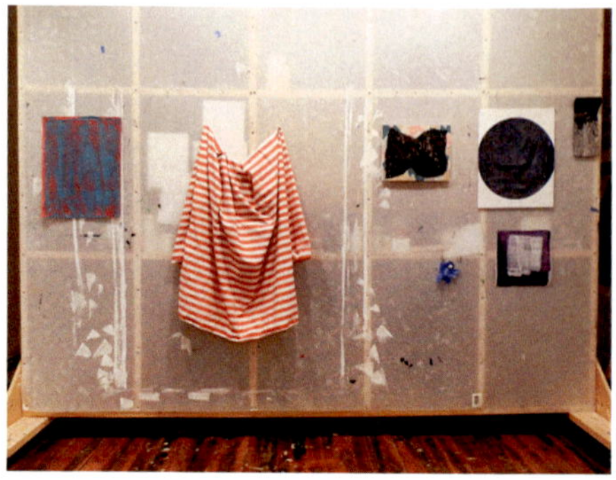

Daniel Huthinson's Studio, Hamilton, ON, 2015.

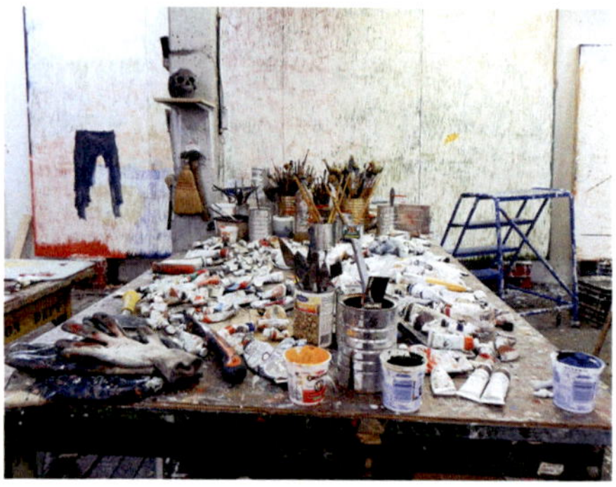

John Brown's Studio, Toronto, ON, 2014.

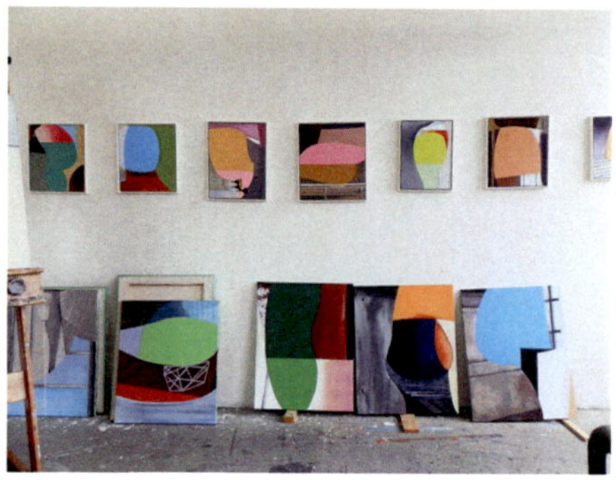

Renee Van Halm's Studio, Vancouver, BC, 2015.

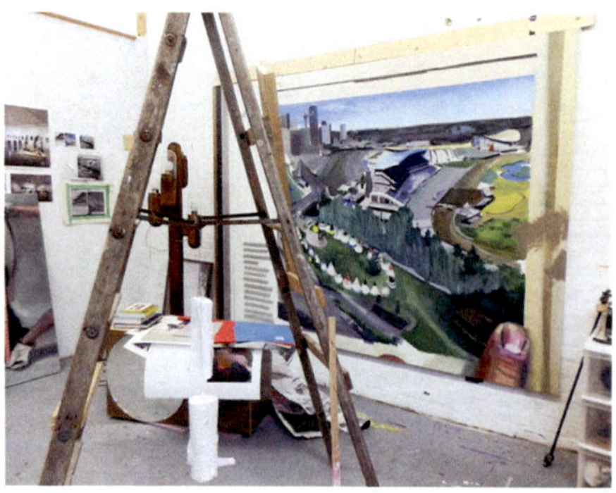

Mark Neufeld's Studio, Winnipeg, MN, 2014.

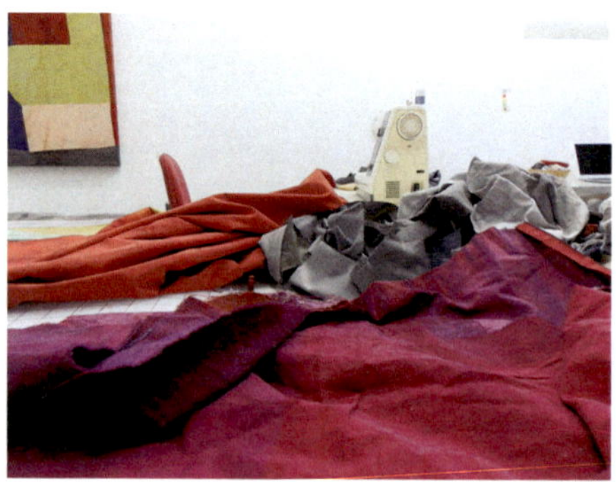

Colleen Heslin's Studio, Montreal, QC, 2014.

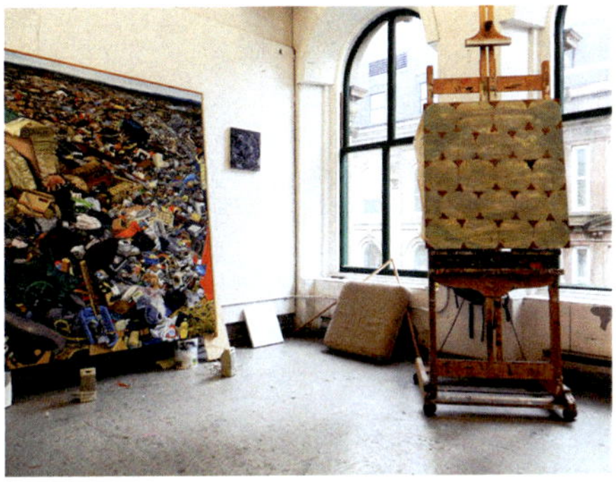

Colin Dorward's Studio, Halifax, NS, 2014.

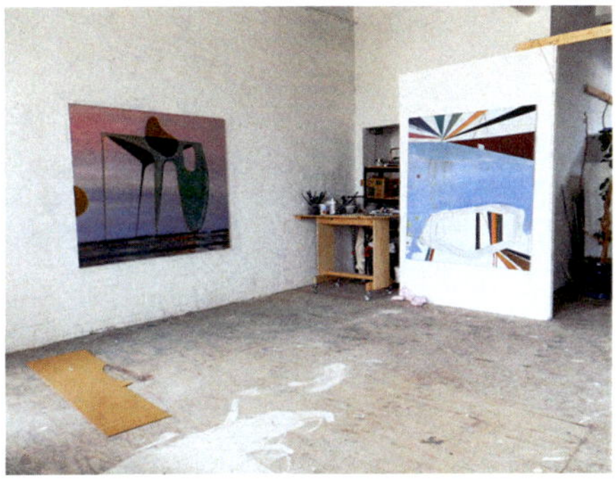

Holger Kalberg's Studio, Winnipeg, MN, 2014.

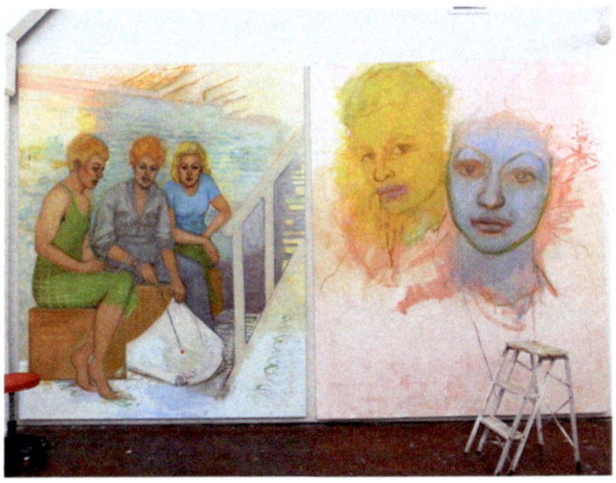

Eliza Griffith's Studio, Montreal, QC, 2014.

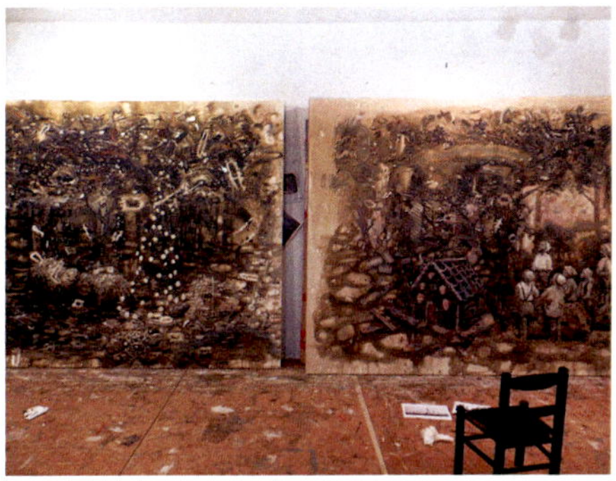

Carol Wainio's Studio, Ottawa, ON, 2015.

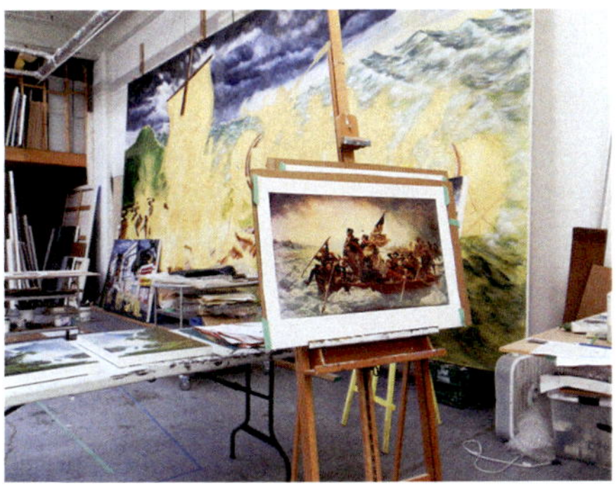

Kent Monkman's Studio, Toronto, ON, 2015.

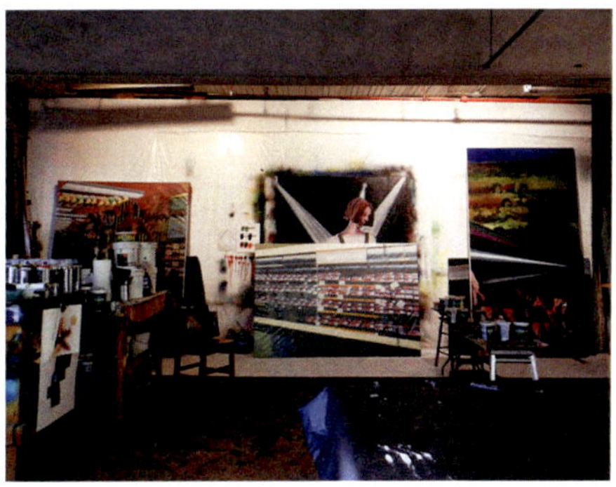

Christine Major's Studio, Montreal, QC, 2015.

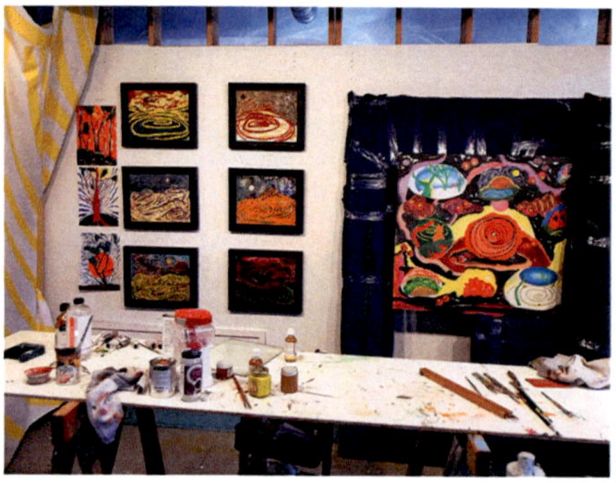

Sandra Meigs' Studio, Hamilton, ON, 2021.

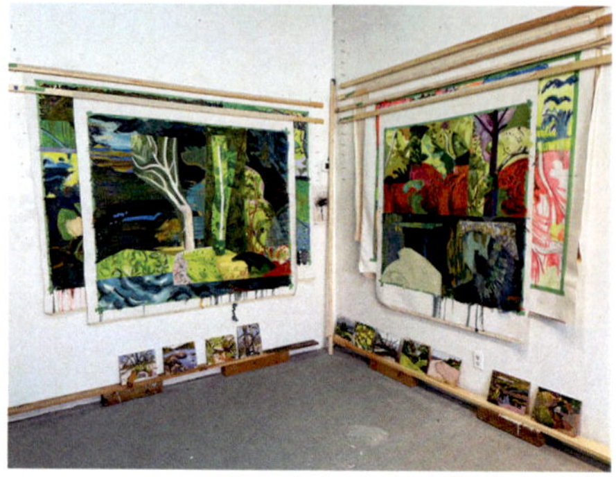

Monica Tap's Studio, Toronto, ON, 2022.

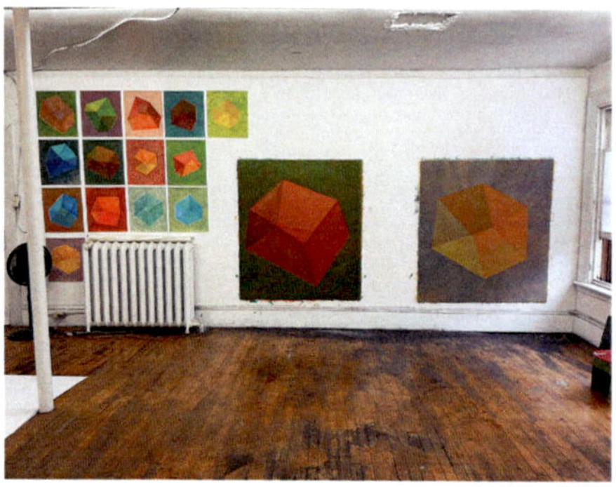

Jinny Yu's Studio, Ottawa, ON, 2022.

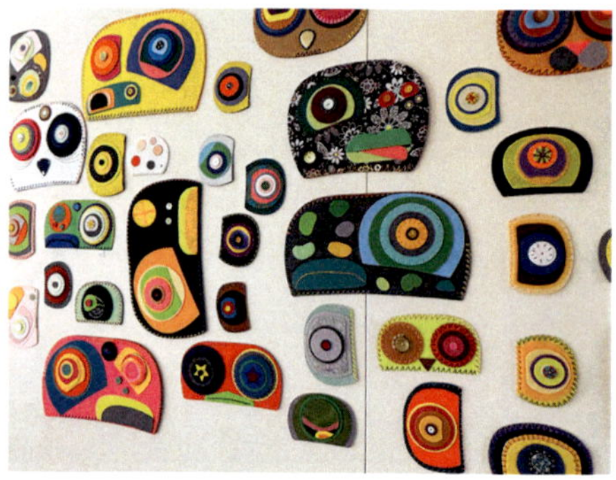

Charlene Vickers' Studio, Vancouver, BC, 2022.

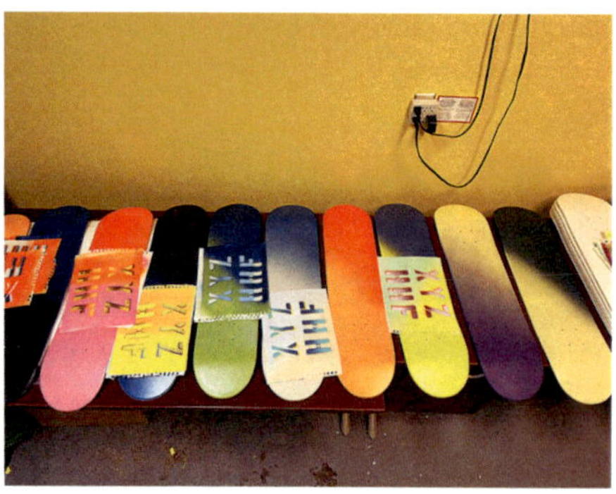

Mark Igloliorte's Studio, Montreal, QC, 2022.

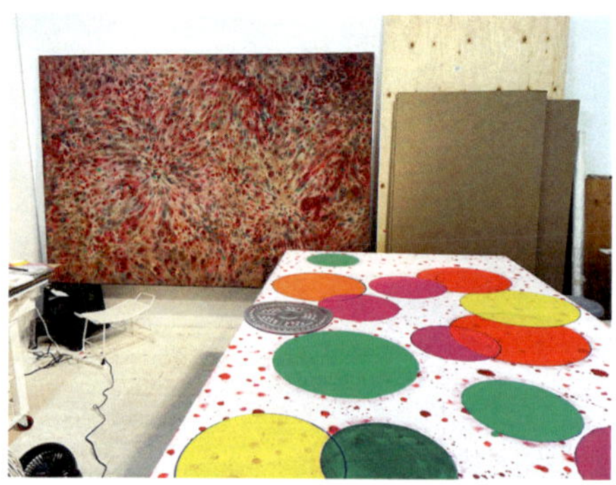

Landon Mackenzie's Studio, Vancouver, BC, 2022.

SECTION 1

STUDIO AS PLACE: DWELL IN YELLOWNESS

A studio is a place where the materiality and history of the space co-exist within the constant flux of the artistic process. Professor of media studies, Elizabeth Ellsworth (2005), describes how places become pedagogical when they 'create the experience of the learning self by putting inner thoughts, feelings, memories, fears, desires, and ideas in relation to outside others, events, history, culture, and socially constructed ideas' (p. 37). I similarly propose that a studio becomes pedagogical through the relations formed through working with materials and ideas through artmaking. In a studio visit in 2014 in Victoria, British Columbia, Sandra Meigs described the power of artmaking to take us elsewhere:

> *I think it's a huge ideal, but I think that art is a transportative place. And if you were to go into the world's best ever art show you would be transported to an actual different world and I think that's what the artist strives to do, to take the imagination there. I think there are those moments where your whole self is transported to someplace else. It's a pursuit of knowledge, a different kind of knowledge. What kind of knowledge? I think it's knowledge outside of daily everyday life. It's for discovery. People go to the Gobi Desert to discover what that landscape is like, so I could go to the land of Pink to discover what pink is like. Or if I do a huge yellow painting that is 47 ft. wide, I discover what it's like to dwell in yellowness.*

Meigs captures the magic of art practice, and the possibilities and potentials of artmaking to allow us to imagine something different. She highlights the significance of place and time in artmaking and the power of art to take artmakers (and viewers) elsewhere. Further, she emphasizes how artmaking is a process of dwelling. Dwelling is a way of being. Within the space of dwelling, one can take time to be present in the moment, allowing our bodies to embody our environment and to give time to art, conversation, and the pursuit of curiosities and obsessions. A studio is a space in which to dwell and to give time to wandering thoughts, experimentation, and the feeling of the materials and making processes.

The concept of dwelling in colour was similarly addressed in a 2014 studio visit with Saskatoon-born artist, Leah Rosenberg while on a residency at the Vermont Studio Centre (cover image). Throughout the residency, Rosenberg discussed her process, art, and baking. From going on a run, or eating food of a particular colour, to noticing colours of buildings, Rosenberg waits for colours from her daily life to prompt her artmaking. Throughout the residency, she painted the studio a colour from her day and then taped off a strip of that colour each night before repainting the space anew the following day. Removing all the tape after the full month, she revealed a colourful, visual trace of her month. Through this process, she transformed the studio itself by painting it a different colour every day in response to colour from a day in her life. Through this process, the studio became a trace of her daily life and a prompt for a sensory experience. She explained that she used to work at a bakery, and she sought to create an experience wherein people would love art the same way they love cake. Regarding the immersive transformation of the studio throughout the month, Rosenberg said: '*When you find yourself somewhere new with an empty studio, nothing makes it feel like yours like painting it a different color every day.*'

Regarding artistic research and art education, Jack Richardson (2011) argues that the materiality of space must be considered as a means of understanding the complexity of experiences in the world. Richardson states: 'Objects, the environment, and human agents produce and are produced by space through an unending negotiation of function and meaning' (p. 5). Studios are one such place, wherein the materiality of the space's history and the artistic processes animate the space. Artist Amy Granat (2010) addresses how our experiences become materialized in the studio: 'There is emptiness and history, acting together ... This history, my memories, they still insert themselves in this space' (p. 259). In this way, a studio is not simply a room, but a place. Lippard (1998) describes place as 'the locus of desire' (p. 4). It is within these places she feels a 'seductive embrace' (p. 5). According to Lippard: 'Space defines landscape, where space combined with memory defines place' (p. 9). Our experience in a place becomes a sensory, embodied, and experiential interaction, and within that place we may project our own subjectivities onto the surroundings. A studio is a place where art educator Sylvia Kind (2018) says there exists a productive tension between a desire to settle and a desire to move. The studio becomes a place in which to nest while also imagine elsewhere. It is a place that fills me with 'muchness', that feeling of liveliness as our bodies turn toward particular moments, as a force that emerges through an affective encounter (Thiel, 2018). 'Residuals of muchness might be pleasure, happiness, accomplishment but also might be frustration, disequilibrium, determination. Muchness is a force that makes someone or something stick with and come back for more, despite obstacles' (Thiel, 2018, p. 27).

Ellsworth (2005) examines architectural and artistic spaces as a form of 'speculative pedagogy' to affirm the role of the body, affect, and subjectivity within pedagogy. She suggests that within pedagogical places, we change and learn: 'In this mind/brain/body meld with objects, spaces, and times, the self is understood as a becoming, an emergence, and as continually in the making' (p. 4). For Ellsworth, architecture becomes pedagogical when the events within create pivot places that allow new understandings to emerge: 'It becomes the force that sets interior self-experience in motion to encounter the outside "not me". Pedagogy stages encounters with the unthought – encounters with the future as in the making' (p. 38). Ellsworth refers to anomalous places of learning as places that may act as pivots that activate experiences and prompt the development of relations between inner and outer, between ourselves and the world. Pivot places 'transform knowledge, self-experience, awareness, understanding, appreciation, memory, social relations, and the future' (p. 37). And through this process, she proposes that places become pedagogical through the ways that we come to know differently through the never-ending relations formed through interactions between inner and outer realities. I propose that a studio may function as a pivot place that connects the inner and outer realms through interactions with materials, the pursuit of curiosities, and the provocation of memories and experiences. Artist Carolee Schneemann (2010) describes a studio:

> It is empty, it is filling. It is the constant site of permission – permission of uncertainty and the rarity of the circumstances in which I can address only my materials and the influences which may or may not bring them into a new form ... the strands are pulling at research, at dream, synesthesia, at political outrage ... The studio is full of nests.
>
> (p. 154)

Ellsworth (2005) emphasizes embodied sensations and the relationship between the thinking and feeling self as she implicates the body, emotions, place, history, and experience in learning and artmaking. She recognizes how memory, fear, desire, and pleasure may emerge within pedagogical places. She highlights the emergence of pedagogy that happens in a particular place and time and that is 'fueled by a fundamental curiosity about things and processes – in this instance, emergent pedagogical elements and qualities – that we do not yet understand and that provoke us to think or imagine in new ways' (p. 5). Pivot places become apparent as pedagogical when viewed as an experience-in-the-making, as hinges that prompt us to think and feel differently.

In this section, drawing from the notion of the studio as a hinge, I discuss what that place may become through artmaking. Firstly, through my lens as the researcher, I discuss the studio visit as a way of engaging with the place and subjectively mapping artistic practices. Secondly, I situate the studio as a part of an ecosystem, highlighting the relationality of artistic practices and contrasting previous notions of an art studio as isolated and separate from the world. Lastly, I discuss how the artmaking process transforms the studio through its ability to transport us elsewhere. I address the following questions:

> How does a studio visit function as a material-based interview that allows artists to situate their art practice in relation to the studio through a dialogic knowledge-in-the making?
> How are studios part of an active and ever-changing ecosystem?
> How does artmaking activate the studio and transform it into a pedagogical place that acts as a pivot that connects the inner and outer and has the potential to transport us elsewhere?

1

Grab That Moment When You're Aesthetically Shocked (Studio as Mapping)

> *Through mapping the experience of being an artist – our sensory world, ideas, and understanding of life – it is possible to develop a story of the imagination. This non-linear story holds both the practical knowledge of creative process and the search for meaning. We come to listen closely to and understand the deep impressions on our imaginations, our themes, the discoveries that come through making, and the lights and shades of our particular world view.*
>
> (West, 2011, p. 12)

Studio Visit as Subjective Mapping

As one of the largest countries in the world with a relatively small population, this journey highlighted both of these qualities. Canada, which is characterized by a diverse and ever-changing landscape, has a small and interconnected painting community. I began my travels in 2014 on the Pacific Coast of Vancouver Island, which is known for its old-growth forests, before heading through the Rocky Mountains of British Columbia and Alberta and to the flat prairies of Central Canada. I visited Calgary during the Calgary Stampede, which provided an interesting backdrop to the studio visits. I found a thriving art community in Winnipeg, the geographical centre of Canada. And I engaged with larger art communities in the cities of Toronto, Ontario, followed by Montreal, Quebec, which has distinct, yet interconnected, Francophone and Anglophone art communities. I proceeded to the East Coast to the small coastal city of Halifax, which is known for its lobster fishing and the world-renowned art school, Nova Scotia College of Art and Design University (NSCAD). I finished the cross-Canada venture in Newfoundland, a province on the rustic Atlantic Coastline. Immersing myself within artists' studios, I recognized the relationships between studio spaces and the cities in which they lived, affordability being a significant factor in studio culture. I visited many buildings re-purposed as art studios, including an old Ukrainian Temple in Saskatoon and an old elementary school in Elora, Ontario. I visited artists who were on temporary artist residencies, including one on the Scarborough Bluffs in Ontario called A Fool's Paradise, a cottage/studio that had been inhabited by Canadian artist Doris McCarthy for 70 years until her death in 2010, at which point it became a heritage site and residency.

A studio visit is a particular kind of interview, one that is located within the materiality of a particular place. Regarding studio visits, artist Marjorie Welish (2010) states:

> A working definition of the studio visit might be that it presents an occasion for the artist to show his or her art to a critic and to engage in a dialogue with this informed audience of one ... But what actually happens in a studio may be hard to pin down. Unstated, uncodified, and subject to on-site improvisation, the exact nature and purpose of the studio visit may always remain elusive.
>
> (p. 182)

I embraced this on-site improvisational process as I engaged in active dialogue with the artists and the spaces. I approached artists, specifically painters, based largely on familiarity with their work and research into public, commercial, and artist-run galleries, recent awards and Faculty in Fine Arts programmes at universities. Thus, many artists interviewed are also art educators within post-secondary institutions and draw from their experience to contribute to my discussion of artistic pedagogies. Many of the artists interviewed had been quite mobile, moving between cities and towns for education, residencies, and exhibitions, thus allowing for a fluid interconnectedness between the places and artists.

I propose that a studio visit is a research methodology that aligns with and performs new materialist theories that emphasize emergence, materiality, and relationality. A studio visit by nature is responsive and improvisational. It is a conversation that emerges in relation to the participants and the materiality of the space. A studio visit is a dialogue between artists, artworks, and objects. The place-specific quality allows it to exceed a traditional interview approach as the materiality of the studio actively shapes the nature of the interview. Further, my own subjectivities as an artist educator actively shaped and engaged with the interview. I was both a learner and a researcher. In a studio visit with artist Ben Reeves in Vancouver, 2014, I noted that I couldn't stop looking at the painting behind him, to which he responded: '*Yes, the paintings are telling their own stories.*' This multiplicity of information from the objects, the place, and the spoken word sets up a space of difference and disjuncture, as what is being said doesn't always line up with the objects in the room. This disjuncture was noted by Reeves, who asserted: '*Tangents in the studio are a natural part of it.*' To address practice-based interviews within artistic research, Hannula et al. (2014) examine practice-focused interview methods, arguing that all practitioners should perform interviews in their respective fields as a means of expanding, developing, understanding, and generating their practice. They describe the open-ended nature of practice-based interviews as not being about describing an objective experience, 'but experience as the base of constant play of leaving and returning, getting closer and gaining distance, but always staying with it – staying with the productive dilemma and its time and place-bound articulations and actualizations' (p. 41). They address ways that interviews reveal how reality is plural, connected to the past, present, and future, and enacted 'through the social imagination of a particular structural space' (p. 41). Within the interviews discussed herein, the studio was a particular context. The place, the art, and the objects in the studio shaped the stories revealed through the interviews.

The analysis of the studio visits was similarly performed through a new materialist lens, one which allowed for a creative assembling of the data drawn from interviews and the studios themselves. Springgay and Zaliwska (2015) approach the analysis of data through the concept of diagramming, wherein working with data is emergent, abstract, and generative. Through this perspective, I work with the data generated through studio visits as 'data-in-the-making' (p. 137) and 'data as open-ended assemblages' (p. 140). Thus, my analysis of the data is creative, nonlinear, and open-ended. Through the lens of the diagram, I engage with the data as a form of mapping. Further, I recognize how, as a researcher, I am implicated in the data as I learn through the practice-based interviews that inform my own artistic practice (Hannula et al., 2014) and embrace how researchers may 'co-compose ourselves with the data' (Springgay & Zaliwska, 2015).

Fear of Forgetting

In a visit to London, Ontario in 2014, Patrick Howlett invited me to his exhibition at Museum London in Ontario titled *Part Time Offerings*. This exhibition challenged viewers to consider the roles of the artist, particularly painters within society and how artmaking exists within complex systems. The exhibition contained several installations, from office space to art fair, to studio, to home furnishing, to demonstrate how art is produced, displayed, and distributed in the world. While on first glance the exhibition appeared to be a critique of ways that art is performed, distributed, and consumed in society, upon closer look and in discussion with Howlett, it became clear that it was more about his story as an artist, travelling, creating art, and participating in a variety of communities. It was about what it means to be an artist navigating society. His personal stories weaving through the work show various memories, from growing up attending an art high school in London, Ontario, to finding a new art community upon moving to Fredericton, New Brunswick to teach art, or remembering his father making painted copies of Modernist art to match his wallpaper. Regarding this work, he said:

> *I was thinking through what it means to be an artist in a time and a place and in Canada. And being interested in the small histories. Artists talking to each other and having conversations was something I wanted to be a subject. So, even my dad's painting was part of a history. Part of the show was making the physical place in which art exists. I think there are some good things about virtual stuff, but the experience of seeing things and talking to people in person, I wanted to be part of the subject. So, it's about learning things from that local person that is around, and it is about knowledge and passing on practices. I was thinking about my history intertwined with other histories.*

This exhibition visit with Howlett (Figure 1.1) underscored the relationality of art practice, the significance of conversation, and the role of place in artmaking.

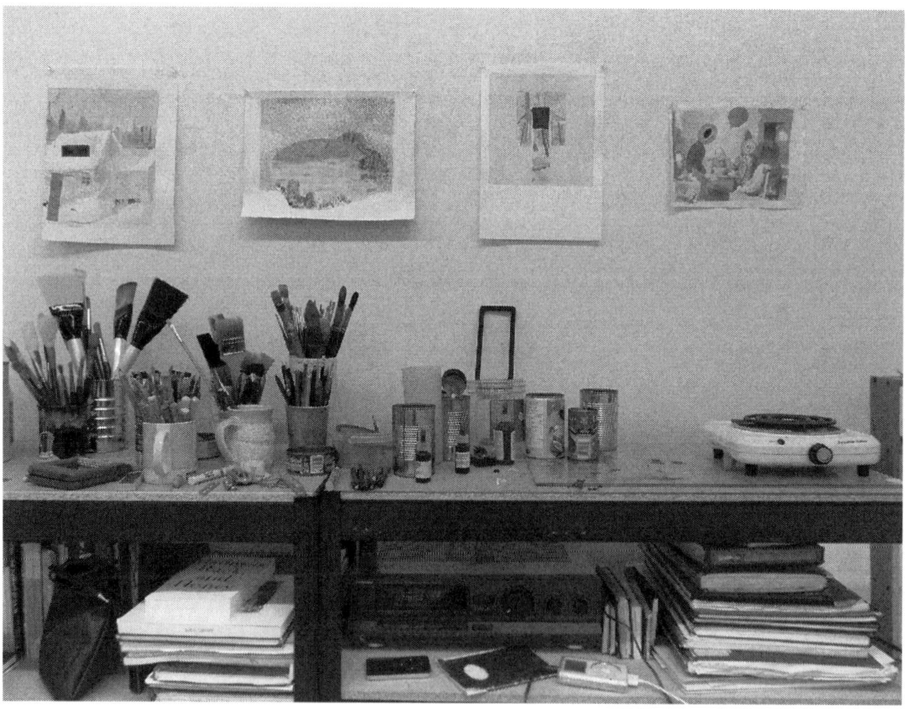

FIGURE 1.1: Patrick Howlett's Studio, London, ON, 2015.

In a studio visit with Jennifer Lefort (Figures 1.2 and 1.3) in Gatineau, Quebec (2014), she emphasized the role of place in her work as she discussed how the city stimulates her painting practice. At the time of the visit, she was excited she would be moving into a new studio collective called Temporaire ('temporary'), developed by a group of artists who also held musical events, that had existed in multiple locations in temporary, run-down old industrial buildings. Lefort described another studio she had had in Toronto years earlier in a building called Thunder Thighs that housed costumes for theatre sets. To get to her studio, she would wade through Viking costumes, mid-1990s outfits, prom dresses, disco dresses, furs, and wedding dresses. Lefort felt energized by the people constantly coming in to find costumes. In her large abstract paintings, Lefort is interested in in-between zones between painting and drawing, between structure and disorder. Her paintings, while abstract, emerge from observation and experience and seeing how marks behave differently in different paintings. While her work is not directly related to place, the place in which she works bleeds into the work. She reflected on times living in large urban areas like Berlin, Toronto, and Montreal:

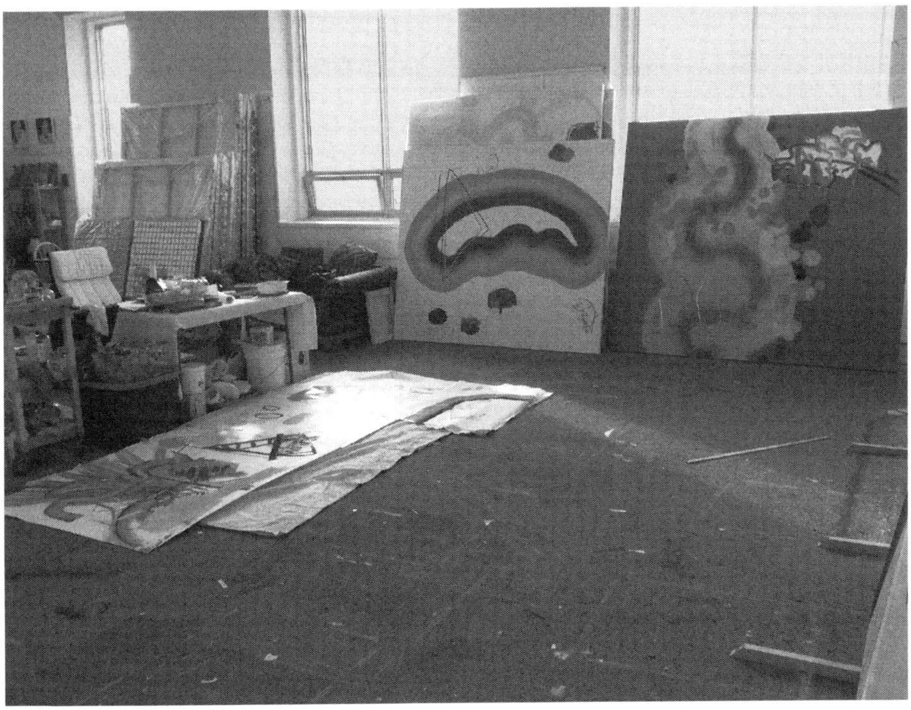

FIGURE 1.2: Jennifer Lefort's Studio, Gatineau, QC, 2014.

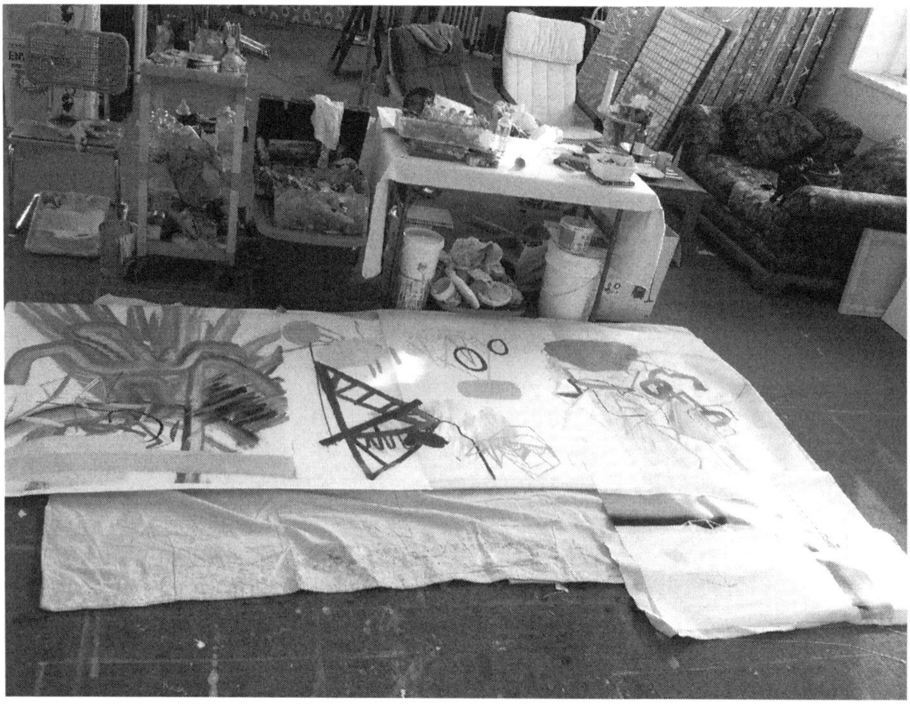

FIGURE 1.3: Jennifer Lefort's Studio, Gatineau, QC, 2014.

> *I could see what it was about Berlin that seeped into the work and informed a number of things, from palette to gesture, to relationships, to layering. So, my process comes from experience. That idea of being in a busy environment, usually an urban space, is that there is a density of things happening simultaneously and you pick up on things ... I'm interested in the experience of painting and experiencing painting. So, where I am and how things are, affect me directly. Art comes from somewhere else, and I need something to feed it.*

I met with Linda Martinello in her Toronto-based studio (Figures 1.4 and 1.5) in 2014. Martinello's work presents an experiential response to places that have historical and personal significance for her. She talked about how she first felt a sublime experience when she went to a small town in Italy following the death of her grandmother and felt a deep connection to that place. Martinello described herself as a hunter and gatherer; however, rather than collecting objects, she is collecting experiences. Contemplating how we all experience place differently, she explained how her work emerged through an improvisational process of working and reworking imagery based on '*data*' collected in the field. She had travelled

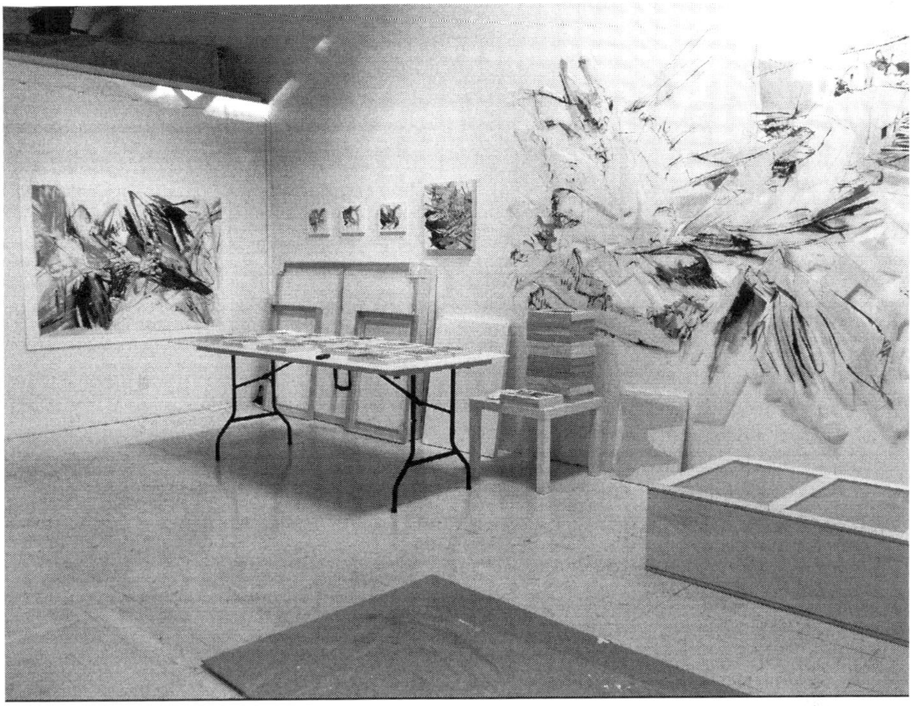

FIGURE 1.4: Linda Martinello's Studio, Toronto, ON, 2014.

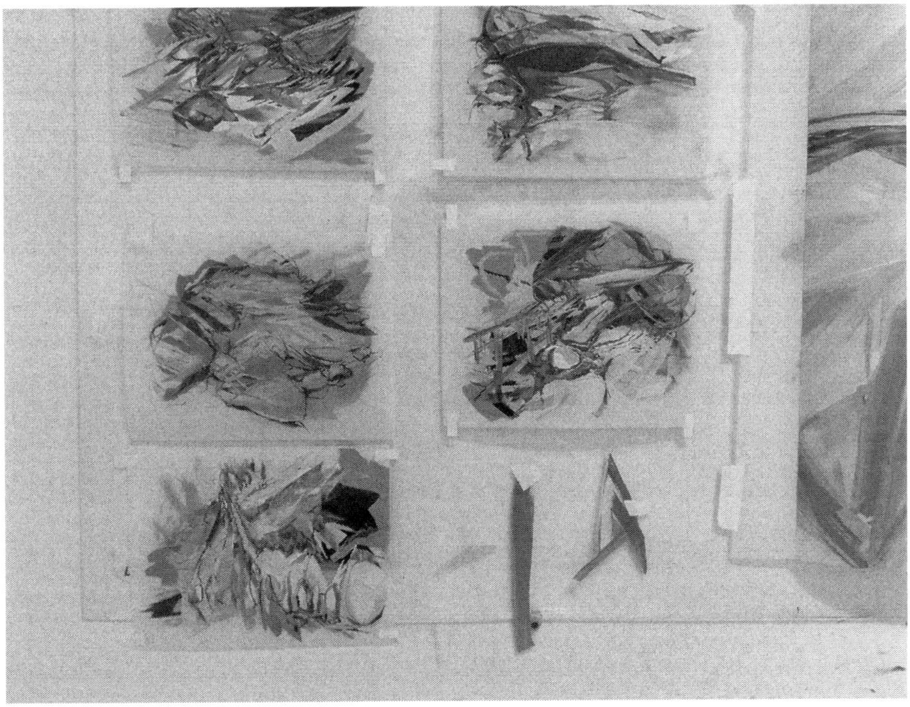

FIGURE 1.5: Linda Martinello's Studio, Toronto, ON, 2014.

to different places of historical, cultural, and geological significance, in particular places with personal, familial connections in Mexico and Italy. Through her process, rather than capturing the image of the place, she would recreate her sensory experience of that place. The return to the studio was a way of making sense of her experience through stirring up the sensations again, re-experiencing these moments and physically responding to those sensations. In these intuitive moments, she was lost in the moment, making sense of that desire to go there. Martinello said she was driven by a '*fear of forgetting*'.

I visited David Blatherwick in 2015 in a backyard studio (Figure 1.6) that he had recently finished building in Elora, Ontario. He shared recent paintings that were drawn from walks around his second home in the Dominican Republic, where his partner is from. There, he'd go for walks through a mangrove tree forest to observe the mangrove trees, which have a complex root system. His work had recently shifted towards paintings that emerged from observational drawings made on site that he would re-interpret in the studio. For Blatherwick, the lighting in the Caribbean allowed him to paint in a particular way that shifted his colour palette. Considering his travels, walking in different places, and absorbing the

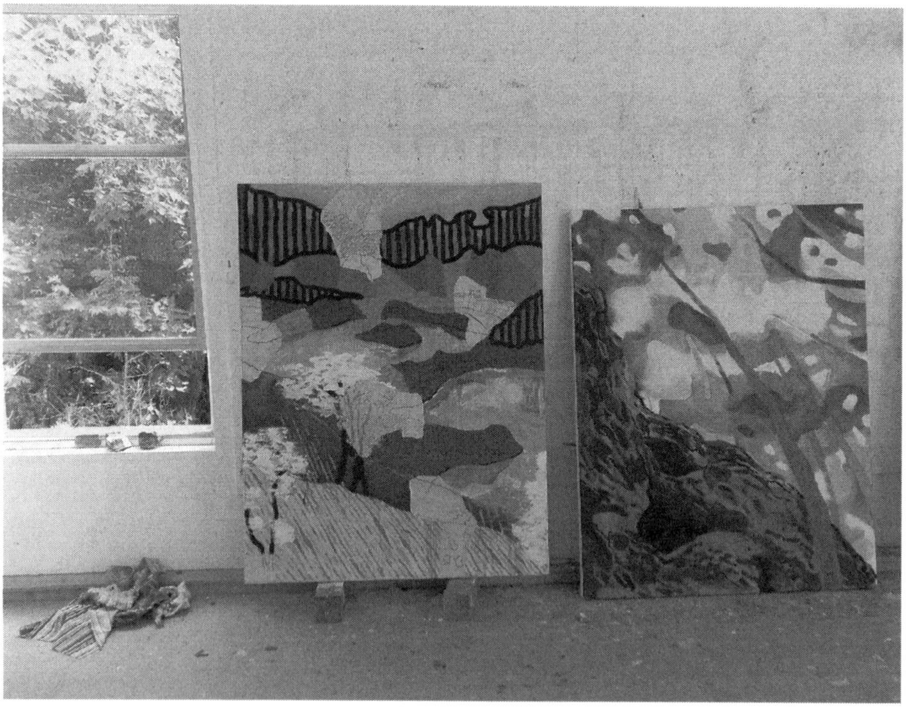

FIGURE 1.6: David Blatherwick's Studio, Elora, ON, 2015.

light in a particular place, he said: '*Whatever the pull that is taking you outside of the art scene is probably the most interesting.*' Blatherwick's paintings emerged through his process of observing light, colour, and shapes in his natural environment. Regarding his experience in the Caribbean and re-experiencing that place within his studio, Blatherwick said:

> *What happened in Dominican Republic was an aesthetic shock. You arrive there and you had no idea that things looked like this or acted like this. And then going to the West Coast, to the rainforest, I had never seen that before either. So, you have to grab that moment where you're aesthetically shocked. You arrive there and see things you didn't know existed. Like weird forms that trees take. I don't know if I want to get addicted to needing it, but the aesthetic shock is extremely important to me. These images and impressions will stay with me when I return to my studio. So, they're stored in my head and regurgitated later in an entirely different context. It's more interesting to come back to it back home in my studio. It stays in my head and gets mashed around with all kinds of other things. You don't have to hang on to the literal reality. The more distance you have from it the more it becomes an impression.*

Drawing from Martinello's discussion of '*fear of forgetting*' and Blatherwick's discussion of an '*aesthetic shock*', I thought about the cross-Canada studio visits in relation to mapping. Art theorist, Simon O'Sullivan (2006) addresses mapping as a process rather than representation:

> Art practice as a form of cartography then, the creative mapping of our connections and potentialities, a mapping that pays attention to regions of intensity (the distribution of affects) and to trajectories of future becomings, as well as to those already delineated continents of representation and signification.
>
> (p. 36)

I draw from O'Sullivan's description of a generative and creative map to address the wandering and exploratory way that I engaged with this research as a form of 'self-reflexive mapping' (Barrett, 2007a, p. 5) that situates my studio practice in relation to other artists and their studios. As I travelled to the studios, connections emerged between places, and I began to see the studio as both situated locally in whichever city I visited and as part of a community of studios that were invisibly connected across the country. This journey was a form of mapping through conversation, through getting lost trying to find studios in hidden places throughout the city, and through drawing connections between the ideas, images, objects, and artworks within the studios.

Addressing the teaching and making of painting, artist and educator, Daniel Sturgis (2016) says: 'Painting can be seen as condensed knowledge, as every brushmark, every choice, is loaded with history and its interpretation' (p. 11). Here, Sturgis emphasizes the ecology of a painting as a web of influences. In the same collection of essays about teaching painting, Gordon Brennan (2016) similarly argues that painting is a process of working with webs of interwoven knowledge:

> If you study art properly and in serious depth you learn about the history of princes and the history of serfs, of astronomy and astrology, of mathematics and magic, topography, agriculture, architecture, clothes and manners, animals and birds, saints and martyrs, religions and philosophies.
>
> (Robertson, 1988, as cited in Brennan, 2016, p. 18)

Through these examples, Brennan implies that artmaking is a transdisciplinary form of inquiry. In a studio visit in Halifax, Mathew Reichertz, similarly said: '*When you become an artist you become an expert in the things you need to learn to do what you want to do.*' This thought was echoed in conversation in a studio visit with Rick Leong (Figure 1.7), who said:

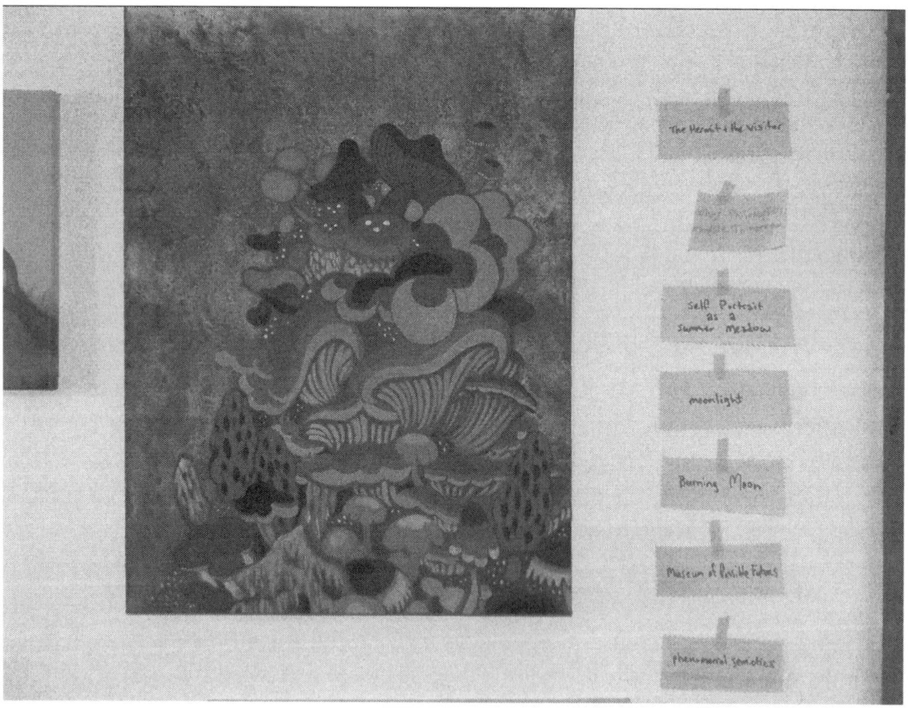

FIGURE 1.7: Rick Leong's Studio, Victoria, BC, 2014.

One of the things I love most about being an artist is we are actively encouraged to pursue any of our interests. We can explore our interests in psychology, sociology, science. We can pursue it, investigate it, but not be bound by rules of that discipline, and bring it into some kind of holistic practice. And then you can see the cross-pollination of those things, how each one can affect each other.

Cross-Pollination

Throughout my trip, studio conversations led me in many directions. I sifted through garbage sights and piles of fabric. I was led through mythical forests and into dark basements. I was guided through maps of sunken ships and sailors lost at sea. I was invited to consider artmaking as a form of dancing. I was explained quantum physics and chaos theory. I considered the relationship between neuroscience and artmaking, between math and artmaking, between physics and artmaking, and between theatre and artmaking. I was brought into artists' travels around the world. I was told that Calgary is the sunniest place in Canada, taken into Winnipeg's snowy winters, and talked about the rustic coastlines of Newfoundland. I was taken back into ancient archaeology, Gothic architecture, Renaissance painting, and Modernist art. Conversations quickly jumped from personal stories to humorous anecdotes, to philosophical texts, to contemporary art theory. Several artists talked about how for them, artmaking was at the intersection of their interest in science, politics, history, sociology, and psychology. They often described studio practice as a way of thinking through the world.

In Kamloops, Andrea Kastner (Figure 1.8) began our studio visit by showing a photograph that motivated one of her paintings in which a house was being towed by a boat, explaining that she had thought this is how they used to move houses in Newfoundland but that later she learned that was not true. It wasn't until I was on the other side of the country in St. John's Newfoundland, that I was told by an artist, in a seemingly unrelated conversation that her story was in fact true. In a visit the week after my visit with Kastner, artist Chris Cran in Calgary took me to the studio of artist John Will in Calgary. Just before leaving, Will pulled out an exhibition catalogue. Within the catalogue, he had old photos that he had come across from a century earlier and had pieced them together into a story. This story included a cruise ship across the Pacific Ocean, a murder mystery, an earthquake, and a search and rescue team. The descriptions accompanying the photos were both fact and fiction; it was his own subjective interpretation of what he had found, but through doing so, he created a relationship between himself and the photographer from a century earlier.

This melding of fact and fiction made its way into conversations with several artists. David Kaarsemaker told a story he had read about an explorer living in a

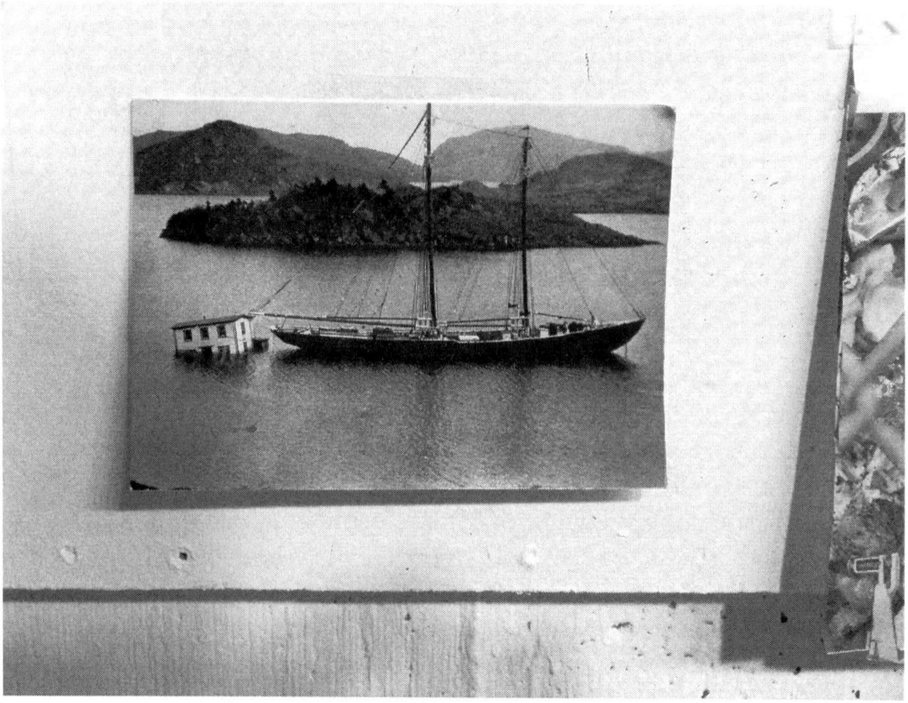

FIGURE 1.8: Andrea Kastner's Studio, Kamloops, BC, 2014.

house made of ice. When he'd breathe, the breath would freeze on the walls, and it kept growing in on him, getting smaller and smaller. Kaarsemaker remembered this story when he moved to a house by the ocean on the coast of Newfoundland with big glass windows. The story and his own reality merged in his paintings of interiors that were ghostly white and embodied a claustrophobic feeling. Artist collaborators, DaveandJenn similarly explained how a painting emerged through weaving chapters of their life, such as being evicted from their home and mouse infestations, with ancient mythology and archaeology. Carol Wainio discussed how she connected seventeenth-century children's book illustrations with images in articles she had recently read in the newspaper about current events and contemporary farming practices. In Halifax, Adam Gunn described a movie he had seen where a man's brain had been replaced by a robot brain, and about a dream he'd had as a child where he woke up and wasn't a real person but rather a pile of jelly with wires coming out of it. Within Gunn's cramped studio (Figure 1.9), I felt like I was brought into a science fiction laboratory, filled with shelves of toys taken apart and pieced back together, and brain-like piles of foam spray dramatically lit up like a still life.

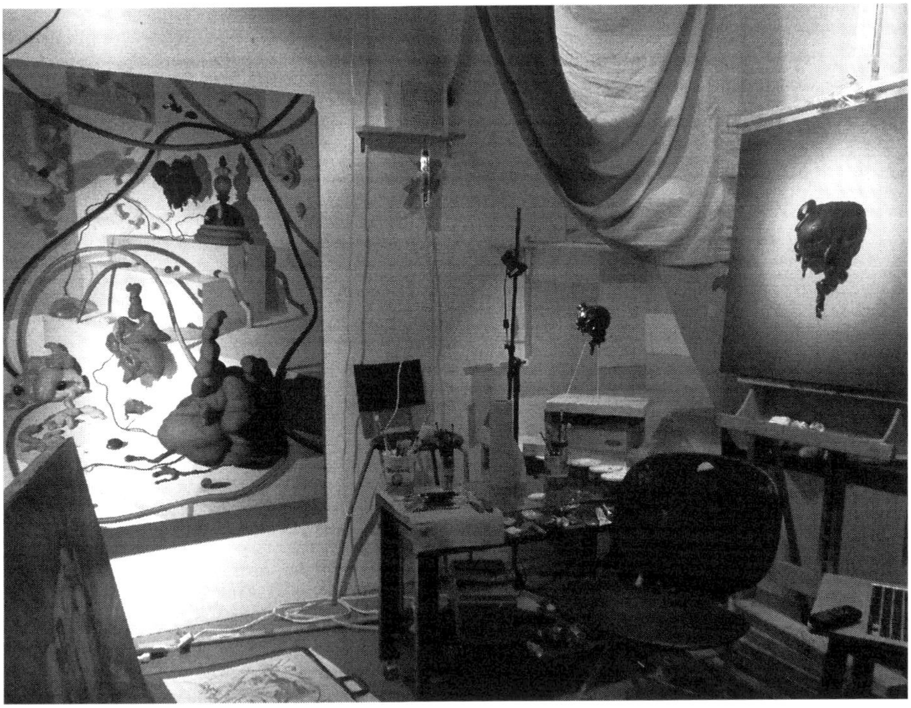

FIGURE 1.9: Adam Gunn's Studio, Halifax, NS, 2014.

I left several visits and pursued further research into people and places discussed. Artists described pieces of Canadian history and challenged me to reflect on how mythologies are constructed. I learned from Laura Findlay about a famous ship in Canadian history, the Edmond Fitzgerald that sank in Lake Superior. Findlay drew me into this mystery that had engulfed a small town where they continue to discuss the several possible theories for the sinking ship, based only off fragments of wreckage gathered through deep water dives. These interests seemed to parallel conversations with Carly Butler who made art about navigation systems and being lost at sea. In Ottawa, Gavin Lynch explained how his research had taken him back to his hometown to investigate stories behind Yellowhead pass and the story of fur trader Tete Jaune. Artists reflected on making art in different locations that shaped their practice. I went to Will Gill's studio where he told me about a residency called the Arctic Circle aboard a tall ship that goes to the Arctic. A guard would stand watch over the artists in case of an encounter with a polar bear. Gill shared photographs of World War I ships covered in 'dazzle camouflage', decorated in a way that mimicked Modernist abstraction, a strategy used during the war to confuse enemies about the distance and orientation of the ship. I met with Kym

Greeley, who on our first visit shared landscape paintings from her time on Fogo Island, Newfoundland. On a second visit, her work had shifted towards domestic spaces following the birth of her twins. She said that the pink of her painting had taken two days to mix. Later, on that visit in St. Johns, iconic Canadian artist Mary Pratt drew me into the stories of her life living in Newfoundland through her still life paintings of cooked salmon and apple pie.

I listened as artists discussed how their art emerged in unplanned and nonlinear ways. Sean Weisgerber described how he was at the grocery store one day looking at an apple, which led to dipping fruits in paint, which then led to creating an elaborate pulley system in Saskatoon to dip his paintings. Ufuk Gueray said that he came across an essay that led him to a desire to paint sausages, and he subsequently began ordering artificial sausages from Germany. Ashleigh Bartlett (Figure 1.10) explained how sharing a studio with a fashion designer, combined with her background in figure skating, led her to collecting fabrics, creating fabric sculptures, and which led her to theatrically cut-up paintings. And Suzanne Funnel shared a trunk full of a collection of letters, old teaching assignments, and drawings that people do extemporaneously to explain things. She explained how she would be at Tim Hortons, for

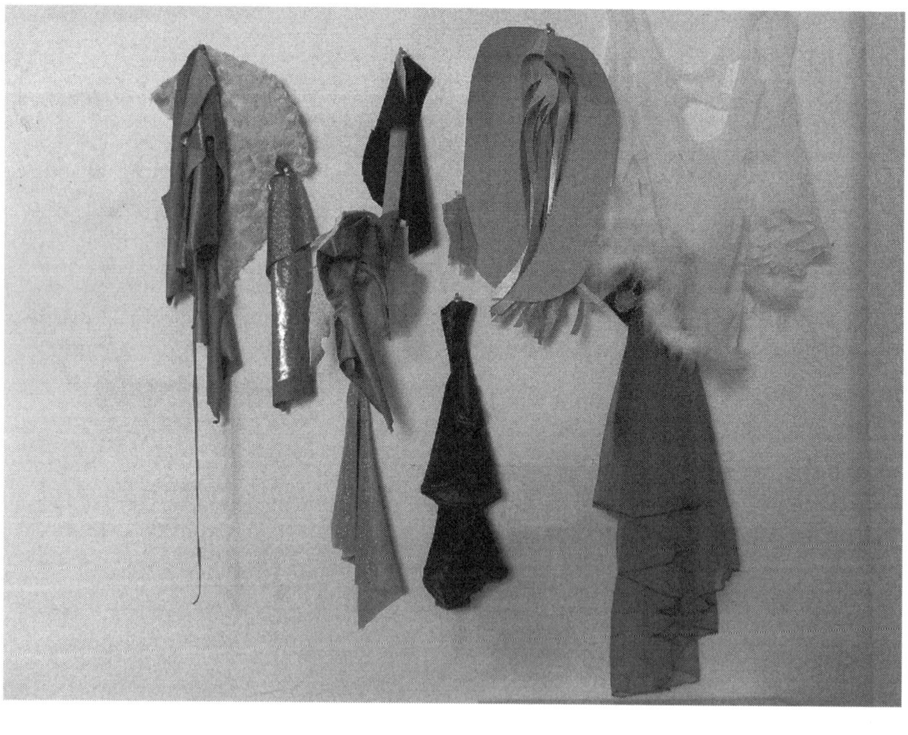

FIGURE 1.10: Ashleigh Bartlett's Studio, Calgary, AB, 2014.

example, and would observe conversations where construction workers created a drawing on a napkin explaining how to fix an elevator. She would ask them if she could have the sketch to add to her collection. In Halifax, Mitchell Wiebe said he had once had a studio in an old postwar underground bunker and wouldn't leave this underground haven for days at a time. Sarah Cale had inhabited a studio down the hall from a psychotherapy office specializing in 'Primal' or 'Scream' Therapy. Her art practice would be interrupted sporadically by long ear-piercing screams. Patrick Cruz described how he went to clown school after art school, and in clown school, they would spend the first 15 minutes every day laughing involuntarily. It helped to see art through humour, similar to the clown philosophy, which made it easier to digest heavy theories, philosophies, and experiences.

Will Gill described his fascination with the times in life when you come really close to the edge and in the hardship people experience in their surroundings. Cynthia G. Renard remembered how as a child, alone, they would invent worlds with pillows and furniture in their living room that involved islands and sharks. And Janet Werner reminded me of watching Romper Room as a child, staring into the mirror until I saw something. Artists took me back to my own childhood of Nintendo games and discussed their childhood interests in comic books and 1980s horror movies. John Kissick and I talked about how it is hard to break away from our childhood influences and how 1970s punk and disco music created an entry point for him to talk about painting and abstraction. As he drew parallels between his paintings and this music, he said: '*I was punking my disco and discoing my punk.*' He claimed that in his generation learning to paint in the 1980s and 1990s, it was hard to make abstract paintings that weren't ironic. He said his brightly coloured, delicious-looking paintings work if '*they are winking at the viewer*'.

Montreal artist, Dil Hildebrand described his work as an infinite game or an ongoing educational puzzle. Patrick Howlett used the game of squash as one of many metaphors to describe painting. As I looked through Robert Taite's studio in Winnipeg, I thought about how I could continuously re-arrange his artworks to create new formations, like an infinite puzzle. Mark Mullin (Figure 1.11) described his painting process as a series of events responding to the next event and unfolding like a theatre performance, an obstacle course or an interactive video game. Describing the actions of the video game in reference to his paintings, he said: '*This entered the that, which then tumbled off of this, then something else is witnessed by the thing coming from above and pushed out the thing that is leaving from below.*' Mullin described artmaking as producing infinite questions.

Eliza Griffiths said that art proliferates unquantifiable and unpredictable possibilities. She described her desire for a '*sensation*' of a thing rather than a '*description*' of a thing, and that in order to achieve that, one must go around it. Ben Reeves addressed the way that artists often speak '*around work*' rather than '*about the*

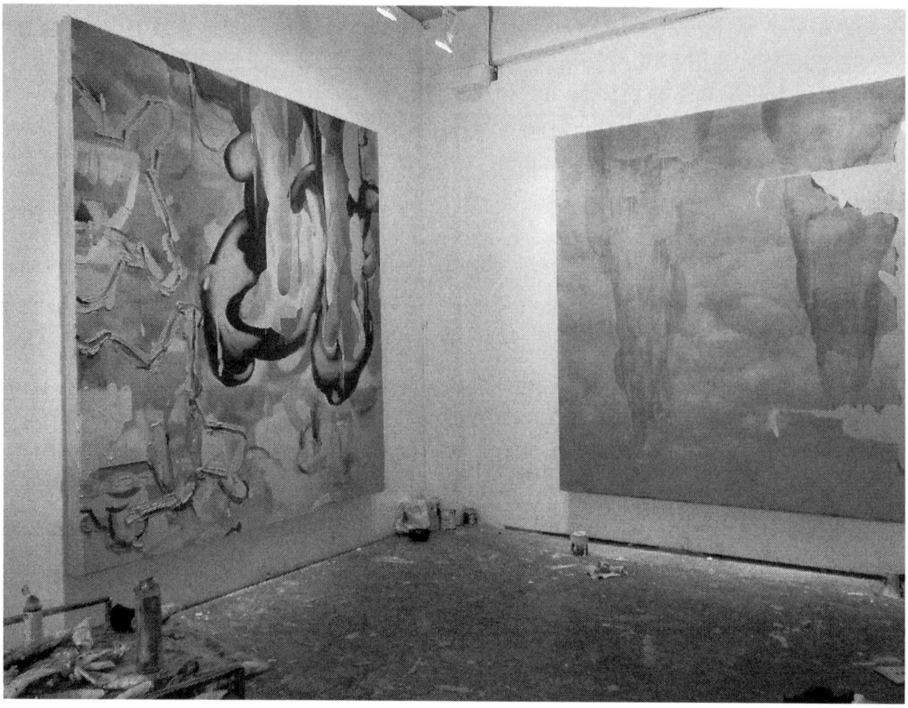

FIGURE 1.11: Mark Mullin's Studio, Calgary, AB, 2014.

work'. Through the lens of curiosity, Coats (2023) embraces the tangents, the distractions, and the wandering tendencies of learning:

> Distraction becomes a capacity for sensing and drifting with the unfamiliar or uncanny, rather than favoring the unifying nature of attentiveness (Lewis, 2020). In this sense, curiosity's divergent tendency is enacted as a state of attentive distraction to other possibilities.
>
> (p. 21)

Similarly, through these conversations, unpredictable insights emerged through stories artists told that went around the work, but nonetheless weaved in and out, intersecting at various points and providing context to the artistic processes. These wandering conversations and tangential stories that occur around the work rather than about the work often offer insights into the nonlinear way knowledge emerges through artistic practice through the process described by Rick Leong as '*cross-pollination*'. As a research methodology, the studio visits align with a particular nonlinear and material-based process inherent within studio practice.

2

Move the Conversation Even in a Tiny Way (Studio as Ecosystem)

> *Every ecology is creative. And every creative ecology is an event, forever changing all of its elements as it co-creates the next moment. This is how I define creative agency. This too is why I find it no longer reasonable or useful to measure creativity in any human-centred, or individual, exceptionalist way. It ignores the truth of this always-creative interconnectedness.*
>
> (Harris, 2021, p. 5)

Co-create Our Studio Ecologies

In the book *Creative Agency*, art education professor, Dan Harris (2021) confronts historical and individualistic notions of creativity and instead prompts readers to consider how creativity emerges and evolves within a community, as an ecosystem. Further, through emphasizing interconnectedness, they address creativity as an active and changing process. Harris uses the term 'never-ending' to address their creative ecosystem as they describe how their current ecosystem consists of gardening, walking, writing, cooking, their chair, their family, friends, students, their neighbourhood, the beach, the kayak, etc.:

> There is no end to the list of the elements that make up my ecology, and my meditation practice around this awareness shows me that any creative act or atmosphere or assemblage is also never ending, always changing, becoming with its ecological elements.
>
> (Harris, 2021, p. 5)

Harris addresses the history of creativity studies which has focused on gifted exceptionalism, innovation and entrepreneurship, creative economies, and individualism, but they reject those characterizations of creativity for not considering an ecological or collective approach.

Similarly, the history of art studios, through a European lens, has been dominated by stories of creative genius and individualism since the Renaissance (Cole & Pardo, 2005) rather than focusing on the interconnectedness of creative communities. Art historians, Michael Cole and Mary Pardo (2005) date the 'invention' of the art studio to the Renaissance. In their edited book, they examine how mythologies of the Modern artist were constructed through depictions of the studio from the Renaissance through to the nineteenth century, during which time the term 'studio' emerged which referred to the space where a scholar worked. This scholar persona was depicted in images of the studio throughout the seventeenth to nineteenth centuries, which were not real representations of the studio, but rather fictitious spaces that depict collections of artefacts, relics of scientific study, maps, literary references, and imagery that reflected the artists' in-depth knowledge of the world, the artist as a solitary scholar (Wood, 2005).

In 1979, artist Daniel Buren wrote an essay entitled 'The function of the studio' that addressed the role of the studio and described it as an isolated and private place where the work originates and that is characterized by limits, frames, and enclosures. More recently, art theorist Lane Relyea (2010) challenges the myth of the isolated space of the artist studio and instead addresses the relational quality of artmaking:

> No longer does the studio appear as an ideological frame that mystifies production, a space where realities of social or mass production are supposedly held at bay in favour of an antiquated craft model that showcases the individual artist's creative genius. And no longer is the studio seen as belonging to a 'system' ... as a space characterized by box-like enclosures, of 'frames and limits', each assigned a discreet place in some rigid, stable, and all-determining structure or order. What system or structure does exist today is more properly described as a *network*.
>
> (p. 220, original emphasis)

Relyea describes studios as situated within a web of connections and as characterized by change, multidirectional movement, transmutation, and integration.

While Relyea's acknowledgement of the network in which a studio exists highlights the interconnectedness between artists and institutions, Harris (2021) suggests that this creative ecology is not simply conversations between artists and art communities but is instead a way of viewing our entire lives as a creative ecosystem. They contend that to pay attention to our creative ecologies is to connect creativity to our everyday experiences, a re-imagining of creativity as lived experience. They say: 'Our ecologies always co-create our experiences, our work, our feelings, our atmospheres and accomplishments' (p. 20). Moreover, through this lens, Harris proposes that we may model a different way of living and researching, 'proceeding by experience, observation, curiosity, and being present' (p. 21).

I view studios as participants in a creative ecosystem, a web of connections. I write through the lens of my ever-changing community as an artist and art educator. Reflecting on travelling over 6,000 km to cities across Canada, I am struck by the interconnectedness of artists across the country, and through these encounters, the artists I visited each become a part of my own creative ecosystem. As a female artist who began studying an art history that largely focused on European male artists, I am particularly drawn to voices that extend this art historical ecosystem to reflect the experiences of those who have been excluded from art history. I examine studios as part of an ever-changing ecosystem through discussing a series of interviews that highlight the interconnections between artists and the places in which they make art, all of which are ever-changing.

Paralleling Two Different Lives

The interconnection between generations of artists and the relationship between studio and place was highlighted in a visit with Ehryn Torrel (2016) at the Doris McCarthy artist residency in Scarborough, Ontario, just outside of Toronto. As I drove up to the old cottage studio on the Scarborough Bluffs, I was struck by the ways stories are passed down through the echoes of the past, held within studios. On the path leading up to the cottage, named Fool's Paradise, a plaque read:

> This property sits on the ecologically sensitive, geologically significant Scarborough Bluffs that display sediments left by glaciers over 70,000 years during the last phase of the Pleistocene epoch. Aboriginal peoples may have inhabited this site as early as 8,000 B.C. Scottish immigrant James McCowan settled this land for farming in 1833, calling it 'Springbank' because of the springs running from the ancient shoreline of Lake Iroquois (predecessor of Lake Ontario) to the north. In 1939, Canadian artist Doris McCarthy purchased the easternmost part of Springbank, which her mother called 'Fool's Paradise' because she considered it to be such an extravagant purchase. McCarthy's home and studio grew over the years and in 1998 she donated Fool's Paradise to the Ontario Heritage Foundation for heritage and artistic activities.
>
> (Ontario Heritage Foundation n.d.)

This plaque greets us as we enter this studio, signalling that we are not just connected to this artist who moved onto this land almost 100 years ago, but rather that we are interconnected with the 1,000s of years of history. This history connects the geology of the land to the Indigenous people inhabiting the land for thousands of years, to British settlement of the land, and finally, a young female artist going against the norm and moving to this land to follow her own path. The ecosystem of this studio extends through time.

The cottage overlooking the bluffs had more recently become an artist residency. It was there that I met artist, Ehryn Torrell (Figures 2.1 and 2.2) who resided at Fool's Paradise for three months and shared the studio with the ghost of the previous inhabitant, Doris McCarthy. Mixed with the familiar smell of Ontario cottages was the distinct smell of an art studio. This little house was at the intersection of these two places. Doris McCarthy had bought the land in 1939 against the wishes of her parents to pursue her life as an artist. Throughout the house there is evidence of McCarthy's life preserved within the heritage site since her death in 2010; books, paintings, portraits, furniture, and knickknacks adorned the rooms.

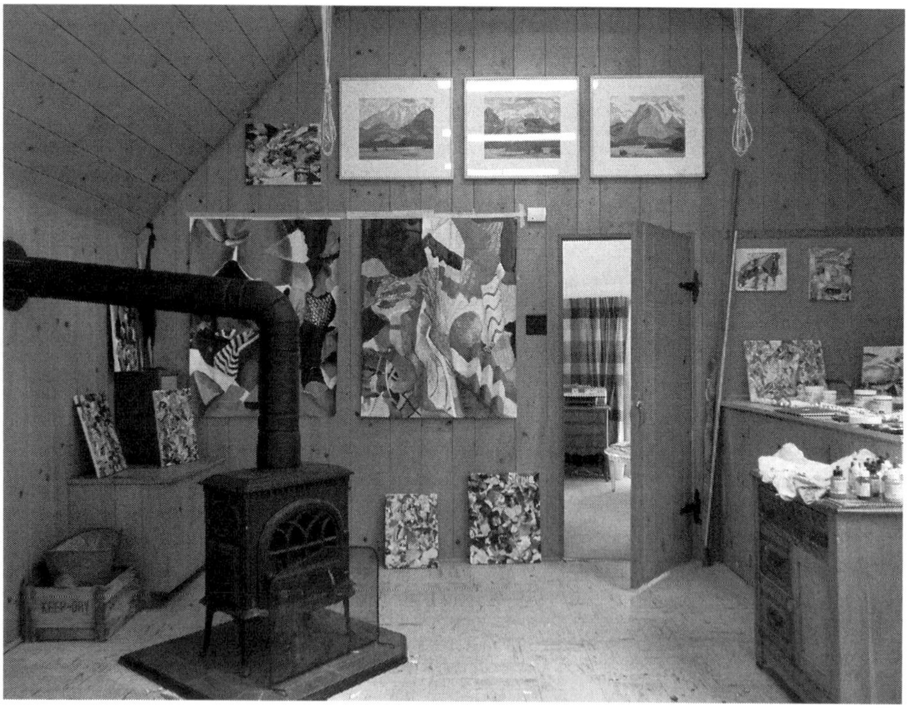

FIGURE 2.1: Ehryn Torrell's Studio, Doris McCarthy Fool's Paradise, Scarborough, ON, 2016.

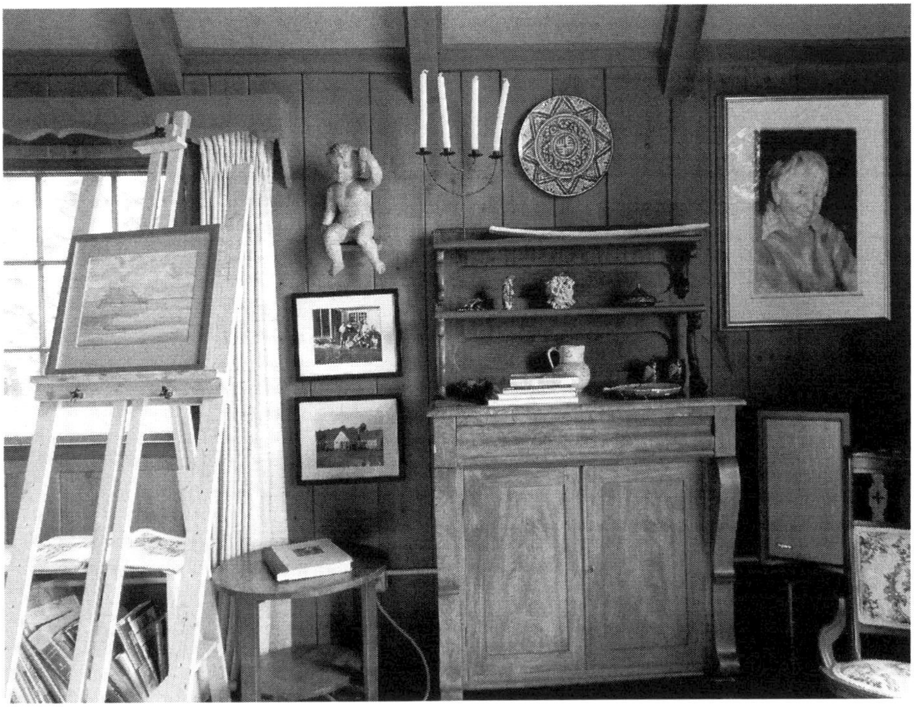

FIGURE 2.2: Ehryn Torrell's Studio, Doris McCarthy Fool's Paradise, Scarborough, ON, 2016.

However, by turning it into an art residency for other artists to inhabit as a studio, it became something other than a museum. It became an active studio where the memory of McCarthy continued to be re-activated by the artists now working in the space. Within *Handbook for Fool's Paradise* written by Doris McCarthy before she died, she explained how the house had evolved over the course of her 70 years there. She introduces it saying: '*This house grew by bits and pieces as I could afford to give myself more needed space. It is therefore unconventional in many ways and will be better enjoyed when its eccentricities are understood.*' Torrell felt connected to this place because her parents had grown up around there and her mother was buried a few kilometres away along with her grandparents and other family. In a sense, Torrell felt as if she was coming home. McCarthy became inextricably linked to her work and her routine. Looking around the room, the images made by McCarthy next to those by Torrell created an interesting juxtaposition.

In our conversation in this old studio cottage, Torrell took me back through the years of her work as an artist. In her paintings, she addresses the materiality of space through her investigations of place and architecture. When she was studying for her Master of Fine Arts (MFA) at the Nova Scotia College of Art and Design, Torrell began to explore her interests in place and architecture: '*My core subject was memory and longing and real attempts to articulate experience in space and experience in place and understand what that means.*' Her interest culminated in work about a house she had seen in the north end of Halifax that had fascinated her because the whole back was taken off like a doll's house, a magical symbol she thought was both attractive and scary. A few months later, it was all boarded up. She started taking videos of herself walking around the space, and as she did this, she talked to people in the community who would share gossip and fictional rumours about its history. For her, this place embodied the interwoven stories that existed within a particular place. Torrell started making paintings of it as it was being demolished. One is a 19-foot painting of the house being torn down in which she had also intertwined fragments of her own experiences.

> *It was like a few decades of neglect and history was exploding. But then interwoven within this wreckage I inserted things, imaginative things that could happen inside rubble, for example, bits of a wedding dress sticking out. I was tying together my experiences, and all those little subjects became woven in.*

Regarding the projection of her own experiences onto this house, Torrell said: '*There is an associative power, ascribing meaning to something that isn't yours. Empathy became so important in this project.*'

Architecture was an ongoing subject within Torrell's practice: '*I feel like construction and demolition and building and unbuilding is a universal language.*' Architecture became a way for her to connect her experiences with others through the connections that have emerged in places. The concept of paralleling two different lives was apparent in the way she inhabited the home and studio of artist, Doris McCarthy. Torrell reflected on how her attachment to this place came from her own experiences and projections onto it, through a connection to her own family cottage that had become a contentious space. In the living room of the cottage studio, there was a portrait of McCarthy, staring out at future inhabitants and her book collection remained for artist residents to use. There was an album of *New Yorker* cartoons from 1925 to 1950. Torrell was drawn to a book from the 1940s about women in antiquity. She also found an old book with an image of an archaeological dig, and she realized that this image allowed her to view her current work in a new way as layers of material were covered and uncovered like an excavation. In the cottage, Torrell found an old 1920s Singer sewing machine and a drawer full of bobbins, thread, and fabric left behind by McCarthy. She began cutting up old paintings and sewing them together to create quilted collaged paintings. I asked Torrell how being at the McCarthy cottage had affected her work.

> *So, there's this legacy that I'm now part of and can contribute to. When I came, I wondered if I would find this visual material and create my own collage material from the memory of the area. I wondered whether that personal subject matter would leak into this collage process. But what I found so interesting is that it's been really about me re-calibrating with myself through making work. I find myself thinking about the advice I got 10 or 15 or 20 years ago from someone. Or I'll be making something, and I'll be thinking that it's like I'm making a painting from when I was 23. So, it's this dialogue over time. And that's moved me to tears.*

Painting Speaks Back to Its History

While studios have often been discussed within art theory as isolated and individualistic, researcher Jenny Sjoholm (2013) addresses the interaction between isolation and sociality within studio practice, which she describes as existing in an ongoing productive tension. Arguing firstly that an overemphasis is placed on knowledge and learning as a social activity, she advocates for a recognition of the value in self-directed practices within the close, intimate, and personal space of the studio. She emphasizes the contemplative nature of studio practice. On the other hand, she argues that the studio is always culturally embedded within its context, within a community, a city, and a nation. Within this community, the studio and the artist are situated within a web of social connections. These connections are explicit, through mechanisms such as research outside of the studio, exhibitions, teaching practices, studio visits, and other social practices. In addition, she describes 'invisible socialities' that situate artistic practices within wider beliefs, conventions, and artistic references that are always present within an artistic process. It is these invisible socialities that I propose allow for a more complicated social network to exist between studios and the ecologies in which they are situated.

In her studio in Vancouver, British Columbia, in 2015, Allyson Clay (Figure 2.3) addressed how she navigated the artistic ecosystem of Vancouver throughout her career. In her studio, there were paintings that featured text as a way of engaging with the language used to describe painting. She had been drawn to a book called *Abstract Painting in Canada* (Nasgaard, 2008) which uses expressive and dramatic language to describe paintings. Clay read one excerpt from the book that described an accompanying painting: '*Splashed and scraped and overlayed with streaked applications of blue and yellow.*' Another read: '*Red falling back like the bottom of a shallow stream.*' Clay found the language to be both evocative and exciting

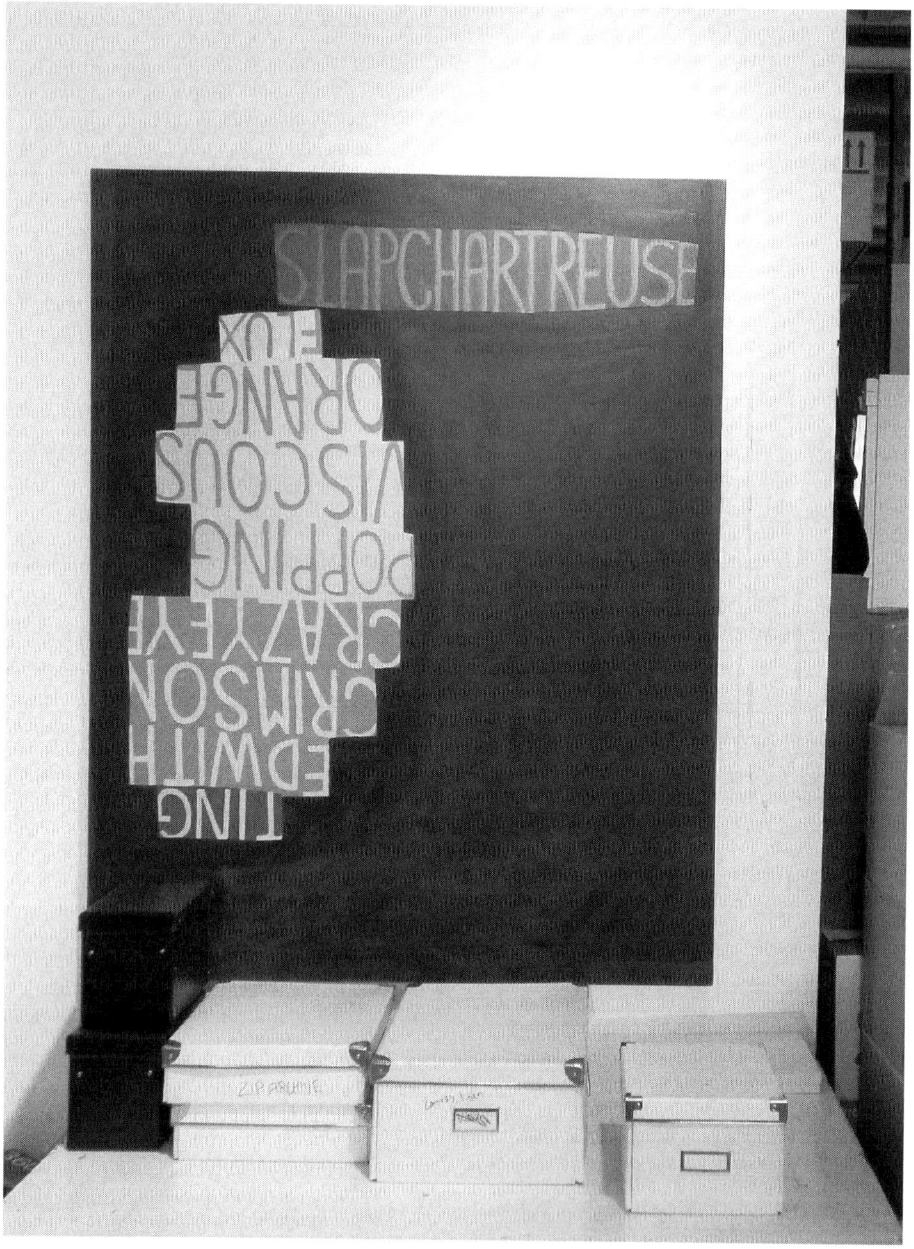

FIGURE 2.3: Allyson Clay's Studio, Vancouver, BC, 2015.

and began to work with the text, enclosing it in shapes on the canvas: '*I see the shapes as the constrictions of abstraction that are left over from abstraction and Modernism. I'm playing with that and interfering with it, making very awkward compositions intentionally.*' One painting in the studio read: '*Slap chartreuse, tinged with crimson, crazy eye-popping viscous orange flux.*'

As Clay developed as an artist in the 1980s in Vancouver, she navigated and intervened in the dominant art histories of painting. Through engaging with artmaking as an ongoing conversation with art history, she re-invigorates a history that has been omitted while finding her own voice as a painter working within Vancouver that at a time was dominated by conceptual photography. During our visit, Clay shared her 'intervention' into an old art history book by Doreen Ehrlich, *Masterpieces of 20th Century Painting* (1989). As a commission for the Lethbridge University Art Gallery in Alberta, Clay had thrown the Ehrlich book in the Old Man River and photographed it as it floated underwater. The book was damaged in this process; however, at Clay's request, the gallery mailed the dried but altered book back to her. The Old Man River book *Drowning* became the first part of her project with this book, where she attempted to apply a physical gesture of disruption to a dominant western and masculine narrative of traditional art history. She pulled out the book that was dry, but puffed, puckered, and torn from water damage. Eventually, over top of the worn-out pages, she painted monochromatic shapes she had abstracted from other artworks by twentieth-century women painters to counteract an internalized art history and restore some omissions from this narrative, in a decisive painterly gesture. Clay writes about this work:

> It's a physical alteration of the material of the book and the progress of its time; re-ruining, re-placing. It's like a voice-over in paint. Paint is viscous. Oily halos form around the images I make. The paper is sucking the oil from the paint in the ruined book. Suck, suck, suck; Mondrian, Picasso, Baselitz. Oil seeps into O'Keefe, Riley, Rothenberg, softening everything. I am laying a map of leaking borders – traces from the spaces of women – across pages of a familiar internalized art history.
>
> (Clay & Warland, 2015)

Clay sees herself as one of many artists actively involved in re-compositions of otherwise normative, male-dominated, and colonial historical narratives.

In Toronto, Monica Tap (met in 2014, 2015, 2022) (Figures 2.4–2.7) similarly described her story of navigating the various artistic influences that shaped her as an artist. Tap discussed her experience going to Nova Scotia College of Art and Design University (NSCAD) in 1982. NSCAD, founded in 1887, would become the first degree-granting art school in Canada and it became an international centre for postsecondary art education throughout the 1970s. Rejecting traditional art

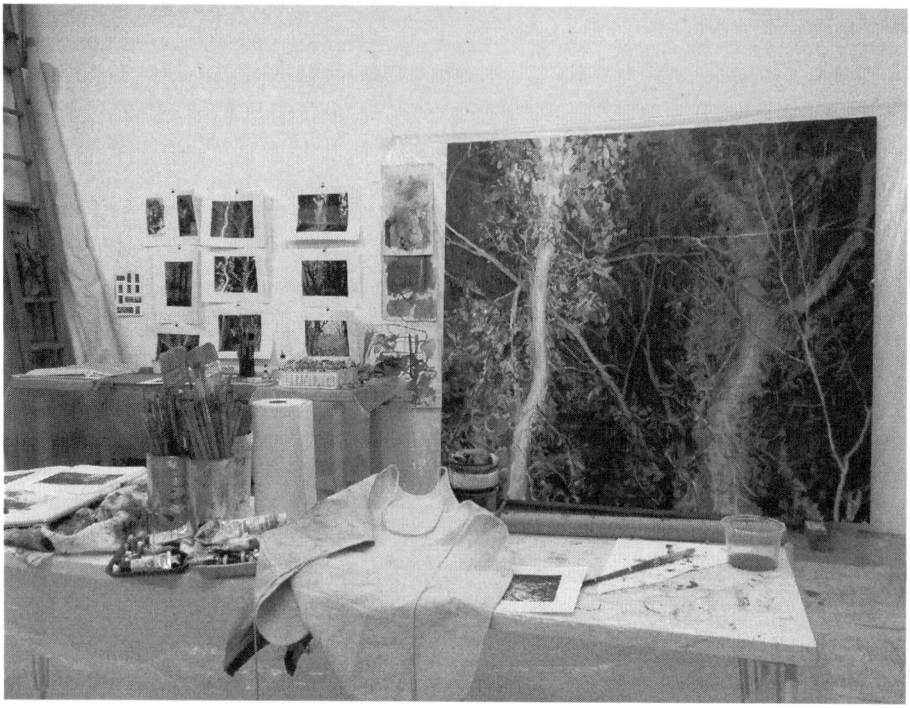

FIGURE 2.4: Monica Tap's Studio, Toronto, ON, 2015.

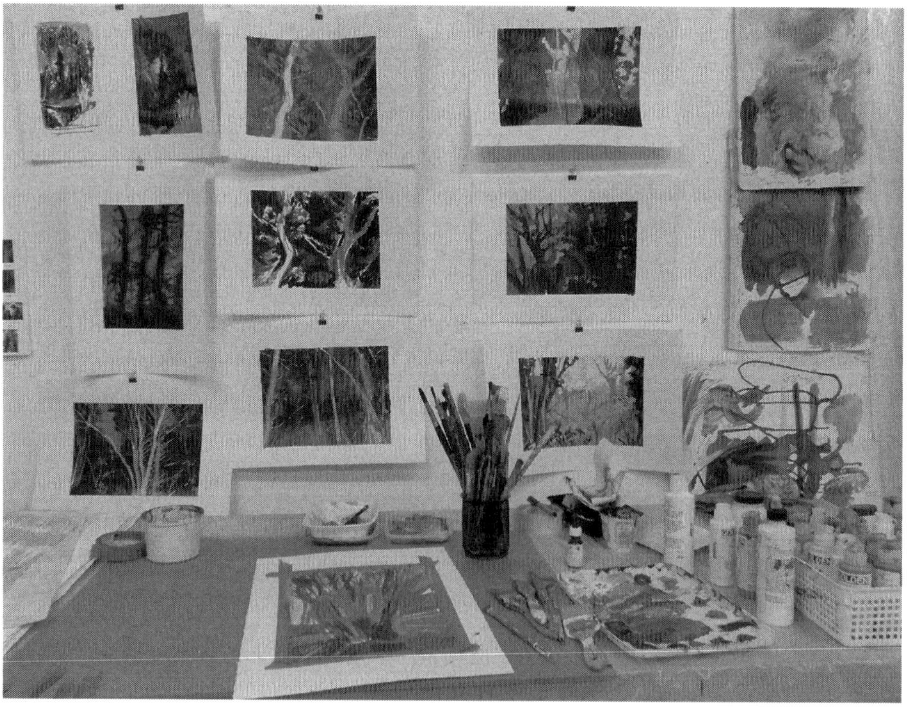

FIGURE 2.5: Monica Tap's Studio, Toronto, ON, 2015.

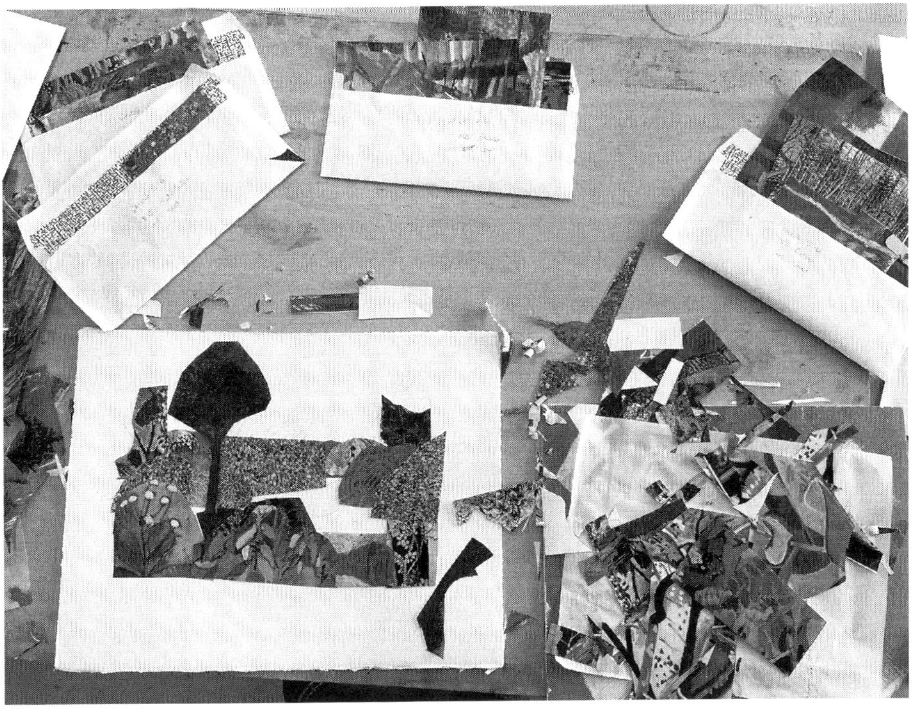

FIGURE 2.6: Monica Tap's Studio, Toronto, ON, 2022.

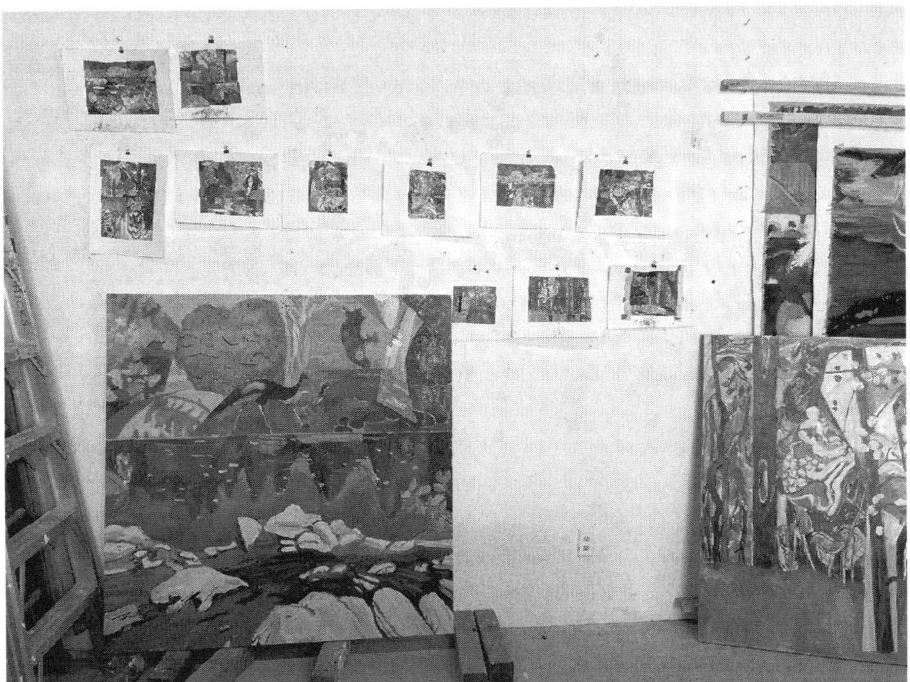

FIGURE 2.7: Monica Tap's Studio, Toronto, ON, 2022.

school pedagogies, practices, and mediums, it became a centre for conceptual art. For Tap, the value of going to art school is about being part of a community, a broader discussion, and a history bigger than that moment. By responding and connecting through the multitude of art historical references within her work, she said: '*Painting always talks back to its history*.' While in some cases her work explicitly references artworks, in other cases, the art's historical references hovered in the background, becoming embedded within the making of the work.

Through her paintings, she navigated histories of landscape, abstract expressionism, and conceptual art through a focus on the marks used to make up a painting. During her graduate work in the 1990s, Tap responded to the paintings by Dutch seventeenth-century painter Rachel Ruysch who was known for her paintings of flowers. Tap dissected the marks made by the artist on the canvas by projecting paintings by Rachel Ruysch on top of each other, abstracting the flower imagery of the painting by focusing on the layering of the individual marks that had made up the image. Through this process, the paintings began to reference Abstract Expressionist marks while also subverting the masculinity associated with that twentieth-century Modernist art movement. Unintentionally, her work increasingly moved into the genre of landscape while also resisting it as she continued to focus on the marks made on the canvas. For example, while teaching a landscape drawing class, she became fascinated by marks used by artists between the seventeenth and nineteenth centuries to translate the giant space of the landscape onto tiny pieces of paper. Along with the students, Tap made a dictionary of marks to signify trees, leaves, etc. and this became a starting point in her work. At that time, a postmodern deconstruction of painting set the context of how one made paintings. However, through this process, she also created conversations between art historical moments. Through re-engaging with marks from earlier generations of artists, she abstracted and reconstructed the meaning: '*I was most interested in bringing together these drawings from different periods and making them cohere and have conversations with each other on the space of the canvas*.'

Her work evolved to painting stills from videos taken out of the window of her car, seeing the landscape in relation to time and space. Throughout her career, her work appears to shift from a more conceptual, removed, and disconnected experience in the landscape, toward a more personal and lived experience with the land. Shifts throughout the years in painting discourse which shaped the ecologies of painting practices were reflected in that change, from conceptual, to discursive, to a more experiential approach. Tap described her newer work as examining her complex engagement with the world. Her process entails assembling fragments from '*outtakes from painting's history with elements from my snapshots, colour notes and memory*'. She explores how landscape may trigger memory while also revealing how aesthetics may have shaped our understandings and engagements with the landscape.

In a studio visit with Tap in Toronto in 2022, her work continued to be in conversation with artists from the past, but in a way reflective of how she views and experiences her natural surroundings. In 2018, she visited a garden in Bremen, Germany, that has the largest rhododendron collection in the world. She described a moment where she felt like she was inside a painting. She realized she sees the world through the artists who had painted it throughout history.

> *Painters often give us the eyes to see and I've always appreciated how an artist can allow us or invite us to see the world through their eyes. I thought it would be fun to see what would happen if I put on the artist glasses relative to this particular place that seemed already to be a painting.*

This led to cutting up coloured reproductions of paintings and glueing them on top of photographs of this garden. Through this process, she continued to reconstruct space, bringing together personal photographic references with references from painting's history. Within a single painting, she might bring in a foreground from artist Paul Gauguin or the colour of trees from a David Hockney painting, or a pond found in Jean-Baptiste-Camille Corot's landscapes. She named the paintings after particular artists such as *Helen's Pond* because of the blue that was similar to Helen Frankenthaler or *Charles' Tree* after Charles Burchfield. Through this work, she depicts the world through the various lenses through which she experiences it, continually forging new relationships with the past in the present. Her studio thus showcases the ecosystem of these relationships that emerge through making. Through this lens, Tap's work might be a powerful analogy for processes of artmaking that situate our way of seeing the world in relation to others' experiences. Regarding artists' participation in a studio ecosystem and learning to contribute to an ongoing dialogue of artists, Tap said:

> *These paintings are phrases that are uttered. They are parts of a conversation that extends beyond you. It's not just the conversation you have with the canvas but it's the conversation that came before this that allows this painting to exist. This painting may help to move the conversation, even in a tiny way, but it doesn't exist on its own and it's that kind of generosity that I think is a necessity at the heart of art making.*

The relationship between the studio and interconnections with art history as a generative mechanism emerged in a discussion with Vancouver-based artist Elizabeth McIntosh (Figures 2.8 and 2.9) in her studio in Vancouver in 2015.

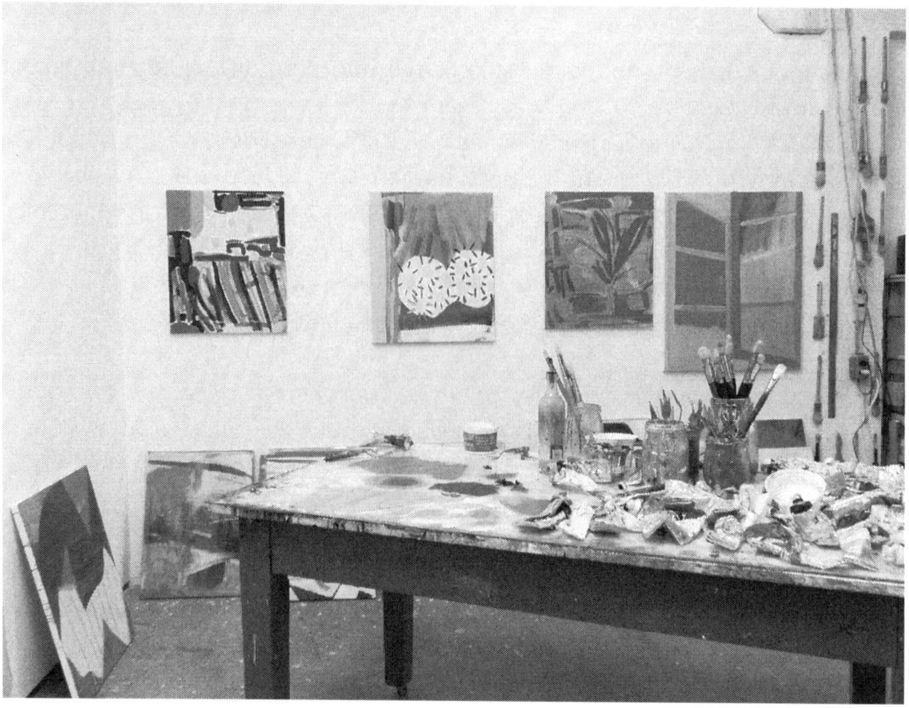

FIGURE 2.8: Elizabeth McIntosh's Studio, Vancouver, BC, 2016.

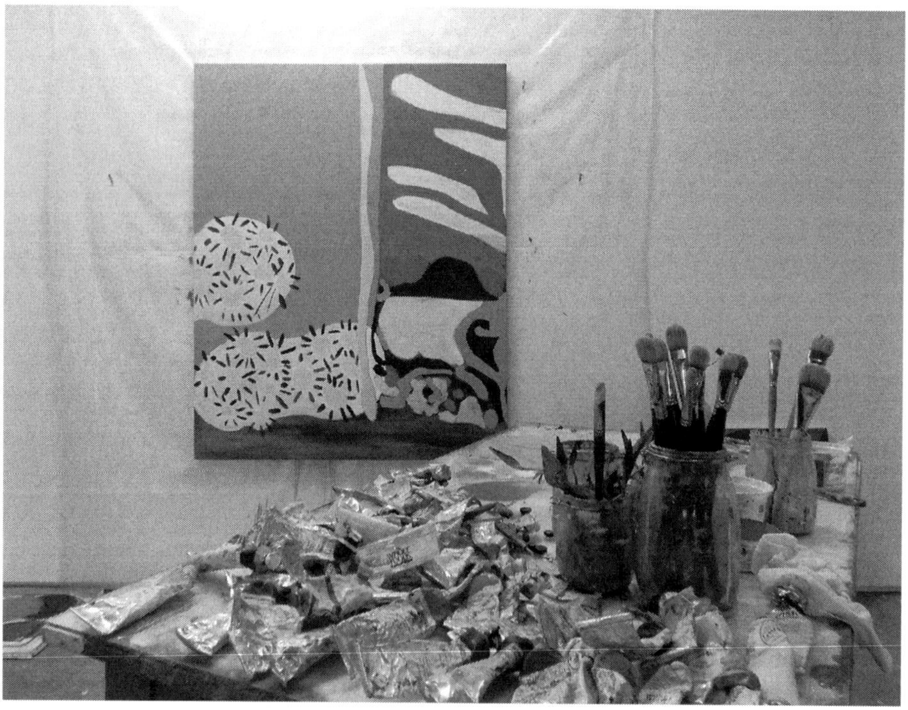

FIGURE 2.9: Elizabeth McIntosh's Studio, Vancouver, BC, 2016.

McIntosh's studio was filled with her colourful paintings, each at varying levels of completion. As a teenager, she attended an adult summer painting class and was influenced by her instructor's interest in artist Milton Avery, a Modernist artist known for his colourful, simple abstract paintings often of the landscape. During this class, McIntosh would sit for hours painting, but she wasn't trying to capture the scene. She would instead look for shapes in the landscape, looking at the overall scene and trying to simplify it to basic forms. For example, she would make a bush with bright pink or use simplified shapes to represent things. She said, '*in a way, that's still what I do*'. Describing her interest in colour and shapes, McIntosh's paintings come out of the process of making them. While she makes decisions as she paints, sometimes the painting would suggest a direction or possibility for something else.

At the time of our visit, McIntosh had been grappling with questions about whether a painting is different if it is planned versus one that is conceived in the making. She had been reading a book about Modernist artist, Henry Matisse, where he talked about how a sketch has the most urgent and necessary information, as evidence of a process. '*He talks about how a sketch is immediate and all the thinking is in the mark because it's being conceived as it's being made.*' She learned that Matisse would do double of most of his paintings, the first one being sketchier than the second. In reflecting on that, she wondered if the second one doesn't have the sketchy quality because something had been resolved. She wondered if a preplanned gesture was empty of expressive potential. She described how the improvisational thinking process is embodied in the painting:

> *That way of thinking, that is a way of making. In the case when it's not planned, it's a kind of record. There is physical evidence because you can't actually get rid of it when you make a painting like that. It's all there in all the layers. It's not like when you're editing an essay. All the decisions are embedded in the paint.*

In a recent exhibition, to examine these questions, she had shown doubles of paintings, the first was improvisational and the second pre-planned. In this way, her work examines how a thinking process is embedded within the work. The improvisational process allows her to leave herself open to move with what's happening and allow the process to lead her through, rather than start with a pre-determined goal.

McIntosh continually makes direct references to other painters, often Modernist artists such as Paul Klee, Pablo Picasso, or Henry Matisse. One group of paintings came out of a sticker book she had found of famous artists, where kids were supposed to find the stickers to make the painting complete. This became a tool for her to abstract from existing paintings as she would make paintings in response to shapes from these artworks. Regarding improvisation, she said:

> *My friend talked about how it's impossible to improvise alone because improvising is something that developed in jazz music and it's a kind of group activity. So, I talk about how I feel like I'm improvising with artists from the past.*

An ecological view of studios highlights the way that places and studio practice are in constant change, in movement as new relations are formed. This process exists as an ongoing conversation between past and present, and between communities of practice. An ecological examination of studio practice shifts away from dichotomies between individual and collective art practices and instead, locates our individual experiences and events within an ecology of interconnections.

3

Create a Parallel World (Studio as Portal)

> *Architecture becomes pedagogical, pedagogy becomes architectural when together they create a fluid, moving pivot place that puts inside and outside, self and other, personal and social into relation.*
>
> (Ellsworth, 2005, p. 38)

Studio as Site Where Incompatible Realities Play Out

French philosopher Gaston Bachelard examines how familiar places become sites of imagination as he addresses the relationship between the inner and the outer realm in relation to space and as he explores how the poetic imagination emerges within places we inhabit. In his book, *Poetics of Space*, Bachelard (1957/2014) addresses how we experience a particular place as our internal experiences confront our external environment. Through examining the intimate spaces of a house, Bachelard proposed that the poetic imagination emerges through the interaction of the real and the unreal. He uses the term topoanalysis to describe the psychological study of our relationship to places. In particular, he examines 'sites of our intimate lives' (p. 30), arguing that our memories inhabit space rather than time as intimate places become sites of projection. As a place that artists inhabit through the act of making, I propose that a studio may be a place where we examine our inner worlds and outer worlds simultaneously. Or a place where we may be here and elsewhere at the same time. Or a place where memories and imaginings become intertwined. Poetics comes from the word *poesis*, which means 'to make'. For Bachelard, poesis is a two-way process in that in the process of making, we are also 'made'. Historical views of imagination often exist as either imitation or invention, however, for Bachelard, the imagination is both 'receptive and creative' (Kearney, 2014, p. xx), absorbing our world around us while at the same time re-creating it in the process.

> The poetic re-imagining of stairs, passageways, porches or dressers bring together powers of memory, perception and fantasy that criss-cross in all kinds of surprising ways, sounding previously untapped 'reverberations' (*retentissements*). Imagination is a laboratory of the possible inviting us – through reverie and poetry – to give future to the past.
>
> (Kearney, 2014, p. xx, original emphasis)

The term '*reverberations*' is a generative way of thinking about an art studio wherein inner and outer realms generate a poetic and creative engagement with space. Through *reverberations*, artistic practice is responsive and imaginative in relation to our engagement with place, experiences, materials, and the painting process. In a studio visit in Victoria, 2014, artist Rick Leong discussed the inner and outer:

> *It's about being in between inner and outer realm. It has a lot to do with memory, and it has a lot to do with something that is external, but it comes from the inside. I find that in-between state so interesting. That inner realm can be just as valid in terms of human experience.*

In this way, a studio may function as a pivot place (Ellsworth, 2005) that activates inner experiences.

Around the time of our visit to Vancouver in 2014, Fiona Ackerman (Figure 3.1) had recently exhibited a series of paintings that engage with how a studio is transformed through artmaking. These paintings were made from studio visits with other artists and examine a studio as both subject and process. Rather than an exact visual representation of the studio, however, the paintings were her response to the studio. Ackerman described a time two years earlier when she was feeling stunted, lost, and uncertain about her painting process. She said she had 'longed for moment of ecstasy when a mess of a painting, like a ship lost at sea, begins to find its way' (Ackerman, 2012, n.p.). She came across an essay by French philosopher Michael Foucault about heterotopias which states:

> There are also, probably in every culture, in every civilization, real places ... which are something like counter-sites, a kind of effectively enacted utopia in which the real sites, all the other real sites that can be found within the culture, are simultaneously represented, contested, and inverted. Places of this kind are outside of all places, even though it may be possible to indicate their location in reality. Because these places are absolutely different from all the sites that they reflect and speak about, I shall call them, by way of contrast to utopias, heterotopias.
>
> (1967, as cited in Ackerman, 2012)

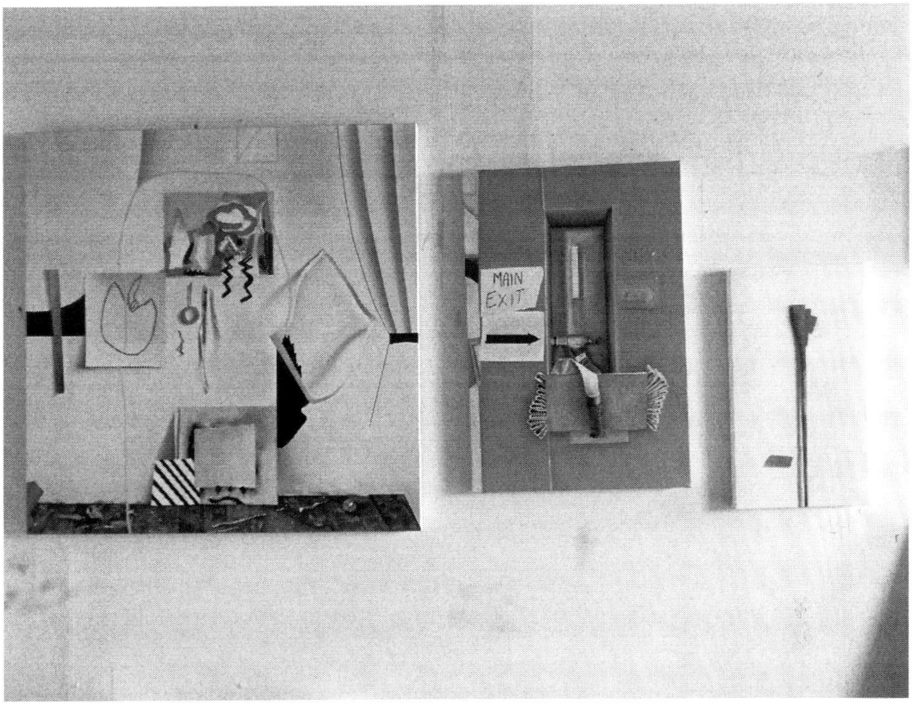

FIGURE 3.1: Fiona Ackerman's Studio, Vancouver, BC, 2015.

Ackerman reflected on how a studio might be considered a Heterotopia, the real and the imaginary. She looked inward towards her studio practice and reproduced gestures, marks, and shapes from previous paintings as a way of both recognizing her inventory of marks and generating new meanings from them. Through this process, she said: '*The world of the studio began to reveal itself onto the canvas.*' She then began to paint various objects, notes, and imagery from around the studio and allowed imaginary narratives and symbolic associations to emerge. For example, she would see an anthropomorphic figure on a piece of paper taped to the wall. Or a doorway would become a sail of a ship. Through recreating her studio within her studio, she had found her Heterotopia. The studio was a place where '*incompatible realities play out*'. Ackerman (2012) describes the studio: 'In these hidden think tanks, an artistic exercise meant to reflect something true or philosophical about the world outside its doors runs amuck. Tangents of association mix with struggle and play. The result is discovery and need not be more.'

While she began her exploration of studios by turning inward to her own studio, Ackerman then expanded her exploration and visited others' studios. She called herself an art-thropological explorer and voyeur. Through her subjective lens, these new spaces were inventions rather than literal physical representations. She was '*not holding a mirror to the studio, but a distorting lens*'. Although the artist was not present while she visited, she said a relationship formed between the artist, their work, and her own through getting to know their work, their palette, their approach, and their materials within their studio. The title of the show, *It's Not You It's Me* emerged as a recognition that it is always through Ackerman's lens: '*Is this your studio or is this my painting? It's a Heterotopia. How you see yourself in your studio can be re-invented.*'

Portals That Have the Capacity to Transport Us Elsewhere

For artist David Elliott (Figures 3.2 and 3.3), artmaking, and by extension, a studio may take us into a parallel world. He described this parallel world in our studio visit in Montreal in 2015.

> *When it comes to art, painting specifically, I like the notion of a parallel world. I live in this world, but I like the notion of a parallel space. Whether it's the space you visit when you dream, a space you imagine, a space you feel when you're in love, whatever that enriched world is, it's that kind of heightened reality, that is like a parallel space.*

He explained this notion of a parallel universe by referring to a quote by twentieth-century German painter, Max Beckmann who described how painting may create a fourth dimension.

> *Beckmann says when you compress space, when you take the 3D world and try to put it in 2D space, he says it's impossible. So, in that transfer of 3D to 2D, something is going to break down. There's going to be holes, there's going to be fissures, there's going to be gaps, there's going to be cracks in the reality. And in those cracks, he says, you can enter the 4th dimension. Time and space begin to dissolve and you're out of the concrete world into another world. So, by setting things in the painting so that they are not necessarily readable in space, so that there is a questioning of where things are located in space, he says when the mind is faced into that kind of decision-making, when the mind is put in that position, it pushes you into another dimension because you can't resolve it. When these things are fractured, when there is a confusion of space, your mind is pushed and forced somewhere else. For me, that is one way that parallel universes get structured.*

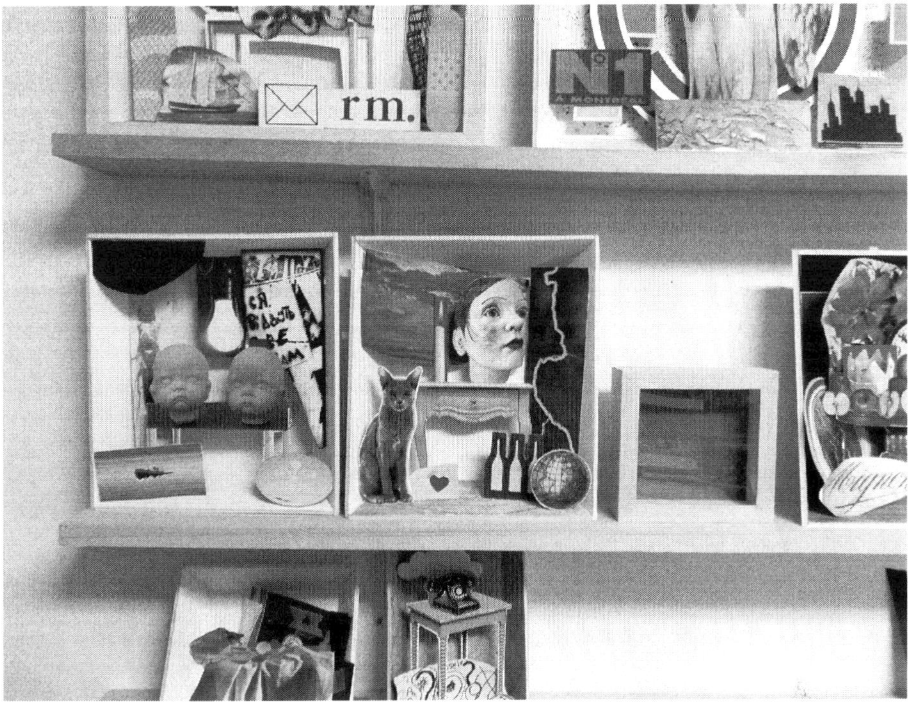

FIGURE 3.2: David Elliott's Studio, Montreal, QC, 2015.

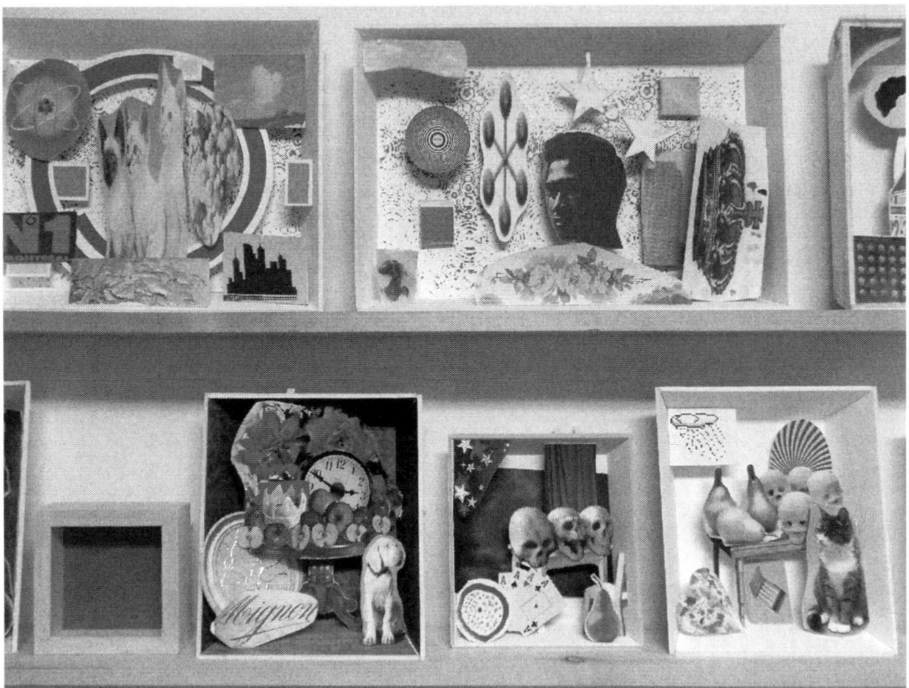

FIGURE 3.3: David Elliott's Studio, Montreal, QC, 2015.

For Andrea Kastner (Figures 3.4–3.7), studios are filled with portals that have the capacity to transport us elsewhere. Within her studio, her paintings function as portals or wormholes that may take her on travels to other places. Through these portals and links within the studio, time doesn't function in a linear way, as paintings may shoot us forward or backward in time and take us somewhere else. Kastner described herself as a code breaker, a detective, an observer, and an inventor of fictional worlds. I first met her in her home studio in Kamloops, British Columbia in 2014 where she showed me her collage-like paintings. Explaining how ideas all form and merge together in her mind, Kastner compared her brain to a garbage truck.

> *You know when you see a garbage truck pull up and the men throw the garbage in the back of it and then the truck itself mulches it, the thing comes down and all the bags break apart and all the garbage mixes together and you have the old things and the new things and the important things and the not important things mixing together. That's how I picture my brain working.*

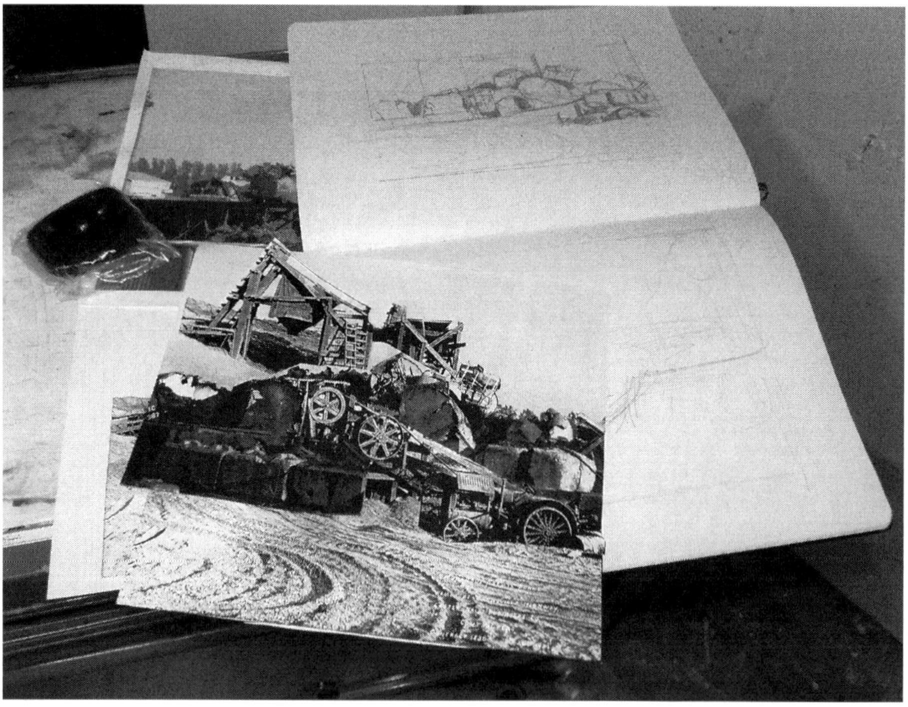

FIGURE 3.4: Andrea Kastner's Studio, Kamloops, BC, 2014.

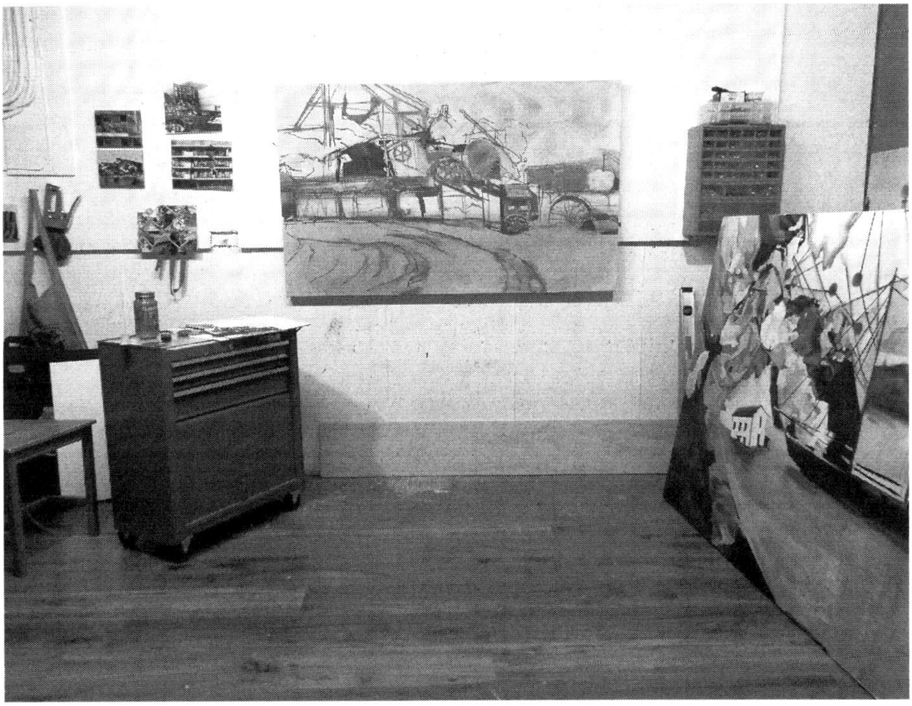

FIGURE 3.5: Andrea Kastner's Studio, Kamloops, BC, 2014.

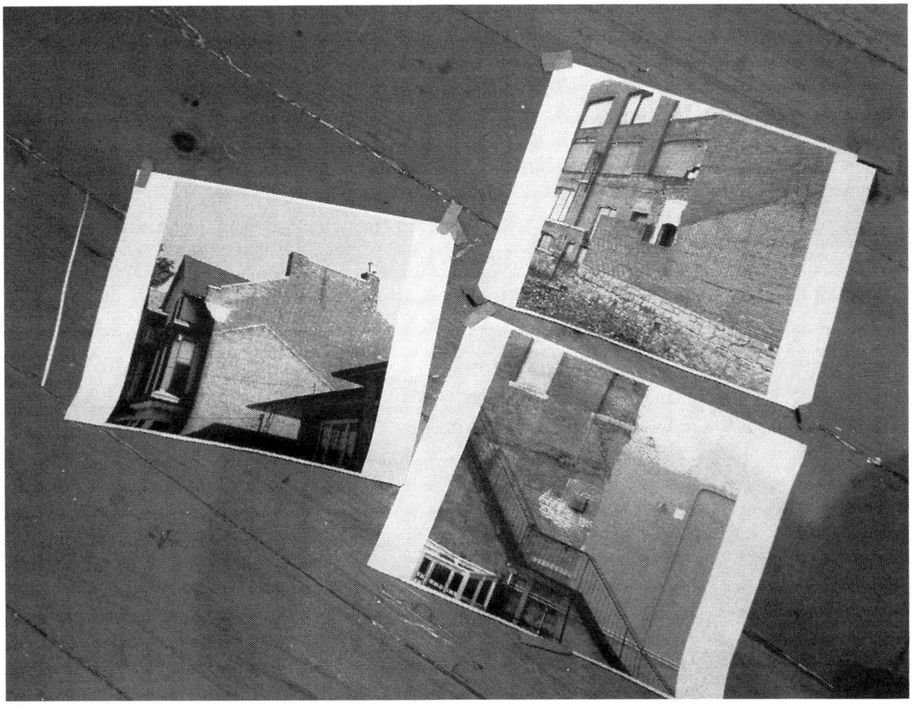

FIGURE 3.6: Andrea Kastner's Studio, Hamilton, ON, 2016.

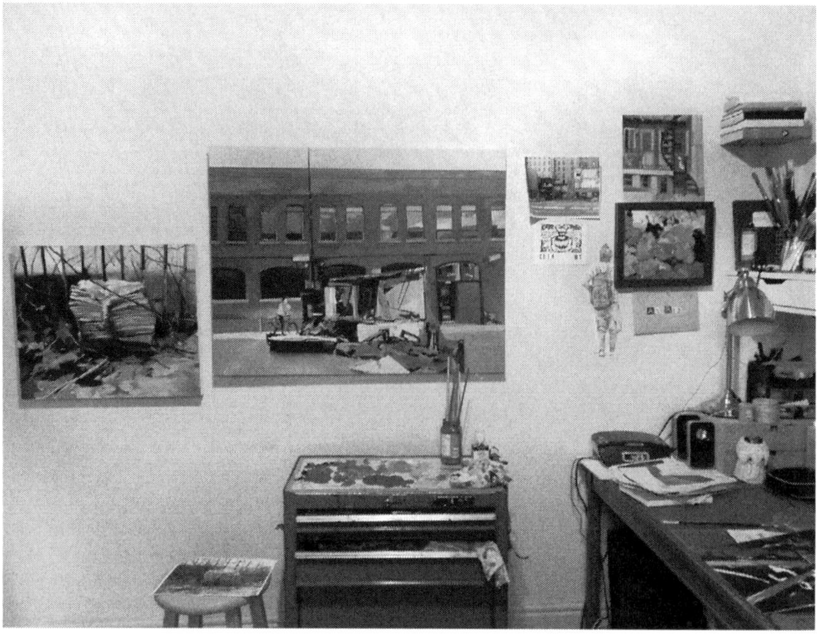

FIGURE 3.7: Andrea Kastner's Studio, Hamilton, ON, 2016.

Kastner began our studio visit by sharing a mysterious printout that she found in a neighbour's garbage that she mistook for a connect-the-dots. She described the mournful moment when she attempted to connect the dots and realized that it was not in fact an image but was just a random assortment of points on a page. While unable to apprehend the meaning of this document, she held onto the letter and used the nonsensical assortment of lines and dots for a future painting.

Throughout her undergraduate studies, Kastner had done a series of paintings of alleyways which were a metaphor for how our minds work. She called the alleyways, the anti-façade, where things are left that are not presented to the world. Years later, upon moving to Edmonton, she continued this fascination with exploring the city as a pseudo-anthropologist finding meanings in what is discarded. She took garbage bags from neighbours' homes and would go through the garbage searching for clues.

> *I was thinking of them as maps in some ways. They were like mind maps. I was thinking of them as these secrets of the subconscious or unconscious or as embedded codes. Somebody once told me that I'm an anthropologist of the bowels of society.*

Throughout the years as she moved to different cities, Kastner continued to explore the unnoticed sides of the city with a curious eye. Her paintings merged several photographs to create surreal and invented places, however, occasionally, she would find a surreal place that already exists in the world.

> *I'm looking for bits where the surreal, a kind of mind map collage happens in real life. Or where it happens because I make it happen. But the ones that I paint that are not collage are because the real world had already done the work for me.*

I met Kastner almost two years later, in 2016, and she had moved to Hamilton, Ontario. Kastner was working on a new series of paintings that she called *Everything Is Pregnant with Its Contrary* that expressively address the inner and outer realm, the relation between real and imaginary and between past and present. This phrase related to a quote someone had written on the wall of her studio in Edmonton, Alberta, that she had jotted down in her sketchbook, and it stuck in her mind. For her, the quote means that within everything there is a seed of the exact opposite of that thing and that there is a balance when something goes too far toward one thing and then returns. Through exploring architecture and cities, she thought about how cities swing from demolition to regrowth and then back again. This was occurring in Hamilton at the time, and she would walk the streets taking photographs around demolition and construction sites. Specifically, Kastner applied this concept to photographs of 'ghost houses', where evidence of a previous building that had been torn down was imprinted on the wall. She explained: '*So, on this house, the neighbor's house left that mark. The brick is different, because of sun. One house gets torn down and the other house next door remains, but that ghost house is still there.*' She shared images of these ghost spaces: ghost door; ghost factory; ghost chimney. '*So basically, I'm going into those secret spaces and inserting its contrary. I'm going to take images of places in the neighborhood and make that cycle of construction and deconstruction be manifest.*'

Kastner explores the people and places that surround her; however, rather than represent those worlds, she invents new ones based on connections she makes and inserts her own surreal imaginings into them. We discussed her interest in codes and symbols and how this relates to how she thinks about painting and creativity, particularly her interest in finding symbolism in the things that surround her.

> *I think I go through phases of getting very involved in codes or code-breaking or symbolism. I have an innate tendency to assign meanings to different things and care about them a lot. I really do love making connections between things. My brain does that a lot. I assign secrets.*

Sandra Meigs (Figures 3.8 and 3.9) similarly addressed how artmaking may explore the relationship between the inner and the outer realms. For her, artmaking

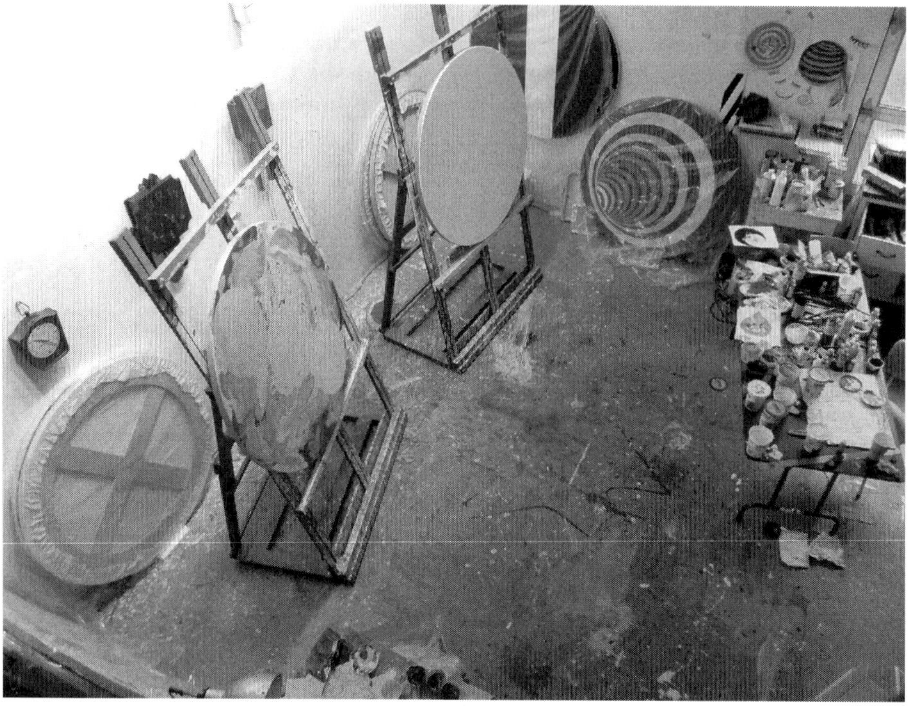

FIGURE 3.8: Sandra Meigs' Studio, Victoria, BC, 2014.

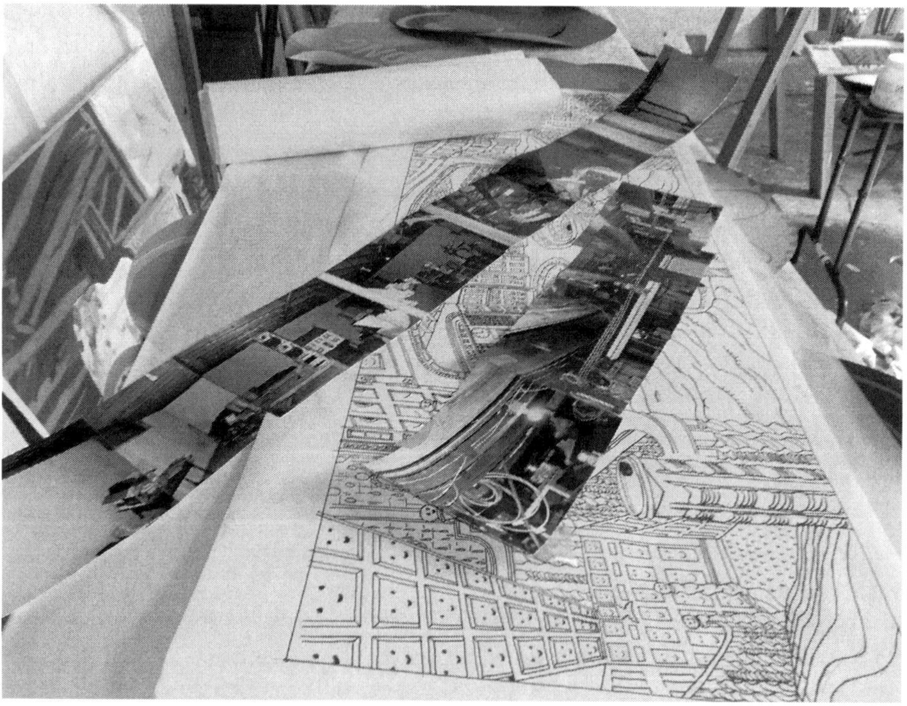

FIGURE 3.9: Sandra Meigs' Studio, Victoria, BC, 2015.

is a search for discovery: '*I think art in general, and most good artists are after the unknown. They're after discovery in some way.*' We began our visit to her Victoria studio in 2014 by discussing an exhibition from ten years earlier titled *A Strange Loop* based on the book *I am a Strange Loop* by Douglas Hofstadter (2007). The term 'strange loop' refers to a reflexive process of understanding ourselves in relation to the world. For Meigs, the strange loop represents the relationship between our inner and outer world that occurs through artmaking. Regarding this exhibition at Carlton University Art Gallery and the concept of a 'strange loop', Meigs said:

> *The idea of this loop around the microcosm that we understand as the 'self' and the macrocosm that is the world is an important realm for the artist to explore. I believe that, within this loop, the imagination takes form ... His thought has potential for art as a model of the viewers looking at the art and it influencing them at the same time.*

Meigs created paintings of nineteenth-century mansions as metaphors for this loop that is generated through the interaction between the outside world and the mind. She went to Newport, Rhode Island to draw from stick and shingle mansions.

> *In the act of drawing you're projecting your mind onto the surroundings at the same time as the surroundings are influencing what you are drawing. So, I saw that parallel as a model in the way I was thinking of the world and my relationship to it.*

Meigs' husband had recently passed away and she realized that she could project that grieving process onto personal spaces. She began working from a crawl space in the house they had shared because she had strong feelings about those spaces. She had to crawl on her stomach to access them, making it an even more intimate experience. The crawl space became a place in which to process her feelings and grief. She created four mural-sized monochromatic paintings with architectural spaces and text drawn on them in white. Each painting represented a stage of grief as she projected her grieving process onto the architectural space.

A year later, Meigs' studio had transformed. The studio was filled with hundreds of circular paintings, balls, clocks, and other circular forms. She wanted her upcoming exhibition to feel like going to a party with an overwhelming abundance of visualizations. She had also been reading about quantum physics and meditation and that wove into how she was thinking about painting. '*I decided to generate with as little planning of outcome as possible, a multitude of pieces with the only thing in common is that they are round.*' Through meditation, she had found that she could indulge in other worlds through the creation of immersive spaces with infinite possibilities.

> *I was thinking very abstractly about physics, space, time and matter, and the circular form related to painting. For me with a circle, there is more of an absence of scale. This can be a subatomic particle, or this could be a planet. I started being interested in quantum physics and quantum worlds and possibilities and black holes and things like that. I think at least in our daily lives, we are Newtonian in our thought. We are still tied to the Cartesian idea that we are a body with a mind. But post-Newtonian physics has kind of disproven all that. And so, quantum possibilities got me thinking about the idea that everything is an illusion, so what you think you see is really just data organized in a certain way.*

Her candidness in discussing her personal experiences and how it affected her paintings reveal a vulnerability in her approach to painting. For Meigs, personal experiences are intuitively embedded in the work.

> *How do we access intuition? Artists have visual talents, a closeness to that part of experience. Intuition is not irrational thought, but it's a kind of thought that is beyond the world. Because we all have an unconscious mind. That's what intuition is, and it's tapping into that and allowing it full credit. But in our culture, it plays a much lower value. You can look at dreams and how important they are to living our lives. When you imagine, when you start a painting, it doesn't come from stuff you know, because if it did you probably wouldn't want to do it ... I've always used my personal experience as a way of finding content to make work about. In some ways, it comes through my sense of humour because life is so absurdly funny, and to bring in personal experiences, I think it enriches my art. There's a difference between indulgence and expression in art. So, what I try to do is find the proper form where something can become universal.*

SECTION 1

CONCLUSION: DWELL WITHIN TIME, SPACE, AND CONVERSATION

A studio is a place that exists in a particular location and time. Moreover, I propose that a studio is a node within an ever-changing ecosystem that allows us to examine our inner worlds while in ongoing dialogue with the world. Thus, studios become pedagogical when they transform our understandings and ways of being in the world (Ellsworth, 2005). For Ellsworth, knowledge is alive; knowledge-in-the-making is the experience of ourselves in the making. Through 'focusing on the means and conditions, the environments and events of knowledge in the making, it opens an exploration into the experience of the learning self' (p. 1) and through examining the affective experience of learning, pedagogy embodies 'experiences of being radically in relation to one's self, to others, and to the world' (p. 2). Through this lens, a studio is similarly alive and ever-changing in relation. Thus, I return to the discussion of 'speculative pedagogy' (Ellsworth, 2005) to discuss how a studio may act as a hinge. Ellsworth asks, 'What places are capable of acting as this moment's "hinge"? What environments and experiences are capable of acting as the pedagogical pivot point between movement/sensation and thought?' (p. 8). Ellsworth contends that through examining architectural spaces as places of learning, she is not proposing a model or an example. Instead, she presents an argument for considering them as speculative places, ones that prompt us to think differently about learning, and in turn, the places of learning.

> Creating room for speculation enables an educator to explore her understanding of the places in which people encounter enjoyable learning experiences and the means through which she, as an educator, could imagine making and using such places ... My intention is to open up such an area of speculation about pedagogy.
>
> (p. 9)

Through this perspective, I consider the relationship between the pedagogy of studio practice and the pedagogy of a studio classroom in a way that emphasizes affect, materiality, embodiment, and relationality. For Ellsworth (2005), '[l]earning never takes place in the absence of bodies, emotions, place, time, sound, image, self-experience, history. It always detours through memory, forgetting, desire, fear, pleasure, surprise, rewriting' (p. 55). She highlights the emergence of pedagogy that happens in a particular place and time and that is fuelled by curiosity and a provocation to imagine differently. Studios become apparent as pedagogical when viewed as an experience-in-the-making, as hinges that prompt us to think and feel differently. Art educator Jack Richardson (2013) draws from Ellsworth's discussion of the hinge as a metaphor for anomalous places that allow for an interaction between our inner world and the exterior world. However, rather than focus on place, Richardson focuses on time and how processes of artmaking may change how we experience time.

> Privileging the processes associated with artmaking over the product is commonly invoked in discussions surrounding best practices in art education. Ostensibly this is to suggest that the constructive value of artmaking is primarily revealed in the development of ideas and skills over time and it is within this development that learning and understanding occurs. However, while this is a frequent refrain in art educational practice, the function of time within the process is left largely unexamined, and its understanding is largely relegated to notions of chronology and progress.
>
> (p. 90)

Richardson shifts away from conventional notions of time that focus on chronology towards a focus on more convoluted notions of time as '"unhinged" from chronology' (p. 92). He suggests that experience produces a particular time that may intertwine past, present, and future. Furthermore, he questions the Eurocentric notions of time that are calculated and ordered and that promote a view of time as related to productivity. He instead focuses on creative time:

> Thought is a creative rather than reflective practice, that is, it produces rather than identifies difference. As such, its function does not simply move the thinker forward in time, where time represents a form of continuity underlying and affecting all thought. Rather, thought, like time, itself transforms both thinker and experience – a transformative process more accurately articulated as learning that opens up the future to difference and variation rather than reflection and reiteration.
>
> (p. 106)

Richardson leaves us with the following question:

> Perhaps in order to bridge, or more accurately obliterate, the process/product divide, we might consider that, in addition to asking 'What kind of product is produced over time?', we might also ask 'What kind of time is produced through process?'
>
> (p. 107)

I similarly propose that time functions differently in a studio. The relationality and materiality of the studio prompts a different way of inhabiting time and space. This unstructured time may push against a linear and objective-oriented pedagogy. The time of artmaking is discussed in the next section to address the studio as a process.

Throughout this section, I have proposed that studio visits are a methodological approach that allows for an artist practitioner to learn in relation to others' practices. Through this process, I suggest studio visits may be a form of mapping, situating ourselves within an ever-changing dialogue. Through this lens, I propose that studios form an ecosystem of interconnected studio practices. And I suggest that a studio may act as a hinge, one that allows us to be transported elsewhere through the time spent dwelling within art practice and the materiality of the space. Through the examination of studios as a hinge, I propose that a studio offers a particular learning experience. Thus, I ask how such a philosophical position, or speculative pedagogy, may be applied to studio art education. In relation to studio-based learning, I propose the following propositions: Re-imagine a studio classroom as an ecosystem, one that extends outwards in every direction; Embrace a studio visit as a pedagogical and practice-based methodology that invites studios into relation with others; Dwell within the time and space of learning; Consider a studio as a hinge, a pivot place, wherein artmaking may turn a studio into a portal to somewhere else.

SECTION 2

STUDIO AS PROCESS: LIVE TIME

Regarding the long process of creating her large-scale paintings, Vancouver-based artist, Landon Mackenzie said: '*They have to literally live time*.' Studios exist within a particular time and place. To emphasize the time of artmaking is, in turn, to recognize the process. For artist and professor of philosophy Erin Manning (2016b), artmaking is a series of events. Emphasizing the process of art practice, Manning describes minor gestures as subtle movements and experiences that affect us in the moment. Moreover, she views the objects of artmaking through a processual lens. Through this perspective, art practice is an ecology, always changing, in motion, and in relation to the place and materials of practice. Regarding painting within an ecology, she says: 'The painter-paint-canvas ecology is an ever-changing one, from sitting to standing to looking to feeling to touching to seeing' (p. 40). Manning focuses on the doing of art as she asks what art practice may be when viewed as an activator of a particular experience and a way of living. She suggests that artmaking is a way of living in the moment and engaging with the world through ongoing questioning. Through viewing a studio as the stage for an event, 'an object is always to some degree not-yet, in process, in movement. In the midst, in the event, we know the object not in its fullness, in its ultimate form, but as an edging into experience' (p. 48). For Manning, an ecology of practice embraces art practice as a way of knowing that may challenge a predefined understanding of what counts as knowledge. She asks: 'What if knowledge were not assumed to have a form already? What if we didn't yet know what needed to be taught, let alone questioned?' (p. 9). Through the lens of time and process, 'art is *a way* of learning' that 'acts as a bridge toward new processes, new pathways' (p. 47, original emphasis). Regarding the nonlinear process of artmaking, Manning says:

> It is about balancing several books, or several passages, or several ideas, or several textures, at the edge of the desk, on the floor of the studio, and wondering how else they might come together, and what else, together they might do.
>
> (Manning 2016b, p. 39)

In this way, a studio becomes a moving assemblage that may be continually made and remade through the experience of artmaking.

Considering a studio as an event aligns with a performative lens of art practice and new materialist perspectives that examine our relationship to the world as responsive, active, and changing. This lens emphasizes *performativity* rather than *representation* as a more apt way of discussing our experiences and responses to the world. For Barad (2007), performativity describes how individual entities are constantly changing in relation to and in response to other entities. She proposes that rather than the world being made up of separate individuals that exist prior to their interactions, that instead individuals are constantly changing because of and through their encounters in a process she refers to as intra-action. Intra-actions reveal a responsive and interconnected relationship between ourselves, others, and the world. She says:

> *Performative* approaches call into question representationalism's claim that there are representations, on the one hand, and ontologically separate entities awaiting representation, on the other, and focus inquiry on the practices or performances of representing, as well as the productive effects of those practices.
>
> (Barad, 2007, p. 49, original emphasis)

To focus on the performative rather than the representationalist means focusing on 'practices or doings or actions' rather than on 'correspondence between descriptions and reality' (p. 28). Barad uses the term diffraction to describe the ongoing changes produced through relational intra-actions between bodies, materials, and ideas, and the effects that these intra-actions produce. It is a process of ongoing interference that continuously generates new processes and effects.

I draw from the work of Barad as I explore the complexities of working with the materials of painting as ideas and experiences become embodied in the process. Through this lens, painting is a performative practice. Barbara Bolt (2004, 2007, 2013), lecturer in Visual Media at the University of Melbourne, similarly emphasizes the embodied and performative process of artmaking that occurs through handling materials. Thus, a performative view of studio practice allows us to engage with the embodied, affective, sensory, experiential, and emergent learning process. Highlighting the processes of studio work, Sjoholm (2013) performed a study of studio-related knowledge. She describes the studio as a 'microcosm of an artist's self-directed work in progress, creativity, knowledge, thought and expression' (p. 2). Comparing the studio to a personal laboratory, she describes the knowledge produced in the studio as investigative, experimental, and drawing on the following knowledge practices: 'contemplation and elaboration, critical thinking and bodily engagement, instruction and improvisation' (p. 2). Sjoholm highlights the generative thinking and learning process of studio work and how the studio itself embodies this ecology.

Within this section, I discuss the studio as a process, as an event in which new knowledge and understanding emerge. I begin by discussing the term 'performativity' in more depth as it relates to studio practice. Next, I discuss studio practice as a curiosity-driven, generative, and responsive process. Lastly, I examine the role of not knowing within the process of studio work. Through this section, I propose that through an understanding of the performative process of artmaking, we may engage with artmaking as a process and examine the role of the studio in enabling and activating experiences. This section is guided by the following questions:

> How does engaging with painting as performative embrace the studio as a way of thinking that is curiosity-driven, emergent and process-based?
> What conditions of studio practice allow for the generativity of artistic processes?
> What role does 'not knowing' play in studio practices?

4

Hold a Wine Glass as Tight as You Can Without It Breaking (Studio as Performative)

> *In the fury of painting, rules give way to tactics and the pragmatics of action. The painting takes on a life of its own. It breathes, vibrates, pulsates, shimmers and generally runs away from me. The painting no longer merely represents or illustrates reading. Instead, it performs. In the performativity of imaging, life gets into the image.*
>
> (Bolt, 2004, p. 1)

You Can Never Step in the Same Studio Twice

Ethiopian American artist Julie Mehretu (2016) uses poetic and sensory language to describe the experience of making:

> Sensory experience, emergent sensile form, tactile, acoustic, auricular, lingual, sensatory, olfactory, auditory, haunting knowledge, premonition ... Find the break, the gap, the fissures, undoing and pulling apart – open force of unraveling potentiality. Improvisation can be radical possibility. Painting as performative time.
>
> (p. 275)

New materialist theories examine our relationship to the world as responsive, active, and changing and emphasize *performativity* rather than *representation*. Within studio practice, a performative lens emphasizes process and becoming and recognizes that meanings are in flux and changing. Barbara Bolt (2004, 2007, 2013, 2016) describes art practices as 'performative'. Rather than simply a representation (a mirror image of the world), artistic processes are performative in their capacity to provoke and generate experiences. Rather than viewing artmaking as simply representing an image or experience that pre-existed the making, artmaking produces experiences. Moreover, performativity asks what artmaking does rather than what it is or what it means, and addresses how painting activates an embodied and affective experience. Thus, artmaking moves beyond representation, and a performative perspective recognizes how a painting emerges through the process, and how meaning similarly emerges through making. Bolt (2004) says:

> At some undefinable moment, the painting took on a life that seemed to have almost nothing to do with my conscious attempts to control it. The 'work' (as verb) took on its own momentum, its own rhythm and intensity. Within this intense furious state, I no longer had any awareness of time, of pain or of making decisions.
>
> (p. 1)

Bolt (2004) argues that throughout the twentieth and the early twenty-first century, practice has been effaced. She critiques the ways theory may stagnate practice, in what she calls the 'theorization effect' (Bourdieu, 1990, as cited in Bolt, 2004, p. 4). Through theorization, the 'fuzziness' of practice is replaced by fixity and stasis. Proposing that there is a logic of practice, she wonders how practice can be articulated or whether practice escapes theoretical contemplation altogether. Bolt addresses various twentieth-century approaches to evaluating artworks, from Greenbergian to Bauhaus to semiotic, in addition to sociological or anthropological approaches that are more concerned with the place of the artist in society. Addressing this history, Bolt argues that what has failed to be considered within these discussions of artworks is the space of the studio, the bodily engagement, and the material practice of artmaking.

I propose that a studio is a performative space, one that embraces the material, sensory, affective, and thinking processes that emerge through making and in turn, how the painting develops through the act of making. Bolt (2013) refers to material thinking as a performative process wherein understandings emerge through working with materials, arguing that we 'come to know the world theoretically only after we have come to understand it through handling' (2007, p. 30). Artist-educator McClenaghan (2016) suggests that to understand the process of painting, we need to shift from representational thinking toward practice in order to examine the learning process of painting. And, to engage with practice, we must understand the life of the studio:

> Practice is in time. It is durational. Artworks are frozen in time. They represent practice but they are not practice … They stand in for that which is absent. Practice is

> always somewhere else. Hence the exposition of practice brings about the collapse of representation.
>
> (p. 36)

He proposes that we examine practice as a 'speculative process of searching' (p. 34). To highlight the temporariness of practice, he says:

> Heraclitus wrote that you can't step twice into the same river. If we attempt to isolate part of the river for examination we find that we have only water. We can examine its properties and qualities just as we can in the case of an artwork but this brings us no closer to understanding it as a process.
>
> (p. 33)

Educator and artist Kaustuv Roy (2024) argues that the 'magic' of artmaking similarly lies within the ever-changing process and can be understood from within this process:

> Just as the current of water cannot be felt without actually coming in contact with it and being carried along, the magicality of art cannot be sensed without encountering the stream of vital emanations that is characteristic of the Eros of creativity.
>
> (p. 1)

For Roy, the magical is not the paranormal, but rather our potential for surprise that emerges through the process of making. I propose that we can never step into the same studio twice as it is a place that is in a constant state of becoming. Performative ways of thinking and being in the world challenge an understanding of thinking as representational and static and instead views artmaking as an active extension of our experiences, or simply an experience in itself. Art educator Donal O'Donoghue (2015) says: 'The act of representing an experience experienced at another time is, of course, the living of an entirely new experience' (p. 104). Through this lens, the studio is a site of activation; the process of making activates new experiences.

Unless You Make an Action, You Have No Way to React

In a studio visit in 2022 with Vancouver-based artist, Shoora Majedian (Figures 4.1 and 4.2), we discussed how artmaking is an ongoing decision-making process. Through engaging with memories, life experiences, and decision-making in the studio, she works through questions from her past. Majedian grew up in Iran

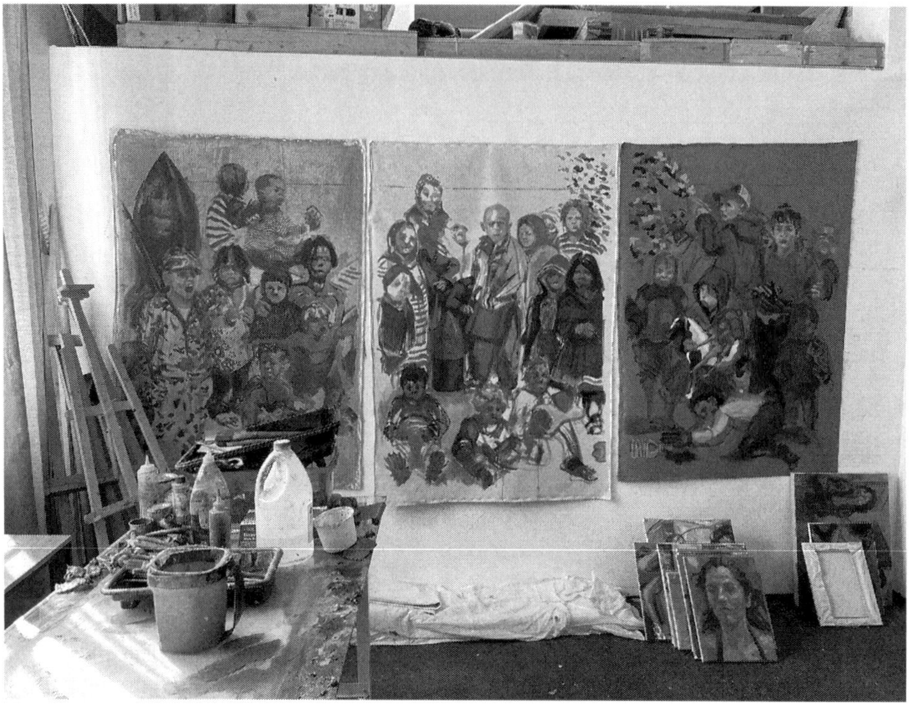

FIGURE 4.1: Shoora Majedian's Studio, Vancouver, BC, 2022.

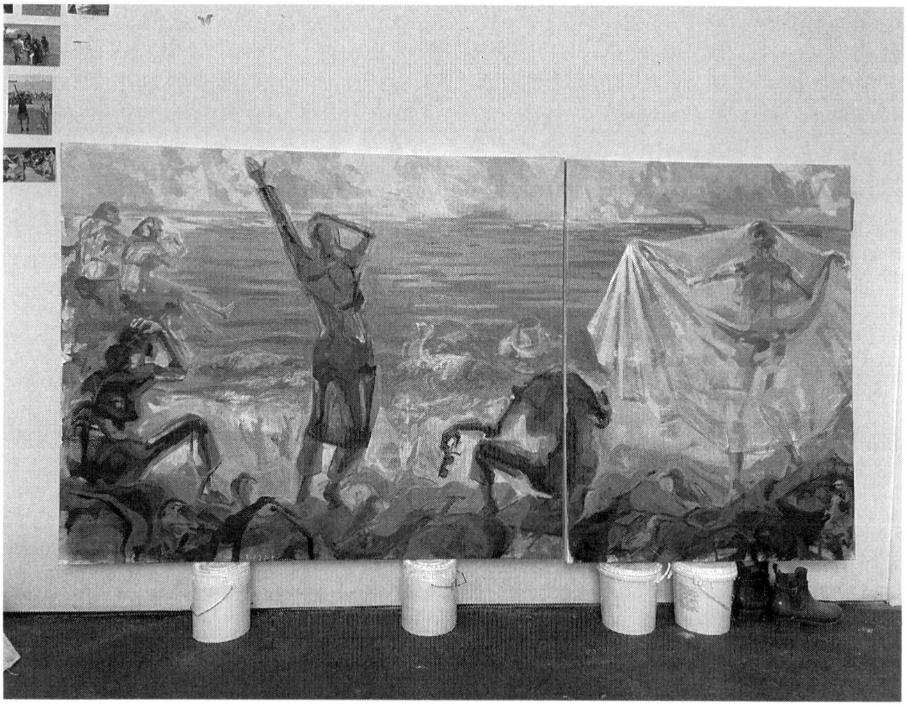

FIGURE 4.2: Shoora Majedian's Studio, Vancouver, BC, 2022.

during the Iran–Iraq war and post-war before moving to Canada. Her studio was filled with paintings drawn from memories of her life in Iran through the lens of her current position in Vancouver. On one wall of the studio, she had a painting of herself, her mother, and her aunt, part of a series of women looking in the mirror. Along another wall of the studio was a painting of women bathing in a body of water which represents a public swimming prohibition, where women were not allowed to swim and were restricted to observing the view and watching men swim. And on another wall was a triptych of children from various countries who have experienced war. She drew from her own memories, while also using painting as a way of processing her experiences and creating a dialogue with society.

> *For me, true and honest art emerges from my life experiences. I believe that within simple, ordinary stories lies an abundance of meaning waiting to be uncovered. Through the act of creating in the studio and within the painting itself, I've discovered a path to explore the questions I've carried from the past. I think through painting. As I sit and make decisions – selecting forms and colors – each element seems to convey a message to me. It doesn't always provide answers; more often, it raises new questions, especially about what my society has endured. In essence, painting begins with my lived experience, and the imaginative process allows me to make transformative changes along the way.*
>
> *I'm currently in a transitional phase. I used to believe that art shouldn't be political, and while I still think it shouldn't serve as a direct political statement, I'm exploring ways to engage with political themes more subtly. At times, I feel the need to respond to current events, not let the current history be forgotten. But I am also aware that a great painting has the potential to endure over time, and the challenge lies in creating work that carries both.*

For Majedian, the responsive decision-making process is at the core of painting. She often starts with an ink drawing. This process allows her to work from memories of her childhood, each memory leading to another. When I asked her why she paints, she connected the ongoing decision-making within the studio to her challenges in making decisions day-to-day.

> *My reflection on the image extends beyond storytelling; it encompasses the decisions I make and my commitment to persevere, even in the face of difficulty. This practice instills confidence during challenging times, both in my personal life and in systematic thinking. Within the painting, I see a reflection of the contrasts and struggles I confront, which prevents me from adhering to a single method of painting. Decisions have always posed a challenge for me, but painting has taught me to embrace uncertainty and look beyond rigid frameworks. Growing up in a society steeped in binary thinking, I've discovered that painting offers a non-binary perspective filled*

with endless possibilities. Each piece becomes a journey of creation, destruction, and reconstruction, unveiling the freedom to explore, experiment, and discover – reshaping my approach to both art and life.

This process can be fraught with insecurity, frustration, and exhilaration, through the not-knowing of what it might become. I propose, as does Majedian, that working through this process in the studio may provide comfort within the indecision and uncertainties of life.

Fiona Ackerman (Figures 4.3 and 4.4) addressed the responsive, decision-making process of painting through an analogy. In a studio visit in Vancouver, Ackerman compared painting to calculus as a way of discussing improvisation within the studio. In her first year studying at university, Ackerman took a calculus class. Her understanding of calculus is that it is a form of problem-solving and a study of how close you can get to something. That's how she treats painting. It is compositional problem-solving.

It's a way of thinking that appeals to a certain mind. I loved doing calculus problems; you keep going and get through this whole process. It was so abstract. It had a logic in itself.

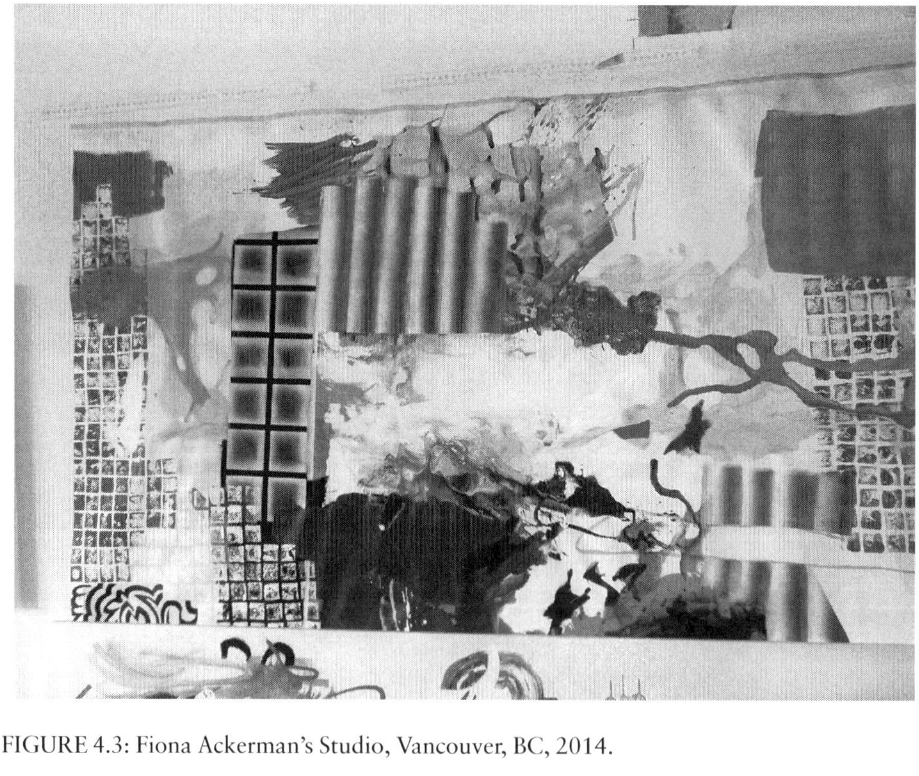

FIGURE 4.3: Fiona Ackerman's Studio, Vancouver, BC, 2014.

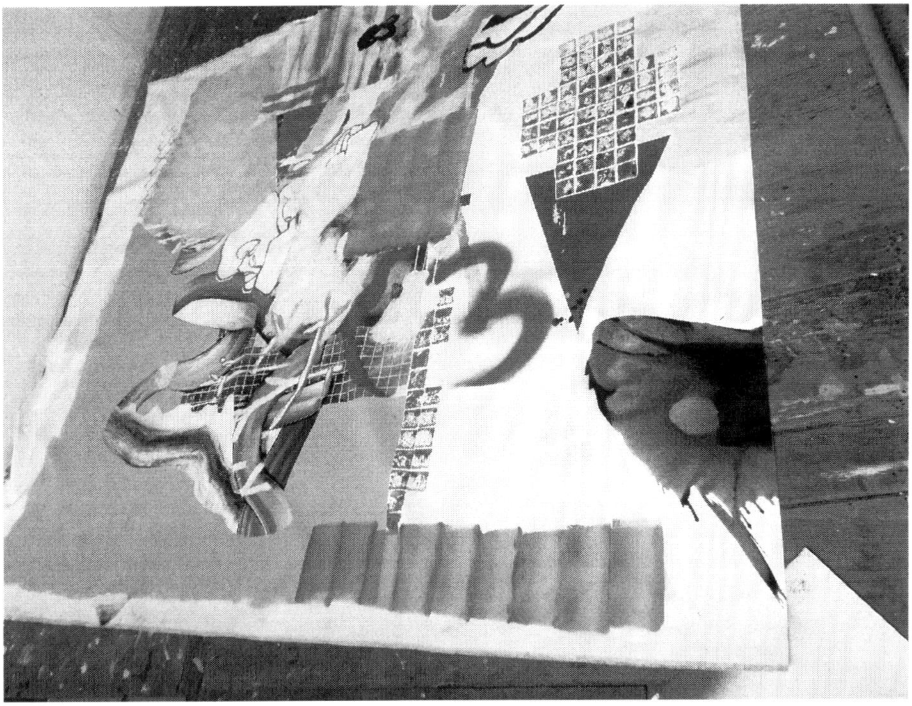

FIGURE 4.4: Fiona Ackerman's Studio, Vancouver, BC, 2014.

> *I feel like what I've learned from years of painting is that just because X worked in one painting, that doesn't mean it's going to work in another painting. So, I have to look at the painting I'm doing and say: What is the problem I'm dealing with here? What is the language I'm speaking? Then you work through that problem. You're going through it with this general idea and you're trying to get it done before it just slips away. It's just on the edge of your mind. You're building up, adding everything because you don't know what's important yet and then you end up paring it down and then at the end it is so clear. So, it's a process of feeling your way through. Everything is a reaction, so unless you make an action you have no way to react. And the reaction is what pushes it along.*

Ackerman said that seeing how close you can get to a good composition is like seeing how tight you can hold a wine glass before it breaks. That analogy alludes to the intensity of the painting process; every decision is fraught, as through the process she gets close to something that works while recognizing that it could fall apart at any moment. It's an intensive ebb and flow of working with materials and imagery. Manning (2016b) addresses this intensity as she considers how intuition may guide the affective response in artmaking: 'Intuition is the fold in experience that allows for the staging of a problem that starts a process on its way, or curbs a process into its difference, creating the germ for a practice' (p. 57).

When I Rush and Try to Complete Them, They Get Smothered, They Don't Breathe

In a visit to Montreal, Quebec (2014), Eliza Griffiths (Figures 4.5 and 4.6) discussed psychology, film, and time in relation to artmaking processes. Her paintings are figurative characters that she builds up over time, often revealing the process of making them through drawn lines and notes. The process generates the image; the characters emerge through the making. Regarding the characters, she said:

> *They're fictitious characters. They are armatures for psychological explorations. They're meant as partners in dialogue. It's a bit like theatre of the absurd. There is a non-specified narrative suggestion, but they're a way of exploring thought, gender, power dynamics, desire and trauma. They are extremely intuitively made. I let them become what they're going to be. So, they're staging while I'm making them. I might have a concept, but then the gender changes, the costumes change and the gaze moves. It's really for me like material philosophy without ever providing answers. It's a way to think while I'm making marks and to bring to life these faces. What's going to finish it is not obvious, because when I rush and try to complete them, I think they are getting a bit smothered. They don't breathe. And what's important to me is that they stay active. A lot of time if you're too familiar with what you're doing they don't feel alive.*

Addressing the relationship between figuration and abstraction, Griffiths has two factors that are important in the work: the figures are compelling, and the abstract qualities revealed through the mark are just as important. '*The thing I like about both abstraction and figuration is you pull people into an illusory thing but then push back with the paint. So it's experiential.*'

Griffiths draws a lot of her material from sources of film and music. She discussed one painting that at first reminded her of a cheesy 1970s horror movie, but later, through changes made, felt like a Brechtian play. She described another series of works she did about psychoanalysis, drawing from cartoons in the New Yorker of people in psychiatrists' offices. For Griffiths, the stories are subtexts that are often embedded in how the figures change. Her paintings are built up through the layers of making, often changing multiple times, transforming the moods and emotions. In addition to these popular culture references, her work is grounded in research in psychology, psychoanalysis, and neuroscience, drawing from her interest in human experiences and how they respond to events. Her work complicates

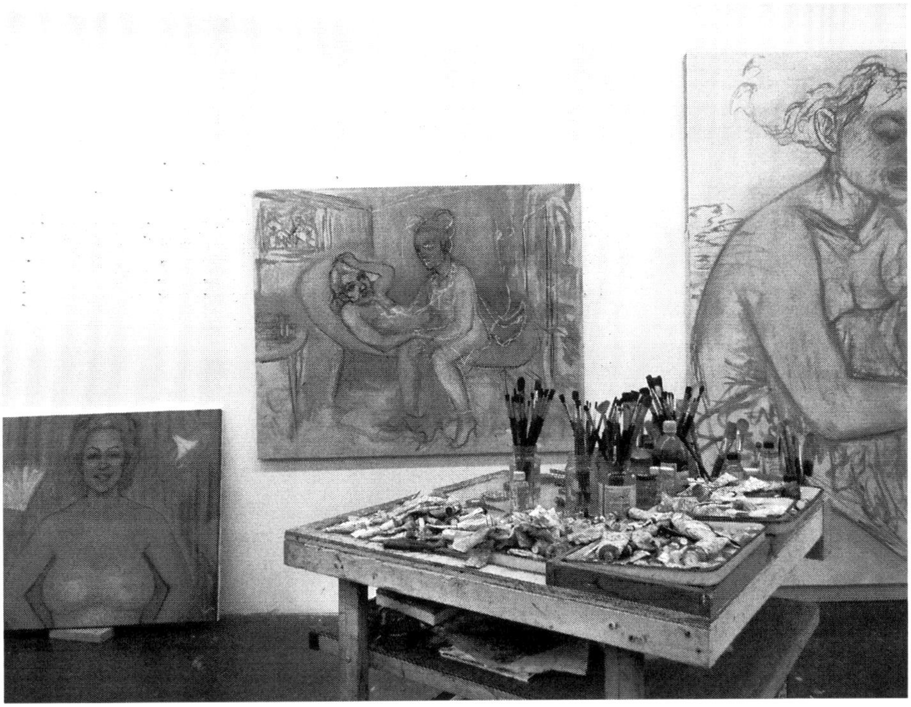

FIGURE 4.5: Eliza Griffith's Studio, Montreal, QC, 2015.

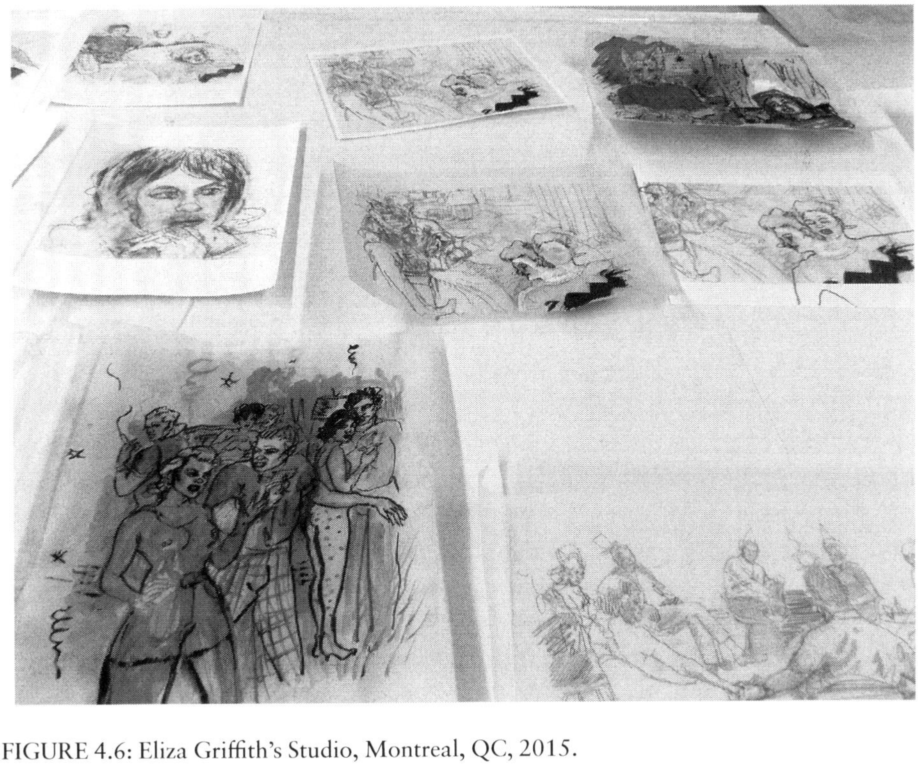

FIGURE 4.6: Eliza Griffith's Studio, Montreal, QC, 2015.

several binaries such as connection and alienation, desire and mistrust, and these complications emerge through the responsive process.

> *It's the call and response. It doesn't execute the idea. It generates the idea. It's a conversation with the painting. It proliferates possibilities that you can't predict because the medium is really active. It's very hard to control, and you can't visualize the unquantifiable possibilities of this combination or that combination. It's like I'm being Dr. Frankenstein. When I think about the finished thing, the object, I have a very different relationship to that, because I don't really care about it as a picture really. The reason I'm interested in doing this, and the reason for my interest in psychology, is that I'm interested in human brains and conversation and experiences. I like the idea that these paintings are triggers for people to have that back-and-forth with.*

Melanie Authier (Figure 4.7) similarly addressed her call-and-response approach to painting in her Ottawa studio in 2015, within an old school repurposed as art studios. For her, while there is background research done outside of the painting process, the research that happens in the studio is all about experimentation that allows the paintings to emerge. Authier's abstract paintings are characterized by colour and movement, each one exuding a unique energy. Her process reflects a performative approach, wherein the making of each painting is an event as she responds to new challenges. Years earlier, Authier worked on cruise ships following university and this experience became very influential to her painting process as she examined various definitions of beauty and the sublime.

> *I began to explore that territory because of the experience of being out at sea. You feel very small. It's a humbling experience. Then you think about issues of infinite space, and you think about scale. I became really engaged with these ideas.*

Authier doesn't represent the landscape or recreate a specific experience. Instead, she seeks to explore the effects of those experiences as an '*afterburn of that experience*' in a way that generates a new experience through the making. Thus, rather than work from the source material, she has a type of space in mind and begins with an initial colour, form or mark, and the subsequent layers respond to the previous marks. '*It gets filtered through an abstract visual language. It all gets played out on the canvas in a question-and-answer scenario.*' Through this process, the work positions itself on poles of oppositions, particularly in relation to types of colour or mark. For Authier, limitations or guidelines are generative mechanisms that set up challenges:

> *I like to set up parameters so there is a certain playful antagonism between myself and the work from the get-go. I think ultimately it traps a certain energy in the work*

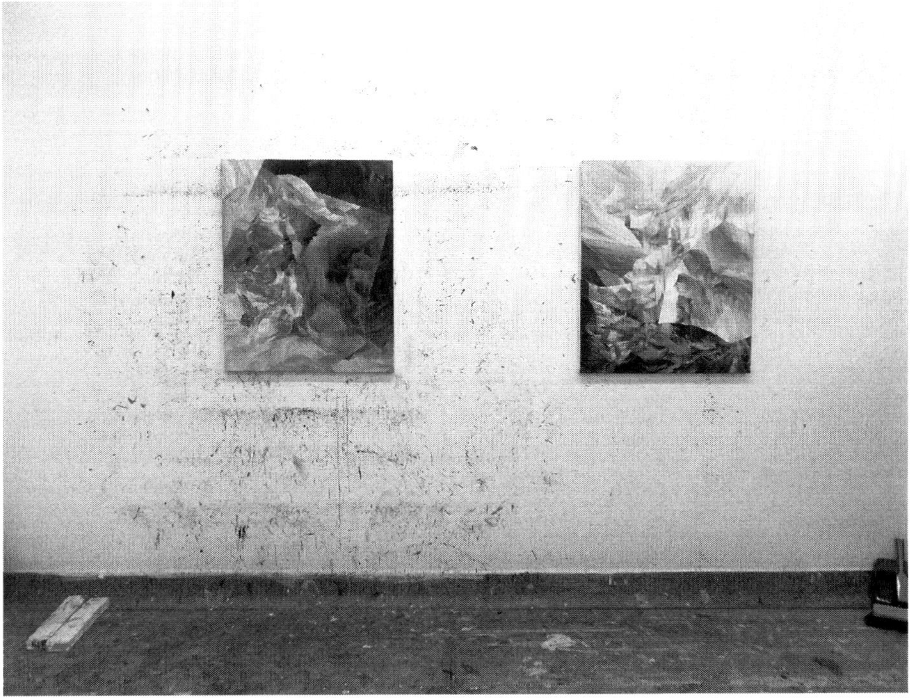

FIGURE 4.7: Melanie Authier's Studio, Ottawa, ON, 2015.

if there is a bit of struggle. Struggle can be positive. I like taking risks, I like painting myself into corners, I like setting fires and figuring out how to put them out or figuring out how to paint myself out of a corner. I like making wrong decisions for compositions or putting down a colour that in theory shouldn't work with the painting's colour palette. By doing this, I challenge myself to discover unexpected colour pairings and hues. I like to set up these games for myself and then figure out which rules are meant to be broken and why.

Regarding her intentions, Authier said that a dialogue emerges between herself and the painting through the process:

Life presents a lot of contrasts, and I think those become the impetus for the contradictions in my work. Chaos verses control, sublime verses the everyday, artificial versus natural, the geologic versus the atmospheric. But I think I'm just interested in creating something that can't be found in the 'real' world that creates an outlet for me and perhaps for my viewers. When I'm painting, I'm painting for me. And I'm working for the painting, because we're in discussion, we're in dialogue. It's a back-and-forth process. But when I think of the viewer, I think of each painting as a proposal or an invitation and that's exciting to me.

What Can Happen When They Encounter Each Other?

As a performative process, I view painting as an encounter and the studio as a site for encounters to occur. Contemporary painter, Mary Heilman says that every painting is an autobiographical marker, a memory of a place or event. The interaction between herself and a painting is described as a '*pas de deux* with natural force' (van den Boogerd, 2013, p. 19). She described a conversation with a painting: 'I am very happy to sit and look all around at painting after painting and allow them to speak to me, as I silently verbally or non-verbally talk with them, say things to them and to myself' (Heilmann, cited in van den Boogerd, 2013, p. 23). The term conversation emphasizes an exchange, a back and forth, and a dialogue. Jan Verwoert uses the term host to address this process:

> [The] canvas is the space of hosting. The canvas hosts the social that assembles in front of it. I would suggest that we shouldn't just think of the canvas as the surface of depiction, but as a strange social, the curtain, the veil, the projection screen, or even the table on which you serve the community the food, or the stage on which the community can assemble. Or if you look at painting as this social stage where different spaces exist next to each other.
>
> (Verwoert, Walker Art Center, 2013)

I take up this proposition, however, I expand that notion to propose that a studio may too be a host, one that invites the event of artmaking. Throughout time, a studio hosts a series of events, thus highlighting the in-process quality of a studio. Regarding the life-sized pieces of cut-up paintings hung on the wall of her studio, Ashleigh Bartlett (Figures 4.8 and 4.9) said: '*I think they act as characters.*' Her paintings take on a life-like presence. In Calgary, Alberta, in 2014, Bartlett's studio was filled with pieces of fabric hanging in clusters on the wall and paintings of abstracted, anthropomorphic figures. Bartlett had been a figure skater as a child and those childhood experiences with performance influenced her art practice:

> *I'm not interested in nostalgia, but I've been thinking about things I spent a lot of time doing and looking at, and I wonder why it is that we have these systems for doing things, whether it's the dramatic costuming or the theatricality.*

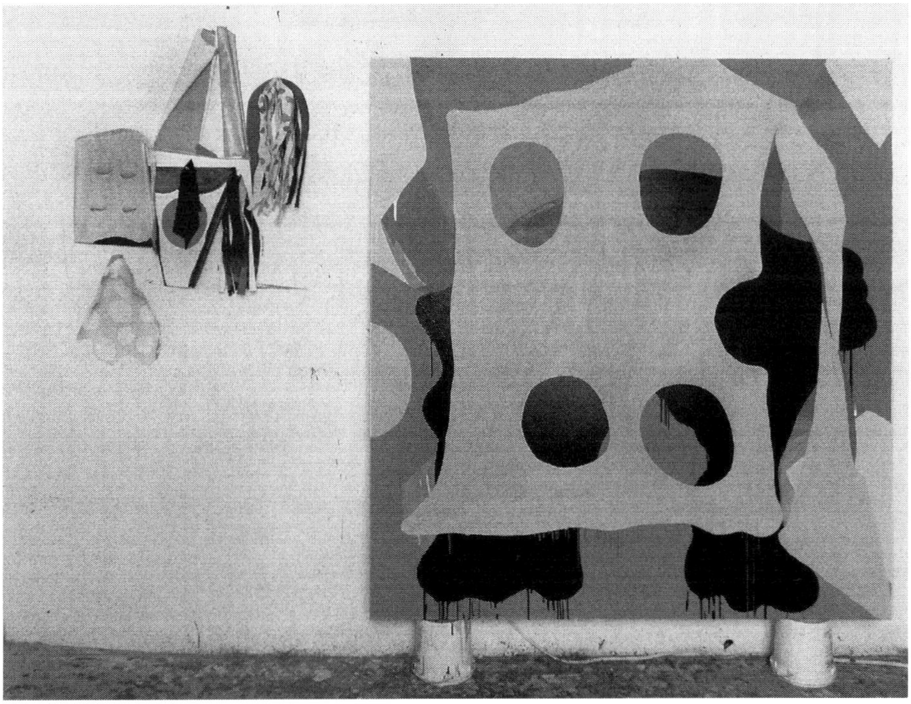

FIGURE 4.8: Ashleigh Bartlett's Studio, Calgary, AB, 2014.

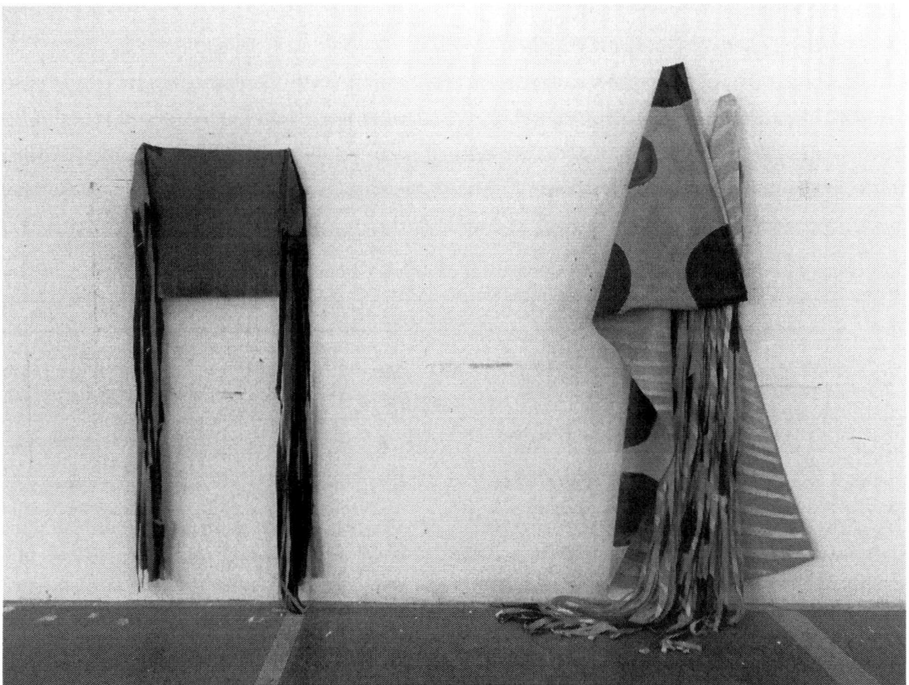

FIGURE 4.9: Ashleigh Bartlett's Studio, Toronto, ON, 2015.

As someone who had grown up on the cusp of the digital revolution, she was interested in a particular kind of flat cartoon imagery.

In 2015, I met Bartlett for a second time at a studio in an old elementary school on Toronto Island. The works had expanded beyond small pieces of fabric on the wall and were now cut-up paintings hung along the wall that looked like life-size puppets. The work had become more figurative as she created forms that are reminiscent of hands and body parts. Regarding these works, she said:

> *I think posture is interesting because it attributes to the body and the figure things you observe about people. It comes from my experience with dance and skating. But there's also this other way of thinking about the posture of an object.*

Between our two visits, Bartlett had moved to a new city and was spending a lot of time alone. These paintings prompted Bartlett to examine how she engages with others in the world as she realized that moving to a new city and not knowing many people, she began observing others from a distance. She started to engage with her paintings in a similar way, as life-like characters. The old elementary school which had an institutional quality was transformed into a theatrical space, as an active and messy art studio. The puppet-like paintings that were hung on the wall animated the space, turning this classroom into a performance, an encounter with the paintings as characters. When she first started these works, she called them her '*Summer Friends*' because they started taking on human attributes. '*I think that comes from a sense of observing people.*'

The term conversation includes a variety of types of interactions, at times calm and stimulating, while at other times tense or oppositional. Some of the words that allude to types of conversation that emerged in my interviews were: encounter; interrogation; interruption; improvisation; negotiation; breaking the ice; chatter; speaking; confrontation; yelling; silence; relationships; lying; and hosting. For example, when discussing how she constructs a painting, Carol Wainio said she wants to see what elements in the painting will say to each other, or Sandra Meigs said that her recent work is a party of all the parts hanging out together. Allyson Clay described how the text in her work interrupts a reading. Dil Hildebrand said we need to listen to what the painting is trying to tell us and Jennifer Carvalho expressed how she needs to spend time with an image to understand its mood. Monica Tap explained how she was told by another artist that he knew a painting was done when it stopped yelling at him; this statement resonated with her.

Art theorist Simon O'Sullivan (2006) says that artmaking is an encounter. He describes encounters as being different than moments of recognition that simply reconfirm our beliefs, values, and understandings of the world. An object of recognition is a representation; it represents what we already know. With an encounter, on the other hand, our systems of knowledge and ways of being are unsettled. An encounter allows us to see or think about the world differently. For Estelle Barrett (2013) artmaking involves a two-way dialogue between the maker and the painting. According to Barrett, through the process of making, our experiences in the world may be transferred through the work. However, she also argues that the work might simultaneously reflect back to the artist perspectives or understandings of the world that may not have been apparent prior to the making. As an encounter, it is a conversation between the artist and the artwork, and between the materials and the process. Thus, a studio sets the stage for encounters and generates conversation.

In a visit with Alexis Lavoie (Figure 4.10), in Montreal, in 2014, we looked at his collage-like paintings that combined childlike imagery to create dark, eerie, and fragmented narrative spaces. On our second visit, in 2015, his work had changed. He had several paintings depicting close-up images of skin. Regarding this work, he said: '*Skin is where the history of our experiences is inscribed.*' For him, painting is the most direct relationship between body and mind. In other works, his paintings continued to show playful, collage-like, bizarre, and unbelievable scenes,

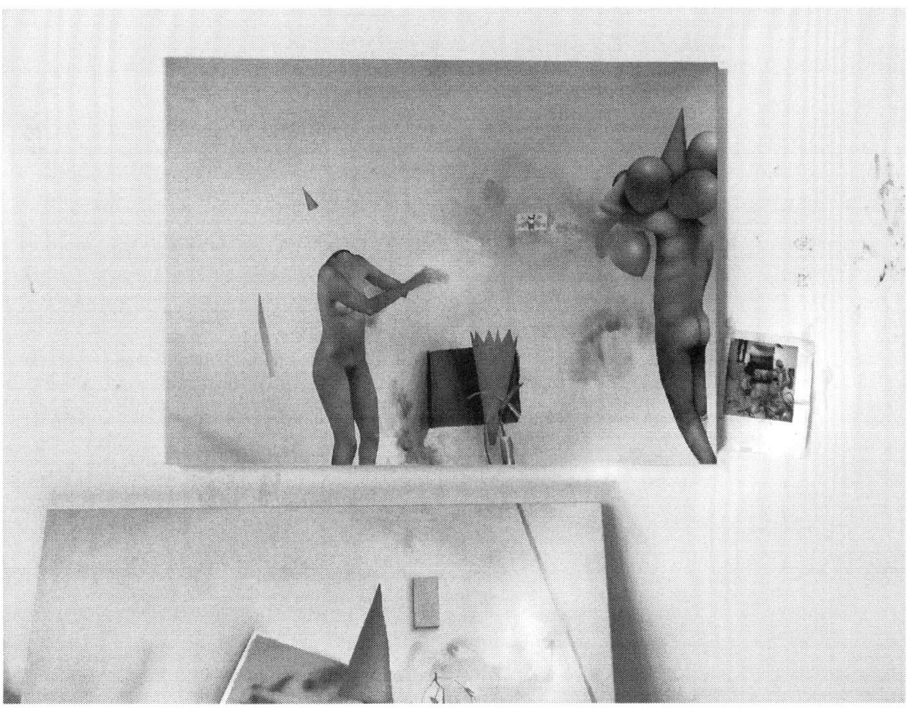

FIGURE 4.10: Alexis Lavoie's Studio, Montreal, QC, 2015.

but now these scenes were generated with other people. He had invited people to parties where he created experiences with improvisation, play, and objects. He would give them activities to do, such as finding a hidden ball to generate playful interaction, like both a game and a performance. While alluding to childlike play there is also something eerie about the interactions, and for Lavoie, it's important that the paintings are ambiguous and uneasy. He described this experience as magical as he addressed the question: '*What can happen when they encounter each other?*' Manning (2016b) asks: 'What else can be created sympathetically in the encounter?' (p. 44). I similarly ask, what can be created when the studio is viewed as a host to an ongoing encounter between the artist, the space, the materials, and the paintings.

5

Take One Small Idea and See How Fertile It Can Be (Studio as Generative)

> *[Curiosity is] a multifaceted and complex emotion, disposition, and capacity that emerges from a range of intentions and creates a spectrum of effects ... Thinking with human and nonhuman bodies, a spectrum of curious intensities emerge that press against established boundaries to trace their conditions of emergence, while becoming an index of their pliability, porosity, and rigidity.*
>
> (Coats, 2023, p. 13)

Viral Entities That Inhabit the Mind

Performativity within artmaking draws from the premise that matter and meaning are constantly changing through ongoing intra-actions (Barad, 2007; Kleinman, 2012). Barad proposes that rather than the world being made up of separate individuals that exist prior to their interaction, individuals exist because of particular interactions. As such, entities are in a constant state of becoming in relation to encounters with other entities in a process she describes as intra-action, a perspective that views the world as constantly changing and in process. This process highlights the particularity of studio practice that exists and is responsive to a particular time and place. Moreover, Barad discusses diffraction as a way of attending to the ways that differences are produced. Diffraction can be taken up in relation to studios as both a physical phenomenon, and metaphorically as a way of thinking about learning through making. As a physical phenomenon, Barad describes diffraction as the ways that waves combine when they encounter each other or bend and spread when encountering an obstruction. Diffraction illuminates a performative view of the world as always changing in relation to its encounters, producing ongoing differences and change. For example, diffraction addresses the way that two stones thrown into water at the same time create two ripples, and as the ripples overlap a new pattern emerges as the relative difference between the overlapping waves. With regards to this way of knowing, Barad (2007) says: 'Making knowledge not simply about making facts but about making worlds, or rather, it is about making specific worldly configurations ... in the sense of materially engaging as part of the world in giving it specific material form' (p. 91). From a research lens, reflective understandings entail a subject examining a world to be grasped, understood, and represented. From the perspective of painting, a reflective practice creates a picture of the world as a representation. A diffractive way of viewing artmaking is to engage with it as relational, situated, and responsive to ongoing changes. It is generative rather than fixed.

Addressing the potentials and possibilities inherent within artmaking processes, art educator Garoian (2015) uses diffraction as a way of moving art beyond representation. Drawing from Barad's (2007) description of the intra-action of waves as they overlap or are interrupted by a barrier, he says that diffraction is a performative process. It is an '"entangled ontology" of perpetual differentiation' (p. 491), wherein actions are responsive and generative. The differentiation occurs through the indeterminacy that is generated through ongoing interruptions, interferences, and interactions that emerge through artmaking. Applied to studio practice, I propose that intra-actions highlight the ongoing relationships formed between materials, making, and our embodied experiences in the world. As such, studio practice is an ongoing process of perpetual differentiation (Garoian, 2015), continuously producing new configurations in response to particular actions. Thus, on a metaphorical level, diffraction also reveals the entanglements and complexity within the ontology of knowing (Barad, 2007) and in turn supports an ontology of making.

Barrett (2013) similarly explores material engagement in artmaking to address experiential qualities of making. Barrett describes the active and experiential quality of artmaking as performative: 'Unlike images that operate via established symbolic codes and that serve to communicate information, the aesthetic image is "performative": it emerges through sensory processes and gives rise to multiplicity, ambiguity and indeterminacy' (p. 63). Extending Bolt's discussion of performativity in relation to material practice, Barrett questions the privileging of distant, impersonal observation of the world and suggests that this approach be replaced with one that is a material approach that emphasizes interaction and action. Barrett emphasizes an embodied experience-in-practice that allows for the emergence of new ways of thinking and understanding that recognizes subjectivity as a process that is in relation to encounters with the world. For Barrett, this is an active process wherein the world enters the artwork, and in turn, the work sends effects back onto the world.

A new materialist lens of painting emphasizes responsiveness, and, in this way, it is an active and generative process. Perez de Miles and Kalin (2018) challenge purely linguistic and representationalist approaches to understanding art and research as they address new materialism within art education and research. They argue that modes of thought from western Humanism need to be reconsidered, through a 'radical reconfiguration of the linguistic turn, critical theory, self-reflexivity and epistemology' (p. 4). They emphasize the ways that objects have agency and relationships occur through an intra-action between subject and object.

> The shift from the linguistic turn and representational thought open up to diffractive methodologies that make evident that entanglements such as matter and meaning or matter-meaning (Barad, 2007), materiality and discourse or material-discursive (Braidotti, 2013) are processes that are iterative, unbound, in-the-making, and relational. (p. 6)

Thus, the studio becomes a space for a 'speculative process of searching' (McClenaghan, 2016, p. 32) that produces multiple iterations and possibilities through the process. Regarding studio practice, Emmanuel Osahar (Toronto, 2022) similarly said: '*It's about a personal longing and navigating of a desire that never gets fulfilled.*'

Art theorist, Jan Verwoert (2005) describes artmaking as a complex decision-making process, wherein forms and concepts emerge through a continual response and negotiation between the emerging parts of a painting. Verwoert also describes emergence as the process wherein structures cannot be derived from single parts but instead emerge through the interaction of elements within a complex and interwoven system. This interwoven system reflects a constantly changing ecology. In Ottawa, Carol Wainio spoke to the infinite possibilities that emerge through painting.

> *It's my way of working through some of this stuff. I want to know what happens when I make it material. I find images interesting, even the most banal. I'm fascinated by choices when there are a million choices. It's like the multiple universe theory in physics. Every step of the way you could go in so many different directions. That's more pronounced in paint. There's something about the accidents that happen that might take you somewhere else.*

In a studio visit while he was participating in an artist residency in 2014 in Halifax, Nova Scotia, Yukon-based artist Colin Dorward (Figure 5.1) similarly

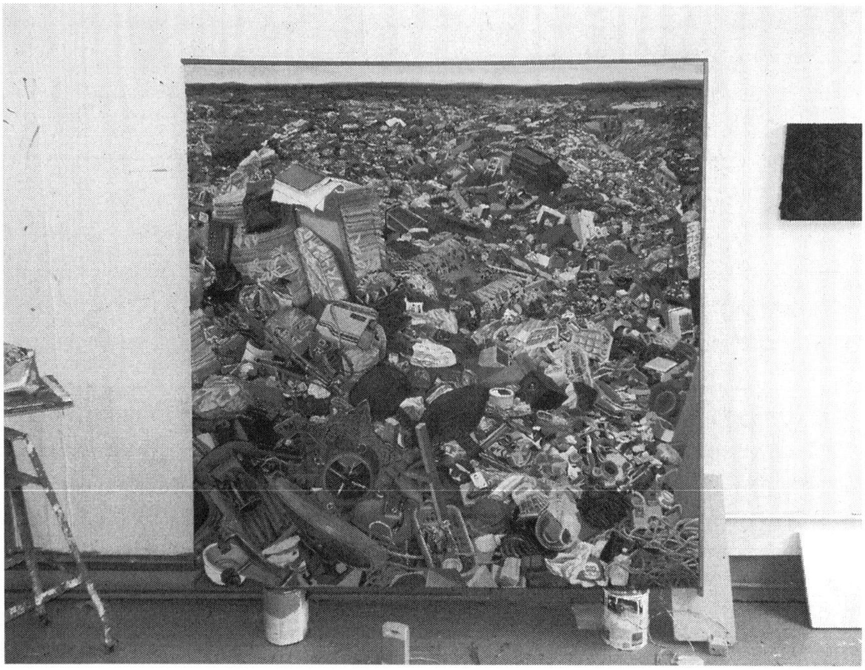

FIGURE 5.1: Colin Dorward's Studio, Halifax, NS, 2014.

addressed how visual imagery takes on a life of its own within his mind through painting:

> *That's the thing I love about painting, it trickles into that part of the brain that thinks about visuals a lot and it's sometimes so behind the scenes that we don't even know what our own influences are until … it takes years sometimes to notice what it was that triggered you to paint something. Images are like these secret, viral entities that inhabit the human mind, and painting becomes a basis for their continuation.*

For Dorward, the process of painting allows for the propagation and transformation of imagery. A studio is thus a space for this propagation of imagery to thrive.

Where Images Come From, Their Migration, How They Rupture, and Where They Deteriorate

Within his studio practice, Montreal-based artist, James Gardner (Figures 5.2 and 5.3), speaks to the emergence and generation of imagery. Gardner's studio

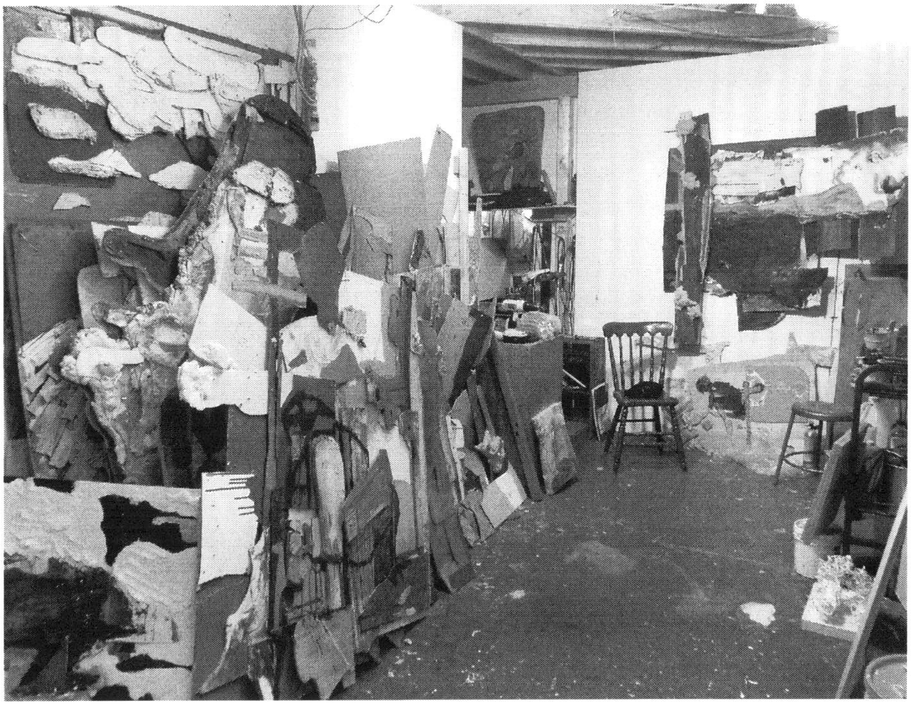

FIGURE 5.2: James Gardner's Studio, Montreal, QC, 2014.

embodies action. Filled with old paintings, piles of wood, tools, and paint, Gardner constantly works and reworks old paintings into new configurations. Pointing at a pile of wooden scraps and old paintings, he said:

> *Sometimes being in a studio for a while, a painting can lean on another painting and they start to fuse together, and that can be a starting point to move forward. So, the ecology of the studio can be a driving force of the work. I'm not trying to just represent things. I'm not trying to capture ways of perception. Or explain things to the viewer. I'm more interested in how the act of painting in itself is the experience and how I can find new experiences through the act of painting.*

I met Gardner in 2014 and 2015 at his Toronto-based studio. At the time, he lived and worked with an artist collective called VSVSVS in a building converted to live-in studios. His paintings were made on plywood and through the action of building up the painting, an image emerges for him. Referring to one painting of a group of trees, he said that the image needs to remain

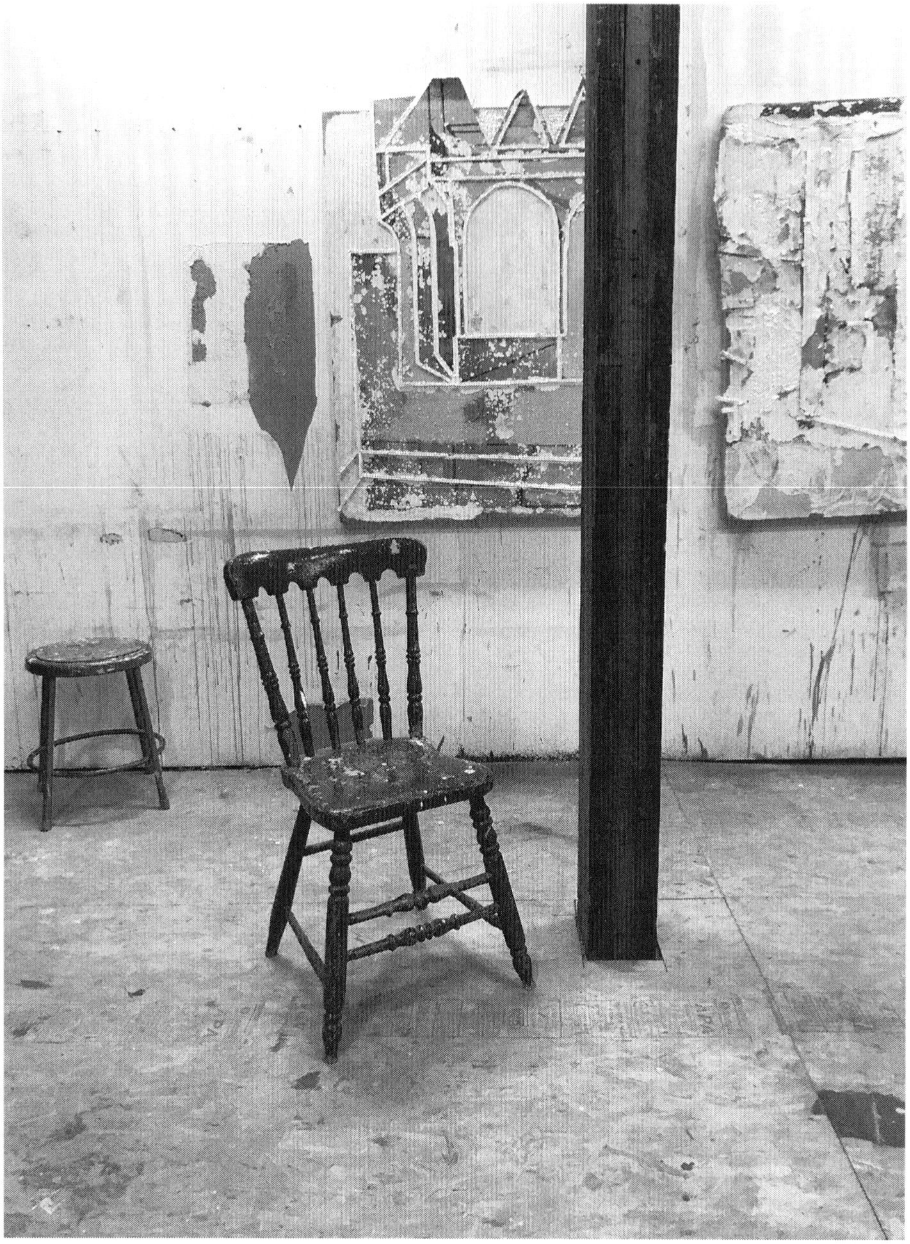

FIGURE 5.3: James Gardner's Studio, Montreal, QC, 2021.

ambiguous rather than fixed. Addressing thinking through making, Gardner said:

> *It's a way to explore ideas about myself. The process of painting and sitting in the studio can be reflective or meditative. People think of meditation as a passive process whereas I experience it as a very active process. The rigorous exploration and paying attention to the processes is a great way of thinking about consciousness.*

Gardner spoke about the strange slippages and coincidences that occur within the studio. He is particularly interested in the inner experience and how that manifests itself through studio practice or how the outer world seeps into the work. He used the word '*transference*' to explain how all his experiences in the world, from a tree he would bike by daily, to billboards he passed on the way home, to images in magazines, manifest themselves through painting. In this way, he said the studio is like a pressure cooker. He uses alchemy as a way of discussing his engagement with materials.

> *I think it is really interesting how you can understand processes through material. Ideas of change, metamorphosis and transformation may be understood through language but are really material things. I think there's something about alchemy that can help us develop a new language to talk about what happens in the studio.*

I met with Gardner again years later in his Montreal-based studio where he had delved deeper into this research into alchemy throughout his graduate work. The biggest shift in his work had been that, rather than letting images emerge through the act of painting, he was now creating an image bank from which to draw. The previous year, he had done research at the Warburg Institute developing an image archive related to alchemy that draws from historical imagery. Aby Warburg was an art historian and art theorist who created a library that would become the Warburg Institute where he had a huge cabinet full of historical images. Gardner spent time in the library, scanning books and creating his own esoteric image archive that showcases historical images related to astrology and alchemy and mapping that imagery through time. He views images as active, generative, and connective rather than fixed.

> *You may end up with one image, but because of astrological meanings, there are all these precedents to that image and later developments. So, when you research one image, you realize how it's connected to all these other images, and it just goes out and out and out. And then as it is reflected inward, you add on your own types of symbolism and personal affinities. So, the meaning making is really strange and almost indescribable to other people. It's very generative.*

Gardner's work had shifted from allowing imagery from his surroundings and popular culture to seep into the paintings towards work that was grounded in a cultural and historical understanding of how images emerge. However, the common thread throughout the work is that it engages with the in-flux and changing nature of imagery. In his studio, there was a cage filled with rock formations. He explained that the cages are called gabions and are used on riverbeds to prevent erosion. The sculpture worked as an analogy for this change.

> *I'm watching where images come from and their migration and how they rupture and where they deteriorate, both physically and through a cultural understanding. New images emerge and combine old images. Images have this great evolutionary, migratory life. French philosopher, Didi-Huberman uses this great analogy where he compares the life of an image to a geological formation. He thinks of it in terms of the erosion of the edge of a river or a pebble in a whirlpool getting tumbled about. It's the same pebble but it's slightly worn down in the same way as an old astrological image. We might not even know where it comes from but it's still being used. So, I use these rock formations as a means of promoting that way of thinking of images as being located in this deep geological time and being part of a really long conversation.*

Self-Imposed Limits as a Way to Generate Stylistic Freedom

In 2017, I went to an artist talk by Winnipeg-based artist Ufuk Gueray (Figures 5.4 and 5.5) with whom I had previously shared two studio visits. In his presentation, he described being in a transition period:

> This presentation will discuss how Kazimir Malevich's 1928–1929 painting *Head of a Peasant* joined me on my current path towards an uncertain artistic future. This charming but awkward piece has become my personal guide to overcoming boredom, nihilism, and artist's block in the studio.
>
> (Gueray, 2017)

He explained how he made drawings and paintings of this peasant, as he imagined him as a '*real-life companion*'. Throughout the next year, as he formed a relationship with the figure in Malevich's painting, he continuously took him apart, re-imagined him, and re-configured him.

> He showed me that art can be simultaneously regressive and avant-garde; that an image can be both awkward and cool. Rediscovering this image made painting

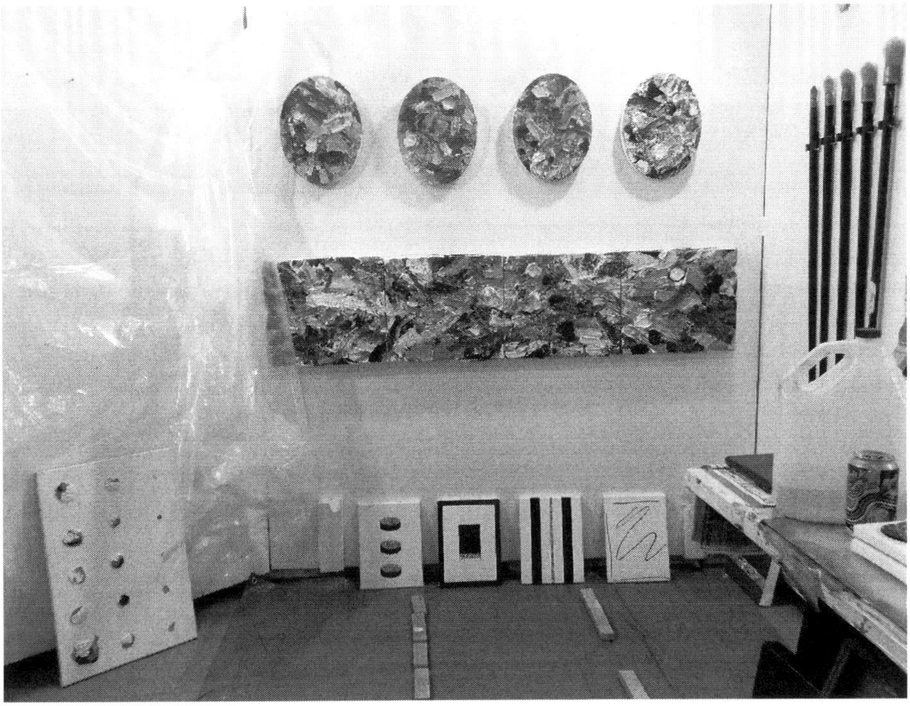

FIGURE 5.4: Ufuk Gueray's Studio, Winnipeg, MN, 2014.

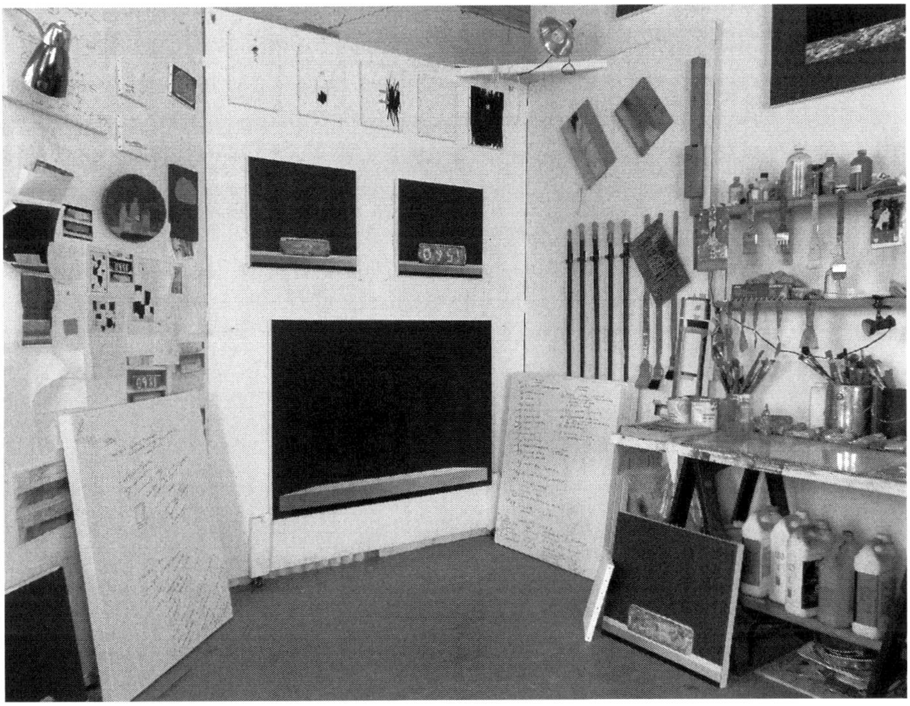

FIGURE 5.5: Ufuk Gueray's Studio, Winnipeg, MN, 2015.

> feel like a party I wanted to attend. It helped me get past the things that were blocking my artistic progress and made being in the studio something to celebrate again.
>
> (Gueray, 2017)

Through his painting practice, Gueray repeatedly dissects one image or motif to examine several artistic, historical, and social issues. The subject of study becomes an allegory for his process of diagramming these connections. Through working with one motif, he uses,

> self-imposed limits as a way to generate stylistic freedom. In the studio, painting often happens in a responsive way, through improvising, going along with textures, forms and shapes, and responding to ideas that get carried over from one piece to the next and morph into different things.
>
> (Gueray, 2017)

Gueray began our first visit to Winnipeg, Manitoba, in 2014 by giving me a piece of cut, fake sausage. He had ordered it from a speciality food replica store in Germany. He first became interested in the sausage as a motif after reading an essay by John Berger in which there was a passage about a struggling painter, who couldn't make money from selling his work, so he painted food shop window displays. In this essay, the artist was pictured as so poor and hungry that he was driven by a desire to paint images of food that looked real. This passage stuck with Gueray and planted a seed for this body of work that came to be called the *Market Series*. In the studio, there was a painting with several circular pieces of sliced sausage, which he described as literal deconstructions (cutting the sausage). There hung four oval paintings with expressive abstract marks that appeared as pieces of sausage, and another with a long rectangular strip along the bottom with a similar fleshy expressive mark. The work simultaneously referenced abstract expressionism, hard-edged abstraction, and minimalism, and thus the sausage became a way of exploring twentieth-century art history, as well as art as a commodity. Working from this very specific restriction (the sausage) freed him up to explore all these other subjects:

> *This work is limited in its formal elements. It is a very similar colour palette from painting to painting, and it's usually very toned down except for these pinky tones. But within those restrictions I felt like I had a lot of freedom, and somehow working within these restrictions, made it easy to come up with the parameters for the next painting.*

The second time I visited Gueray, in 2015, he was working on a new series informed by the generative process of the market series. He had taught a course in lithography that past year which led to working with lithography stones as a motif.

> *The way it works is that it's a very specific limestone from one quarry in this area in Bavaria, Germany that is essentially near exhausted at this stage. And it was a very popular medium starting in the 1880s and it was popular well into the 20th century. In the 1970s you were still taught it in art school. They would break, and every time you put on a new motif, you'd draw on it, then you'd have to grind it down, so they'd lose 1/20th of an inch each time. I became interested in that because I liked that they are all from this one place but now are all over the place, so there is something biographically linking them. I also liked that whenever you grind the surface it becomes super smooth and clean and becomes a brand-new surface that no one has ever laid eyes on, but when you look at the edges, there are people's names on it, numbers, bits of tape, ink and gunk. I thought that contrast is interesting. You're seeing the stone that has had X number of layers of images on it but gets pulverized away over the years. And they were these objects I could put in a painting, but I liked that they were about process. Particularly in painting, the death of painting keeps coming up with this constant regularity, and it's not like it ever really dies, but then there's a medium that is really on its way out. So, I thought this is a medium that is actually going to die out just because physically the material is going to die out. So, I thought maybe this is an interesting series about death and art and death of mediums. Or obsolescence.*

Regarding the generative process of working with a single motif, Gueray said:

> *That series consisted in taking one small idea and seeing how fertile it could be, doing new reformations of that one motif. All these derivations came from that one motif. So, I had to come up with something new that was informed by the conceptual form of this work but was something new that kept my interest alive.*

Arrive at Something That's More Specific and Less Generic

I visited Janet Werner's studios (Figures 5.6–5.9) in Montreal three times over the course of several years (2014, 2015, 2021). Through our studio visits, we discussed the learning, thinking, and feeling process of painting. Her paintings of figures, often sourced from fashion magazines, go from the beginning point to some other endpoint, and during this time, something happens that transforms them into something else. For her, the process is fraught with feelings of inadequacy, failure, and hopelessness, but she keeps going because she loves the game.

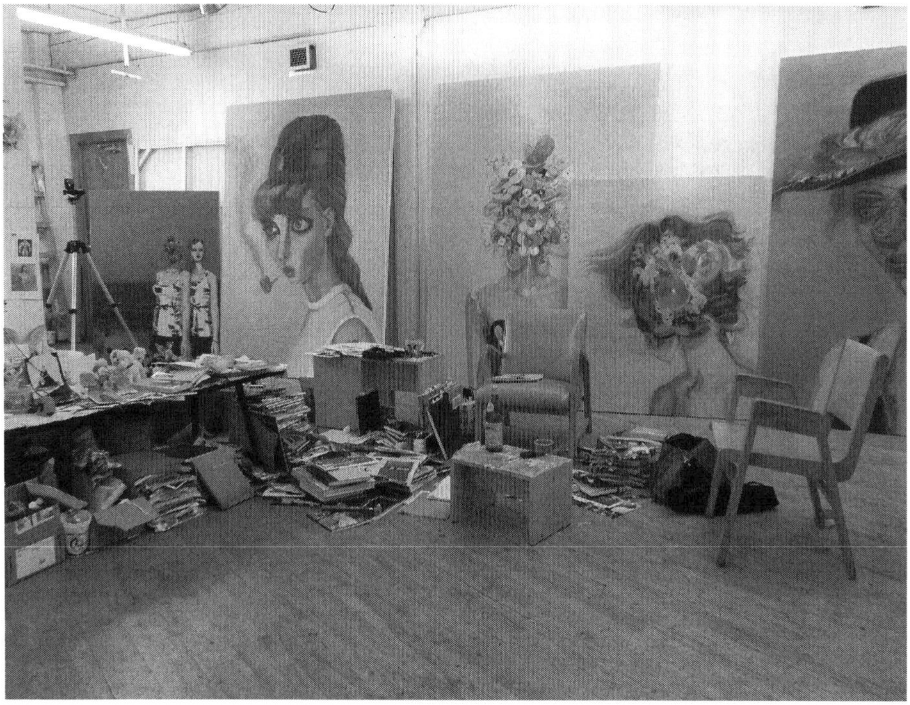

FIGURE 5.6: Janet Werner's Studio, Montreal, QC, 2014.

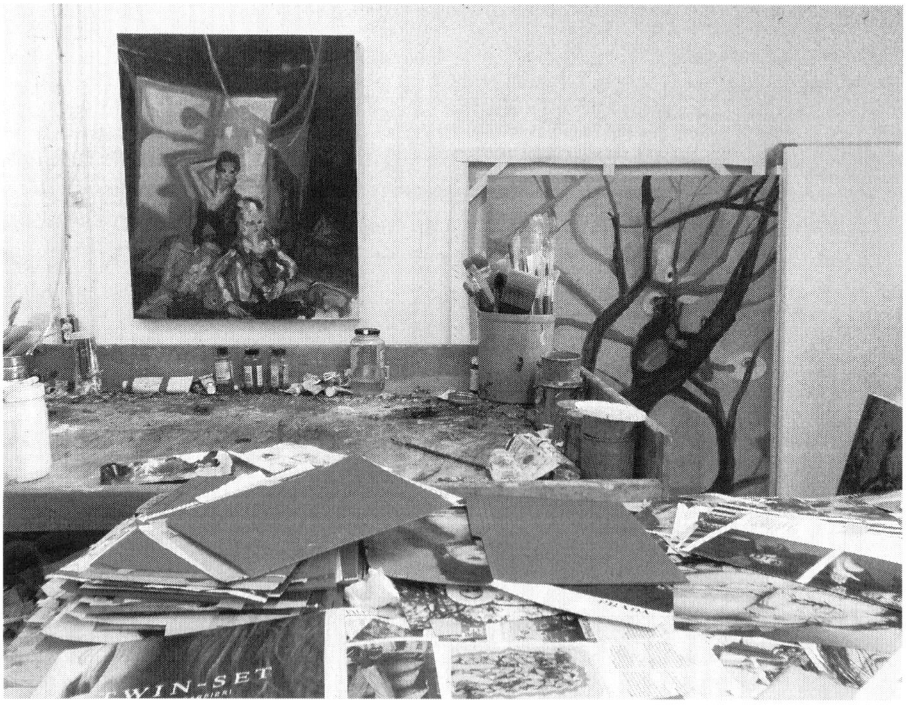

FIGURE 5.7: Janet Werner's Studio, Montreal, QC, 2014.

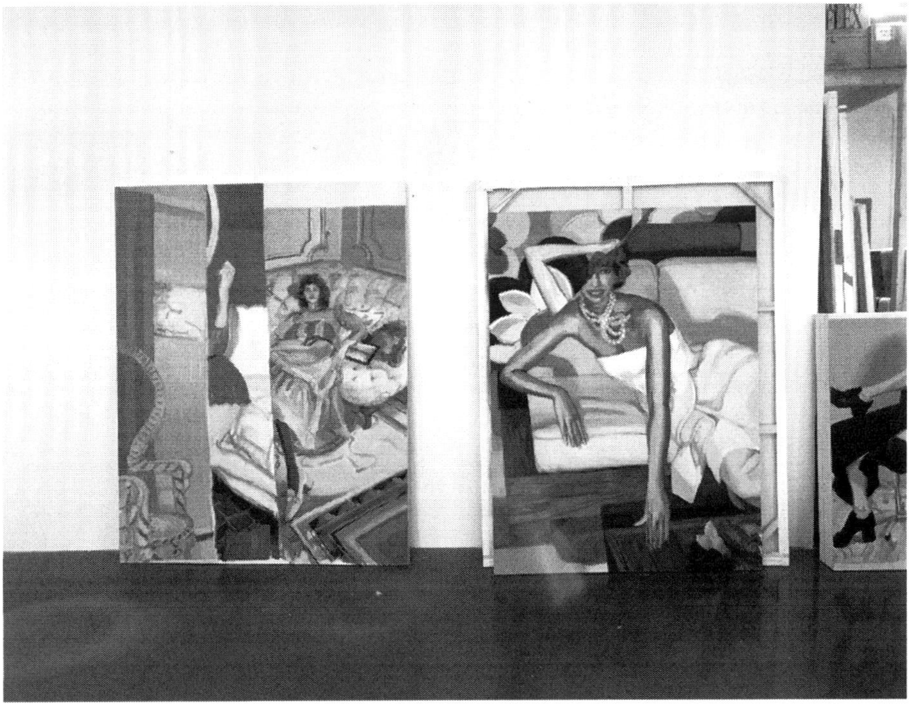

FIGURE 5.8: Janet Werner's Studio, Montreal, QC, 2015.

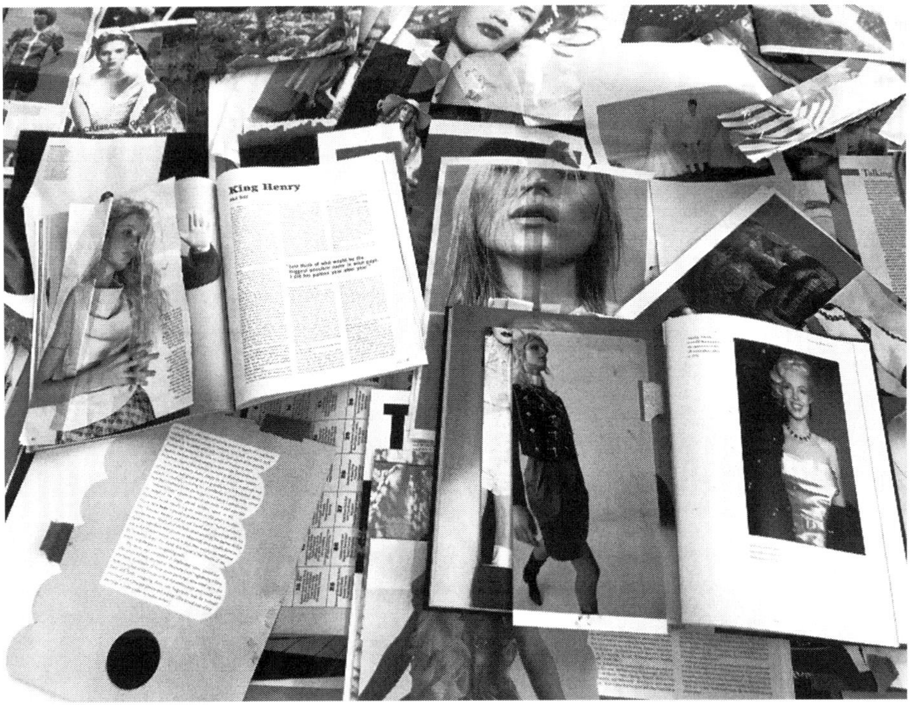

FIGURE 5.9: Janet Werner's Studio, Montreal, QC, 2015.

Werner has a complicated relationship to portraiture, as her paintings are of figures, but not specific people.

> *What they do have in common with the portrait is the formal framing of the figure. It's a solitary figure. So, it's somewhat within that convention, but it also works against it. It's subversive in some ways, because it is not about wealth and glamour.*

She is interested in portraits because they are a locus of meaning, communication, and honesty: '*So, why the portrait? For starters, it's not so much about portraiture as it is about an encounter.*' Werner expanded on her interest in painting the figure.

> *I've always been fascinated with very primal direct things and non-linguistic experiences. So, the eye-to-eye communication that is preverbal or that happens on another level is inarticulate. I'm really interested in the inarticulate. And all that communication and experience is very real and very true but we don't have language for. The story is contained in the person, and I'm interested in how you can talk about your interior life through external appearances.*

The invented-through-the-process figures are composites combining source material from fashion magazines and books as she works with glamourized and idealized images of beauty. Although she has painted animals and the occasional male figure, Werner has mostly painted women as she believes women function better in culture as '*vessels of the imagination*'.

> *If you look around at all the images that are produced in our culture, it's mostly images of women, and one of the reasons is because, as someone once said, 'men look at women and women look at women.' Not to say we don't look at men, but men tend to have a very stereotypical role in the image world. Masculinity and images of power are often associated with men. Whereas woman project all kinds of things. Sometimes it's a vulnerability, sometimes it's power, sometimes it's beauty. Whereas guys are very limited in visual culture in terms of what they're allowed to do, how they like to be seen. Women are freer in a certain way and also more tied. It's also because I identify with women, and I usually have to be able to identify with the characters. I try to invest the figures with some sort of power and vulnerability at the same time.*

Through the making process, Werner complicates the image through distortions, costumes, gestures, masks, and covering the face in different ways. For her, these complications introduced into the painting manifest the idea of an interior world. Regarding using fashion magazines as source imagery, she said that as generic people rather than specific people, '*they lend themselves really well to the idea of projection and transformation*'. Through transforming them and removing them from the source material, they become less perfect, troubled and create a different kind of narrative.

> *I hope that through the construction of painting, and this is what the creative process is about, hopefully I arrive at something that's more specific and less generic. Usually when I look at the source material, I find it boring. But the idea is to move from the generic to the specific through the process of painting. I believe that colour is this language that can create meaning, even though it's nonverbal. It can create a mood and meaning just by the physical effects of the colour. So, what is transformed? It might just be a dramatization of something that's already there but taken to a different extreme. It usually involves an exaggeration of some kind. And how is often through scale, through colour, through drawing, through mis-drawing, through accidents, through the time-based process of drawing and painting. When I'm disgusted by this image it is because they are so shallow and they don't have depth, and they want something from you. They want your money. Whereas the painting doesn't really want anything except for you to engage with them as objects, and ideas and images.*

6

Create Problems That Can't Be Solved (Studio as Not Knowing)

> *A life of making isn't a series of shows, or projects, or productions, or things; it is an everyday practice. It is a practice of questions more than of answers, of waiting to find what you need more than knowing what you need to do.*
>
> (Hamilton, 2009, p. 69)

The Captain Knew Too Well Where He Was

In a project at the Lancaster Institute of Contemporary Art, artist and professor Rebecca Fortnum (2009) studied the creative processes of visual artists. Through interviews with artists, she found that a sense of discovery and a search for the unexpected was a dominant motivator for artmaking. Rather than seeking a mastery of materials or technique, she found that the challenges of handling materials, working through problems, encountering doubts, and facing uncertainty are at the core of artists' practices. Furthermore, she believes this search for the unknown is not necessarily out of a belief in the avant-garde. Instead, her interviews showed that many artists have a desire to create work they might not understand, or that may exceed their intentions. She argues that resolution is a fiction, and this fiction perpetuates a continual search for understanding that creates an ongoing tension between knowing and not knowing inherent in the creative process. For this reason, she states: 'The artist is thus in a continual state of process, compelled to repeat because he can never know how (or even if) he has achieved his intention.' Fortnum and Fisher (2013) argue for the necessity of not knowing:

> Where knowledge is positive, the *un*known is often simply the opposite: it is *un*certain, *in*visible, *in*comprehensible. *Not* knowing represents a lack or absence,

> inadequacy to be overcome. However [we] describe a kind of liminal space where *not knowing* is not only not overcome, but sought, explored and savoured; where failure, boredom, frustration and getting lost are constructively deployed alongside wonder, secrets and play.
>
> (p. 7, original emphasis)

I met Carly Butler (Figures 6.1–6.4) in Halifax, Nova Scotia, in 2014 and 2015, and then again in Ucluelet, British Columbia, in 2018. Over the course of our visits, we discussed the role of 'not knowing' in artmaking. She had grown up with a father who was determined to sail around the world. His dream finally came to fruition when she had just moved away from home as a young adult, and she was not able to join him on that journey. This '*almost adventure*' that she never got to go on fuelled an obsession with shipwrecks and being lost at sea. Her grandfather had once been lost at sea for several days during a sailing race. In the studio, she had books about sailors lost at sea and rules of navigation. On the wall of her Halifax studio, Butler had maps of the East Coast of Canada on which she had marked where shipwrecks had occurred and next to them, there were mixed-media

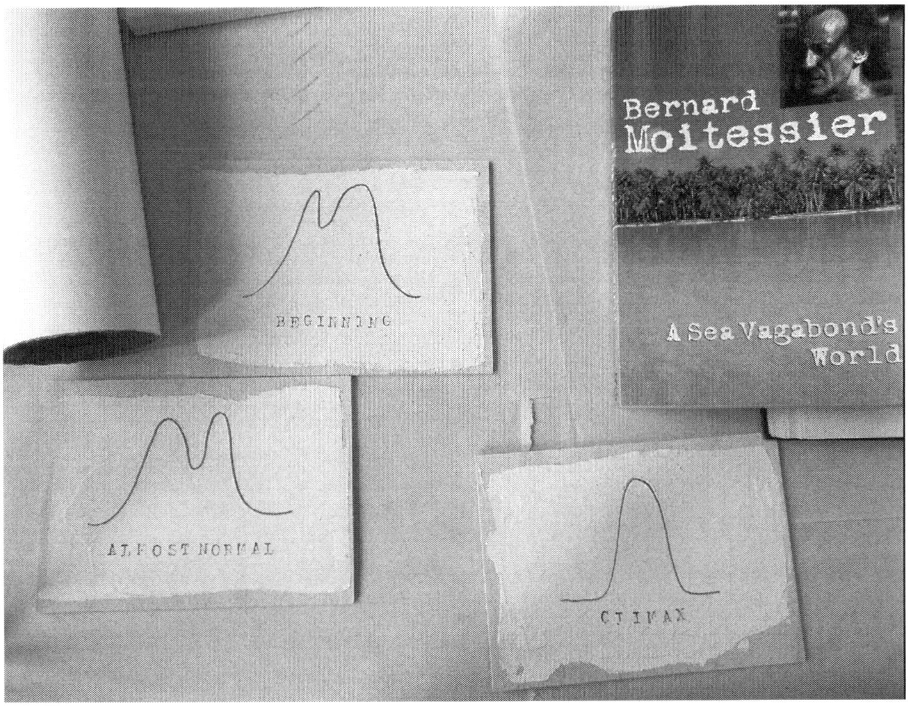

FIGURE 6.1: Carly Butler's Studio, Halifax, NS, 2015.

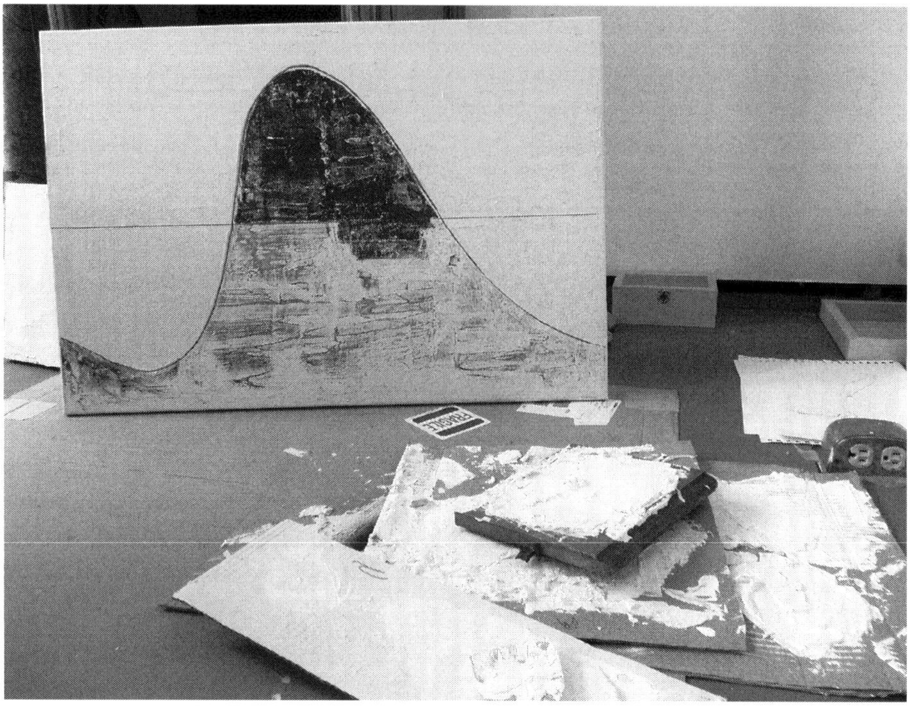

FIGURE 6.2: Carly Butler's Studio, Halifax, NS, 2015.

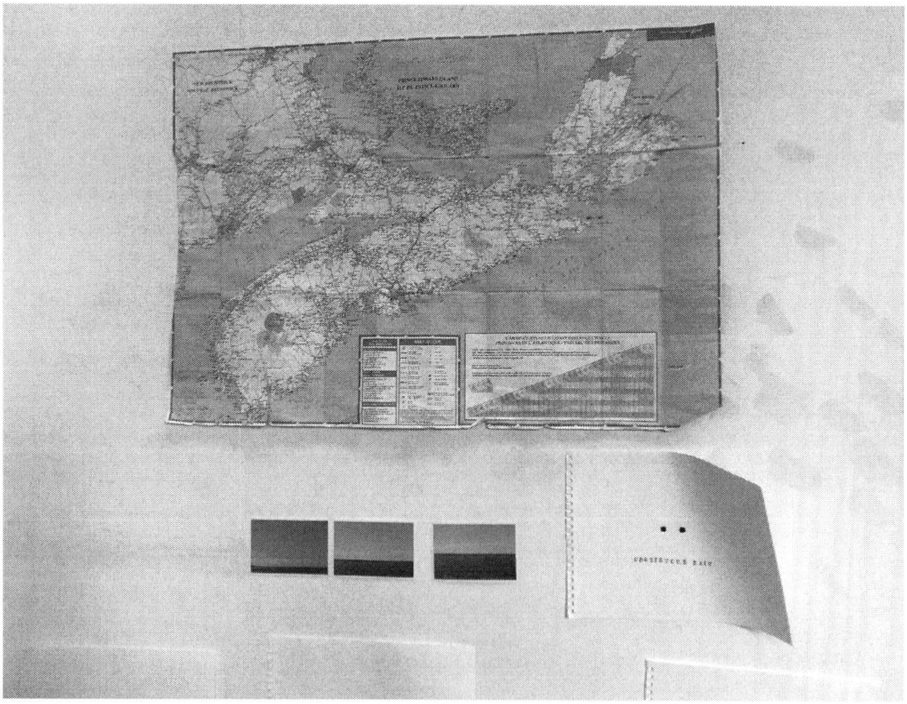

FIGURE 6.3: Carly Butler's Studio, Halifax, NS, 2015.

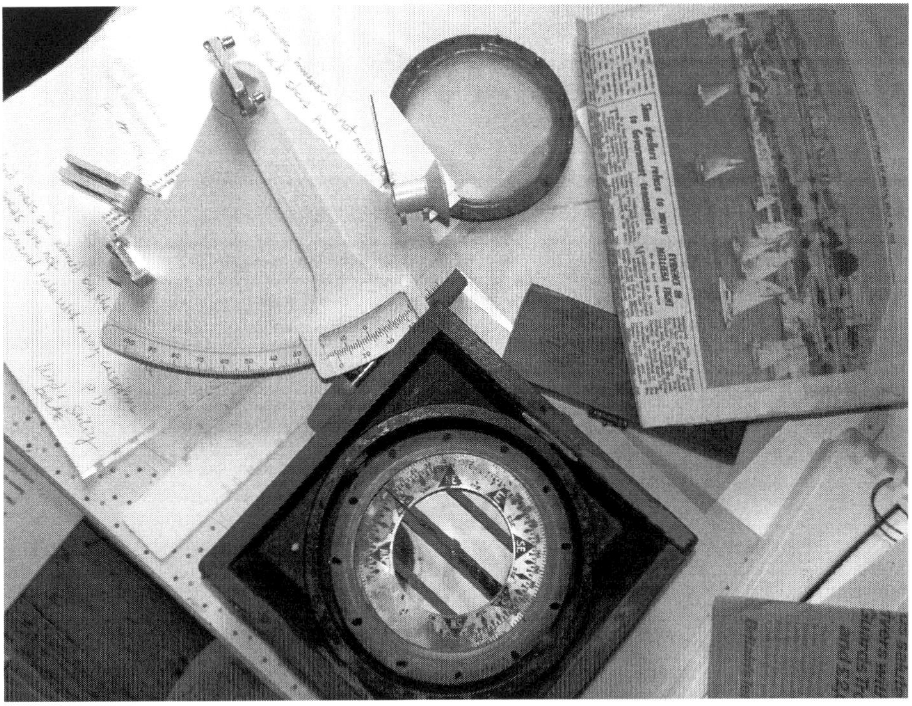

FIGURE 6.4: Carly Butler's Studio, Halifax, NS, 2015.

paintings on which she had inscribed nautical sound wave patterns she had taken from the *Manual of Navigation* that had belonged to her grandfather. The notes and instructions taken from these manuals enticed her partially because she didn't fully understand their meaning which allowed her to project her own meanings onto them: '*It's about not knowing. These things are kind of on the edge of our comprehension.*'

At the time of the visit, Butler had had a recent exhibition entitled *The Captain Knew Too Well Where He Was*, which refers to a quote by Joshua Slocum, a Nova Scotian who was the first person to sail alone around the world. In his book, Slocum describes how he was out at sea and met a '*young cocky captain*' who told him their exact latitude and longitude and that Slocum thought '*the captain knew too well where he was*'. Butler explained her interest in this story:

> *I've been thinking a lot about the idea of getting lost and not knowing where you're going. If you look at GPS and we're getting so reliant on our iphones, we know where we are but we don't know where that is. We can pinpoint it, 'I'm here' but have no idea where that is in the world.*

Butler explores this concept of being lost through using navigational tools. She had recently travelled to Mexico and while she was there her father taught her how to use a sextant to navigate. She showed the sextant and explained that it's used to find out where you are by using the sun and stars. She demonstrated how to use it, showing me how to find the sun, and pull it to the horizon. She had tried it daily and ended up in different places every time, thus revealing the errors in her methodology. '*Part of my practice is that I'm not an expert and it's about what I don't know and it's all about the failures.*' The title of her exhibition *The Captain Knew Too Well Where He Was* highlights how trying too hard to know where we are may limit possibilities. Butler's explorations challenge notions of mastery within artmaking and instead focus on the value of not knowing and uncertainty.

Within Fortnum and Fisher's (2013) anthology that addresses 'not knowing' within artistic practices, Jones (2013) highlights the strangeness and wonder that emerges when we put ourselves in a position of not knowing.

> Part of the 'artistic work' of becoming thus lies in remaining open to the strange in the strangeness; being prepared to lose ourselves in the encounter; risking *not* knowing as the condition of possible transformation ... Learning to see as strange makes us un-at-home in the everyday, and thereby restores it as a potential place of marvel where we might become other than what or who we are.
>
> (p. 18, original emphasis)

Jones argues that to attend to difference without reproducing more of the sameness is to recognize that ourselves and others are '*never* entirely knowable or graspable' (p. 18, original emphasis). According to Jones, 'the vital openness that springs from not knowing needs to be cultivated through an "artistic working", even as it is also the necessary condition of such work' (p. 18). To embrace 'not knowing' is to embrace wonder. Finally, Jones highlights the dialogic relationship between humans and materials as material intelligence. Material intelligence recognizes that material has its own agency and thus working with materials that in themselves are unpredictable opens us up to that space of 'not knowing' that is felt in the body:

> Material intelligence would then belong neither wholly to human beings nor to matter. Instead, it would emerge in the interactions between them, made possible by the way human beings always already *are* bodily and material beings themselves, as well as by an acceptance of not knowing that allows human intelligence *about* matter to be coupled with the guiding intelligence *of* matter. It is this *between*, perhaps, that the creative practices of art and thought can take place.
>
> (p. 28, original emphasis)

When I met with Winnipeg-based painter Holger Kalberg, I asked him why he makes art. He said that his recent work is largely about the question: '*Why am I still making things?*' I asked him if he came up with anything and he replied '*No and I don't want to. If I do that's probably the end.*' Extending this idea, Mark Neufeld asked: '*How do you make knowledge that's not just about ends, to have an excitement with discovery?*' In a studio visit in Guelph, Ontario, Maegan Harbridge described the anxiety she felt as a child being constantly told that one day, she would figure things out, that one day everything would come together and make sense. This anticipation of an eventual resolution or closure haunted her for years. She explained how making art allowed her to approach life from a different perspective:

> *Making art is like philosophy. It's always about questioning. It's not like you're ever going to come to a place of knowing, it's just about the questioning and that in itself is a politics of living ... Why go to art school? It helped me become ok with not knowing.*

In Toronto, Azadeh Elmizadeh similarly described artmaking as open-ended: '*There are hunches, moments of excitement that drive exploration in the studio. But they never conclude as statements or definitive answers to problems.*' Elmizadeh draws from Iranian folkloric literature as a source for her painting, saying that '*literature is more fluid and naturally lends itself to the language of painting*'. Elmizadeh is captivated by the limitless nature of artmaking, explaining: '*Painting has an element of escape – it's uncontainable, expansive. It allows me to communicate something or perhaps even miscommunicate it. While words impose limits, paintings can transcend boundaries of meaning.*' Similarly, Ben Reeves says that paintings tell their own stories. We have to follow the path of the painting and things are often not clear until we do them. He celebrated the importance of not fully understanding why we are doing what we are doing as he said:

> *It seems to me that as soon as I develop a way of doing something that works, I have to give it up to a great extent. Because then it becomes technique and is no longer interrogating the subject. It really is flat and dead.*

Ellsworth (2005) echoes Reeves' words as she examines how places become pedagogical when they transform our understandings. Regarding 'not knowing' within learning, she challenges us to think about knowledge as being alive:

> Knowledge, once it is defined, taught and used as a 'thing made', is dead. It has been forced to give up that which 'really exists': its nature when it is a thing in the making,

> continuously evolving through our understanding and our own bodies' experience of and participation in that world.
>
> (p. 1)

She emphasizes how knowledge-in-the-making is the experience of ourselves in the making and 'opens an exploration into the experience of the learning self' (p. 2). For her, the 'self' emerges through learning, and this is how studios may become pedagogical, by allowing ourselves to learn through embracing messiness, not knowing and exploration.

Dig a Hole and Find Your Way Out

For Montreal-based artist Dil Hildebrand (Figures 6.5 and 6.6) painting is an ongoing learning process. For him, painting is like trying to find someone in a crowd, while not knowing what that person looks like. While he first starts with a sketch as a starting point, he always has the freedom to destroy it, obscure it, or change it as he goes. In our studio visit in Montreal, he explained this idea:

> *The first sketch bears no resemblance to the work in the end. It doesn't have that purpose. It's a sequence of movements and changes. I don't really know where I'm going. It's really just a walk in the woods. It's like a walk in the wilderness where you don't know where you're going and every decision is based on what's there right now. It's not based on the map to tell me where I'm going. I don't have a map. I'm just walking through the woods and making decisions. There are problems with that because sometimes you do get lost; I get lost each and every time.*

In his studio in 2014, there were images that were painted green, like a chalkboard or a cutting mat. He explained that his work is essentially all about learning through doing, a process of learning through taking things apart and putting them back together. For him, that is how learning works. Regarding the in-process painting, he says: '*It doesn't really know what it wants to be*', stating that each painting is a Frankenstein of the previous work that feeds into it. For him, painting is an infinite game, but the object of the game is to keep the game going through play, problem-solving, and unpredictability. In Montreal, Janet Werner similarly said: '*The creative process is like digging a hole and trying to find your way out of it.*'

In an essay entitled 'Making Not Knowing', artist Ann Hamilton (2009) describes making as an ongoing, unfinished story. Artmaking allows something new to appear and come into existence through an urgent engagement with materials and practice. Hamilton suggests that a comfort in not knowing is a driving

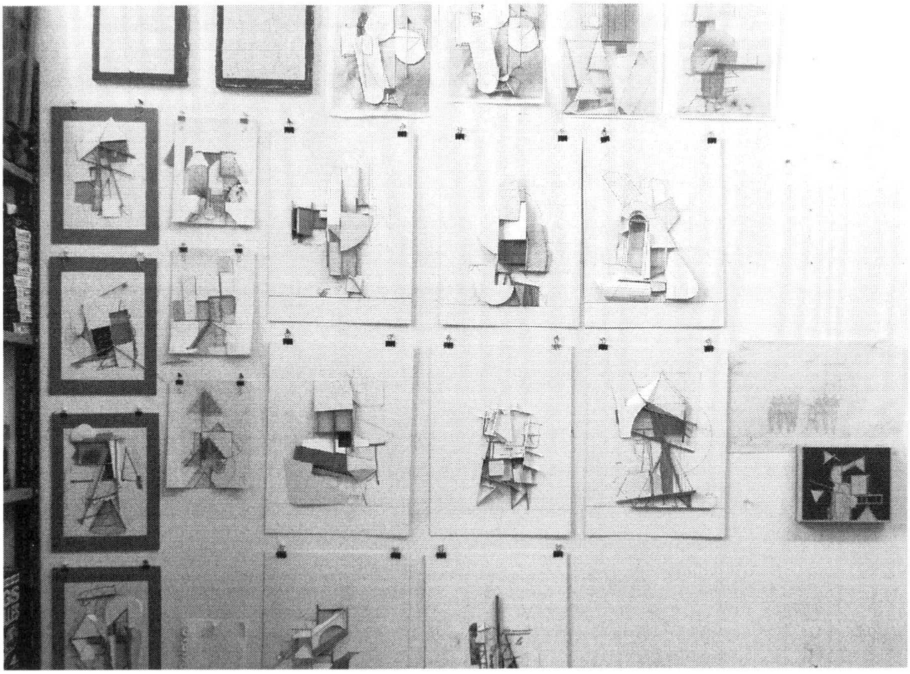

FIGURE 6.5: Dil Hildebrand's Studio, Montreal, QC, 2014.

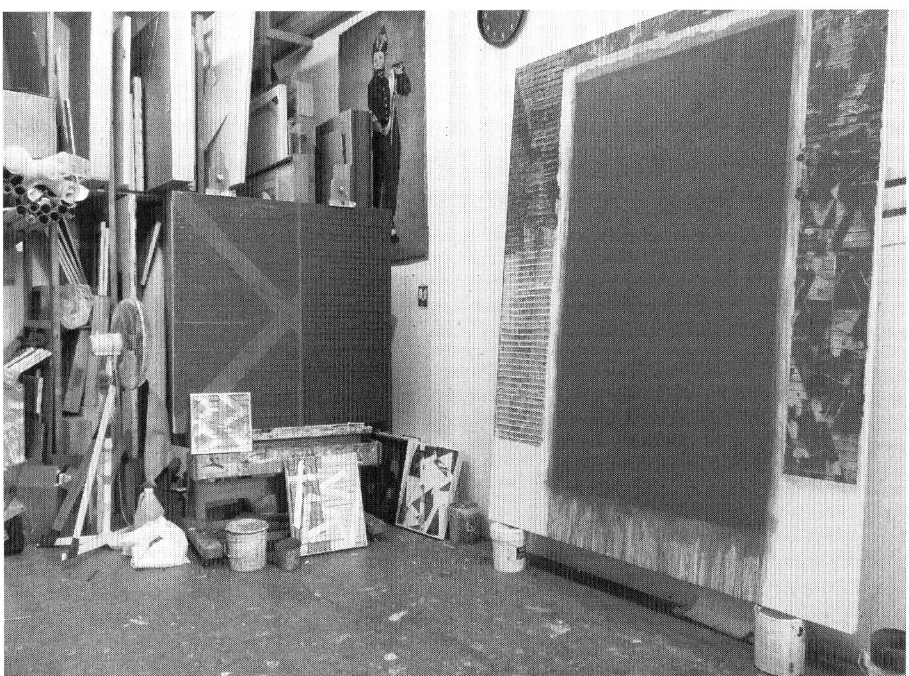

FIGURE 6.6: Dil Hildebrand's Studio, Montreal, QC, 2015.

force in artmaking; one moves from what you know to what you don't know: 'Not knowing isn't ignorance. Not knowing is a permissive and rigourous willingness to trust, leaving knowing in suspension, trusting in possibility without result, regarding as possible all manner of response' (p. 68). Hamilton laments the critique of unproductive time or daydreaming in society and calls for more time to imagine and embrace ways of knowing that are not quantifiable. She admits to the difficulty in explaining experiences that are not quantifiable, easily named, measured, or categorized. Thus, she acknowledges the challenge in articulating how knowledge and meaning are produced through artmaking while asserting the significance of valuing uncertainties inherent to creative practice. Hamilton refers to the butterfly effect, the way a flap of a wing in one continent may change the weather in a different continent, to describe how often small, undetectable variations in phenomena may cause huge differences. She uses the butterfly effect to allude to the emergent process of artmaking as responsive within an ecology.

Artist Emma Cocker (2013) creates prompts for engaging with 'not knowing' as part of her practice as she produces conditions for 'uncertainty, disorientation and indeterminacy' (p. 127). For her, provoking states of 'not knowing' can disrupt habitual ways of being and therefore prompt her to think differently. Significant to Cocker's description of not knowing is the acknowledgement of the challenges and frustrations of 'not knowing'.

> Not knowing might well be the ground from which creativity springs, however, to inhabit the experience in affirmative terms is not an easy task. It is not inherently productive or generative nor does it always lead to new and imaginative lines of flight. Not knowing can be paralysing, prohibitive. It can usher in the feelings of anxiety and embarrassment, the debilitating sense of being at a loss or lost, unable to see a way out or forward.
>
> (p. 126)

Cocker critiques education systems that emphasize the attainment of measurable objectives wherein 'to not know is treated as a deficiency or failure' (p. 126). Through this lens, 'the pleasurable potential of not knowing becomes squeezed into designated timeslots called play, breaks of unruly abandon where what is known can once again be rendered unfamiliar, the uncertain or unexpected met with rushes of brief wonder and delight' (p. 126). She argues that valuing 'not knowing' is a challenge to a culture that sees 'not knowing' as meaningless and as something to be overcome. Instead for Cocker, 'not knowing' is an active space in which to dwell through encountering something unfamiliar or unrecognizable. Furthermore, the goal of art is not to move towards something knowable, but instead to retain something 'infinitely unknowable' (p. 127) within the work.

Cocker connects 'not knowing' to studio practices as she suggests that artists may move beyond frustration and defeat towards something generative through embracing the sensation of not knowing:

> The studio becomes a gymnasium where thoughts and forms like limbs are made to stretch and flex, arc and fold ... The studio creates the conditions of parentheses for dislocating its contents from their habitual surrounds. Here, objects, images, words and sounds can be disassembled and reassembled; stretched; compressed; inverted and rotated; pushed into unlikely proximity, and then prized apart. Familiar forms are worried until they begin to break down and recombine differently; materials are pressured toward their limits, categories tilted to the point of slippage or collapse. The challenge is how to prevent these nascent assemblages from being assimilated all too quickly back into meaning, from becoming classified or (re)claimed swiftly by existing knowledge. The artist strives for that elusive encounter with something momentarily unnameable or unclassified no longer *and* not yet known.
>
> (pp. 129–30, original emphasis)

Thus, a studio becomes a site for ongoing experimentation with the unknown.

In Halifax, Julie Trudel (2015) (Figures 6.7 and 6.8) discussed this space of 'not knowing': '*Art is all about not knowing. I think we raise young people to know. There is not much space for experimentation, for trying.*' For Trudel, her passionate relationship with painting makes it possible to be a painter. She addressed experimentation and the role that vulnerability, insecurity, and doubt play in artmaking.

> *In the day-to-day practice of being an artist, coming to the studio and seeing art, there is a great deal of doubt. Over the course of a painting project, you're trying to understand what other people are doing, trying to understand what you are doing, trying to find your own way into the whole baggage of art history. You start with an idea, you try this, you try that, and you walk through this whole process. And in the end, I've tried every possibility, and when I choose one, it's like, 'ok it couldn't be any other way for this project'. Then I feel confident enough to show it in the world.*

To address the process of working through experiments and trying to find a solution, she quoted artist Brice Martin who said: '*Art is a source of renewable energy.*' A large part of Trudel's process is inventing new tools and processes through experimentation. Her abstract painting practice involves intricately measuring formulas to create paint droplets that move in particular ways to create specific effects that she seeks out. She recounted a story of her frustrations while on an artist

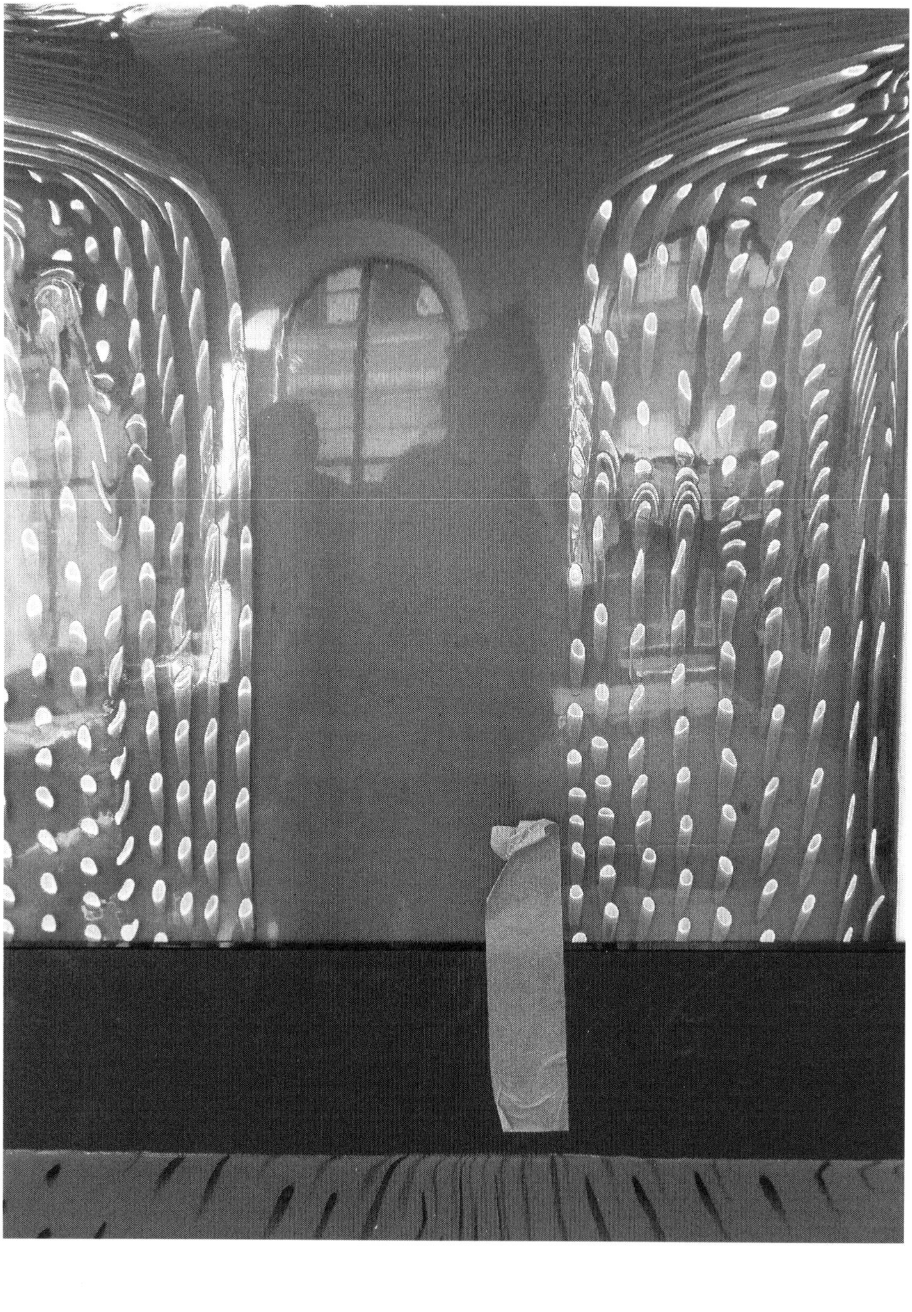

FIGURE 6.7: Julie Trudel's Studio, Halifax, NS, 2015.

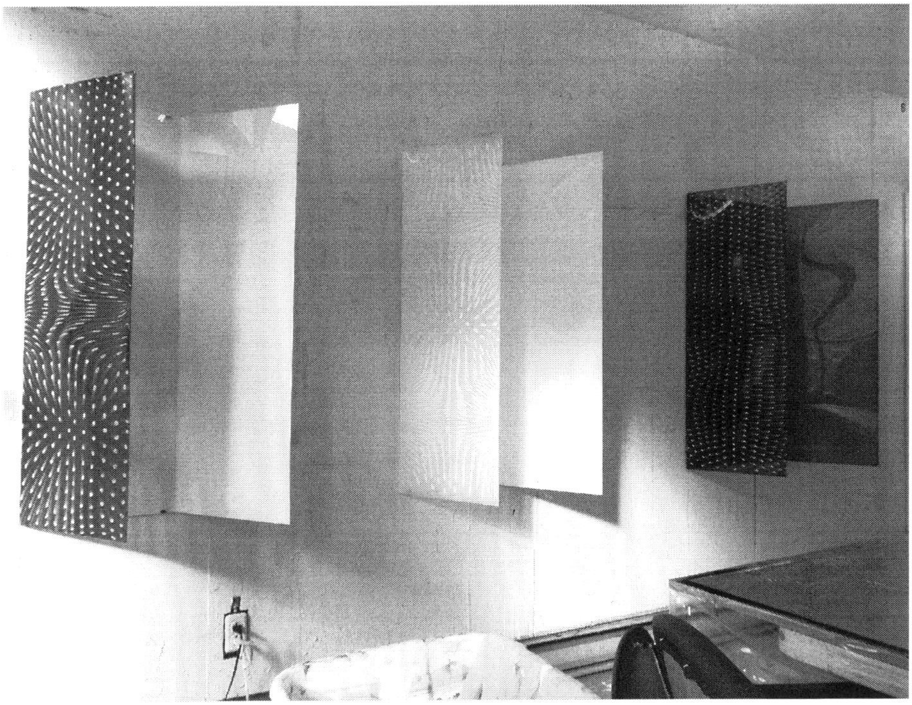

FIGURE 6.8: Julie Trudel's Studio, Halifax, NS, 2015.

residency and was unable to acquire her usual materials. Reflecting on the experience, she realized that she needed to accept what was available there and adapt accordingly. But from those limits, she discovered new processes and directions within her work. For Trudel, working through frustration is part of the process:

> *Many of my paintings are very simple technically but I push the technique so far. Being faced with technical challenges, through my fascination for these processes I have an intensity toward solving it, that I can find my way out. Even if it is abstract, the curiosity I have toward a particular kind of painting, or some kind of colour occurrence, is personal ... When the project is finished, it's finished, it's not alive anymore. But you hope that the painting retains a life of what you put into it. If you work through all the problems as you work through the project, and if in the end what you let out keeps the energy of the questions and the making, then it looks really assertive and confident. But you don't reach that point without making room for a lot of insecurity, uncertainty, searching, being stuck, and all those things that happen. If I can get you into my excitement of doing these things and if I get you into my passion, then it works.*

Seek Out Coincidences and Find Things You Didn't Know You Were Looking For

> *My ideal viewer is a person who has a lot of time on their hands. You're looking for patterns, seeing how it repeats and questioning my motives and asking what the hell is going on. My theory is if you put enough time into it, it gets the wheels spinning.*

This is how artist Art Green (Figures 6.9 and 6.10) described his intentions. In his Stratford, Ontario studio (2015), he took me on a journey into a life of 'not knowing', coincidences and problem-finding. Within Green's complex paintings, several repeated motifs appear: ice cream cones; airplanes; flames; cities; scissors; couples embracing. Over the course of our visit, we discussed his life, teaching, creativity, and art as he offered insights into a life lived pursuing problems that can't be solved. Born in 1941 to an engineer father, and raised in Indiana, Green originally thought he should pursue a more practical route like graphic or industrial design. He went to the Art Institute of Chicago where by second year he was drawn into studying Fine Arts.

He began our interview by sharing anecdotes from his days in art school that capture the spirit of a 1960s art education. He recalled one etching professor who worked with old copper plates from *Time Magazine*. The image would begin as advertisements for Coca-Cola and end up as a paranoid picture of the world. He recalled another professor in a silkscreen class who encouraged them to print with lipstick and mustard. Following art school, Green began working as a teacher in a senior centre. He remembered one woman he taught who was almost 100 years old. She had gone to art school in 1902 but could only get so far because they wouldn't let women draw from the model. He laughed about students' perceptions about what made a 'good' artist, one student claiming that a true artist knows how to draw noses. Green later worked as an elementary school art teacher to avoid the Vietnam draft call. He also became part of a creativity study in the 1960s and explained with cynicism and humour his participation. For this test, they were asked to make a still life and then make a work of art based on it.

> *It turns out the people who spent the most time on the still life were the most creative. The ones who got it done in a zap had an 'idea' of a still life, like wine, guitar, apple, drapery. They solved the problem. I think anybody whose work is interesting has found a problem. In a way if you solve the problem, you have to find another one. So, art is not about solving problems it's about finding problems.*

While in Chicago, Green formed a group of artists called the 'Hairy Who'. The Hairy Who was a Chicago pop art style that engaged with the artists' private obsessions. In search of his obsessions, Green comes across the imagery for his

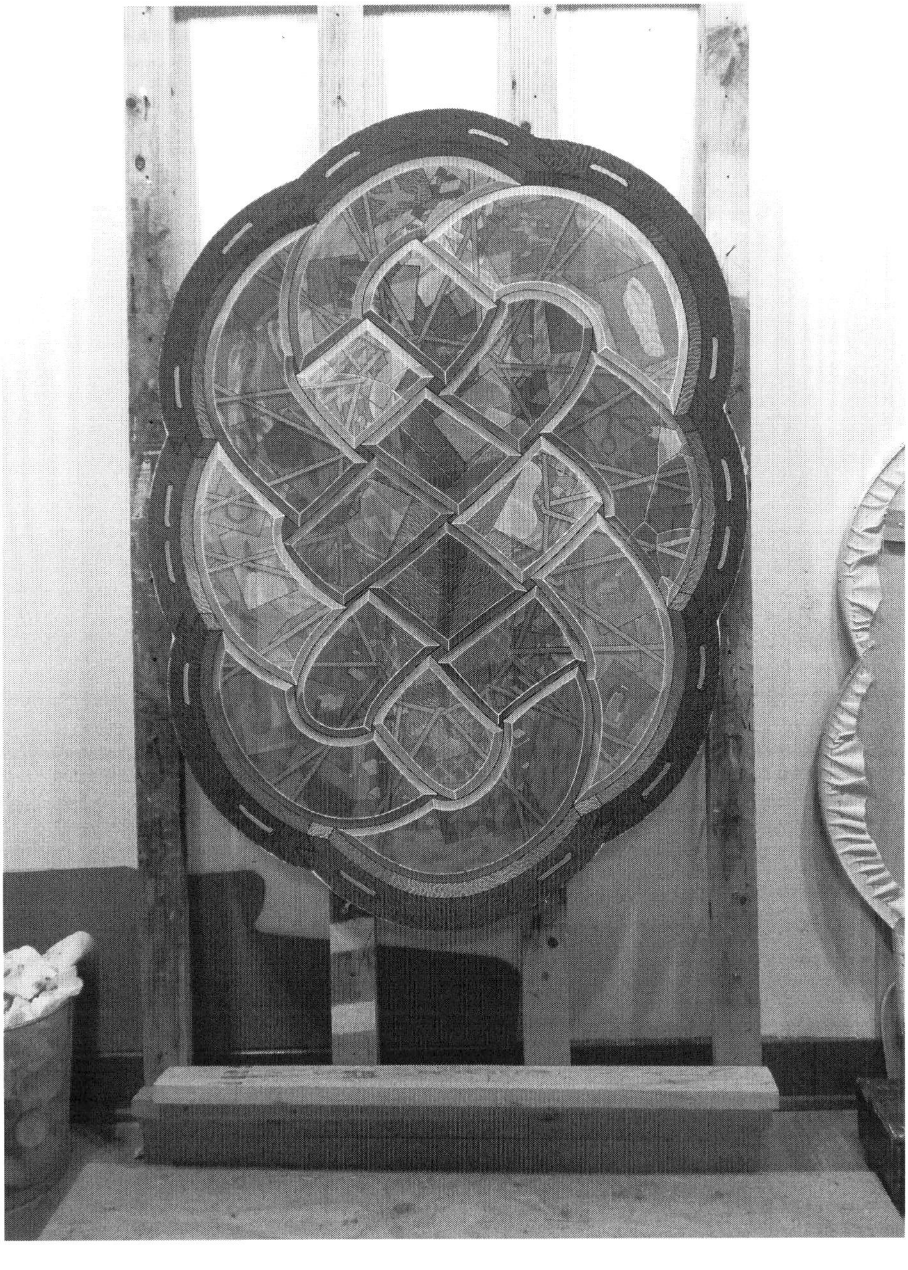

FIGURE 6.9: Art Green's Studio, Stratford, ON, 2015.

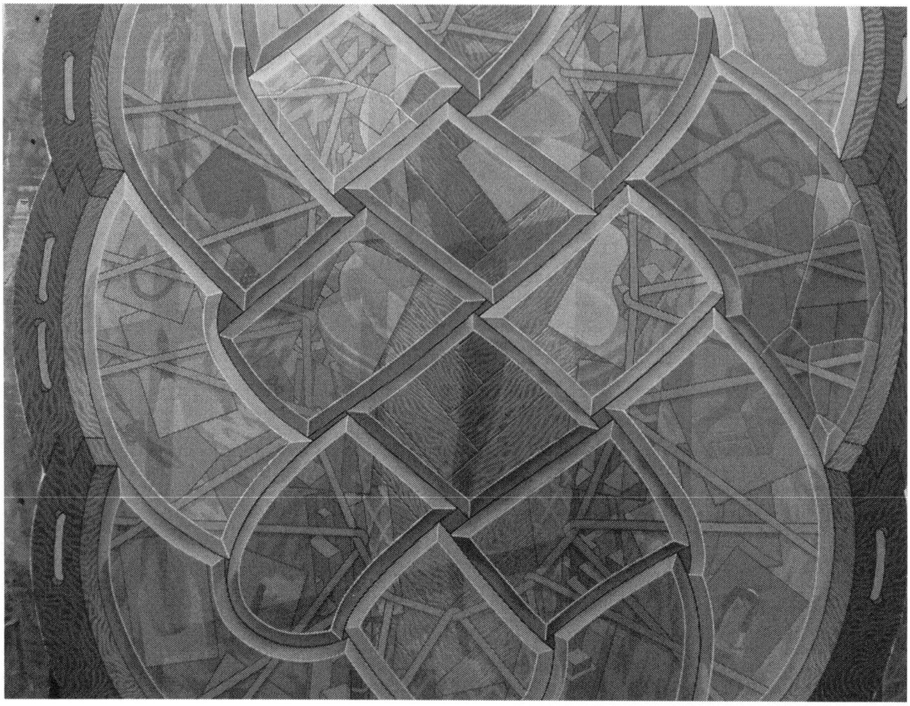

FIGURE 6.10: Art Green's Studio, Stratford, ON, 2015.

paintings through looking at ads and magazines until he has moments that intrigue or confuse him. He described one such moment when he saw an advertisement for soft ice cream and was fascinated by the idealized image. He recalled looking at a magazine thinking about how odd the cigarette ads were. And he remembered seeing an image of a pair of scissors that appeared voluptuous or as if they were ballet dancing. Or he would look at old physics books or tool books and be intrigued by these objects with mysterious uses that he did not understand. These motifs became a repetitive inventory of imagery that reflected his curiosities, intrigues, and surprises. He then played with the imagery on the canvas with geometric forms and repetition, trying to look at something from multiple angles. He spoke nostalgically about the days as a child where there was so much time for boredom and exploration and wondered if technology has removed boredom from our experience. '*It's a good thing to get bored. That's when you come up with ideas.*' Addressing how he scavenges a range of sources for imagery, he said:

> *I really like finding things outside the art world. I like finding coincidences or finding things you didn't know you were looking for. I like libraries. In the library you*

have a chance of coming across things accidentally. Because it's a place that's like an old junk store. You can find things that come in many different paths to that point. And they'll have many different beginnings and many different connections and maybe you'll find something that you were looking for that you didn't know you were looking for.

Regarding his continued interest in painting, he said:

Art is not about solving problems; art is about finding problems that you can't solve. In other words, artists keep working because they have found something they want to resolve. Maybe it's something in their life they want to resolve. They've been carrying around an incredible guilt and want to paint it out. Or it's the relationships to a flat plane or it's a colour relationship. The most important thing you can find as an artist is a problem. I like painting because it takes a long time to do. And when you get into the painting, particularly with these overlays that I do, you encounter problems and then you end up with all these decisions and then you have to change it along the way. Looking at an art object is different than an ordinary object, like a mass-produced chair, because a chair doesn't have as much baggage that went into it. Whereas an art object is full of the decisions that were made over time through the changes and the fact that the person was looking at it all the time and seeing it in different ways. It's like spinning a gyroscope that's going faster and faster with every decision and every move that you make and when you see it, all that energy can knock you over.

SECTION 2

CONCLUSION: EMBRACE CURIOSITY AS A VITAL FORCE IN LEARNING

Through a performative lens of artmaking, a studio takes on a life of its own as the materiality of making continually transforms the space. Similarly, through the lens of learning, a studio is a space that resists fixed outcomes and instead embraces a material learning that is always in flux. It is an active and generative process of learning through artmaking within an ecology of makers. Manning (2016b) addresses artmaking as a way of learning through the process. For Manning, an ecology of practice embraces artmaking as a way of knowing that may challenge our understanding of what knowledge is. She suggests that artmaking is a way of living in the moment and engaging with the world through ongoing questioning. She urges us to consider how practice produces knowledge through an uncertain, inventive, and intensive process wherein we embrace the messiness of being with materials.

A performative lens of learning through making welcomes the messiness of working with materials and responding to the events of art practice. Learning within the studio allows one to dwell within the process in a way that responds to the particularities of that moment of making. Further, through embracing this responsive, generative, and uncertain process of learning, the studio is a space where curiosity thrives. Art educator Cala Coats (2023) discusses artmaking through the lens of new materialism by arguing for the role of curiosity within learning: 'Curiosity is generally defined as a strong desire to know or learn something, but this tepid description underestimates curiosity's emotional and intellectual force of attraction' (p. 15). Coats emphasizes sensory and affective responses to the world and embraces uncertainty, indetermination, relationality, and complexity. Moreover, curiosity may push back against established structures within education as she proposes that a pedagogy driven by curiosity resists a desire to grasp and define the world and instead promotes active engagement with the world.

> Curiosity acts as a capacity for attentiveness and desire; at other times, it relates to an affective strangeness of the world. In this sense, curiosity becomes an embodied attraction and affection, a mode of engaging the world through ecologically oriented, transdisciplinary, and transversal inquiry that links to and flows with the world through vital currents of affect and commitment.
>
> (Coats, 2023, p. 15)

According to Coats: 'Vital curiosity creates flows of desire through and between moments, where the world transmits signals realized through embodied encounters, aesthetic attentiveness, intensive attraction, and a durational drive toward complexity' (p. 13). Curiosity may activate questions rather than answers and embrace emergence and ambiguity. In a visit with artist Sara Hartland-Rowe (2015), regarding teaching studio art, she similarly said that she encourages her students to '*Follow their curiosities*'. Thus, through examining the studio as a space of process, and through the lens of speculative pedagogy, I propose that a studio as a space of learning is a place that sets the conditions for curiosity to guide learning.

Throughout this section, I have examined how the studio is a site of process. The studio was examined as an event through suggesting that artmaking is a performative rather than representational practice. Through performativity, the process is celebrated in a way that fosters emergence, responsiveness, and knowledge-in-the-making. Furthermore, performative processes take as their premise that art produces rather than generates experiences. Thus, I have argued that embracing 'not knowing' is essential to the process of making in a way that prompts us to know or understand differently. Finally, I addressed how artmaking is curiosity-driven which highlights the intensities and affective qualities that propel the artmaking forward. Through considering the process of learning in the studio, I propose the following propositions: Embrace the process of artmaking through emphasizing the experiences and new understandings that emerge through the process; Allow for the performative and generative qualities of studio practice that emerge through spending time experimenting and responding within the studio; Create space for curiosity and 'not knowing' to drive learning through making.

SECTION 3

STUDIO AS MATERIAL THINKING: FEEL THE MOVEMENT AS YOUR BODY RECORDS IT

In a studio visit in Montreal in 2015, Janet Werner described the affective quality of art practice as she said: *'I think that the power of painting, if it has any power and if it has any meaning that isn't in words, it would be that you can feel it. Maybe that's true of any art but I think it's especially true with painting. It is that you feel it.'* In his book *Material Thinking*, Carter (2004) uses the term 'material thinking' to explore a philosophy of artistic process that navigates the relationship between theory and practice and reflects how understandings of ourselves and the world are embodied in the artistic process. Barrett (2007b) argues for a recognition of knowledge produced through material thinking through the handling of materials: 'Sensation, feeling and thought are progressively differentiated phases of our embodied relationship to objects in the world' (p. 1). Further, she underscores that a tendency within postsecondary education and research to focus on product over process has led to a lack of understanding of approaches and methodologies of artistic practice, particularly in postsecondary institutions. Barrett (2013) addresses how the materiality of making produces affective relations:

> In creative practice the subject can be viewed as a passageway where there is a struggle between conflicting tendencies or drives in response to external stimuli and matter

> as it is felt. Moments of resolution or stasis are rooted in affective relations – the positive or negative values that emerge through the encounter with objects in the world. (p. 65)

She questions the privileging of distant, impersonal observation of the world and suggests that this view be replaced with one that is a material approach that emphasizes interaction, action, and experience in practice.

Through bodily experiences, art produces affect (O'Sullivan, 2001). O'Sullivan defines affect: 'Affects are moments of *intensity*, a reaction in/on the body at the level of matter. We might even say that affects are *immanent* to matter. They are certainly immanent to experience' (p. 126, original emphasis). He shifted his views about research and knowledge creation away from a representational lens and towards the mapping of affects that may bring about unfamiliar and new understandings of the world rather than simply reinforcing what we already know. O'Sullivan speaks about the value of artmaking for its potential to shift thought and make change through affective events:

> Art, then, might be understood as the name for a function: a magical, an aesthetic, function of *transformation*. Art is less involved in making sense of the world and more involved in exploring the possibilities of being, of becoming, in the world. Less involved in knowledge and more involved in experience, in pushing forward the boundaries of what can be experienced. (p. 130, original emphasis)

Through new materialism Hood and Kraehe (2017) similarly explore how artists think through materials as they 'pose questions, construct problems, conjecture, investigate, experiment, and many times fail but then make discoveries in the process' (p. 33). They describe dualistic thinking 'imprisoning' most research that separates human from non-human and argue that this poses a challenge to art education research practices by overlooking the '*thingliness of things*' (Bennett, 2010, as cited in Hood & Kraehe, 2017, p. 33). Instead, they argue that for many artists, the attraction to being with objects and creating with materials is what drives their art practice. Hood and Kraehe ask what happens when artists and researchers look at the interconnectedness of things: 'Rather than *representing* the symbolic or cultural meanings of things as otherwise inert objects, a new materialist approach supports speculative questions and methods that seek to make sense of the vitalities of matter and agency of things' (p. 33, original emphasis). They examine one artist's description of objects in his studio through a discussion of the vitality of materials.

New materialism emphasizes our relationship to materials and the effects produced through our encounters with materials. Moreover, it emphasizes the body's materiality and how the body is affected. Springgay (2022) calls for a radical pedagogy based on 'feltness' which promotes a relational and interconnected approach to art practice. Further, she recognizes the role of intimacy in studio practice and learning: 'Intimacy is conventionally described as closeness, affinity, attachment, and familiarity. As feltness – relationality and reciprocity – intimacy becomes a mode of invention and creation that proliferates indeterminately and affectively' (p. 11). To value intimacy within studio practice is to be open to vulnerability and to be affected by artistic processes. Further, to practice intimacy is to recognize 'that everything is in relation, indeterminate, and constantly forming' (p. 11). By proposing that artmaking and pedagogy foreground intimacy and feltness, Springgay proposes that we emphasize the relationality and care within artistic practices and embrace feeling, sensation, and affect: 'It is a proposition that remains open; it is infused with experimentation, emergence, and undoings' (p. 10).

Within this section, I address the role of materiality, the body, and affect within studio practice. I begin by discussing embodied knowledge through the lens of intimacy, affect, and feeling. Next, I explore the messiness of art practice through a discussion of material experimentation within art practice. Lastly, I examine collage as a way of addressing studio thinking as an ongoing process of assembling and reassembling materials of practice. I conclude by emphasizing the significance of embracing embodied and material thinking within pedagogy as a way of moving away from the dualistic separation of mind and body and highlighting the significance of affect in studio-based pedagogies. This section is guided by the following questions:

> How does a studio embrace an emergent and affective approach to learning that fosters feeling, sensation and intimacy?
> How does the messiness of material experimentation disrupt learning approaches grounded in fixed objectives, and how does a relationship form between a maker and materials?
> How can 'collage' serve as not only an artistic medium, but also as a way of viewing studio practice as an ongoing process of making and remaking?

7

Bridge the Gap Between What You're Seeing and Feeling (Studio as Embodied)

> *Movement and rhythm inflect affect and connect, disrupt, and invert life. Affects are the atmospheres generated by particular compositions between bodies. Attuning ourselves to the affective atmospheres around us asks us to be more deliberate about creating the kinds of worlds in which we want to live.*
>
> (Springgay, 2022, p. 10)

Bring Together Thinking and Feeling

In her studio in Vancouver, British Columbia in 2022, Landon Mackenzie recounted a story about going to New York with her mother as a teenager. She went to the Museum of Modern Art and immediately saw Salvador Dali's infamous painting of clocks melting on a beach and then in the next rooms saw Henry Matisse, Pablo Picasso, and Marcel Duchamps. She remembered advice from her mother.

> *My mother said: 'Just really pay attention to what is connecting with you because you will visit this collection for the rest of your life and it will change, what you're attracted to. You have to look at a lot of art to understand art and when you feel that that is the one in the room that you want, you have to remember what that feels like so that when you're making art, you're looking for that feeling.'*

Manning (2009) emphasizes the body's sensory experiences as she explores how bodies change in relation to movements in space. Manning refers to these movements of sensing with the body as 'body events'. She says: 'A body is such a machine, sensing toward infinite recombination. Sense perceptions are not simply "out there" to be analyzed by a static body. They are body-events' (p. 212). Through the lens of artistic practices, I consider how artmaking may similarly be a 'body event'. And the studio is the setting for the 'body event' to be experienced. Tacit knowledge refers to embodied knowledge acquired through the body's interaction with the world. Barrett (2007b) describes artmaking as a form of tacit knowledge:

> Experience operates within the domain of the aesthetic, and knowledge produced through aesthetic experience is always contextual and situated. The continuity of artistic experience with normal processes of living is derived from an impulse to handle materials and to think and *feel* through their handling. Sensation, feeling and thought are progressively differentiated phases of our embodied relationship to objects in the world.
>
> (p. 1, original emphasis)

Swedish artist and curator, Jan Ryden (2014) brings the examination of painting processes into the studio. He argues that rather than looking outward to painting's limits from an outside perspective, instead, we examine painting from its nucleus, from the inside out, looking towards the 'body of paint itself' (p. 46). Drawing on the relationship between thinking and making, Ryden uses the term '*embodied cognition*' (p. 47). He argues that the separation of body and mind through the enlightenment led to a disconnect and he believes that through painting we engage the mind through the body and the body through the mind. He says:

> I believe paintings get a lot of their magic from the fact that we go back and forth between seeing them as images, windows into another world, and as objects and surfaces with a bodily, fleshy presence in the room ... The reason this attracts us might be that painting is closely related to how we think: in metaphors and images that arise from bodily experiences.
>
> (p. 46–47)

Embodied cognition within the painting is addressed through the lens of new materialism by Munro (2022) who argues that painting is a diffractive process as she explores the role of materials in 'embodied perception'. Munro examines a painter's experience during the process as the materials elicit bodily sensations and produce real effects on the body. She describes the sensations produced through working with materials as 'a diffractive pattern experienced as a passage of intensity sensed in the body of the painter when interacting with the material aspects of painting'

(p. 241). For Munro (2022), reflection creates an 'optic event' while diffraction generates a 'haptic event' that allows for the messiness of practice. She highlights the generative possibilities when embracing the feeling of making wherein

> the painter-researcher brings a heightened sensitivity to these diffraction patterns, the potentials, movements and transformations of the material forces within their studio practice. This 'intra-active' engagement generates affective intensities that involve an element of surprise, resonance, shock to thought, insight or epiphany.
>
> (p. 249)

Iconic Canadian artist, Mary Pratt (1935–2018) earned a Bachelor of Fine Arts from Mount Allison University in New Brunswick and spent most of her life in Newfoundland. We met in her St. Johns, Newfoundland home, in 2015. Her still life and figurative paintings show the intimacy of her daily life living in Newfoundland where she lived with her husband, artist, Chris Pratt, and raised her four children alongside her art practice. These still lifes of fish on a plate or jars of jam glow with the time and energy spent creating them. Through the domestic imagery, they also reveal Pratt's story, as a woman raising children while pursuing painting. Her experience as an artist is in dialogue with feminist art practices throughout the latter twentieth century as her work highlights the complexity of her life as a woman, a mother, and an artist through showing her daily experience. Pratt explained with candour and humour a significant moment for her while living in Salmonier, Newfoundland.

> *At first in Salmonier [Newfoundland], I had a hard time finding the time or a place to paint, because I didn't have a studio, but I painted all over the house. All I needed was my easel and a little trolley that had spaces to keep things warm, so I could keep my paints in that and open it out and it could be a pallet, and it was grand. Anyway, one day, when I was cleaning up the house, I went down this very dark hall and there was a door at the end with a window in it. There was a little bit of light coming through that window but basically it was a dark hall, and I opened the door to our bedroom which I had decided to clean up, wash up, do the floor and there was a blast of light. We faced east, and the river was right next to the house, I mean the kids could practically nip a fly right over to the river from the veranda. And the bed was all tumbled out, and I actually got an erotic reaction from what I was looking at. And I thought, 'Oh my god, oh my god, what is this?' ... So, I went back, and I set up the paint and I thought, 'Alright, if the world is going to give me this reaction, I won't paint anything that doesn't. I'll never set anything up, I will wait until the world gives it to me.' And it did.*

Cynthia G. Renard (Montreal, 2014) similarly described a moment where they realized that a particular action was remembered within their body and manifested in the studio. They had recently moved studios and had begun drawing unicorns becoming a representation of Utopias. G. Renard addressed this subject:

> *They are a fantasy animal. They don't exist. Every one of them is representing a Utopian ideal of how to live in the world. But they are impossible. And Utopias too. You try to reach them, but you are never going to reach them. And so it talked about justice in the world.*

The artist had been working at a stable, grooming horses for six months and then without noticing they started painting unicorns in the studio. The act of painting was like the artist was grooming them. G. Renard's body remembered the action as they painted them. '*I was in my studio one time and just realized it's like a stable. Eight months earlier I was grooming horses and without knowing I'm doing the same in the studio.*' They discussed 'body memory', how our bodies remember actions in painting. They remembered another 'body memory' emerging when they were at an exhibition looking at a painting of trees. They said that they were thinking about it afterwards and could feel it in their hands.

> *And then I went to my studio, and it was stuck in my arm. Because you look and you feel the movement and your body records it. The brushstroke is so important because you feel it too. It's like space and time; it's like choreography or dancing. You can record the movement. There's so much information in the brushstroke, it can be very dense.*

For Gary Evans (Figures 7.1 and 7.2), the gap between what you're seeing and feeling is at the core of his process. His lush and active paintings are filled with brightly coloured, organic shapes that hint at real-life neighbourhood places, such as a house, a yard, or a bush. In our visit to Barrie, Ontario (2016), Evans discussed how these brightly painted and fluid shapes capture the space between reality and imagination, and between what we see and what we feel.

> *There's this idea that there is a known reality, whether it's a shrub, a tree, an object, a building or a car. And then there is us, which is implied by the edge of the canvas. And then there's all this stuff in the middle which doesn't really exist. So, we've got a dialogue of what this abstraction is and what the reality is and why I put the two together. And that's something I've always been compelled to do, to bridge that gap between what I'm seeing and feeling. It's that feeling of a space. And the feeling of being in the space and aware of that feeling. And then the awareness of looking.*

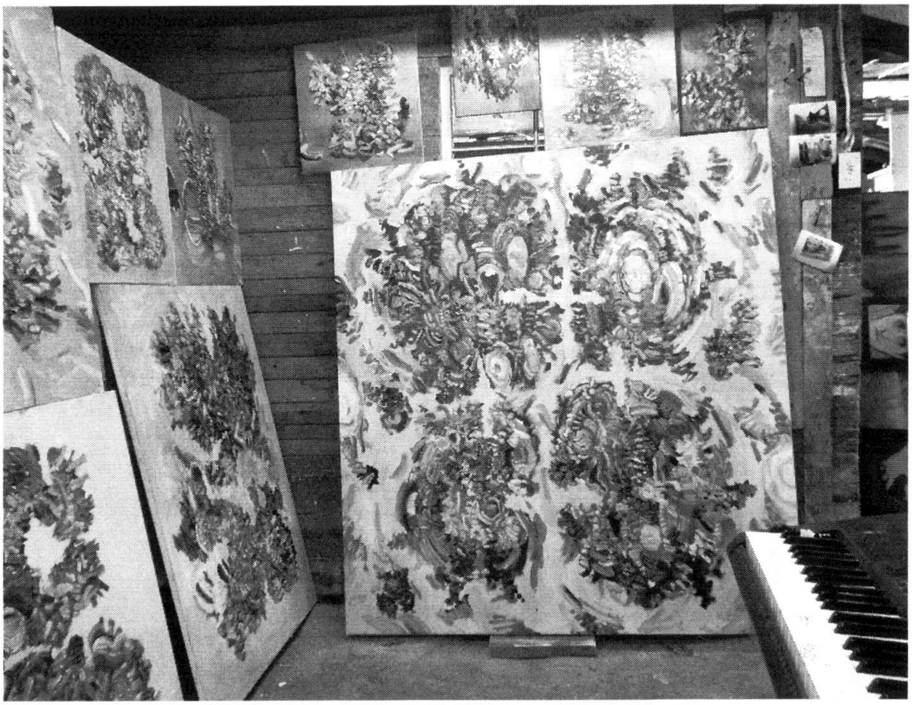

FIGURE 7.1: Gary Evans' Studio, Barrie, ON, 2016.

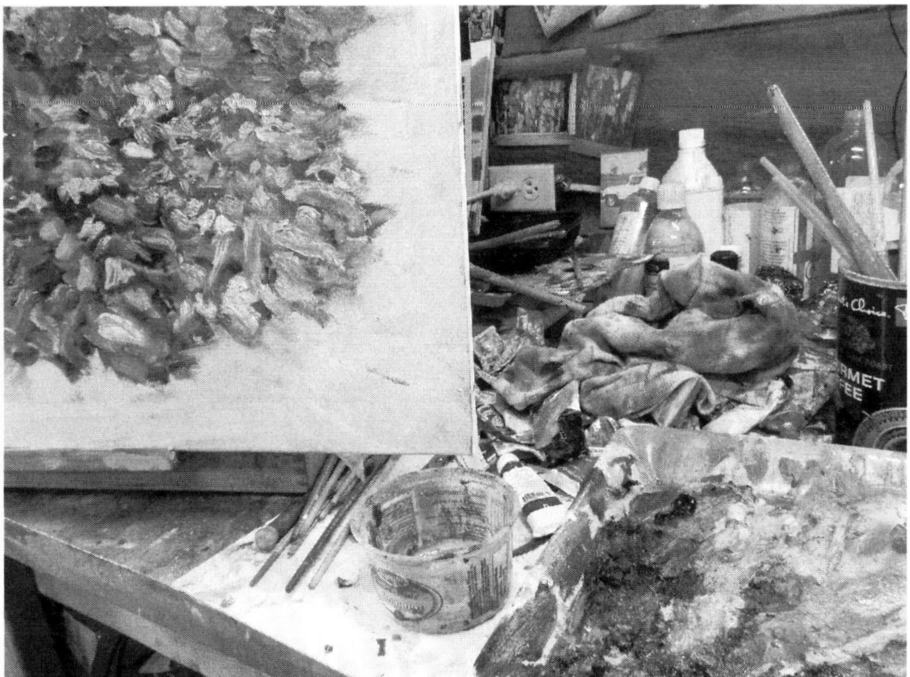

FIGURE 7.2: Gary Evans' Studio, Barrie, ON, 2016.

> *I always thought of my paintings as self-conscious looking. If a picture is this big (gestures with hands), the fact that I feel it as a presence in my world starts a whole bunch of responses: fight, flight, movement, happiness, comfort, discomfort, on a physical level. That's how our bodies work.*

Indirect Information Can Impact Your Senses and Imagination

In Hamilton, Ontario, Daniel Hutchinson (2014, 2015) discussed the relationship between art and the body (Figures 7.3–7.5):

> *I do think a really good, really affective painting can kind of hit you in the spleen or something, or make you feel like your feet aren't on the ground or something, or like you're lighter, or make you feel pain or discomfort.*

Hutchinson described the 'anxiety of influence' as the impossibility of knowing all the threads that come into every decision in the studio, from slides he saw in art history lectures years ago, to fabric in local stores, to everyday bodily experiences. That is how he defines intuition: '*My definition for intuition is everything you've ever learned bubbling up in random ways that you can't possibly understand. I imagine this kind of soup of stuff with this unimaginable depth of knowledge that I'm not fully conscious of.*' To explain his understanding of intuition, Hutchinson described a memory from his childhood. He remembered the feeling of drawing with his hands on the carpet, drawing lines, a grid, a face, and then erasing. Through paralleling his painting process to drawing on the carpet he highlighted the bodily and material engagements of making paintings. Hutchinson reflected on the relationship between the subject of his paintings and working in the studio.

> *There's something that you take for granted when you're in a studio. I want to figure out what that is. So, my work, whether there's a natural subject or a subject from the world out there, I try to always fold this artifice of the studio into it, or an over wrought or overworked sense into it that acknowledges the studio.*

Hutchinson's focus on the studio became more explicit in our second visit when he shared the '*frottage paintings*' he was making. He made these paintings through rubbing against a surface in the studio and allowing the paint to reveal the marks and texture from the surface underneath. Sometimes the surface that he would frottage would be another painting, revealing the textural undercurrents of that painting. In others, he would frottage the studio floors or walls. Reflecting on that relationship between his paintings and his childhood memories of drawing on the *with an inert material and you're trying to shape it. If I'm painting in a particular mode, it can be predictable and stiff. But if I've been painting often and for long periods of time, I'll paint things that I would never have been able to think of to do that completely bring the painting to the level I want to. And that isn't magic, but it seems like magic, and it's the thing I seek. It is this shift that doesn't have any bearing in logic that stops it from being just a representation and becomes something experiential. It's extraordinary focus. And somehow it feels like your brain is wide open. It's just a movement. Your whole body is fully intelligent. It's like your body is intellectualized, every sense is working.*

What happens with painting is this embodied knowledge. If you've been painting for several years, your body knows what to do. So, your brain is acting, your eyes are acting but it's in concert with each other. You may be meandering everywhere, but it becomes this site where you can put a lot of condensed information in that comes out indirectly. So, to support painting you have to believe that it's worthwhile to have indirect information that can impact your senses and imagination.

Change the Way Someone Felt in That Moment

or Springgay (2022), 'feltness' is radical through its emphasis on care, reciprocity, nd relationality, particularly within an education system that doesn't recognize he role of feeling within learning.

> It proposes that the future of radical pedagogy is conditioned by what I call feltness, a practice of intimacy. In an era of increasing neoliberal reforms, the corporatization of the university and of education more generally, and the reliance on impact factors and numerical measurements to assess the value of research and pedagogy, I posit intimacy as a necessary source of disruption.
>
> (p. 7)

or Springgay, affect theories foreground relationships and a recognition of learng as an intimate process that embraces feeling. In her Winnipeg, Manitoba studio, rica Mendritzki (2014) addressed the tendency throughout history, particularly ithin western history and philosophy, to separate mind and body, thinking from eling. Her work is grounded in a proposition that thinking and feeling are nearly entical (Figures 7.7 and 7.8).

In practice, thinking and feeling are together. It's a huge limitation in academia that they are completely separate ... I am not versed in psychoanalysis, but I think what painting has in common with psychoanalysis is that that was a genre that tried to bring together thinking and feeling.

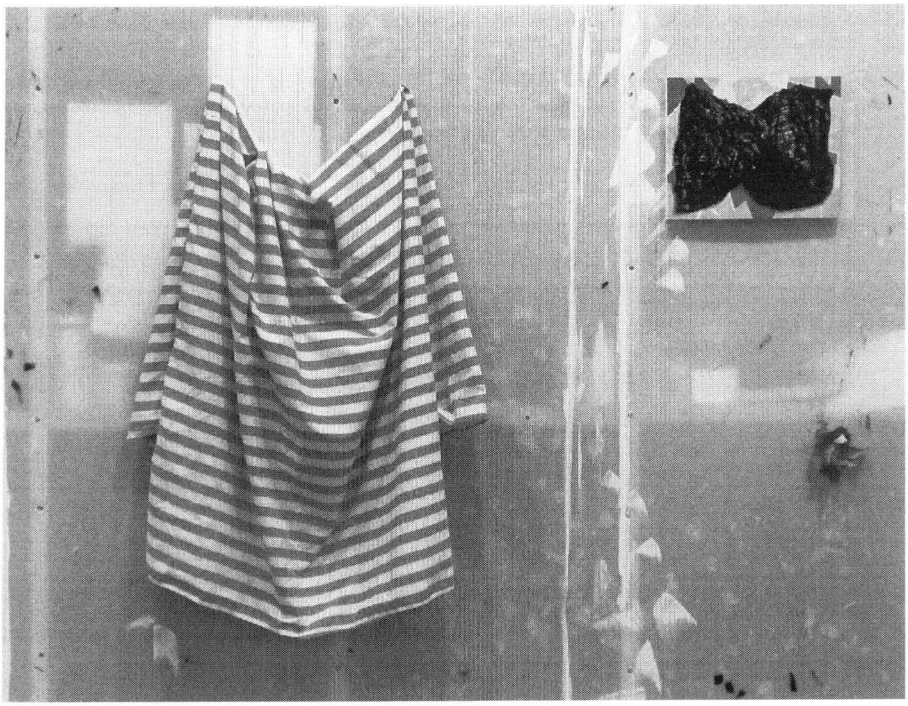

FIGURE 7.3: Daniel Hutchinson's Studio, Hamilton, ON, 2015.

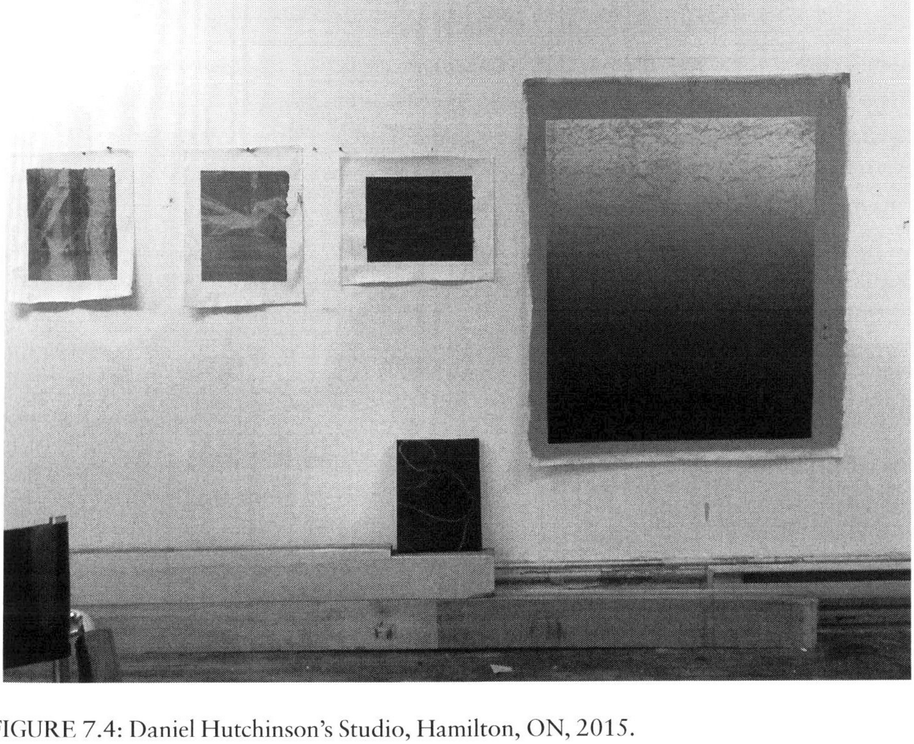

FIGURE 7.4: Daniel Hutchinson's Studio, Hamilton, ON, 2015.

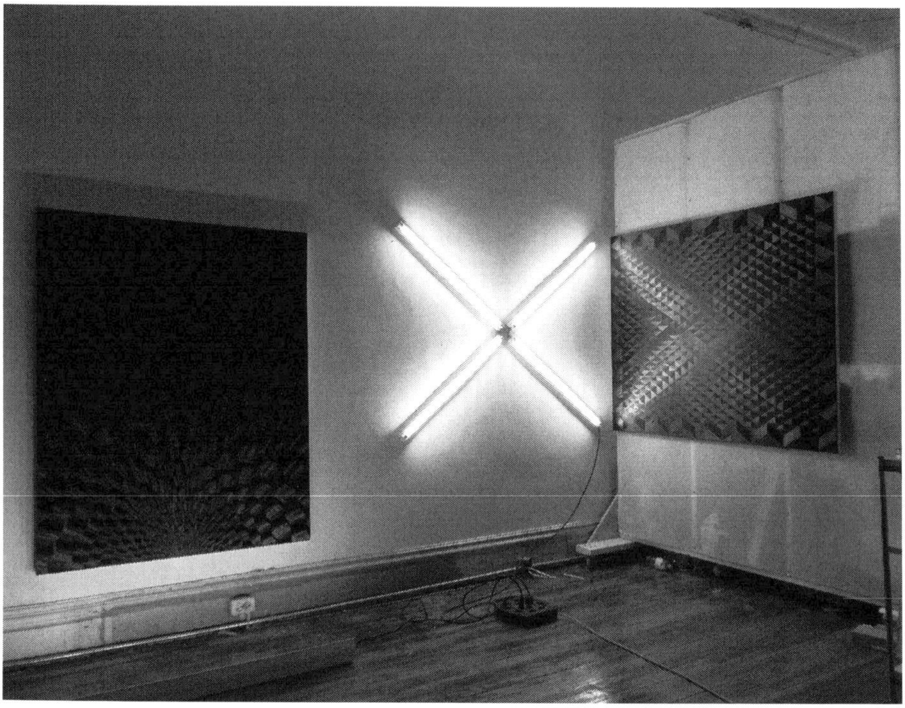

FIGURE 7.5: Daniel Hutchinson's Studio, Hamilton, ON, 2014.

carpet, he said there is something about looking to the world outside the studio and seeing these affinities. Within these frottage paintings, he looked for parallels between the experience or process of painting and bodily experiences. Through the titles of his work such as *Gravel in Your Shoe* or *Clinging to Your Shoulders*, Hutchinson compared his lived bodily experiences to the action of making in the studio. For him, the action or feeling of painting paralleled a feeling in the body that often sticks with us or makes us uncomfortable. '*[It alludes to] how I "felt" the painting with the squeegee or the rake or whatever it is. So, I have to find a title that suggests both looking and feeling.*' By addressing affinities between his body's experiences and how he paints, Hutchinson draws connections between his studio practice and everyday experience. He described his recent work as allegories that address the process and feeling of painting. The allegories connect the act of painting and the act of looking through his bodily memories. Hutchinson further complicates the relationship to the subject as the viewer may look into these paintings that depict simply the act of painting but instead find an image or subject. Rather than being in the studio painting a representation of the world, he instead paints from his interactions with the studio, and what emerges may be an image from the world, a subjective projection onto the painting. Re process, he states:

> *Painting is a vehicle to talk about our particular place in the world, o embodied place in the world. So, gestures tied to a particular body, or find in gestures seems honest. Finding images in there suggests a desire.*

In Montreal, Eliza Griffiths (Figure 7.6) described embodied know way that multiple lines of thought are embedded in the intuitive pro ing. '*You process all this information and research, and it imbues tl that particular effect.*' She expanded on her understanding of intuiti two opposing modes of working, the latter being more productive a

> *For me, with painting there are two states. One is where I'm completely and it's horrible, I don't know what to do, and I just illustrate. So, you wan a place where you're painting but where the decisions are coming from a di than that rational place. There is something particular about work where yc*

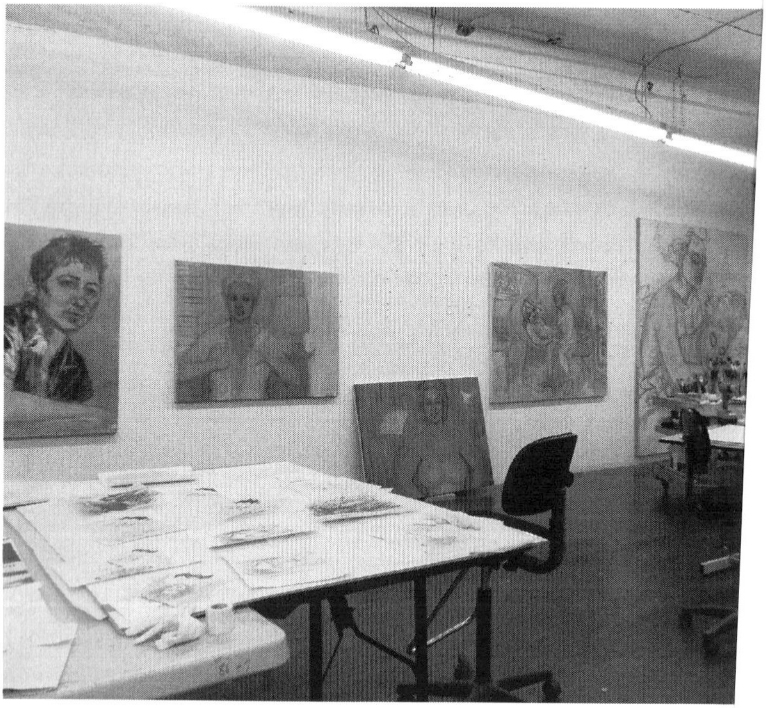

FIGURE 7.6: Eliza Griffith's Studio, Montreal, QC, 2015.

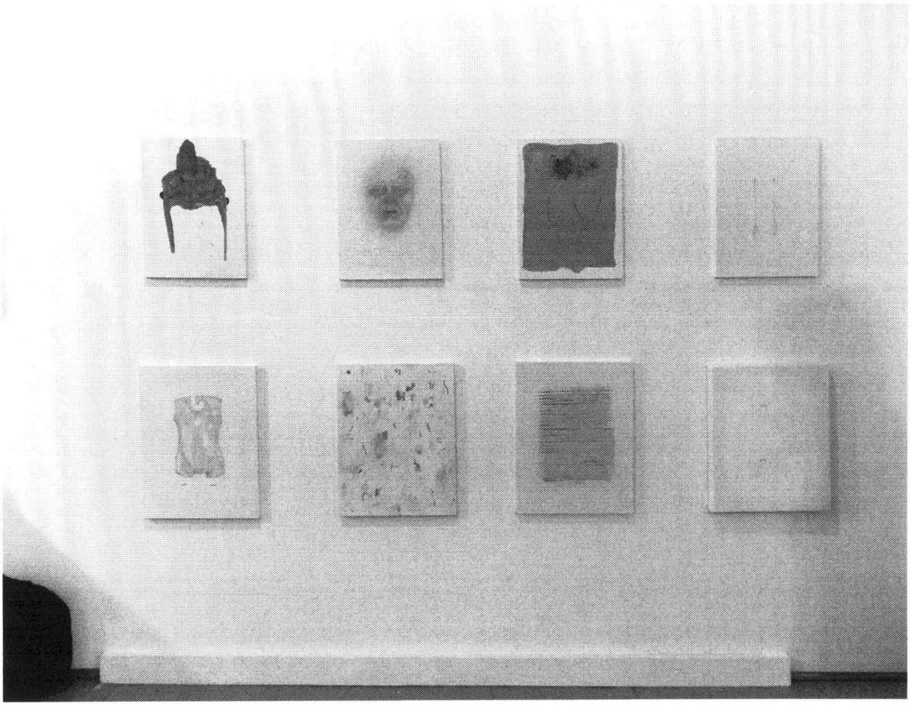

FIGURE 7.7: Erica Mendritzki's Studio, Winnipeg, MN, 2014.

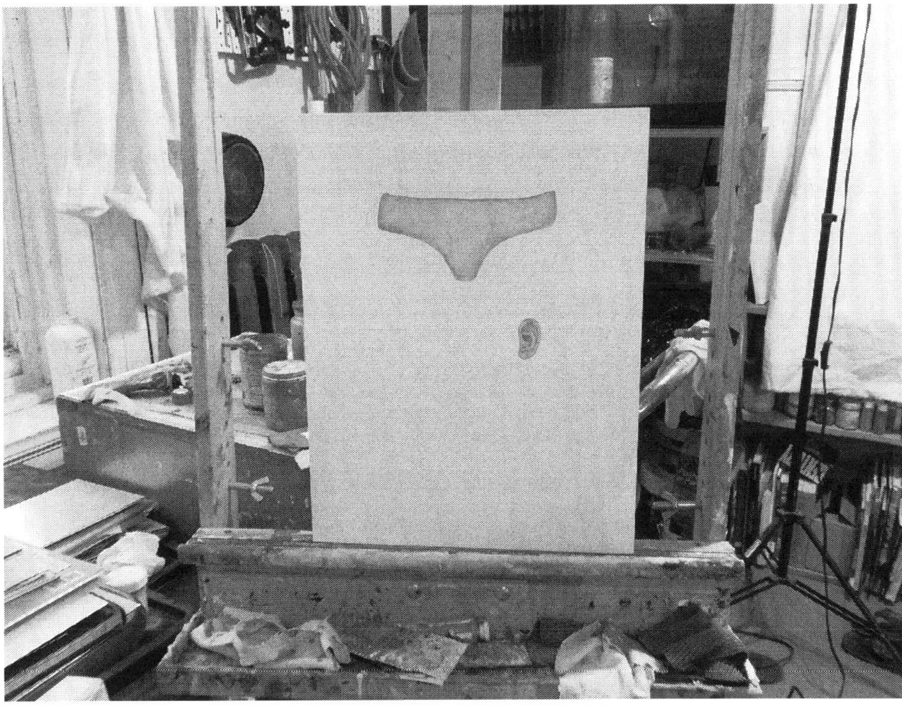

FIGURE 7.8: Erica Mendritzki's Studio, Winnipeg, MN, 2014.

At the time of our visit, she was thinking about the feelings of snowy Winnipeg as she was struck by the aesthetics of snow and how the aesthetics generate feelings. She addressed the complexity of the word 'feeling'.

> *I began thinking about winter and the aesthetics of it and the feelings of it. Here in Winnipeg, you can't see the roads, because it never melts. When it finally melts, you realize people were driving on the sidewalk. I liked this idea of getting rid of clear paths and the fact that the snow reverses what's visible. Your breath becomes visible, footsteps become visible, but pathways become invisible. And Winnipeg is so cold your eyes freeze shut, your hands go numb, and you can't see people's bodies properly, so it's intense, the physicality of it. You're repressed and depressed. It's extreme feeling and no feeling at the same time. Those weird feelings, the intensity, the repression and the suppression all come together.*

Within her studio, Mendritzki had a series of paintings of individual objects. She had one painting based on a picture she came across of 'jelly hands', a long jelly-like hand that could be flung at walls that she had played with as a child. She described the 'feeling' of these limp jelly hands as both active and disgusting. She addressed the complexity of the word 'feeling' as a term, a philosophy, and a sensation.

> *'What are different ways of feeling?' is one of the questions in this work. Physical feelings and emotional feelings are something I'm always interested in. And why or how we draw a distinction between thinking and feeling. So much of Western philosophy is based on the idea that those are separate things, which is so self-evidently false. I find it mindboggling that we don't have a way of talking about the fact that what we think and what we feel aren't separate. I think they are inextricably connected ... That is a topic that is really central to Feminism, what it means to be a woman, and what it means to be a female intellectual. Historically, men get to be the rational ones, women get to be the feeling ones. Obviously, women think, and men feel and that is completely false, but yet we've managed to build an intellectual structure on that basis. So, necessarily it becomes something you think about as a female artist. The work didn't necessarily start that way, but that is where it has ended up, I'm thinking in a lot more head-on way about what it means to be a female artist today. And I'm thinking about the relationship to history.*

For Anishnaabe artist Charlene Vickers (Figures 7.9 and 7.10), the power of art to affect the body is integral to the process of making art as she proposes that through making, art has the potential to heal. Through her work, Vickers explores her experiences as an Indigenous woman. Her Vancouver studio was filled with sewn felt

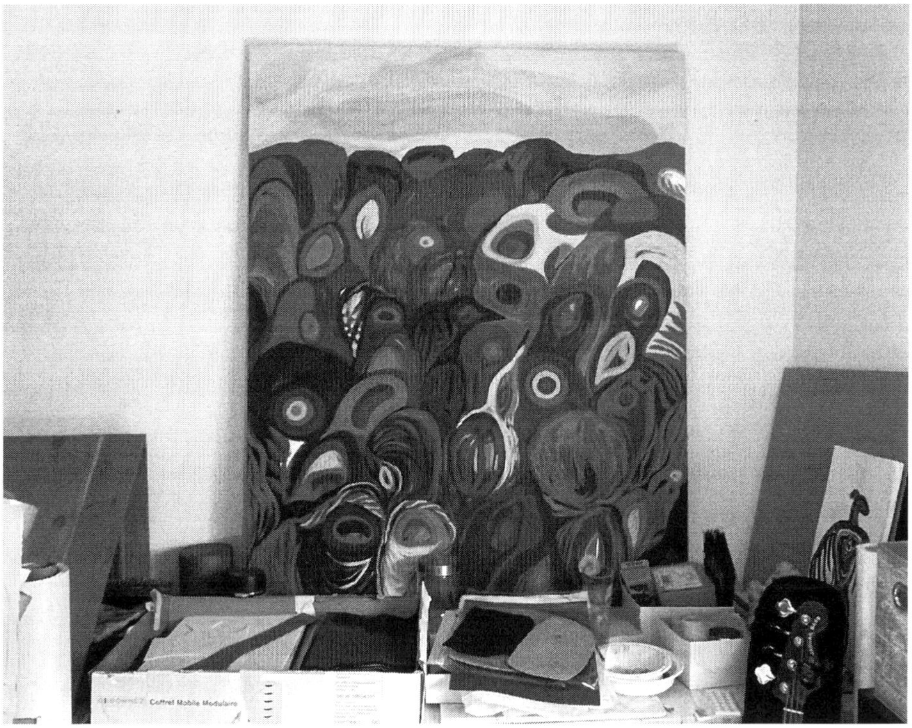

FIGURE 7.9: Charlene Vickers' Studio, Vancouver, BC, 2022.

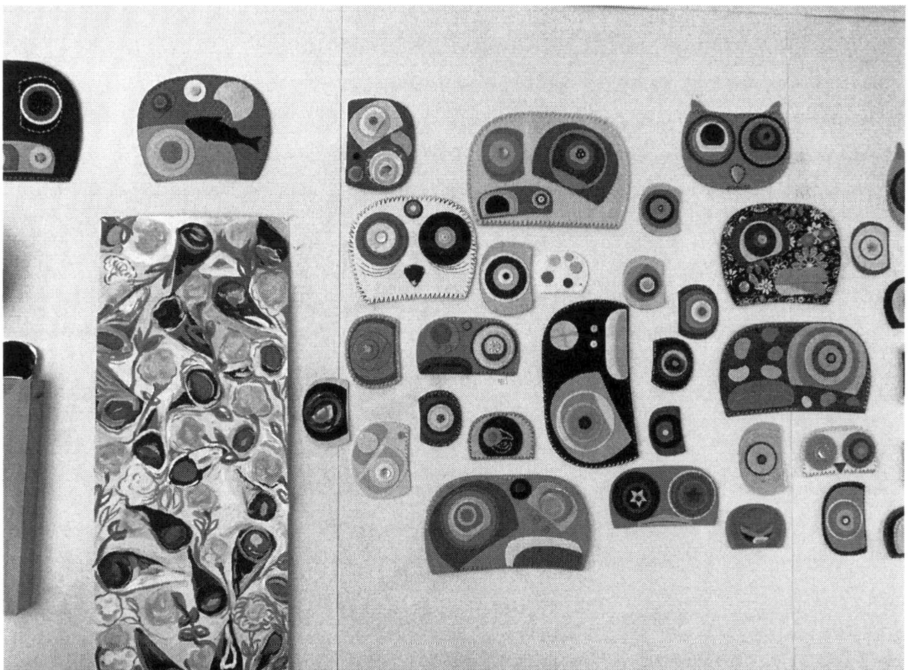

FIGURE 7.10: Charlene Vickers' Studio, Vancouver, BC, 2022.

shapes on one wall and a painting on another wall that showed abstracted animal figures making up a landscape. Regarding the painting, she said:

> *I was thinking about undulating gestures of starting out something and building up forms and it becomes a landscape. Then there's things you see within the gesture; the landscape is giving birth to the animals and the animals are giving birth to the landscape.*

Addressing this work, she said she was influenced by sixteenth-century Dutch painter Hieronymus Bosch's *The Garden of Earthly Delights*; however, she engaged with that painting through her lens as an Indigenous artist. She said:

> *So if I was to make the Anishnaabe garden of earthly delights, what would that be? So, it's coming up with what-ifs on an idea. And playing with the idea of Indigenizing. I was asking myself, what would that look like? I like to play with ideas and language and make jokes to myself.*

I asked Vickers what the role of art is, and she said:

> *I can just speak for myself. If I were to say that my work had any bearing in the world or if it could have any sort of effect in the world, it would be about healing. That it could change the way someone thought about something or how they felt in that moment. That's the importance of art, if you're able to do something to somebody's thinking or the way they feel or have some sort of effect on someone's body. That is a personal thing that you can do with art. So that's the power that art can have. And that is a very human thing that art can do ... For me it's all about how to feel connected within yourself and then have some sort of voice to say something. On a personal level, art has saved my life. There is a word that [Indigenous writer and scholar] Gerard Vizenor has, 'Survivance.' That's what I think healing is, survival. And I think art saves people's lives too.*

8

Make Sense of the Chaos That Is Happening (Studio as Messy)

> *A theory of art is also a theory of surprise. But this surprise is not a petty or commonplace one such as that of a spectacle, but of the order of wonder and revelation, and catching ourselves by surprise. ... It is aesthetic-artist shock and surprise that provokes and teaches, shaking us loose from ourselves, freeing new possibilities and pathways of becoming.*
>
> (Roy, 2024, pp. 21, 119)

Explore Ways of Being Outside Structures of Language

In his Vancouver studio, in 2014, Ben Reeves addressed the messiness of practice as meaning is continually remade through working with materials. He discussed intuition, ambiguity, and painting's ability to elude language.

> *Things happen that you're not even necessarily aware of at the time or that you don't control. A lot of what happens in my work, I reflect on, and I think I understand it after the fact. Just as certain codes of paint will assert themselves; they will equally fall apart. And similarly, the representation kind of knits together but kind of undoes itself at some point. I think there's an interest in exploring the possibilities that the medium has for exploring ways of being that are outside structures of language. Language is such a useful tool, but I always have a lot of difficulty with it because language often wants to supply definitions to things. It starts to draw boundaries between this and that and often definitions are created through oppositions. So, there is a sense that the analytical is not the material or not the intuitive and I think, sitting here talking, that makes perfect sense. But in actual doing, I don't think that*

> *makes any sense. I think they're not so divided and defined and separate. There are ways of using language that are more poetic, and I always think of that as when language starts to escape itself.*

Reeves speaks to the messy, complicated, and nonbinary relationship between the analytic and intuitive.

I propose that to embrace the material and intuitive within the studio is to embrace the messiness of making. Through the lens of messiness, studio practice is an ongoing process of learning in a way that invites uncertainties, emergent qualities, affective, sensory experiences, and ongoing encounters with materials. Art educators, Ayliffe and Mieves (2016) suggest that it is the dirtiness of art practice that allows for an ongoing process of learning and unlearning. Specifically, they discuss the dirtiness of the studio as they ask, 'to what extent the concept of dirt, often defined as "matter out of place" proves to be productive in artistic practices' (p. 55). They draw connections between the messiness of art practice, a refusal of mastery, and an allowance for unknowing and unbecoming within education. They draw from a book by Trotter, *Cooking With Mud* (2000), and explain this connection between dirtiness and a connection to the world:

> [M]ess here becomes not only a means to confront established order, but eradicates and blurs the subject/object distinction ... Mess, disorder, staining can therefore be also seen as a way in which a person, or the artist, responds to the world, in a very individual way.
>
> (Ayliffe & Mieves, 2016, p. 55)

Furthermore, they draw connections between dirty practices and the acceptance of messiness and failure within learning. They argue that messiness is an essential quality of learning within studio processes, specifically painting, and this messiness has a subversive potential within the context of larger systems of education. Through their work they explore this messiness as the 'quality of art as dirty and not adherent to an ideal system and its "resistance to precedent and academic template" (Roberts, 2011), or failure' (p. 55). Through their examination of the dirtiness of the studio, they draw parallels between art practice and resistance to a particular way of knowing. They suggest that the messiness of artmaking allows us to embrace the uncertainties of practice. I refer to messiness as not simply the obvious mess caused by the materials of paint, but also the messiness of thinking, knowing, and being, wherein experiences, ideas, and actions collide with the materiality of the process. This is the messiness of practice wherein the materials of practice become a site of interference.

The messiness of matter is a productive, inventive, and generative interruption. McClenaghan (2016) states:

> Uncertainty and managing uncertainty are the companions to practice. The impression of certainty emerges in resolution and resolution comes at the end. It is the skin of a painting, concealing its underlying anatomy, its inherent evolution and embodied learned behaviours. This is part of the embedded narrative of practice.
>
> (p. 32)

I propose that painting is a messy practice, and through understanding the learning that occurs within the studio, we may become open to the messiness of pedagogy. Through embracing the messiness of learning, I contend that artmaking becomes a way of being in the world, an ontology that resists representational thinking and learning, and fosters performative, embodied, and experiential ways of engaging with the world. Furthermore, this ontology of being resists the need for certainty that has become so embedded within our systems of learning. McClenaghan (2016) states: 'In teaching the practice of painting it could be said that we are supporting a learner engaged in the process of trying to find an obscure or at least obscured destination' (p. 33). Through the experience of learning in the studio, McClenaghan (2016) argues that artists 'speculate, take risks and test ideas in materials in an attempt to give them form' (p. 32).

During a visit with Doug Kirton (Figure 8.1) in Kitchener, Ontario, I was interrupted by the painting behind him. Drawn into the vivid blue in the painting, I commented '*I love that blue*', to which he responded, '*Let me show you*'. Our conversation shifted as he pulled out several tubes of blue paint, showing me their colour, consistency, and potential, shifting the conversation towards the material. Similarly, regarding her studio practice, Landon Mackenzie said she had to come in every day, even if it was just for a moment, to change a yellow thing to orange. Her conceptual process involved continually adding to the painting over a long period of time.

> *I had this one rule, that once I see the magic in a colour I can't use any more of it ... I think I have a very heightened response to colour. I'll get a real rush when I put down the right colour.*

In her studio, Mackenzie had a painting on a table covered in circles and she invited me to use a circular disk to trace and paint a yellow circle onto the canvas. Within the painting, the materiality of colour is integral to the process. In an essay titled 'On color', American painter, Amy Sillman (2016) describes working with

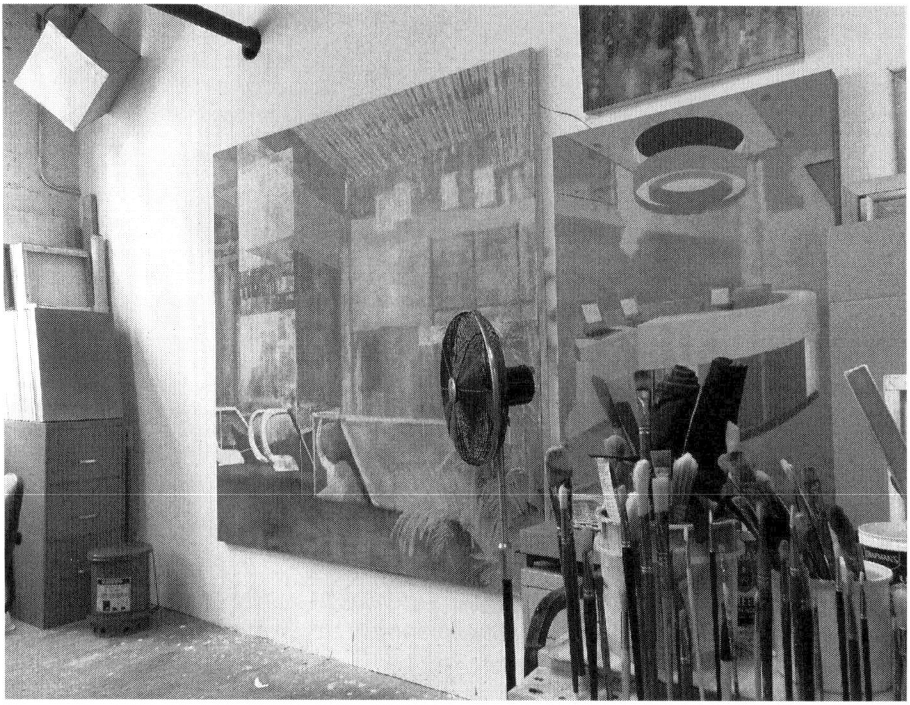

FIGURE 8.1: Doug Kirton's Studio, Kitchener, ON, 2014.

pigment and addresses how one learns to feel and understand colour through the time and practice spent working with it:

> Color as *object* is earthly material stuff. Color as *subject* arches over everything like a rainbow, from cosmic rays to the minerals in the earth to what happens inside your eyes, from religious symbology to philosophical problems, from phenomena to noumena ... To deal with color as a painter is to render these overarching problems as physical propositions, as sensuous experiences synesthetically merged under the sign of the hand.
>
> (p. 105, original emphasis)

In this essay, Sillman captures the complexities of how we experience colour. Furthermore, she addresses how meanings of colour are always changing as she states: 'I am more interested in color as an engine of ongoing change and metamorphosis than as a static theory ... let us welcome the collision of mistakes, accidents, desires, contradictions, destruction, and possible disasters that color embodies' (pp. 115, 116). Sillman views colour as a prompt for sensory and affective experiences. She emphasizes the role of time and change in painting as she compares the process of artmaking to a choreography and describes her method as a physical response to both emotional and analytic change.

Art educator, Garber (2019) similarly addresses how as active participants in the process, materials form an important part of the ecology of art practice. This is particularly true of paint wherein the materials are active, messy, and often uncontrollable. In our visit in Halifax, Mathew Reichertz discussed the ongoing 'failures' that emerge through working with materials. In his studio, his work consisted of multiple cut-out shapes and images painted on metal that depict a walk from the perspective of a dog's sense of smell. Reichertz (Figures 8.2 and 8.3) explained his use of this particular material, relating it to his experience teaching at Nova Scotia College of Art and Design.

> *The whole thing revolves around dealing with a new material in relation to an idea that already came to me. The undiscovered possibilities in the material allow me to approach whatever I'm trying to do, where something is coming in from outside myself that I can't control but that I have to engage. I haven't painted on canvas in*

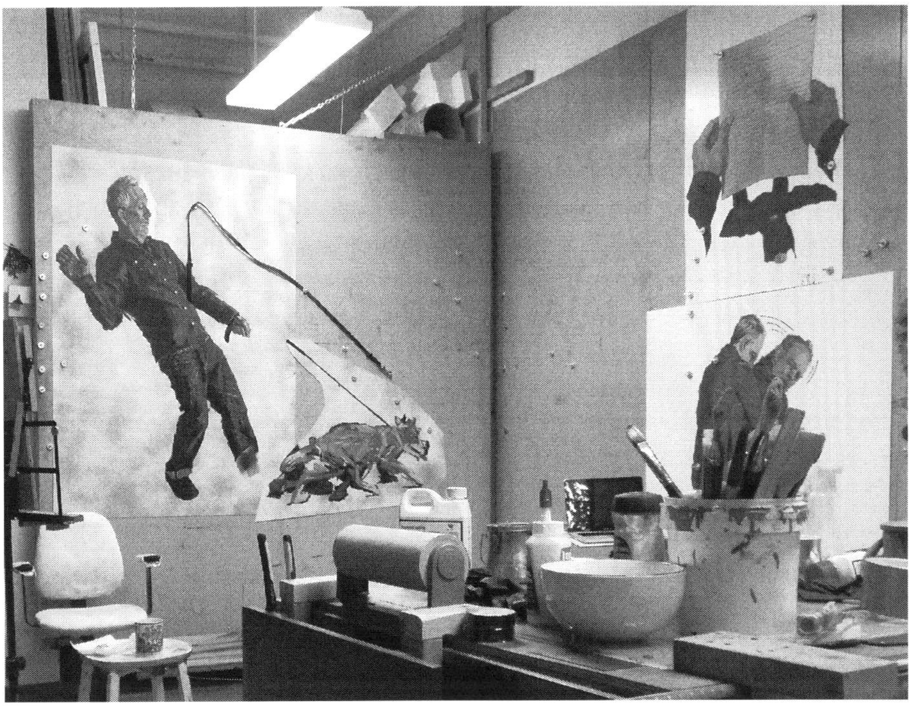

FIGURE 8.2: Mathew Reichertz' Studio, Halifax, NS, 2015.

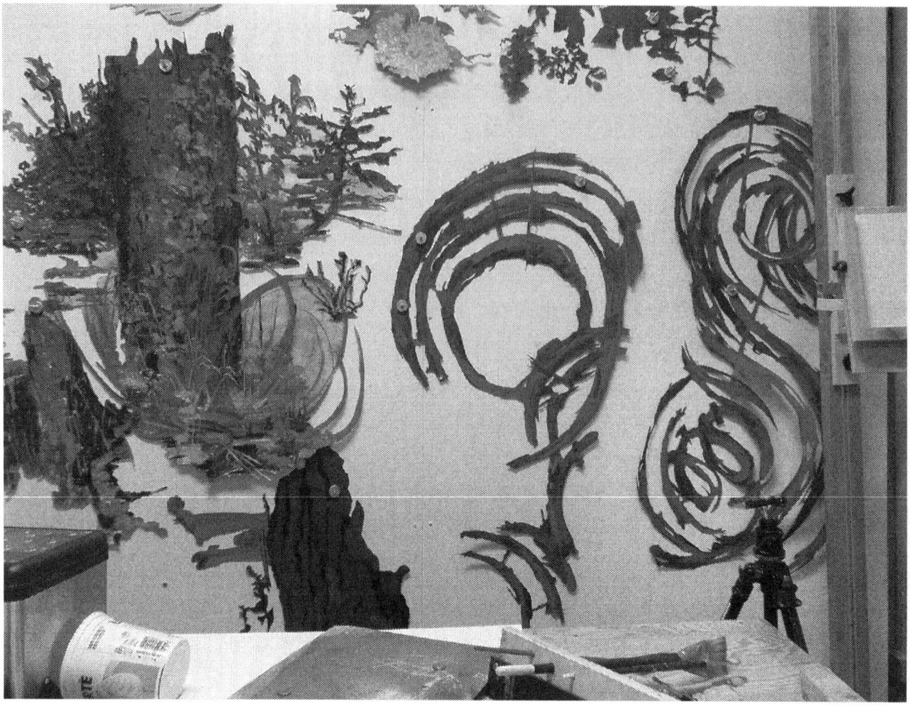

FIGURE 8.3: Mathew Reichertz' Studio, Halifax, NS, 2015.

> *a long time because of how I work in the studio. I need to invite something into the process that disrupts what I'm used to doing, so I can think about it in a new way. Besides some of the sciences, we're so removed from working with materials in the university system these days. In the visual arts, we demand that students take this unwieldy stuff and do something with it, which is a continuous negotiation. Often you have to confront failure after failure after failure and mediate those failures to try to make something and get a positive result out of those disappointments. And that is something you only learn when working with unfamiliar materials. At a basic level, in an art school experience, you're being confronted with materials and given the time and context to grapple with them while trying to make meaning. That is a big part of what I am doing in the studio.*

Newfoundland-based artist Will Gill (Figures 8.4 and 8.5) described his artistic process as an ongoing negotiation between order and chaos, as he reflects on times when humans come close to the edge. Gill's work starts with a seed, an idea, but only begins to make sense as he works through these ideas. '*They just sort of develop until they start to make sense to me. It's more of an exploration or discovery.*' His work addresses

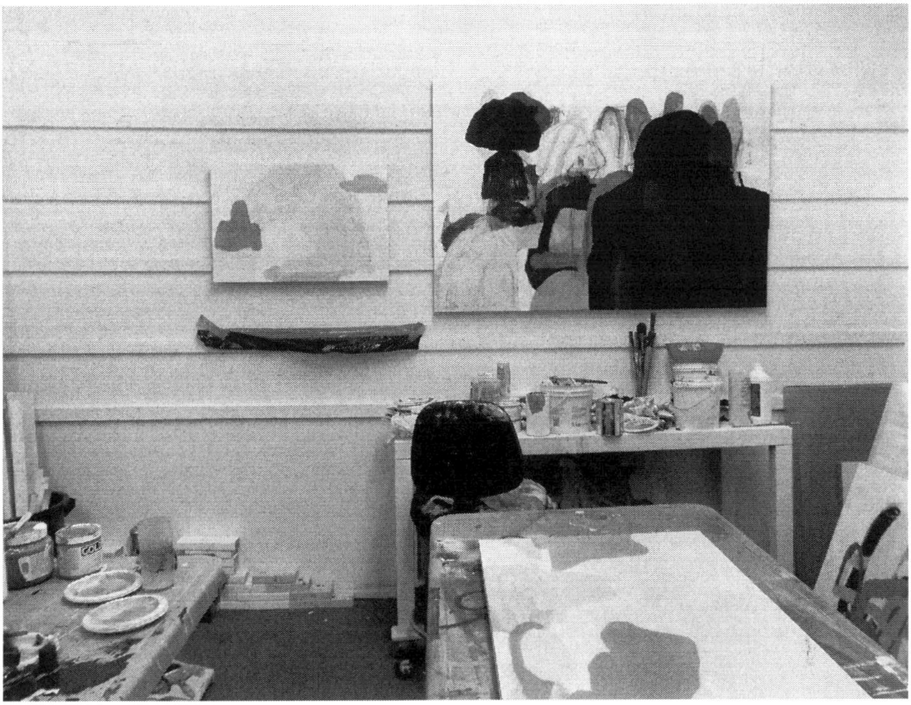

FIGURE 8.4: Will Gill's Studio, St. John's, NL, 2015.

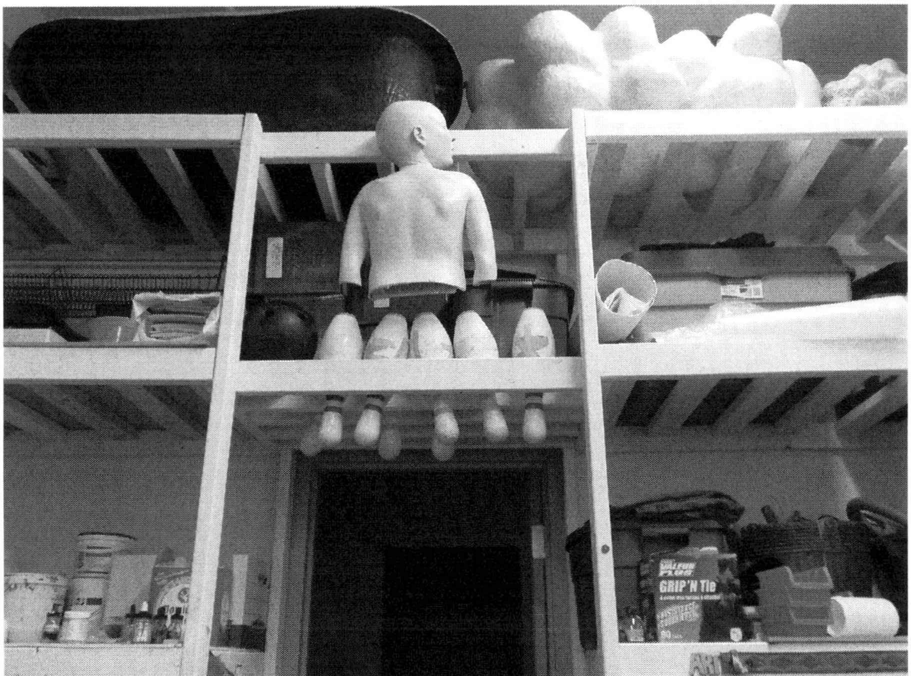

FIGURE 8.5: Will Gill's Studio, St. John's, NL, 2015.

hardships and struggle, particularly in relation to our surroundings, in Gill's case the ocean. He noted that as stories start to develop through making, and as connections emerge, the painting begins to remind him of a particular time in his life. For Gill, leaning into the messiness of art practice is about navigating between control and chaos.

> *I'm interested in letting a certain level of chance happen. Things happen and you have to decide whether to leave it or not, what to cover up, what to add, and it gets more and more complex. I like when it goes very wrong because it makes an extra challenge of trying to make sense of this chaos that is happening. It's always pulling order out of chaos for me. That's almost always what it is for me. And I think it lends itself to other parts of life.*

Part of Being an Artist Is Inventing Technologies

Jeremy Hof's (Figures 8.6 and 8.7) Vancouver (2015) studio was filled with colour, paint, and plaster. It was a playful experiment with materials. At the time, he was

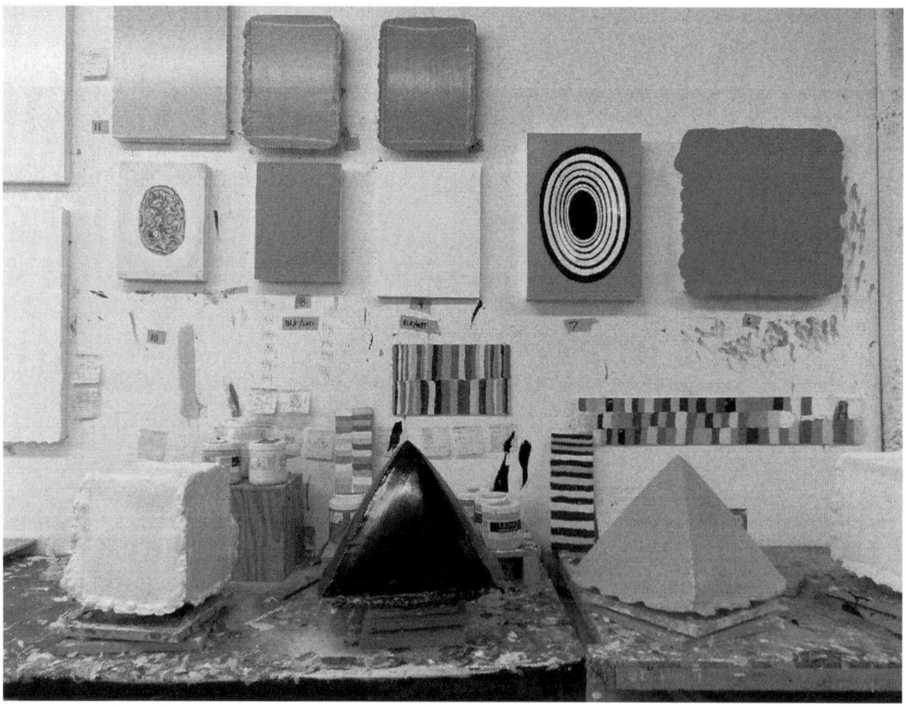

FIGURE 8.6: Jeremy Hof's Studio, Vancouver, BC, 2015.

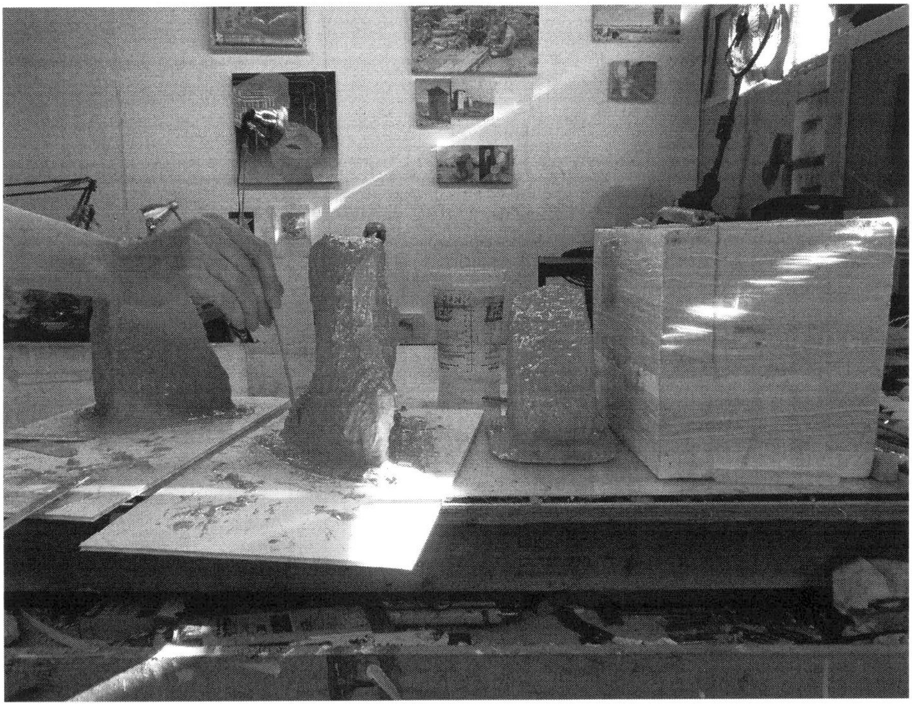

FIGURE 8.7: Jeremy Hof's Studio, Vancouver, BC, 2015.

working on a new project, casting stone sculpture rocks such as soapstone and limestone. He casted the shape of them and poured paint in layer by layer. He described himself as a sculptor trapped in a painter's body. Hof is drawn to material-based things, historical references to sculptural materials such as bricks, but he creates a dialogue with the colour that is embedded within the language of paint. Hof's work is characterized by methodically creating layers upon layers of paint. On an area of a wall in his studio, there was a checkmark list to keep track of the layers. For Hof, the planning happens in advance, selecting the colour palette and then coming in daily to follow through on that plan. Hof addressed the relationship between conceptual and material, an artificially constructed dichotomy that often existed in painting discourse. Arguing against this dichotomy, he proposed that the concept is embedded within the process and materials and his 'maker' need that drives his practice.

> *Painting is such a fluid and intuitive process that uses your body. There are so many natural elements to it that it seems artificial to start from a place of theory ... I'm at my happiest and healthiest when I'm working in my studio. It gives me great pleasure.*

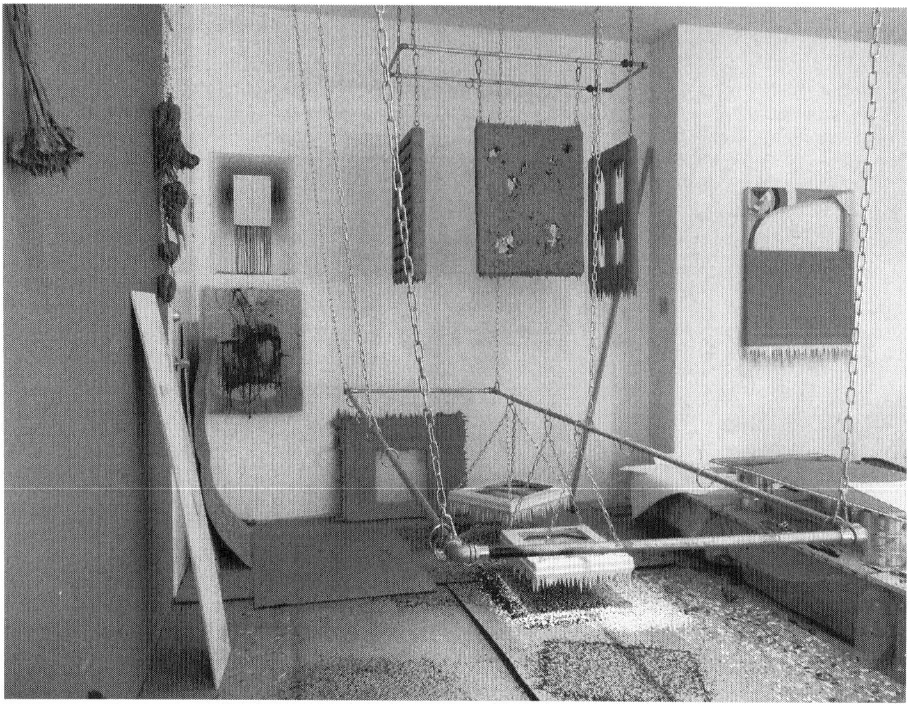

FIGURE 8.8: Sean Weisgerber's Studio, Saskatoon, SK, 2014.

Sean Weisgerber's studio (Figures 8.8 and 8.9) in Saskatoon, Saskatchewan (2014) sat on a stage in an old community centre. He had large tanks that he filled with mis-tint paints that he poured together to create a grey colour. '*Part of what I like about being an artist is inventing technologies.*' He created a complicated pulley and winch system to dip paintings. The resulting paintings that were dipped sometimes 50 times had spikes coming from the bottom made from the dripping paint. When held up vertically, the spikes project outward to the viewer. Weisgerber began this process by dipping fruit. In his studio, he had a pepper, an artichoke, a pineapple, and a dozen roses that had been dipped in paint. He described how this process emerged:

> *I was at the grocery store one day and I was looking at apples and was thinking about wax coating that protects it and makes it last, giving it a shimmer. I went home and I just decided on impulse to dip an apple. And I just kept dipping it every day not knowing what would happen. It started to shrivel up and then expand because of the gases, so it had this interesting interaction. So, I decided to try a couple more, but I felt like I needed to push it further. I was at first more interested in encasing*

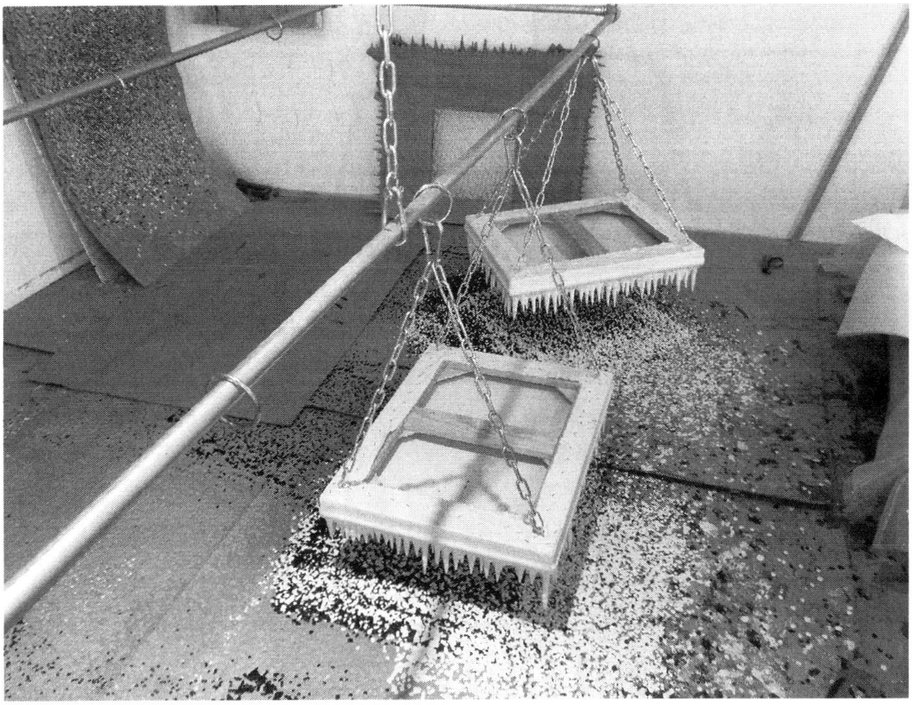

FIGURE 8.9: Sean Weisgerber's Studio, Saskatoon, SK, 2014.

> *something. It's alive in there and has this other skin on top of it. But the spikes started growing and I found that interesting. So, I thought 'what would happen if I did this?'*

High up on a wall hung a quilt that had been half-dipped, revealing the texture and stitched line work through the dipped paint. As a child, Weisgerber went to his grandmother's home after school, and he would craft with his grandmother while she quilted. He had found this quilt at an estate sale, probably from the 1930s, and bought it not knowing what he would do with it, but knowing he had to make an intervention into it. He cut it in half, spray-painted it, and dipped it. Regarding the objects he chose to dip, he said: '*The material has to be charged in one way or another.*' He proposed that in life, people often want a right or wrong answer, however, he prefers the uncertainty and the experimentation that comes with artmaking:

> *There is no right answer. You have to navigate through it. If you know the answer, why are you doing it? Or if you know what it's about, why make it? I find it more interesting to not know what is going to happen. I'm doing a specific thing, this gesture, but there are so many possibilities. It's a way of exploring learning. There's*

> *also a euphoria associated with this work. It's that excitement about looking at things and making things that make you want to keep going.*

For Van Maltese (Figures 8.10 and 8.11) (Toronto, 2014, 2015), collecting has always been a part of their practice, beginning with collecting wallpaper and seeking out patterns and interesting motifs. Later they began collecting objects that formed shapes that intrigued them. For example, they had recently been camping and found a corrugated piece of metal that formed the shape of a window. They brought it back to the studio. Their studio was filled with paintings, sculptural objects that looked like they belonged in a circus or like childhood toys, and piles of found objects and material. For Van, the studio is a space of collection.

> *When your studio is a permanent space, it's sort of a place for accumulation. I collect things, like that hanger and bring it to the studio, then it will sit next to this piece of a table I picked out of the garbage. And then one day all of these things just fit. It's like a waiting room. I don't know when it is going to happen. And sometimes objects resurface. Sometimes you have to go back for that follow up appointment.*

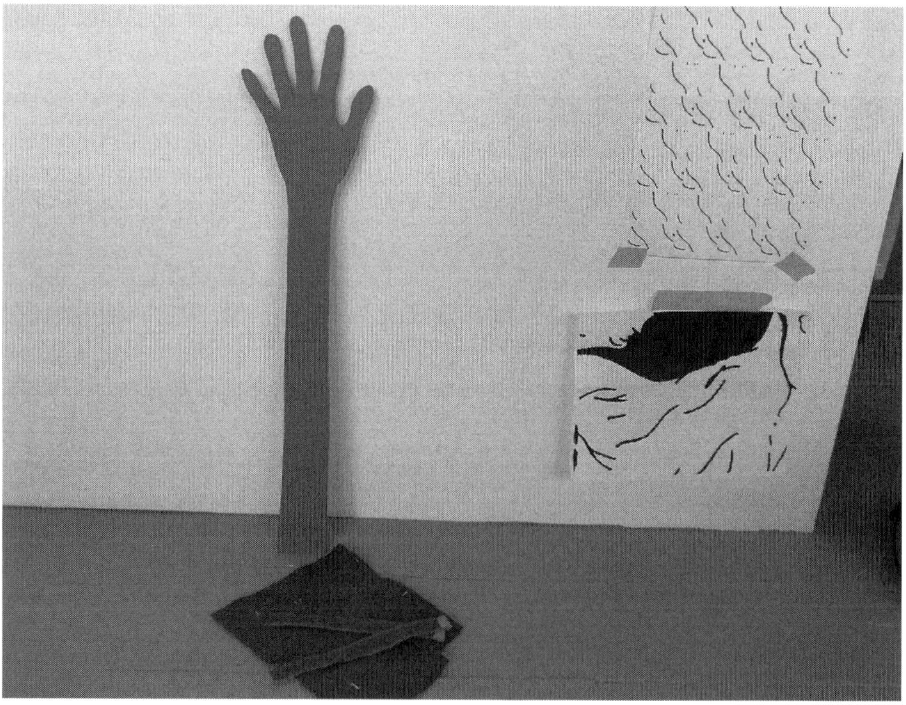

FIGURE 8.10: Van Maltese's Studio, Toronto, ON, 2014.

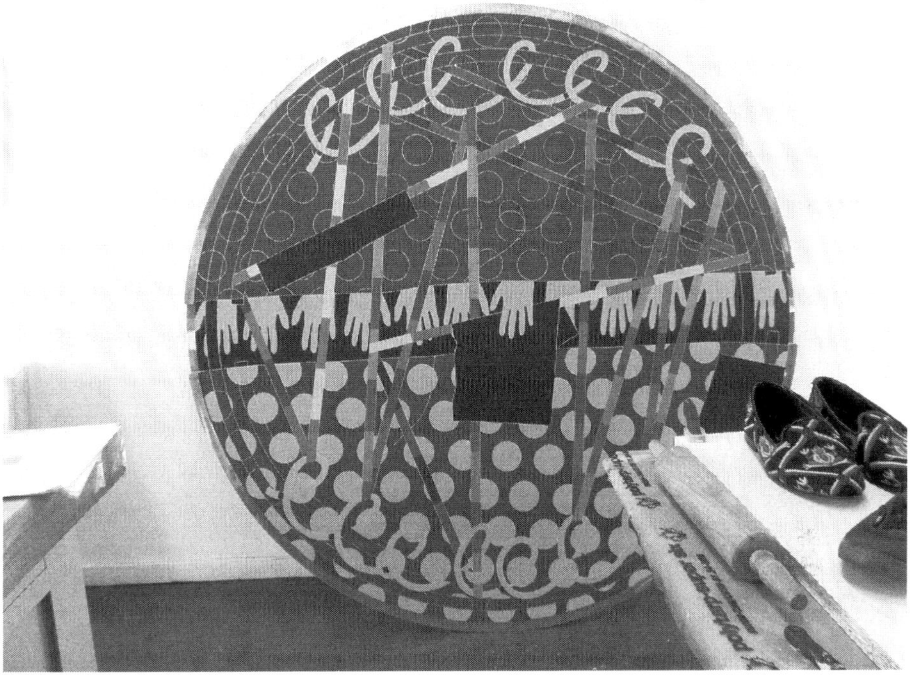

FIGURE 8.11: Van Maltese's Studio, Toronto, ON, 2015.

In Colleen Heslin's (Figures 8.12 and 8.13) Montreal studio (2014), piles of fabric filled the space. She had been sewing since she was 12 years old, but only recently her painting practice shifted towards staining, dying, and sewing. Recently, she was getting more comfortable approaching work without a plan, letting go of control, working with materials, and '*paying attention to what's happening that's interesting and being guided by that*'. Heslin began making paintings with off-cuts of canvas that she dyed and sewed together from leftover material in her studio. She had become disinterested in the surface quality of paint and said that working with fabric '*became metaphorically lighter, a counterweight to other histories that seemed to take up a large presence*'. She started mixing washes, immersing materials in it, doing rubbings outside, or biking or driving over materials as she developed new ways of working. Scraps from one painting would sometimes become the centre for the next:

> *I'm a person that saves things in little bits. There is something satisfying about that, in terms of finding material. Most of it are sheets from thrift stores. I've*

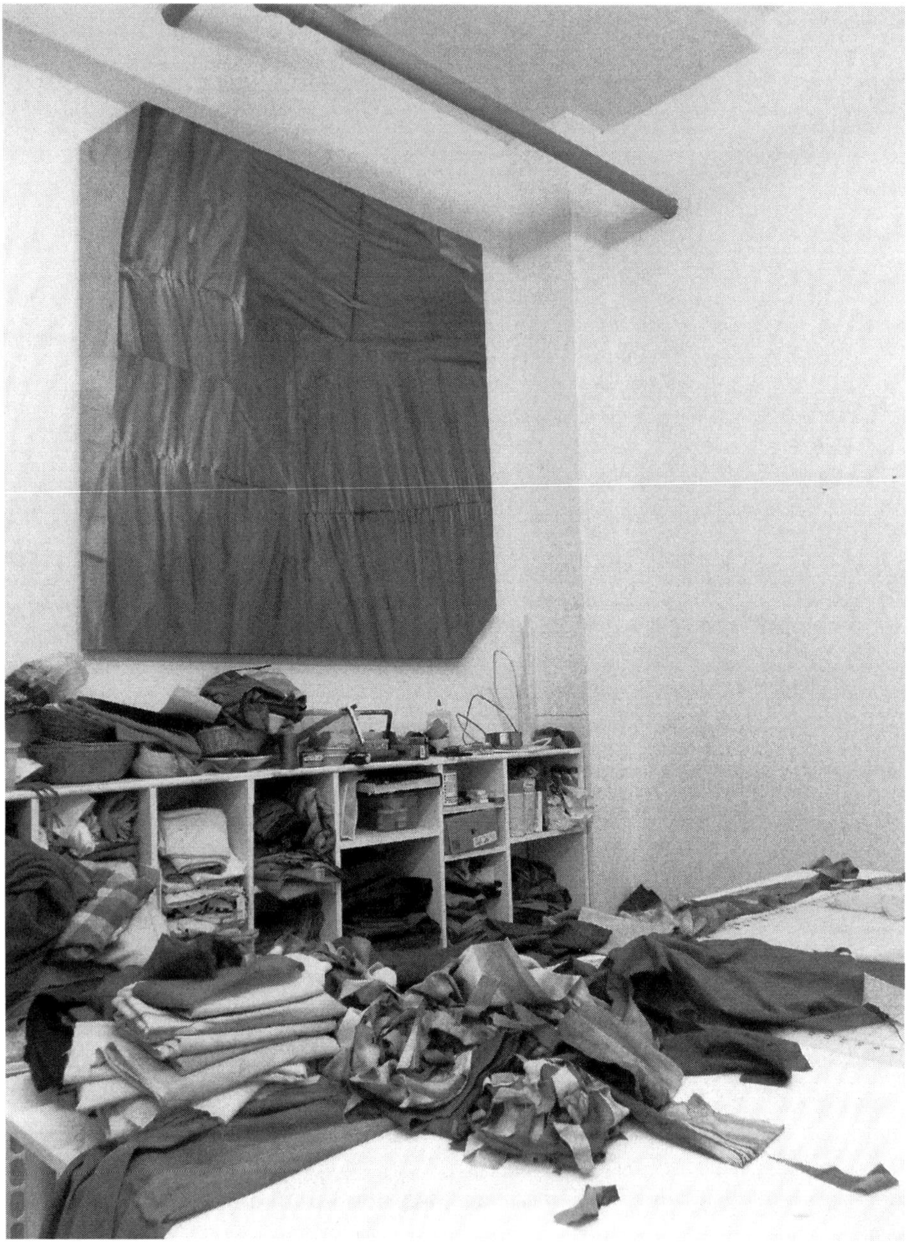

FIGURE 8.12: Colleen Heslin's Studio, Montreal, QC, 2014.

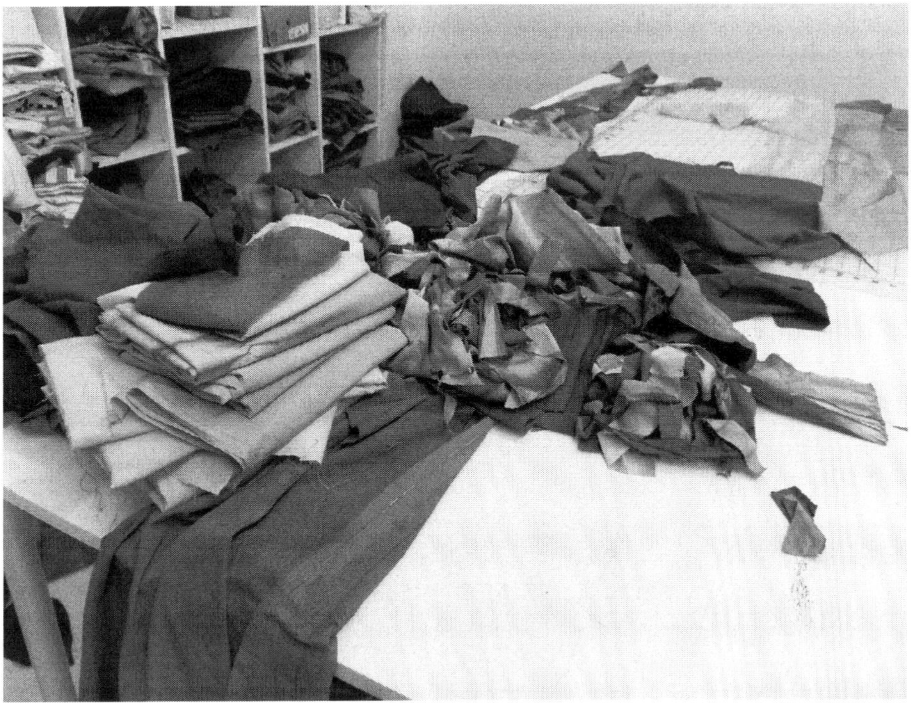

FIGURE 8.13: Colleen Heslin's Studio, Montreal, QC, 2014.

always had piles of sheets. I kept buying sheets. I'd get coloured ones and think I'd use them, but I didn't, so I'd collect them. A thing that happens when you're moving, you're forced to deal with the stuff and notice the things you go toward. You figure out what you want to hold on to. And also let things go ... This idea of being in a disposable culture bothered me. So, I liked working with recycled material, the idea of things being outcast, and being able to invert value in something. Sometimes the life of something is up. But there is potential for it to have different use. Any work that is interesting, is informed by the material that it's made from in some way.

For Heslin, working with different materials is an ongoing process of experimenting.

As an artist you're always on the cusp of figuring out what you're doing. Something about not really knowing how to do something, and things happen that might not have happened if you are following it by the book. Working with materials, that's how you come about it.

It's Not Until You Look Back That It Makes Sense

I propose that the studio is a place that has the capacity to counteract a desire for certainty and where wandering directions that emerge through the distraction of thought or the distraction of materials are generative. It is a place full of curiosities, and a place where one is constantly seeking out unanswerable questions, new problems and generating new connections and new meanings. It is a messy space, both physically and psychologically, and a space of incompletion, uncertainty, and continual change. A studio is a place where the materiality of the studio, the materials of making, and experiences and ideas become entangled in a continual learning process. It is a space that is active, constantly changing, and where artists work through ideas. The messiness of practice alludes to both the messiness of materials as well as the messiness of thought, ideas, perspectives, and meanings that change within an ever-changing and messy world.

Thus, a studio may be filled with contradictions. '*I think I'm perverse. I think I like the thing to be itself and its opposite simultaneously*', said Laura Millard regarding her messy relationship with the subjects of her studio practice. In her Toronto studio, in 2015, Millard (Figure 8.14) said that throughout her career, she

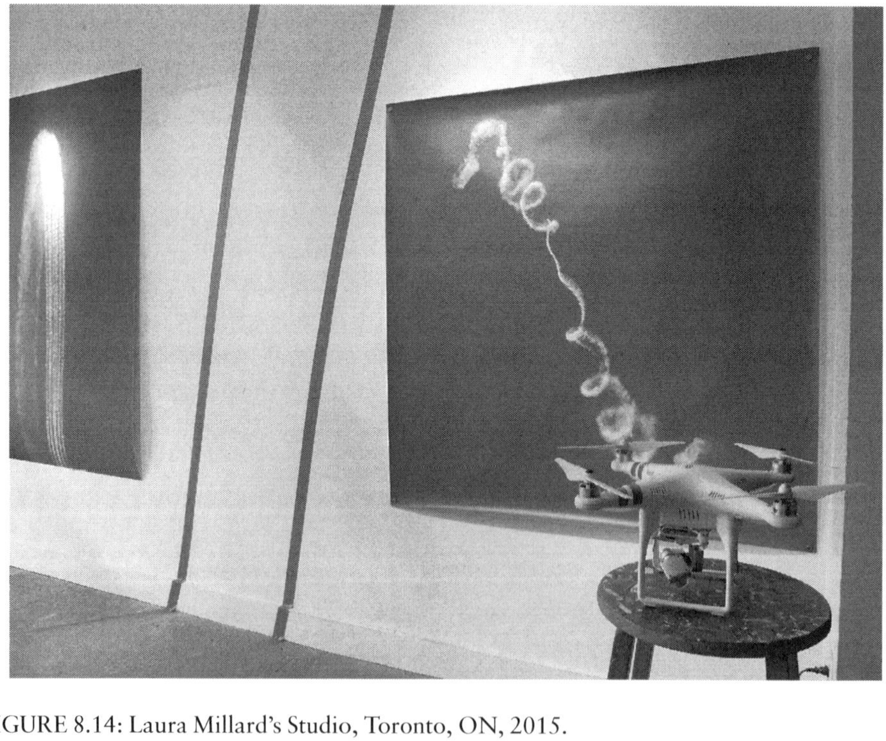

FIGURE 8.14: Laura Millard's Studio, Toronto, ON, 2015.

was constantly confronted with her beliefs about artmaking through an ongoing exploration of her relationship to the land. Through her art practice, she continuously questioned her relationship with the land, largely due to the history of colonial landscape painting. Having grown up in the Rocky Mountains of Alberta, her childhood experiences were imprinted within her and her work. Millard studied at the Nova Scotia College of Art and Design when painting as a studio practice was very much in question.

Millard struggled to find a way of engaging with issues that were important to her in the 1980s such as clear-cutting in western Canada. Trying to disengage from a colonial lens of the landscape, she began working with traces left behind, '*the thing once present, now absent*'. She made a series of works made from photographs taken above frozen ponds of the marks made by ice skaters. These photographic paintings of traces capture a poetic drawing made by the skates when viewed from above. '*That trace is a sort of transcribing on the surface. There's no horizon and there's a relationship to abstraction and to having the body make a line. It's someone else making those lines, someone else doing the drawing.*' In her studio in 2015, Millard had made the shape of an airplane with blue tape. On the walls were images of the smoke lines made by the traces left behind by planes in the Toronto Air Shows. She had contradictory feelings about the airshow as she loathed the shows, while she simultaneously found the spectacle of them fascinating. A drone that she had recently purchased was a central fixture in her studio. She had created videos taken as the drone was rising above the land, again showcasing the traces made within the landscape.

> *I'm very interested in finding different ways of looking at the landscape, in that desperate attempt to escape its romantic and questionable past. I'm standing in the middle of a frozen lake. All the lines are from skidoos. Again, it's that found drawing. But my father had recently died, and I was trying to find out if you could use landscape as this device to give the feeling of the soul leaving the body and drifting away.*

Through her work, she contemplated if artmaking in a particular place may be a way of understanding that place differently:

> *There's a long history of using pathetic fallacy or stand-ins for loss or expressions of loss. Trace and travel and comings and goings and spectacles of futility, those things interest me. But when I do these, I'm just doing it so I can figure out what it is that might be possible to visually create, to communicate the thing that I'm exploring.*

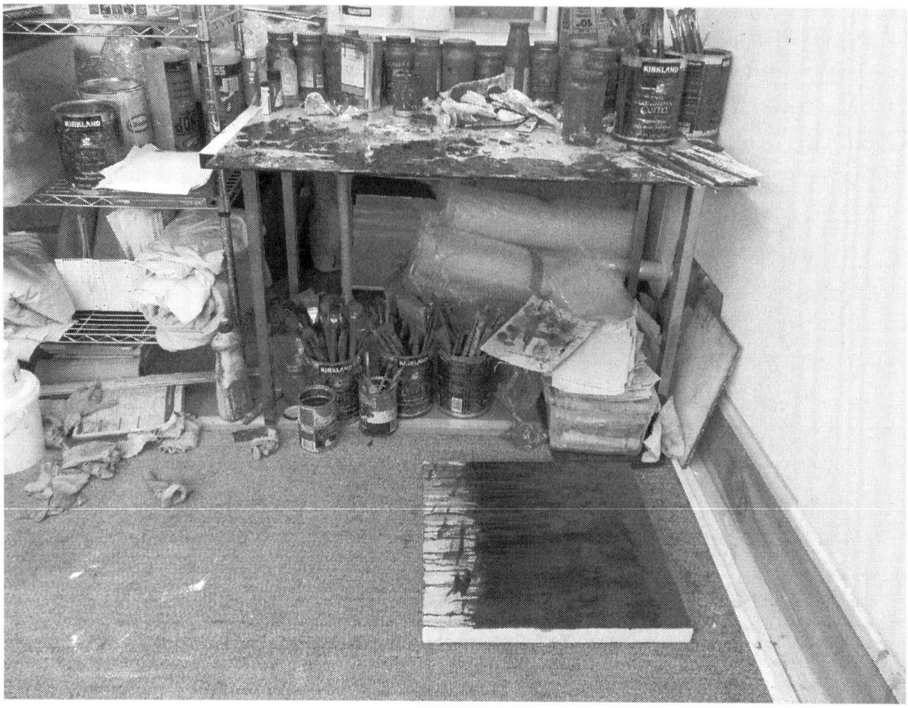

FIGURE 8.15: Jennifer Carvalho's Studio, Toronto, ON, 2015.

In her Toronto studio (2015) Jennifer Carvalho (Figures 8.15 and 8.16) similarly explores our relationship to the land as she addresses themes related to climate anxiety.

> *I'm interested in examining what a landscape is now. As human beings we've come to think of the landscape as a backdrop to human activity, and we can now see the influence of human behaviour on the Earth's atmosphere. So, what does that mean? How do we understand our relationship to landscape, and how if at all has it changed with the looming ecological crisis? I guess I am trying to think through the landscape.*

Her process weaves through several references from movies, to books, to other paintings, to current environmental issues. Regarding her process, she said:

> *There's a basic structure that's laid out as a drawing. But I still don't know what the painting is going to look like until it's done. I have an idea for how I'm going to make the painting, what I'm thinking about and other paintings I'm looking at. My process is very very slow and the paintings are a mess in the beginning stages. I feel*

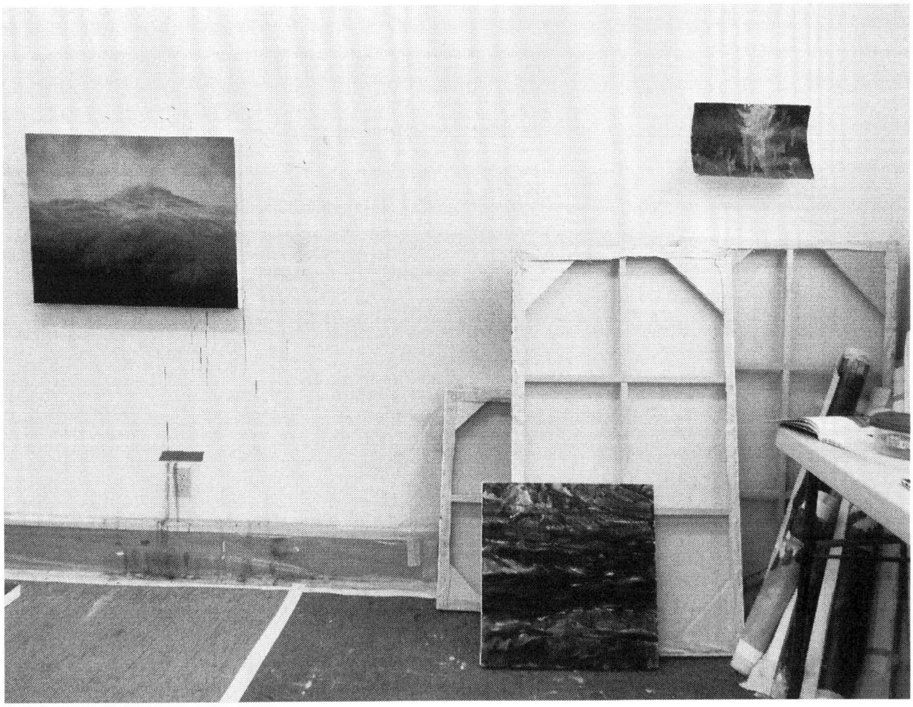

FIGURE 8.16: Jennifer Carvalho's Studio, Toronto, ON, 2015.

> *like I'm spending time with the image trying to understand the mood and a direction for the painting. And then some sort of incident happens, and I can build from that. And then something starts to happen. So, it's slow, and it's a mess and then somehow it starts to come together, and a structure starts to emerge. Someone once said to me in a studio visit that the etymology of the word methodology is to make a path. So, if you think of yourself as making a path through a wild forest, you have nothing ahead of you but wild brush and you're cutting into it as you go, and you can't see the path until you look back. In front of you, you're making some sort of intuitive decision but it's not until you look back that it makes sense, and there is a path. I'm ok with things being a bit messy and having unanswered questions. Over time things will make sense.*

In her recent book, *Faux Pas*, Amy Sillman (2020) addresses the messiness of practice through the lens of diagramming. When she was living in Germany in 2009, Sillman began learning about diagrams. She viewed the diagram as revealing the interconnectedness of everything:

> My mind stretched out with increasingly dizzying interconnectivity; everything started to make a weird kind of sense, and I got it: *everything was related to something else*. The Enlightenment, Romanticism, Symbolism, modernism, Bad Painting, it was all locatable on one big map ... thinking about the diagram liberated my work.
>
> (p. 128, original emphasis)

However, she then recognized that the diagram also makes apparent the social conditions in which a painting exists and that can also be oppressive saying that 'the same problematics that I had faced in painting were back to haunt me with the diagram' (p. 134). She concluded by recognizing that the messiness of painting and the messiness of practice may allow it to escape the diagram:

> I felt intuitively that the answer *had* to be located in some way in something messy: accidents, negations, a spill, some excess found on the floor, some physical inexplicability, the idea of desire, urges, pleasure, which I thought was exactly bound up

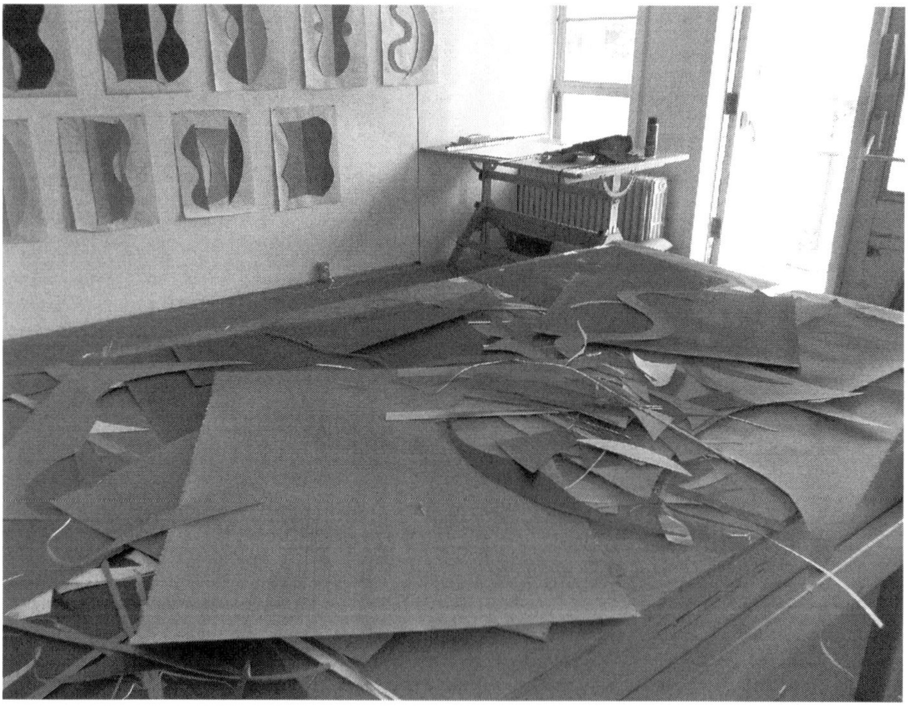

FIGURE 8.17: Jessica Groome's Studio, Toronto, 2014.

> with the not-knowing part of the art-making process ... It's a mess of unknowns, beyond diagrammable.
>
> (pp. 134–36, original emphasis)

This idea was echoed by artist, Jessica Groome (Figure 8.17) who is driven by the tactility of the material, ongoing experimentation, and the constant feeling of chasing something. '*I'm driven by decision on top of decision. How far can I chase this internal process-based search?*'

9

Set Up Two Situations So Your Mind Has to Travel Between the Two (Studio as Collage)

> *Our bricoleur's fancy improvising, jerry rigging incongruous images and ideas, adding and subtracting, attaching and detaching, gluing and nailing, leaning and propping, in order to extend and expand their presumed functions prosthetically, linking the present with the past, the familiar with the strange, to see and understand the one through the other, back and forth, and again.*
>
> (Garoian, 2013, p. 3)

A Belief in an Undefinable Interconnectedness Between All Things

I met Alex Livingston (Figures 9.1 and 9.2) in his Halifax, Nova Scotia studio in 2015, where we discussed his life as an artist. His paintings throughout his career navigated the relationship between representation and abstraction often through examining the mark. Through his work, he looked at reproductions and the marks made to create images.

> *I was thinking about how much the representational image was on a smaller level, abstract; a brush-mark on its own is abstract until put in with other marks. In my earlier works I was interested in serpentine forms or twisting, interlaced shapes, whether it was in a tree or wave or an animal.*

He would draw from the line or gesture within an image and distort that mark to create a quasi-abstract image. Livingston's interest in pulling out the serpentine

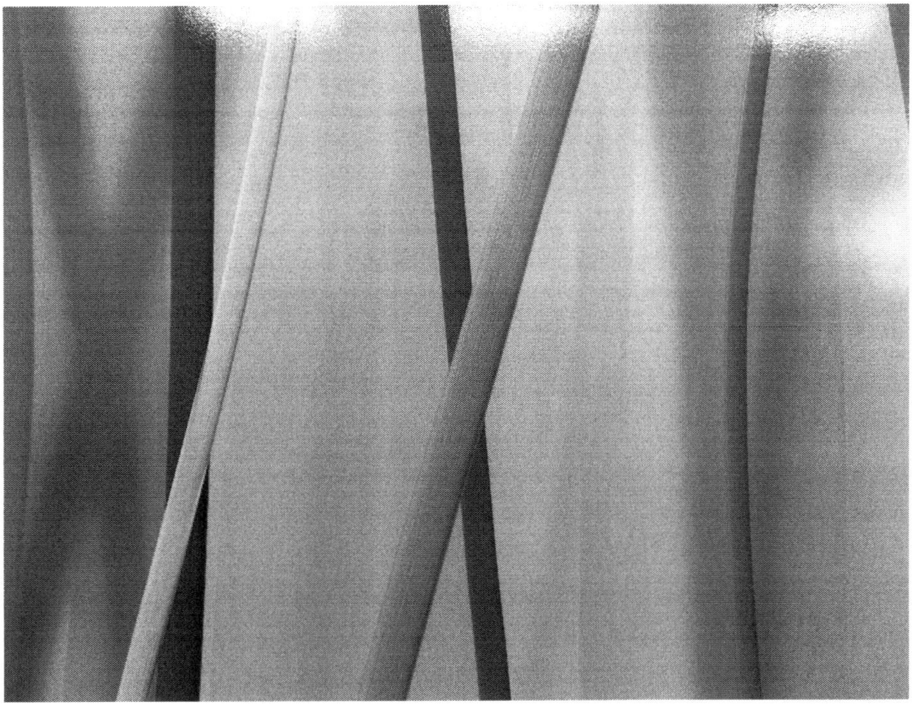

FIGURE 9.1: Alex Livingston's Studio, Halifax, NS, 2015.

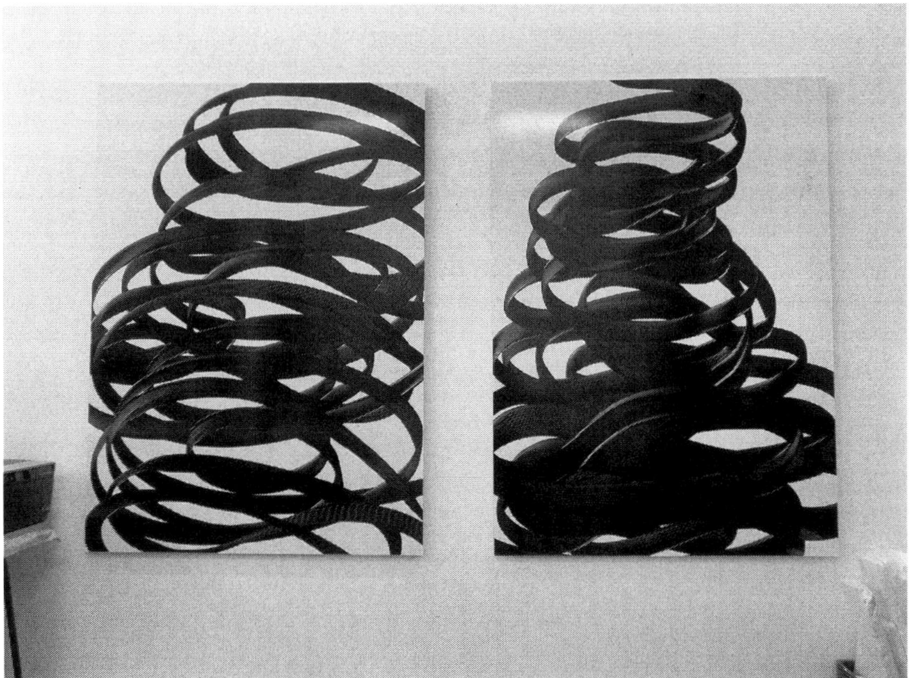

FIGURE 9.2: Alex Livingston's Studio, Halifax, NS, 2015.

and twisting forms from marks led to his current paintings of simple, twisting, and interlocking shapes. Regarding why he makes art, Livingston said:

> *It's the underlying connections in the work. I think there's this notion of the interlaced and interconnected form and metaphorical references to the natural world whether it speaks of structures or growing forms or underwater. Even in the abstract language they are metaphors for interconnectedness. So, I suppose if there is a base note to all the work it's that there is a deep belief that there is a strong and undefinable interconnectedness between all things. We all find different ways of speaking about our relationship to the external world and the internal perceptions in our world, our internal minds and how we fit into the bigger picture. And that is a prime impetus of mine, a way of coming to understand both myself and how I perceive the world.*

Highlighting the interaction between humans and non-humans, Jane Bennett (2010) refers to this affective interaction as the 'thing-power' (p. 3) of objects. She describes how a material relationship formed between a grouping of objects that she happened upon: a glove, oak pollen, a dead rat, a bottle cap, and a stick of wood:

> I caught a glimpse of an energetic vitality inside each of these things, things that I generally conceived as inert. In this assemblage, *objects* appeared as *things*, that is, as vivid entities not entirely reducible to the contexts in which (human) subjects set them.
>
> (p. 5, original emphasis)

An actant, which Bennett describes as an interferer may be human or nonhuman, and its effects are felt on the body, as affect. An assemblage, for her, is created through the affects generated out of the thing-power, the vitality of objects to affect others. She describes vital materiality as the ability of our body to be affected.

Through viewing the studio through this lens, the objects within the studio, the paint, and the space itself become interconnected with the story told by the artists. The studios contain remnants of old works next to new works, sketches, piles of books, and trinkets, all in a seemingly haphazard formation, creating juxtapositions that prompted me to view the studio as an imaginative assemblage. Art educator, Charles Garoian (2008, 2013) uses the term prosthesis to address how artmaking extends understandings. According to Garoian, rather than synthesizing ideas into a singular meaning, artmaking functions prosthetically, extending outward in multiple directions. Through this quality, artistic practice disrupts a desire for a whole and is instead characterized by continuously producing an excess and surplus of understandings. Through this process of extending outward, previously dissociated and contradictory ideas become interconnected and more complex. He describes this indeterminacy: '[It is] constituted by disjunctive, incongruous fragments of images, ideas, knowledge, and understandings, whose complex, irreducible slippages of meaning resist synthetic closure similar to the way in which collage narrative has resisted concrescence (Kuspit, 1983)' (Garoian, 2008, p. 227).

Artists create spaces that extend existing knowledge by allowing for impossible associations, connections, and relationships to emerge.

In a 2016 exhibition by artist William Kentridge titled *No It Is!*, he addressed the complexity of artistic practices as he brought viewers into his studio process. Kentridge describes the studio as an enlarged head filled with fragments of ideas as he uses collage as a way of describing what happens in a studio:

> One thinks of collage as a particularly 20th-century artistic phenomenon. But in its very nature of pasting together different fragments of the world and the possibility of constructing a coherent world from them, it is a central category today, both for artistic activity in itself and for artistic activity as a metaphor for how we think in general. This idea of taking the world as a single element and then splitting it apart is one of the fundamental activities of the studio.
>
> (Kentridge, 2016, p. 25)

I similarly view the studio as a collage, not simply as a way of discussing images, but as a way of thinking that generates new ideas through connections. I visited the studio in Calgary (2014) that Chris Cran (Figures 9.3 and 9.4) had inhabited for seventeen years. He described his process as generated through stumbling on something that interested him. It's about play and about noticing things and waiting for a feeling without overthinking. He shared a quote he often uses in his teaching: '*When a crow lands on a branch and a coconut drops, there is no connection.*' This story is told to explain coincidences. Cran explained his interpretation: '*There is no connection. The point is that we are meaning-making machines. We will put two and two together at the drop of a hat so that we're not held in suspension.*' He described the process of looking, seeing, and finding meanings as the '*connecting thing we do*'. Throughout the space, there were images from old newspapers, photographs, and magazines blown up large. On one wall of the studio, there was a series of faces, eyes looking in various directions guiding the viewer to different areas of the studio. Cran described the stencilling process used to make the dots and stripes and explained that our vision moves back and forth as we either look at the stripes/dots or the image, but we cannot see both at the same time. According to him, the mind cannot pay attention to two things at the same time, as he exclaimed:

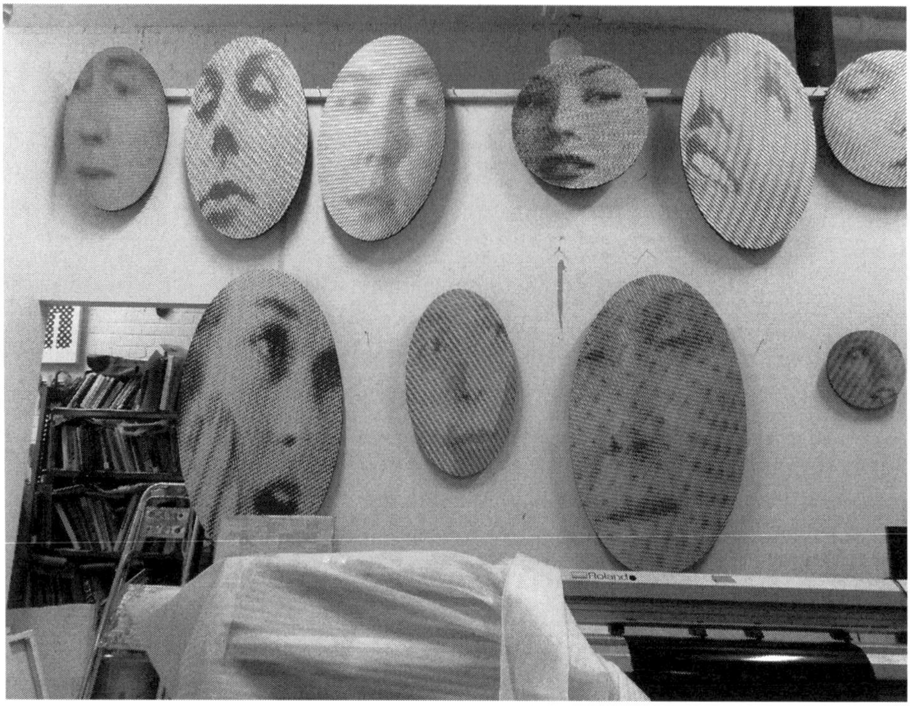

FIGURE 9.3: Cris Cran's Studio, Calgary, AB, 2014.

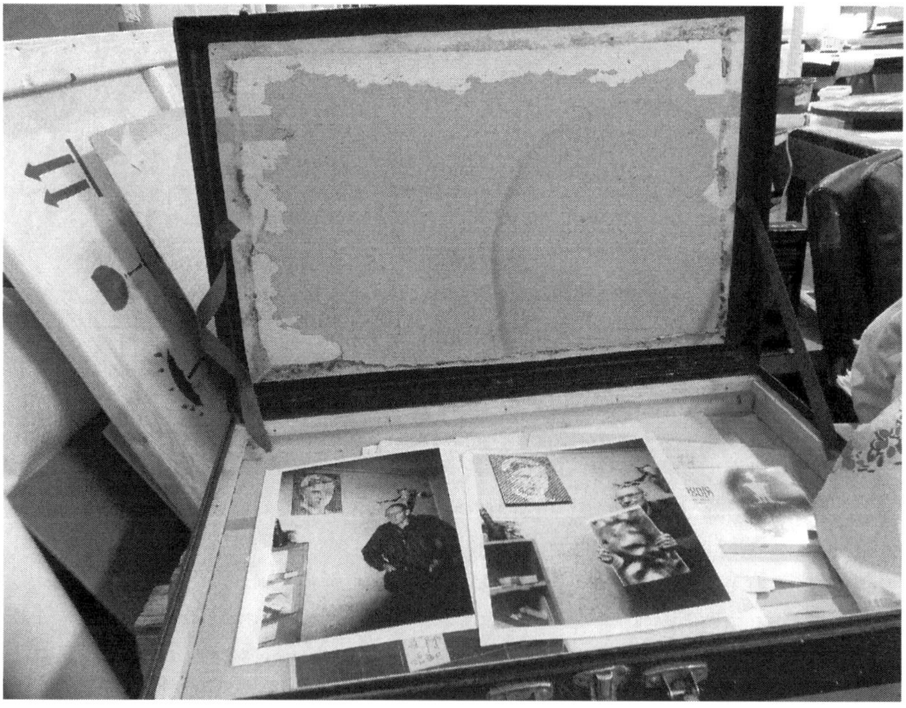

FIGURE 9.4: Cris Cran's Studio, Calgary, AB, 2014.

'If you set up two situations then the mind has to travel between the two and it is entertained in that travelling.'

Transforming All This Noise and Filtering It Through My Own Experience

In her studio in Vancouver in 2015, Renee Van Halm (Figure 9.5) described her artistic process of looking to the world and bringing those experiences into the studio:

> *It's not about going inside. It's about going outside. I've never believed there is something innate in painting. I don't believe it is a psychological experience or that it comes out of your forehead fully formed. For me, it's all about finding things out there and processing them. It all comes from somewhere. It's about putting things together. That's what research is. You take facts and you take things you experience from seeing and looking.*

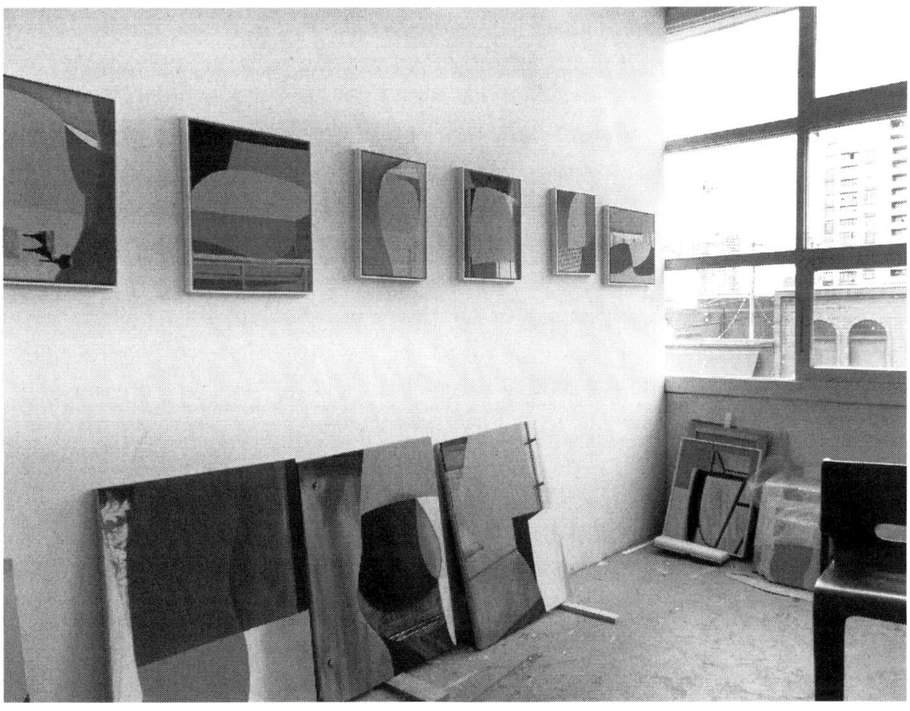

FIGURE 9.5: Renee Van Halm's Studio, Vancouver, BC, 2015.

Van Halm has always been curious about space and architecture. Her studio was filled with a row of her most recent paintings that, while abstract, reference architectural spaces. '*I have an interest in the background of life. What's there that we don't notice? It's disregarded and yet it informs our everyday activities.*' To show how her process began, she shared a painting from 1978 where she drew from historical paintings but took the figures out of them.

> *I've been doing that ever since. You still see elements of that in my recent paintings, where there's snippets of architecture but there's never any figures. And now the figure has been replaced by these big, coloured shapes that can be seen as surrogate bodies.*

Thus, while there was a deliberate removal of the figure, she implies the figure in a way, more recently through imagining the viewer as the figure. '*The viewer becomes enveloped by the experience of the architecture.*' Through her work, Van Halm connects images from magazines, architecture, and colour source material. She was particularly interested in colour filtrations in fashion magazines. She demonstrated how ideas emerge through a series she referred to as *French Curves*.

> *I'm always looking at ways that colour can be defined. That made me collect all these images. And I started cutting out the figure. I was cutting them out arbitrarily, just to get rid of the figure in all of them. And then I started becoming interested in the shapes that come out of the cuts. And then I started using French curves (plastic tools used to cut curves) to make the cuts.*

In relation to ways that she draws imagery from the world and reconstructs them in the studio, Van Halm discussed the title of one series, *Reverse Engineering*.

> *'Reverse engineering' is the term that is often used in computer engineering to describe when you take an existing thing, like taking a watch apart and build a new watch based on what you learned from the old watch. So, I'm taking pre-existing images and making something new with it, but I still have a reference to the original.*

In her studio in Montreal, Christine Major (Figures 9.6 and 9.7) (2015) similarly discussed collage, through the lens of hybridity. By bringing diverse and incongruent imagery together she addresses failures of technology, the body, and painting. Regarding continuing to work with paint, despite the prevalence of technology in art discourse, she said:

> *It's about the body. So conceptually, I keep coming back to painting. I'm working through this idea of source imagery, and appropriation and filtering through*

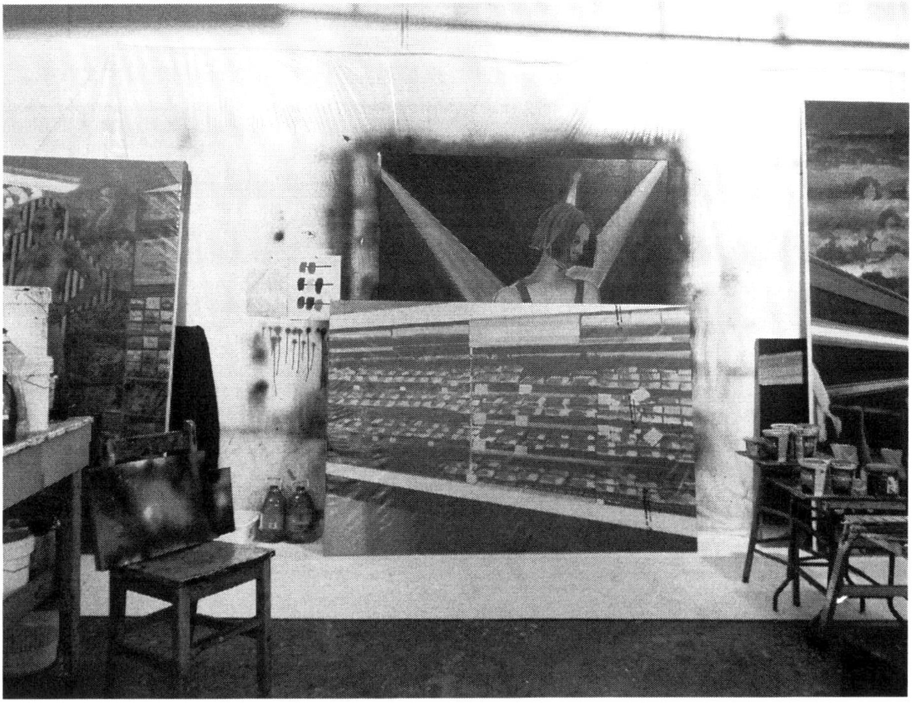

FIGURE 9.6: Christine Major's Studio, Montreal, QC, 2015.

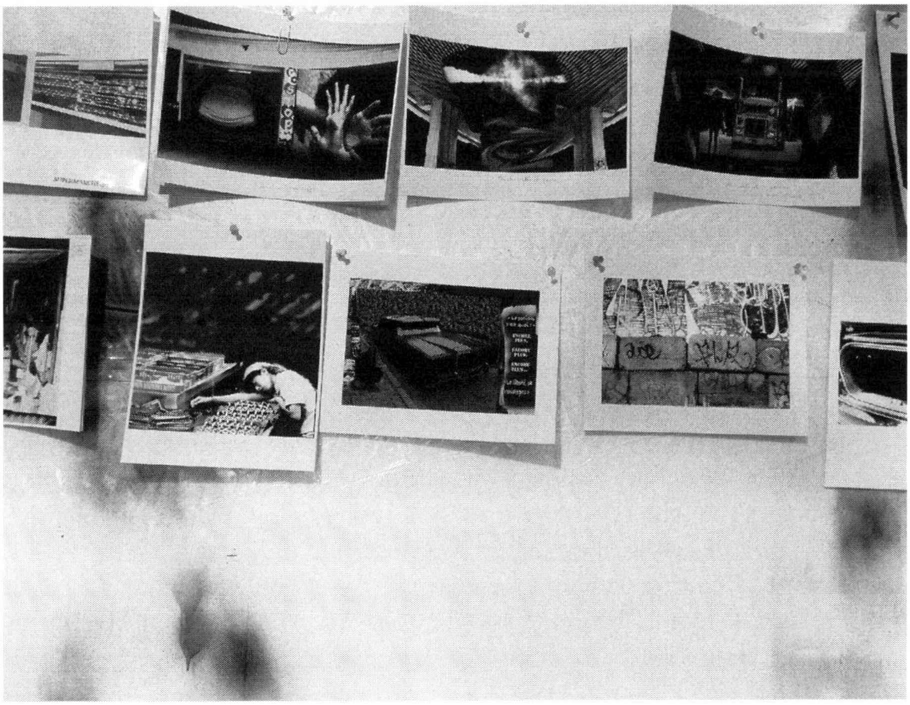

FIGURE 9.7: Christine Major's Studio, Montreal, QC, 2015.

> *technology. My work is a mixture of Feminism and trying to tackle the obsession with technology ... And all of it is about questioning representation and ways of seeing.*

Addressing the drive behind her work, Major discussed hybridity and mixing images that don't go together. '*There is something theatrical about working with the figure and creating scenes that didn't really happen.*' Major had been working with a variety of images, but lately she drew from imagery of roads and car crashes and bringing together images of the micro and macro, or trying to make things visible that can't really be seen. Around her studio, there were photographs of truck stops, roads, meat in a supermarket, and a car crashing into a casino in Montreal. Regarding her process, she said:

> *I like constructing paintings and talking about all sorts of things going on in society. Putting images together creates a great space to have conversations about issues or about the presence of technology and social media in our lives. I've been critical of technology and I'm using paint to feed that criticism. I can't live in the world. I can't deal with this reality, so I need to get energy from this parallel world. I find art politically and ethically so important. I could just be a consumer, but in the studio, I'm digesting this stuff and making it my own. And I feel this empowerment because I'm transforming all this noise and filtering it through my own experience.*
>
> *Making art expands your consciousness and connection with the world. You could just decide to let go and not be connected. Art pushes the connection. I've been thinking more about being present in our body. Feeling the gravity. In a context where people are more are more disconnected from their physical presence through technology, just feeling present in our own body is enough for me. Feeling emotions. That's enough. I'm trying to find ways to be free as much as I can and live in this parallel world.*

It's the Time You Spend With the Image

In her Vancouver studio, Gwenessa Lam (Figure 9.8) (2015) and I discussed memory, images, meaning-making, and what materials evoke. Lam's work addresses ways that we view, interpret, and remember images as sites of both the personal and the collective memory. She draws from found or taken photographic images that she reworks through drawing and painting. For Lam, the relationship between aesthetics, material gesture, and the conceptual framework is intertwined. Pointing to her current work, she explained that she tried out several materials, paint, graphite, and charcoal to explore the effects that the different material evoke.

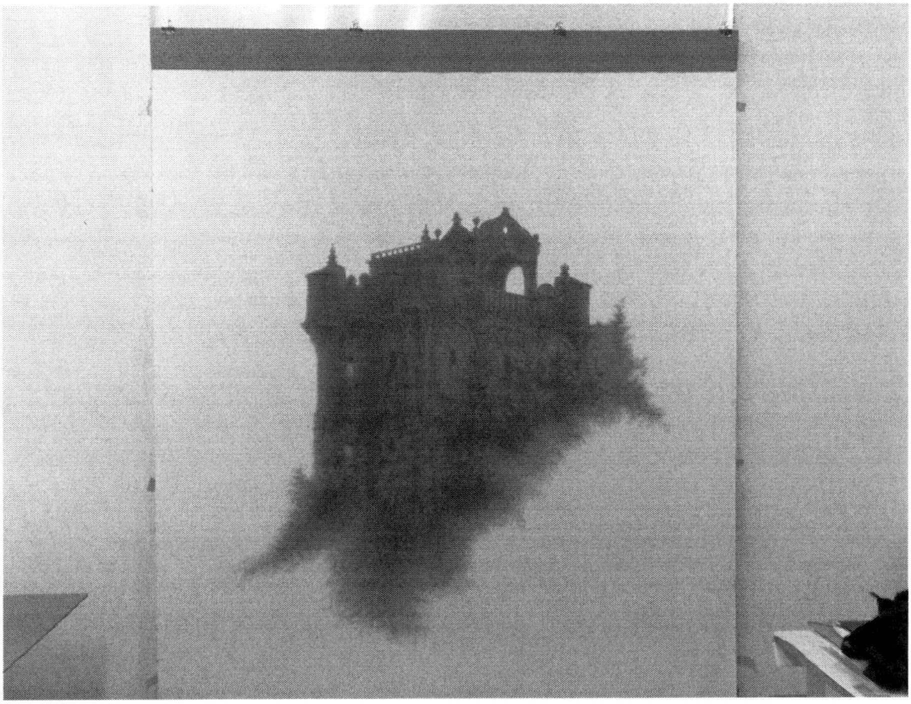

FIGURE 9.8: Gwenessa Lam's Studio, Vancouver, BC, 2015.

> *For me, artmaking is a series of questions. It's a process of trying to comprehend my external environment. It's the material. It's the time that you spend with an image. You live with the image for a really long time. So, there is something about constantly touching the image. The movement of the body across the surface. I feel like I'm physically digesting the image by creating it.*

Earlier in her art career, Lam lived close to a pawn shop where she found cabinets full of old family photo albums that showed milestones of strangers' lives such as baby photos, weddings, graduation, etc. Through looking at these generic and familiar photographs, she was interested in the ways that they highlighted collective memories.

> *By 'collective' I mean an image we can all tap into of a shared experience but that's open to a subjective rereading, misreading, and permutations of it, one that's not fixed ... In a sense I was constructing a fictional memory bank.*

She reworked the images, often through cropping, to destabilize them or take a fresh look at something familiar. Through editing, Lam sought to create fictive spaces out of the existing images to generate a heightened psychological experience.

> *There's a different knowing when I explore the image, especially one that is so fleeting. These aren't precious photos, but it gives it weight to really explore the meaning through spending time with it. I have a bias toward 2D images, specifically the hand-drawn one. There are instances when I find the image of the real is more interesting than the real space itself. There is a different level of understanding when understood through the photographic lens. And then a third remove when I interpret the image through drawing. And I'm interested in ways of looking and how that translates within the bodily mark.*

Later, Lam began making paintings of shadows from chairs, without the presence of the actual chair. These chair shadows took on a human-like quality, becoming a stand-in for a figure. '*I began thinking about the shadow or remnant of an event as a psychological trigger. How would that relate to our relationship to objects or images?*' From there, she began making drawings of shadows left behind by sixteenth-century Chinese vases at the Metropolitan Museum of Modern Art. Her interest in this work came from seeing how ceramics was defined by a particular time and location, but these definitions were slippery as these Chinese vases were in conversation with Japanese, Korean, and Indian ceramics that were being disseminated around the world. The shadow of those images was a way of playing with the remnants or traces of an object that no longer exists. On the wall of her studio was a drawing that emerged following a visit to her parents' village in China in 2007 when she came across towers that had been built in 1910–20 by families who had emigrated from North America, Australia, and different parts of Asia. The buildings were Gothic European but also had North American features. She describes them as a mishmash.

> *So, I called the works* Mongrel Histories. *Because they were bizarre clusters and combinations of cultural experiences that became embodied in these buildings. I wanted to further complicate that by re-cannibalizing them and making a hybrid of a hybrid to question how we categorize buildings from what history. I was interested in the mongrel. Salmon Rushdie wrote an essay looking at the idea of culture and mixing of identities. He talked about mongrel as something generative, not one of impurity or defect but by combining different elements you have something new. I was interested in that in terms of thinking about the buildings being mongrel. There's that line where I'm interested in responding to cultural/historical artifacts that I may or may not have a personal relationship to but by virtue of my mixed experience I'm formulating these ideas together.*

Borrowing Different Patterns, Different Visual Languages, and Putting Them in a Blender

I met Patrick Cruz (Figure 9.9) in 2015 in Guelph, Ontario, where he was currently pursuing graduate work. He addressed what he believes painting can do:

> *I see painting as a way of manifesting a new reality. It's a way of raising an awareness to something that I don't think any other means can. It's interesting because painting has been associated with every section of history. There's an enigma to painting that makes it come back.*

In his studio, there was an odd plant-like sculpture and multiple paintings of a plant. Regarding this work, he said:

> *I was first drawn to my neighbour's aloe vera plant that looks like a swan. There is an interesting play about mimicry. So, I decided to do three of them to mimic each other. Aloe vera is supposed to be the most distributed plant in the world. So, it has a globalized history to it as it is dispersed and used for medicinal purposes.*

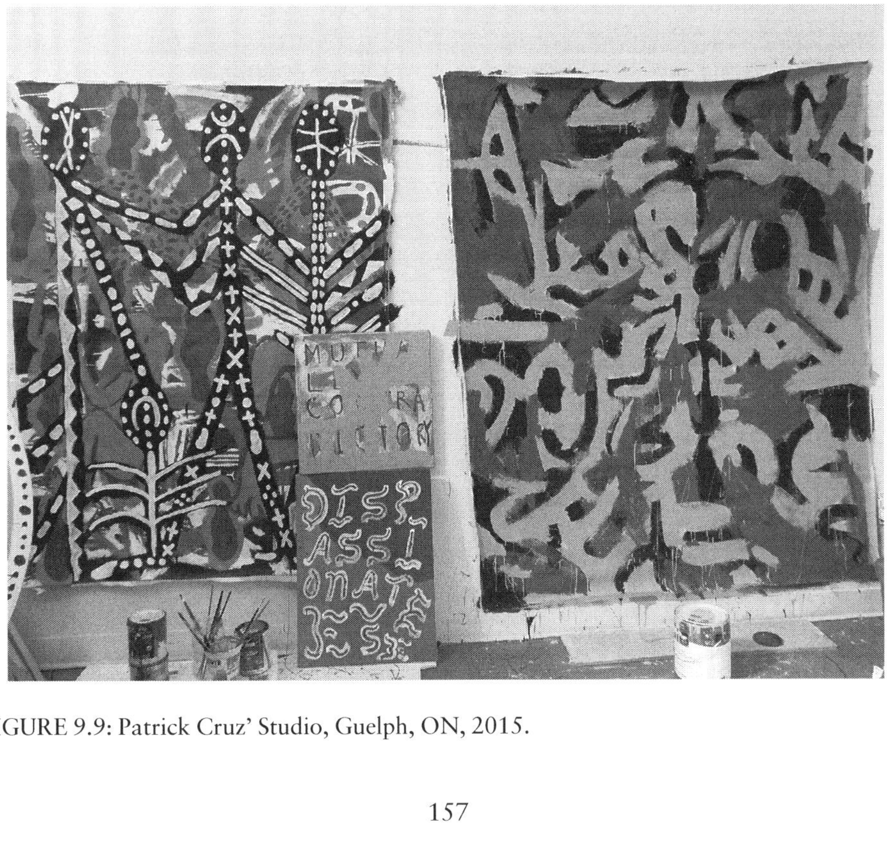

FIGURE 9.9: Patrick Cruz' Studio, Guelph, ON, 2015.

At that time, Cruz was reading about cultural displacement and transnationality as it relates to his experiences as an immigrant from the Philippines. He was also interested in prehistoric cave paintings and its relationship to his current painting practice.

> *I've been looking at painting as an anachronistic medium. It is an old medium that is still used today, and we're trying to revive it and see what it can do. I'm interested in cave paintings because they still don't know what it's for. Some people say it's used for magical purposes or to increase bounty for hunting, or just to document. But I like their basic formal attributes. They're so direct and so clear but so ambiguous.*

Cruz explained that an interest in folk art aesthetics is also a political position, a decolonization of what is considered good taste and what is considered contemporary art. Placing folk art in an institutional context was challenging a colonized point of view. While he doesn't make overtly political work, for him, making art in and of itself is political.

> *How do I form things? How do I define things? I call this a painting instead of a sculpture. That's political to shift an ontological experience of something. For me cultural displacement comes from borrowing different patterns, different visual languages and putting them in a blender. I think that displaces a lot of things. So, it's this idea of scavenging the excess of our culture and putting them together. I think collage has probably been the most influential medium for me after painting. Because it already speaks to displacement. When we tear something and put it in a different place, it changes the context.*

For Cruz, ambiguity is significant in both his intentions and its reception.

> *Ambiguity connects to the idea of transnationalism. For me, ambiguity is a strategy in art. It prolongs the seduction. Ambiguity of shape, of material, ambiguity of meaning. Sometimes I don't even know what I make. So, it makes it even more evident that it's ambiguous. I know my intentions are to transmit my story, my experience. But the takeaway for others; there is a mix. Some think it's a violent response. Some people think it's a happy feeling. Some think it's a threat. Maybe it anchors to that idea of ambiguity too. It doesn't know what it's trying to transmit in terms of an emotional response. But I like that. Some people say art can change the world. Art is not that different than activism. It's just a tool for generating a sense that something is existing, this issue exists and so we talk about it. But activism alone can't cure something. And art alone can't.*
>
> *Art has the capacity to slow down time. I think it has the capacity to distill a thought and examine it in a way that no other place can offer.*

SECTION 3

CONCLUSION: CREATE SPACE FOR MANY POSSIBLE TRAJECTORIES

In society today, particularly in the post-COVID-19 era, with the increase of online education and the celebration of digital platforms, I contend that it is ever more important to recognize the significance of learning within the materiality of a studio space. William Kentridge (2016) addresses how ideas emerge, develop, and generate new ideas through being in the studio:

> Walking, thinking, stalking the image. Many of the hours spent in the studio are hours of walking, pacing backwards and forwards across the space gathering the energy, the clarity to make the first mark. It is not so much a period of planning as a time of allowing the ideas surrounding the project to percolate, a space for many different possible trajectories of an image, of a sequence, to suggest themselves, to be tested as internal projections.
>
> (p. 22)

Through examining the materiality and the affective relations formed through studio work, I propose that a studio classroom similarly embraces materiality, intimacy, and embodiment.

Springgay and Rotas (2015) ask how a classroom may operate like a work of art. Drawing from '"new materialism" or Deleuzian-informed methodologies' (p. 552), they view artmaking as 'a way of thinking about art as an affective event that has the capacity to invent new relations and new ways of learning' (p. 552). Challenging dominant methodologies that privilege linguistic and discursive discussions of art, they align with new materialist methodologies that recognize the role of matter and space in learning. For Springgay and Rotas, framing a classroom as a work of art is based on the premise that art is a relational event: 'When art is understood materially, as an affective event, it becomes irreducible to function, form, and technique. It becomes a force of relations that makes learning felt and inarticulable' (p. 554). To re-imagine the classroom as a work of art is to view learning as relational and affective wherein the students, the classroom, and the art are interactive. Through this lens, education is an emergent event, wherein learning happens relationally, experimentally, and materially. Moreover, this framework recognizes the ecologies of art practice and the ecologies of learning.

Continuing this discussion about the relationality of learning, Springgay (2022) argues that similar to the messiness of art practice, education is messy, emergent, and unpredictable.

> Departing from the view that art is work done by an artist to predictable materials, or that the classroom is capable of being shaped by a teacher, a *classroom as a work of art* renders art and pedagogy in an ever-evolving entanglement of mutating coemergence and co-composition ... artist-teacher-student-classroom become a creative assemblage replete with the potential to open itself to future creative instances. If a classroom operates as a work of art – not as an object manipulated from the outside but as a spatiotemporal site of cocreation – it becomes enmeshed and enlivened with potential future worldings.
>
> (p. 4, original emphasis)

Further, she emphasizes the bodily and intimate process of both learning and artmaking, a stance that posits 'intimacy as a necessary source of disruption' (p. 7) within an education system in 'an era of increasing neoliberal reforms, the corporatization of the university and of education' (p. 7) that emphasizes measurable objectives to assess and value pedagogy. Springgay's emphasis on intimacy and relationality with regard to both individual studio practices and studio classrooms is a radical proposition that brings with it a sense of hope for an education that embraces connection and feeling. She says: 'In articulating research-creation as a practice of intimacy, I am holding space to be touched by the thinking-making-doing of research-creation, as well as the bodies (human and nonhuman) that co-compose the research encounter' (p. 11).

Within a world and education system with an increasing shift towards online learning, I believe it is necessary to consider and understand the materiality of a classroom and the creative ecosystem that emerges through artmaking. Through examining a studio as an intimate and affective space I similarly ask how a 'radical pedagogy is conditioned by what I call feltness, a practice of intimacy' (Springgay, 2022, p. 7) and how a studio may be the site for a 'speculative pedagogy' (Ellsworth, 2005) that embraces affective relations. Through the lens of feltness, messiness, and intimacy I offer up the following propositions for studio thinking through making: Embrace the messiness of materials, making, and learning; Recognize the feeling and sensing body within artmaking; Invite intimacy into learning.

SECTION 4

STUDIO AS DIALOGUE WITH THE WORLD: EMBRACE ART AS A VEHICLE TO UNDERSTAND OUR PLACE IN THE WORLD

In a studio visit in Toronto with artist and professor, Emmanuel Osahor in 2022, he addressed how the studio is essentially at the core of learning through art:

> *I feel that the goal of a studio art education is not actually about the art, but is about the studio. To teach people to be in the studio and to see it as a generative space of production and questioning and searching and finding and elation and anger and frustration. Whatever that space looks like for you, how do you cultivate this space you can go to and make these things happen? The work reflects the space it's being made in.*

The past several years have marked a significant shift within education, shaped by a move toward increased digital and online learning. Within this shifting educational landscape, I believe it is essential to examine the significance of learning within physical and material spaces that exist within a particular time and place and are part of an ecology of learning. And I propose that a studio, as an active, material space of making, is an ideal site to recognize the materiality of learning. Moreover, as Canada and other countries face housing crises, studio spaces are rapidly disappearing from cities due to unaffordability, affecting artists' abilities to find places to work and depriving cities of the vibrant energy that a studio culture may bring to a city. Thus, I return to the questions originally posed in this book: '*What happens in a studio? And how is a studio a way of thinking?*' as a means of examining the broader implications of arts-based learning as a way of understanding our relationship to the world and the roles of art in society.

Through an emphasis on process over product, professor of education, Gert Biesta (2018) argues that 'the educated is not a thing or a product, but a human being with an altered outlook' (p. 13) and through a shift in perspective toward the '*existential quality* of what and who is being expressed' art may guide us toward how to exist 'individually collectively, *in* the world and *with* the world' (p. 14, original emphasis). He argues for an education that is world-centred, suggesting that society is stuck in an instrumentalization of art education and creativity. Instead, he proposes that art education develops a dialogue with the world and that through this world-centred approach, art education allows one to live differently. Throughout this final section, I discuss how art education allows us to understand and re-imagine our relationship with the world as I propose that a studio art education may stand in contrast to increasing tendencies in higher education towards standardization and digitization through its focus on materiality and relationality. Moreover, through the messiness of studio processes, where experimentation, play, and questioning thrive, I argue that artmaking processes may open up ways of learning differently or unlearning ingrained ways of learning. Ayliffe and Mieves (2016) examine the ways studio-based classrooms may disrupt standardized and objective-driven approaches to education. They argue that there is an inherent contradiction within education between the emergent and foregrounding of practice-led approaches to education, while at the same time the reality of higher education that is focused on distinct learning outcomes. They argue that this educational framework does not provide the environment for studio-based disciplines. Through an examination of a study performed through a week-long studio-based painting program, they highlight the qualities of studio-based learning:

> What became apparent … is that fundamental ideas such as providing a personalized studio space, encouraging the experimental handling of materials, allowing the students time to test, mess up, fail, play and develop an individually negotiated art practice have all been effectively sidelined by both educational rhetoric, its systemizing structures and much contemporary art practice and criticism … What we have

> seen is a gradual erosion of art school teaching pedagogies and methods and we are now in a position where fine art and creative education is so warped by the outcome-driven and employability agendas of the current institution that we need to consider what we have lost that is so integral to maintaining this creative 'ecosystem'.
>
> (p. 53)

They address the ongoing critique and skepticism of the individualized art studio that emerged through postmodern discourse while suggesting that within the context of the institution today, the studio may resist standardized approaches to learning through its emphasis on the relationship between individual learning within a community of learners. Their work asks that we continue to investigate these personalized and experiential approaches to learning within the studio.

I begin this section through a discussion of the concept of 'unlearning' as a way of both leaning into failure and the unknown while also questioning what we think we know about learning and how we know what we know (Dunne, 2016). Through the lens of unlearning, I propose that studio art education may disrupt 'established states of pedagogical knowledge' (Atkinson, 2013, p. 138) through the process of searching, experimenting, and working with materials. Thus, art education as a process of unlearning may challenge assumptions about learning (Baldacchino, 2019). Next, I explore how a studio may be a prompt for the imagination as it allows for us to imagine different ways of viewing ourselves and the world we inhabit through an ongoing dialogue between fact and fiction, invention and storytelling. Lastly, I examine how a studio, rather than an isolated room separate from the world, actively engages with the world as I ask artists about the role and impact of artmaking in their lives. Through the lens of Biesta (2018) who argues for a world-centred approach to art education, I propose that artmaking is a dialogue with the world that has real effects on how we live with the world. Further, I propose that studio art education is a unique and integral way of learning through unlearning dominant tendencies within education and re-examining how we live in the world. Through this section, I ask the following questions:

> How does 'unlearning' as a lens for studio practice allow us to both lean into the messiness of material practice and question how we know what we know?
> How might we view studio practice as a prompt for the imagination?
> How does a studio create a dialogue with the world that allows us to live differently?

10

Change Your Relations to the World (Studio as Unlearning)

> *Unlearning calls on us to shake things up, to shake it off, to philosophize with a hammer, to take a leap of faith into the abyss of nonknowledge; it calls on us to let go, to fail, to fail again, for better or for worse.*
>
> (Dunne, 2016, p. 13)

Prisons of Thinking

In her studio in Toronto, in 2022, Monica Tap discussed how her work had changed in response to the world, particularly as it relates to social, political, and environmental issues that had become increasingly urgent. Regarding this shift, she said:

> *I think things that were not being questioned, that needed to be questioned, are on the table in a way that has made things more interesting and urgent. And if any of those big questions are present here in my studio, it's probably climate change. These are not political paintings, but if I'm thinking about this activity of constructing a landscape out of pre-existing parts, it is as if we're trying to remember what was there or how we can keep it from falling apart. Landscape and nature are not a stable thing, it's all in flux.*

Tap addressed how art, as a dialogue with the world, may prompt us to rethink and question how we know what we know. As a concept and philosophical lens within education, 'unlearning' is a way of leaning into failure and the unknown while also questioning what we think we know about learning (Dunne, 2016). For Dunne, 'unlearning' is not simply the opposite of learning but is instead a way of thoughtfully considering how we come to know what we know. Dunne argues that unlearning confronts us to question how we know and embrace the unknown as he says:

> Unlearning is not into learning *out*comes; it's into learn-ing *in*comes. It's into the incoming of the unforeseen, the truly monstrous, the advent of all those wholly others turning up at our doorsteps unexpectedly and demanding our hospitality. Unlearning is *in*to the risk of intrusion and insemination, the insolent overcoming of the known knowns in favour of the *in*-coming of the unknown knowns.
>
> (p. 14, original emphasis)

In his essay 'Un-What?', Jacques Rancière (2016) similarly asks what is at stake within education when we focus on the knowns. Through his examination of ways of learning, he pushes against a presumption that there is '*one* point from which we must start and one definite order that we must follow to acquire knowledge in the right way' (p. 26, original emphasis). I propose that through its materiality which disrupts predefined outcomes, a studio sets the conditions for 'unlearning'. Thus, a studio is a site of 'unlearning' as materials and unexpected processes will always confront the maker, thus disrupting a particular way of learning that relies on pre-planned outcomes and instead generates unexpected directions. To emphasize 'unlearning' as a studio practice means to dwell within the doubt, frustration and uncertainty that is inevitably a part of studio practice. Dunne (2016) captures the hope of unlearning by celebrating the surprises that emerge. It is a particular way of engaging with thinking:

> To love thinking, to speak *philo*sophically, means to love the surprise of thought. It means to be in love with the unsettling *in*sistence of unlearning. To really love learning means opening yourself up to the event and to the hope that something might come to help you stage the becoming of another you and another us.
>
> (p. 17, original emphasis)

I engage with 'unlearning' within art education as a recognition of the ways that we have been taught and how that has influenced how we think about artistic pedagogies, both conceptually and materially. Unlearning is about letting go of a particular way of learning that aligns with pre-planned outcomes with the goal of progressively moving towards mastery. Unlearning in this way constantly disrupts habitual ways of learning. Furthermore, unlearning means asking ourselves how we know what we know and the lenses through which we have come to know what we know. Moreover, through the lens of unlearning, I examine how studio art practice and studio art education challenge widespread understandings of learning. Art educator Dennis Atkinson (2013) argues that embracing the unknown allows for resistance to dominant discourses and practices of learning that emphasize knowable outcomes and rigid frameworks. Atkinson argues for a 'pedagogy of the event' that may 'expand our grasp of what it *is* to learn and lead to the possibility of forming more effective learning communities' (p. 139, original emphasis). He suggests that real learning 'involves a disruption of established states of pedagogical knowledge and practice through which learners are recognized but through which such recognition may also be constraining' (p. 138). Moreover, he proposes that learning and learners are in an ongoing state of becoming and emergence. He makes a distinction between real learning that moves learners into a 'new ontological space' and opens 'pedagogic spaces to the truth of learning encounters and events', and normative learning 'which comprises much of the daily procedures of learning, teaching and assessment' (p. 140). Atkinson contends that learning is an event that opens us up to new possibilities.

In his studio in Toronto, in 2014, John Brown (Figures 10.1–10.4) discussed his ongoing process of creating, erasing, and revealing. For Brown, painting and then scraping away layers of paint is a continual process of editing and an ongoing exchange between his internal life, the materiality of the paint, and his responses to the world. Throughout the years, Brown had been drawn to photographs

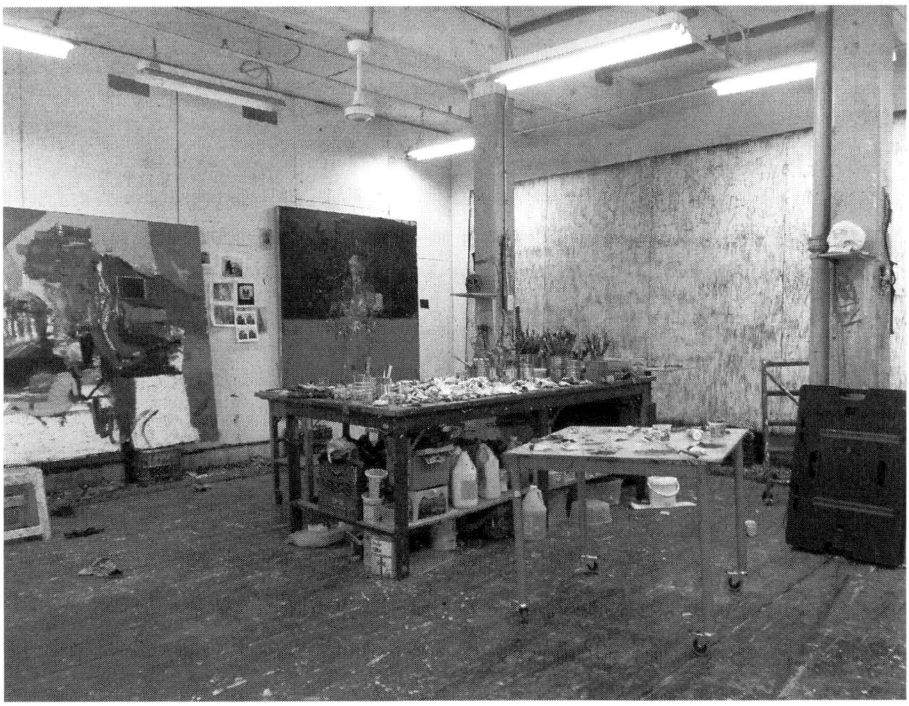

FIGURE 10.1: John Brown's Studio, Toronto, ON, 2014.

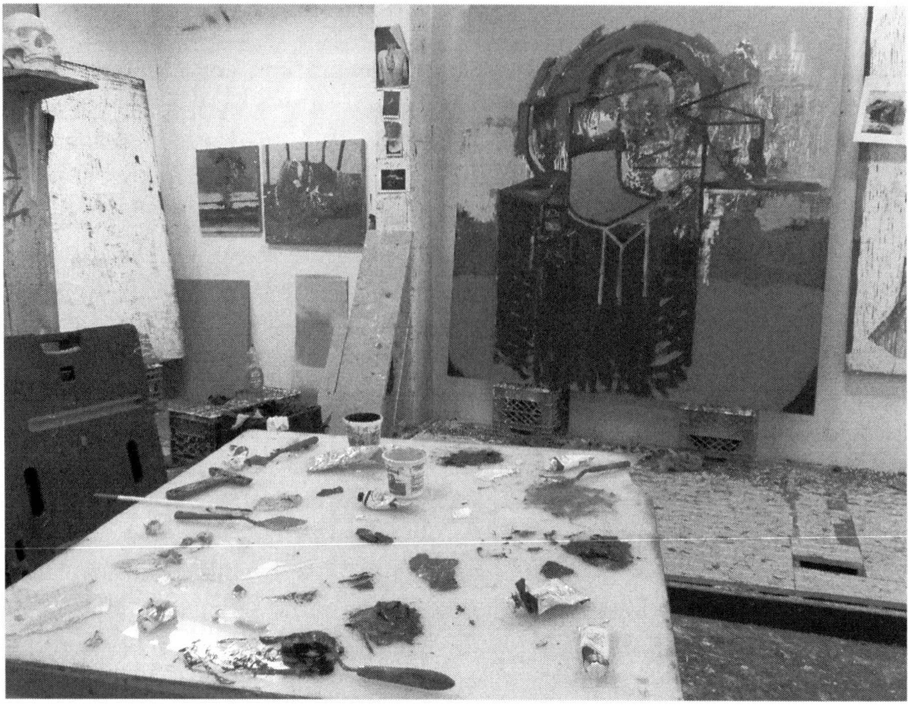

FIGURE 10.2: John Brown's Studio, Toronto, ON, 2014.

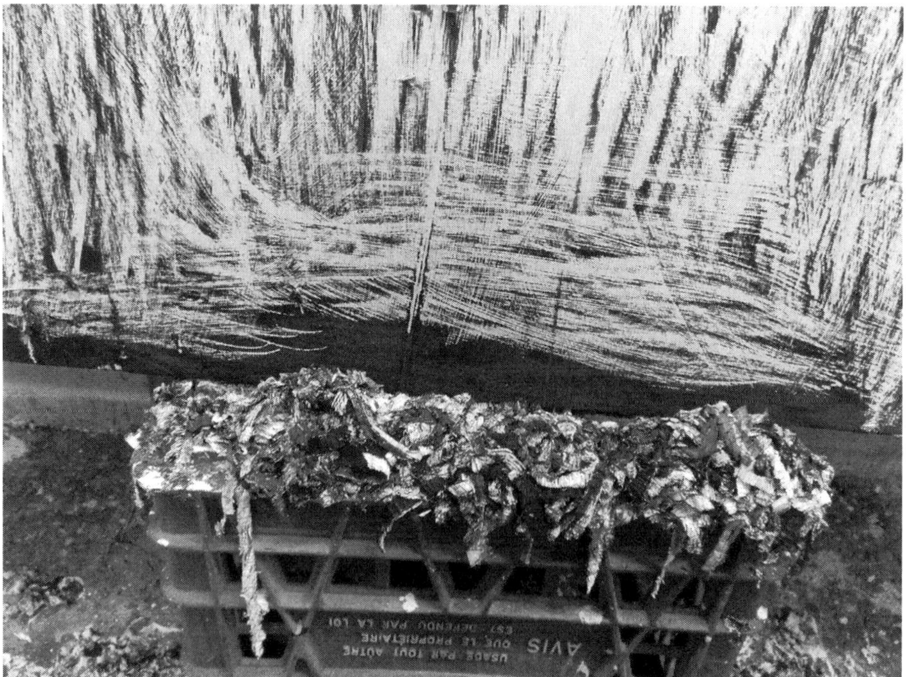

FIGURE 10.3: John Brown's Studio, Toronto, ON, 2014.

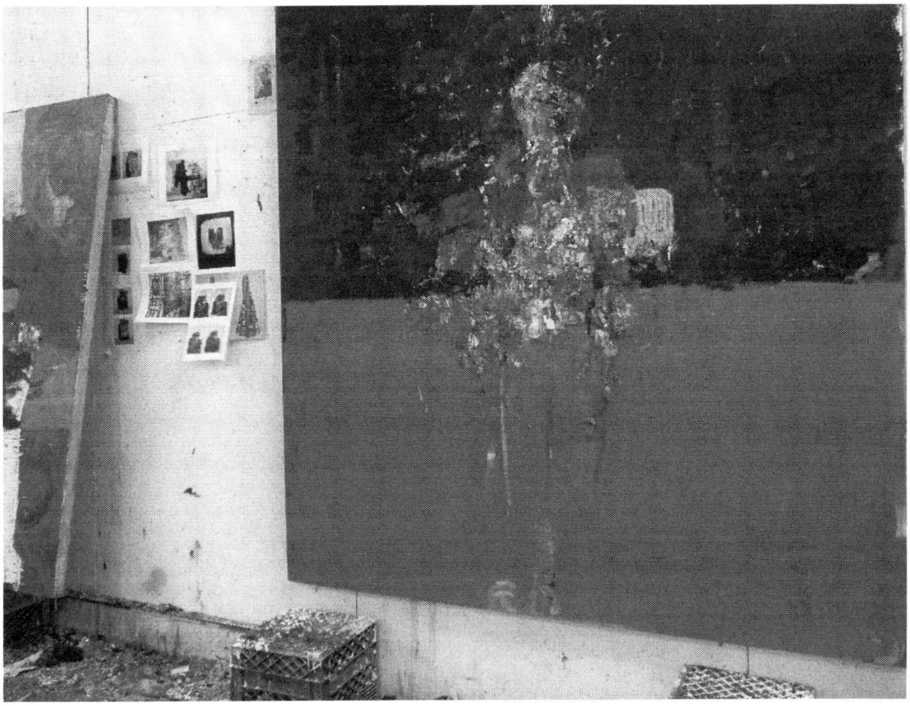

FIGURE 10.4: John Brown's Studio, Toronto, ON, 2014.

from a variety of sources. His process involved painting images and then scraping them off until only abstracted traces of the image remain. In his studio, there were wood scrapings covering the floor as traces of his process. Regarding the scraping process, he said:

> *For me it's a form of drawing. Really early on in my career I had to make a painting for a show. I didn't have a lot of money, but I had some oil paint someone had given me. And I did all this stuff, painting figures, and I didn't like what I did because I didn't know what I was doing with the oil paint. So, I scraped it off. And I liked what that did. So, it went from just the kind of scraping where you could see a lot of the layers of paint coming through, to where it was almost all scraped off. And now it's starting to come back around.*
>
> *The way I paint is really about editing. The scraper is an editor. Scraping allowed me to make the paintings I want to make. It's a balance of getting caught up in the process and wanting to make something that has meaning. The thing I love about painting is that I look at them and I say to myself, 'I made those', but then the next thing I think is 'I don't remember how'. I don't remember how they come about.*

> *I sometimes wonder if how they do come about is that I'm trying to remember the image or the painting and it's kind of on the edge of my consciousness. It's hard to talk about painting because it's one of the ways of making art that can be very improvisational. There are all these things coming in from the side all the time. Sometimes you'll do something and realize later why you did it. And not even what you were thinking about, but something you had seen kind of leaks into it. Paintings have a lot of leakage in and out of them.*

Brown's process of adding and erasing evokes a feeling of searching and discovery through the act of removing an image. He addressed the psychological impact of the process.

> *I think there was a thing about making something and then covering it up and then removing it all the time. I think the early work was all about the inside of the body. It was partly about that, about this hidden body, and about hiding something, then revealing it, then freaking out about revealing it and then hiding it again. But that's embedded in the process. That's a part of what the work is, but I don't know if it's about that. Artwork has a lot of complex meanings and that's it's real value.*

Art educator John Baldacchino (2018, 2019) makes a case for art as a process of unlearning:

> Unlearning is crucial in how representation takes on artistic form by which students unlearn what they come with into the studio – that is, the presumed image of things and what they should be – so that they would then understand what is in front of them. The crucial point of unlearning is how this process of *representation* (which is very different form *imitation*) allows students to critique and articulate what they see, so that reality becomes something they *make*.
>
> (2018, p. 138, original emphasis)

Through this lens, studio practice is an ongoing process of making and remaking one's own learning. Baldacchino (2018) makes a distinction between 'unlearning *in* art' which makes a case for '*education through the arts*' and 'art as unlearning', which he says makes a case for art education (p. 138, original emphasis). Thus, for him, a large part of the value of art education, is that it involves a process of unlearning. And through this process, art as unlearning 'challenges the assumption that we have held about learning' (Baldacchino, 2019, p. v). Viewed through this lens, unlearning is a state of being and does not mandate moving towards knowable goals, but is instead a space in which to dwell. It doesn't lead to resolution, but instead 'unlearning is here understood to be a continuous way of doing and being' (2019, p. ix). Baldacchino posits that considering art as unlearning is to embrace unlearning as a process of making that resists more normative forms of learning.

> To claim that art is equivalent to unlearning is an invitation to forget those taught dispositions by which we have been hoodwinked into the fallacy of certainty, be it expressed through the premises of a foundational tradition or as a sense of continuous progress by which we have developed our habits of making, doing and knowing. Unlearning the certainties by which we were schooled also urges us to exit into a wider world of possibilities. To do so, we have to embrace paradox, as we seek to unlearn what we know without presuming to relearn other certainties or find new canons on which we would secure a measurable outcome.
>
> (p. xii)

In Montreal, 2014, Cynthia G. Renard discussed the role of play and imagination within learning in a studio. They remembered being a child and building fantasy worlds as they thought about the importance of their studio as a way of thinking and being in the world: '*You play alone and you invent worlds. A rock becomes an island and you feel you're on a sea and you can't jump down because there are sharks. Painting is like a game.*' They said that as a child they always wanted a hidden room to hide in. Today, they similarly consider a studio to be a hiding place, '*une cachette*'. They are very nomadic, moving studios often.

> *It's so much freedom. I'm afraid of becoming stalled if I stay too long in one place. It generates a new energy when I move. So, I tend to move a lot. It's a way of thinking and a way of life.*

G. Renard had recently had an exhibition, *Unicorns and Dictators* at the Esker Foundation Gallery in Calgary. The show is described:

> At first blush Cynthia G. Renard's work is a candy-coated world of animals, birds, and simple political slogans: cute but not threatening. But do not be fooled: G. Renard uses colour, pattern, and the reassuring forms of small beasts to disarm. On closer look this work deals in class struggle, social utopias, and the game of politics and power.
>
> (Esker Foundation, 2014)

Through complicated webs of meaning, their work engages with their inner worlds, fantasy, and their frustrations with politics through the lens of dystopia and utopia. They discussed these frustrations by addressing why they make art:

> *Because I can change my relations to the world. I try to create a world where I would want to live. And I can only do it in art. I'm quite limited in the normal world. In the arts I can create another balance of powers, and it makes sense to me. Or create balance in a different way. To mix girl bedrooms with politics, with sexuality, with Utopias, which are all supposed to be separate. And it mixes it with emotion. It brings another order. I think politics should not be reserved for specialists only, so I want to bring it back with the imagination.*

Addressing education and politics, G. Renard related a particular kind of thinking that emerges in their studio that connects artmaking to a way of being in the world. For them, the act of making is itself political. They lamented the way emotion is removed from learning experiences and how binaries and separations exist within learning.

> *People tend to separate everything to think. If they want to think properly, they have to separate politics, sexuality, dreaming. And at the end you think in boxes. It doesn't make sense in the world. We separate one knowledge from the other. Everything has closed itself off. It's bizarre. It's like prisons of thinking.*

Speak Back to History

In 2022, I went to see an exhibition by artist Denyse Thomasos at the Art Gallery of Ontario that showcased her career as an artist before her untimely death in 2012. As a Canadian who had immigrated from Trinidad, Thomasos' work is characterized by abstracted and layered images that reference cages and enclosures, and ways that African diaspora have been contained such as prisons, slave ships, and other architectural spaces. Abstraction allowed for complexity and nuance to address these themes through painting. In an accompanying catalogue, one of the curators of the exhibition, Michelle Jacques addressed her personal interest in Thomasos' work. In the publication about Thomasos' exhibition, Jacques wrote an essay titled 'Moving towards loving painting again, or Dear Denyse' (2022) that includes letters written at various phases of her career as she finds affinities between her own experiences and those of Thomasos. In her 1993 excerpt, Jacques described her frustrations that she had experienced in an art seminar that focused on only formalist analysis of painting rather than cultural experiences. Addressing Thomasos, Jacques says: 'It was such a relief to encounter your work. I don't think I could have borne the assumption that good painting must be content-free any longer, an idea that belies the origins of art of African Diaspora' (p. 69). In her 1993 and 2007 letters to Thomasos, Jacques examines Thomasos' work through the historical relationship between African history and culture, slavery, diasporic experiences, and Modernism. In her final excerpt in 2022, ten years after Thomasos' passing, Jacques writes:

> It is 10 years since your passing and I'm afraid that the ills of contemporary society have caused the world to catch up to the messages of your work … You created space in painting for those of us who were told it could not hold our histories, interests, or concerns. Thanks to you painting and I found each other again.
>
> (p. 83)

Through Thomasos' work, Jacques challenges readers to recognize the inclusions and exclusions within the histories of art as we were taught, and whose stories were untold when painting was solely spoken of through a formalist lens, through means that deny our relationships and experiences in the world.

In a visit with Michelle Peraza (Figure 10.5) in Milton, Ontario in 2022, she reflected on how she addresses complicated colonial histories as a Latin American artist and how that lens shaped her education and studio practice. Peraza reflected on the images she saw growing up and how that shaped how she found her own voice through painting:

> *I feel like as an artist you're a cultural commentator. All I had access to when I was little were Renaissance books from Costco. And I was looking at them and just thinking, I want to see some brown people in this size, this level of realism. So, I thought, this is what I can do to work through this mess of a world.*

Peraza's mother is Cuban and her father is Costa Rican, and as a child growing up in a rural area outside London, Ontario, she remembered spending her childhood hiding out painting her bedroom walls, playing with whatever art materials she could get her hands on. As she developed as an artist, she drew from a Classical Studies background to examine how western thought and aesthetics affected her experience as a Latin American artist. She was particularly drawn to the folds and layers of fabric in Greek sculpture. She focused on high realism, particularly through portraiture. '*The face is so important to me. There is so much that goes into it and so much about your life gets written into your face. I find it very vulnerable.*' In her studio, there were portraits of each of her sisters that she made while part of a mentorship program in Toronto at a Latin American gallery.

> *We were asked to make work about decolonization and disruption. And as a portrait painter, that felt so loaded and I didn't know how to deal with that in one work. So, for me it was about bringing that question first. My family is what I'm really*

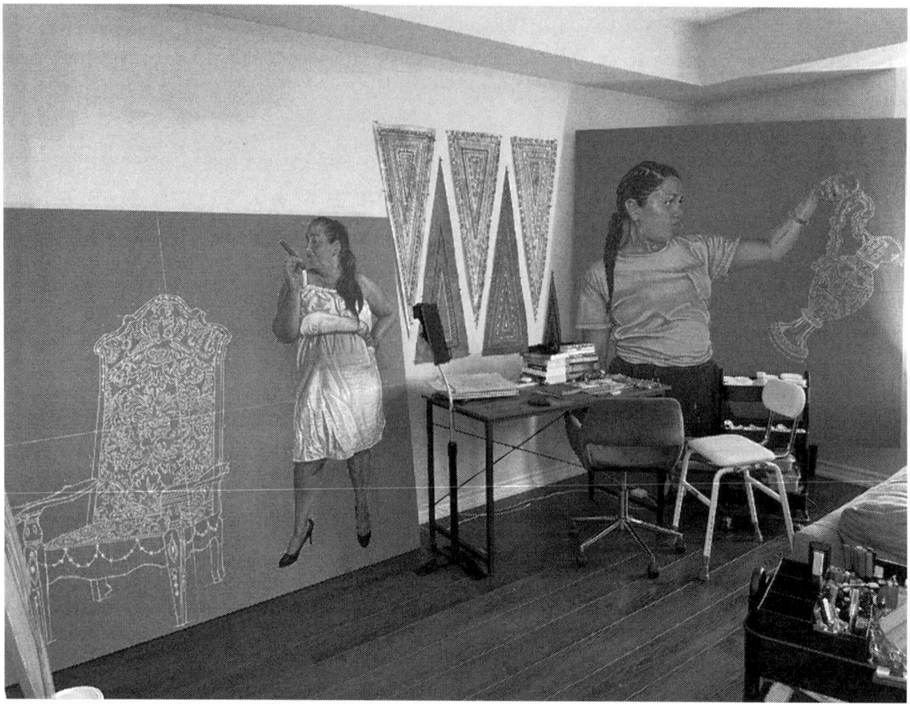

FIGURE 10.5: Michelle Peraza's Studio, Milton, ON, 2022.

> *interested in, so now I was going to look at it from the perspective of our own history, Latin American history, and thinking about the colonial past and putting into question this tension. So, I was thinking about all that had happened with the Indigenous people, all the massacres and diseases and then all that happened with the African slave trade, and then we're also Spaniard. So, it's complicated because we're mixed people, and we identify with both. So, I wanted a tension there.*

For Peraza, skin tone became a way to examine this complexity: '*That whole history that is so loaded comes through our skin. I was just putting a question out, but I don't have an answer ... What does this colonial history mean for the contemporary Latin American person and a painter?*'

Peraza dove into these questions firstly making colour swatches that referenced skin colours and reading about colonial history through a decolonial perspective. She was drawn towards the way that Latin American paintings showed the Spanish influence as they had brought the Baroque style to Latin America; however, it changed as it became intertwined with Indigenous painting styles and imagery. Within the studio, there were two large paintings of Latin American women painted in oil paint, looking at a colonial object drawn in white charcoal, a material that by its nature may be wiped away.

> *Where I'm painting the figure itself, the contemporary Latin American woman is real, but the colonial object is starting to recede. It's charcoal, so it does fall away eventually but the foundation is still very strong. I was interested in having a figure with a face that's really pushing back against a colonial object. And I thought a lot about what the face means as a political way for a marginalized person to push back. I started off with questions about how to deal with it because we also are both the colonizer and the colonized. We have both identities. How can I even see these two ways of thinking and being? There is a loaded history, but they still co-exist in a mixed person. So, I looked at a lot of Baroque paintings that were made and housed in Spain and I took patterns that I was pulling from paintings. But I was also bringing in Mesoamerican patterns. This body of work is critiquing painting and pushing back or speaking back to history. So, it's a co-existence here, but not intertwined. I have no answer, nor do I want one. Identity is not static.*

A Reversal of the Gaze

I visited Cree artist, Kent Monkman (Figures 10.6–10.9) in his studio in Toronto in 2015. In his large paintings, Monkman transforms iconic western history paintings to retell history through the untold Indigenous stories. His paintings insert Indigenous perspectives and experiences into the dominant narratives of the exploration and discovery of North America. Through this work, Monkman addresses how representations of history tell particular stories while omitting others. On one wall of the studio was a mural-sized painting that referenced the nineteenth-century painting *The Raft of the Medusa* by Theodore Géricault which was shown on an image next to the painting. My conversation with Monkman showed the complexity of his relationship to art history as he explained how he could simultaneously embrace and critique historical western European painting. He discussed the tensions he encountered through taking up western history painting to critique colonial lenses of history. Monkman addresses how our engagement with the land is shaped by images of the landscape.

> *Really it was a whole genre of work, paintings of the 19th century where you had American artists and Canadian artists like Paul Kane and George Catlin whose eyes were on Indigenous people and basically giving us the authoritative version of history. So, I realized that art history as it was and how it was perpetuated in the museums was very one-sided. And there were so many historical moments that had*

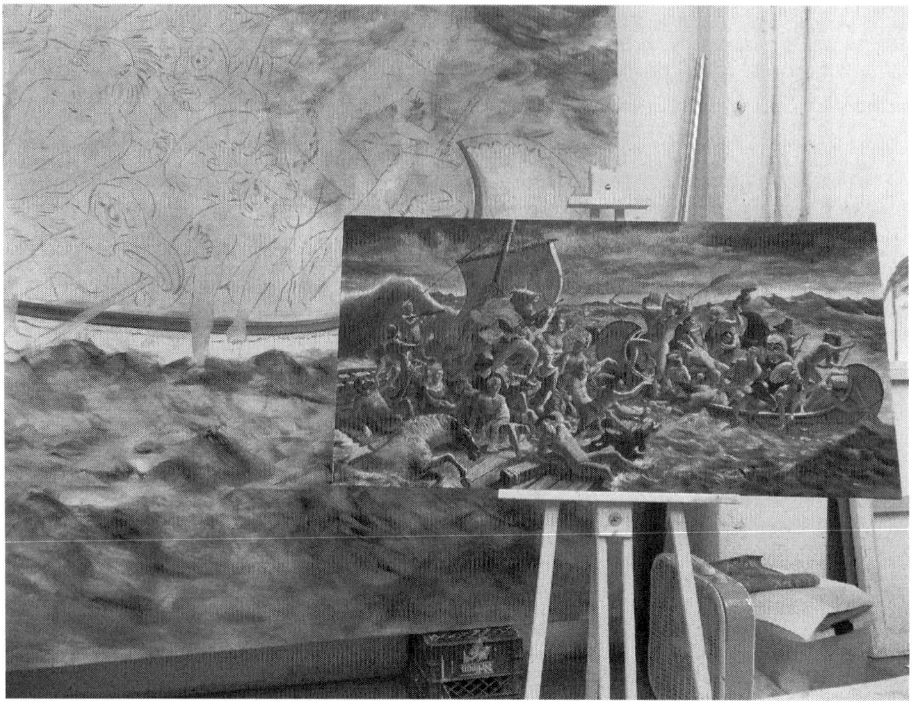

FIGURE 10.6: Kent Monkman's Studio, Toronto, ON, 2015.

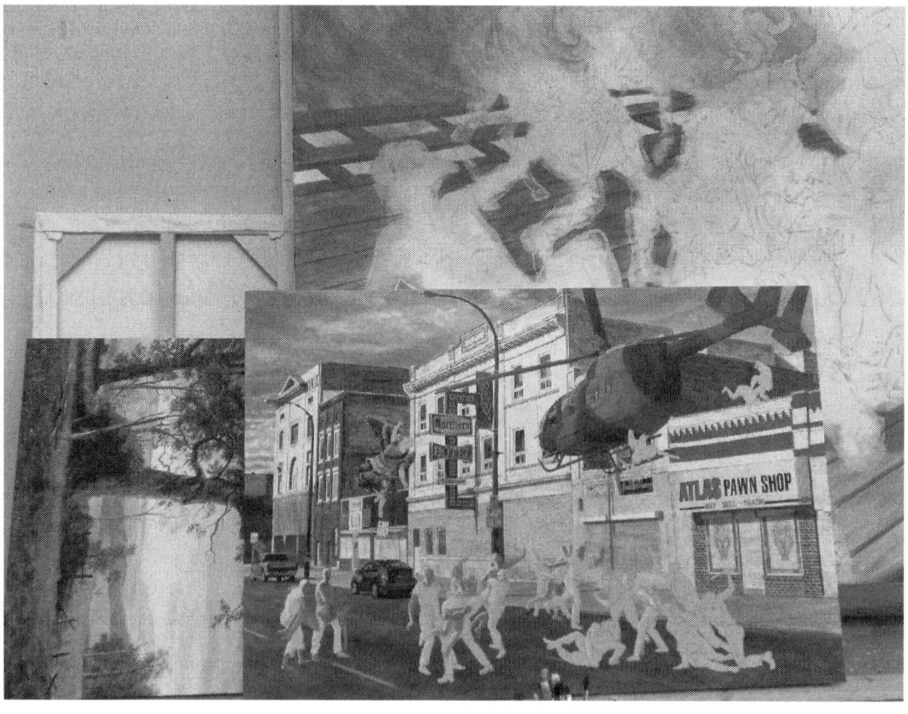

FIGURE 10.7: Kent Monkman's Studio, Toronto, ON, 2015.

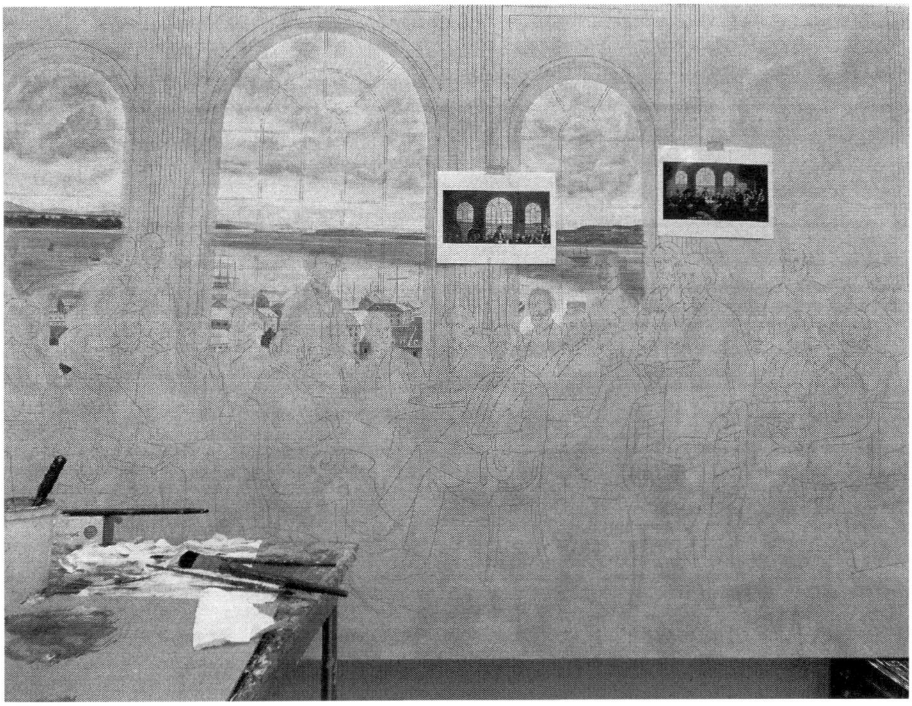

FIGURE 10.8: Kent Monkman's Studio, Toronto, ON, 2015.

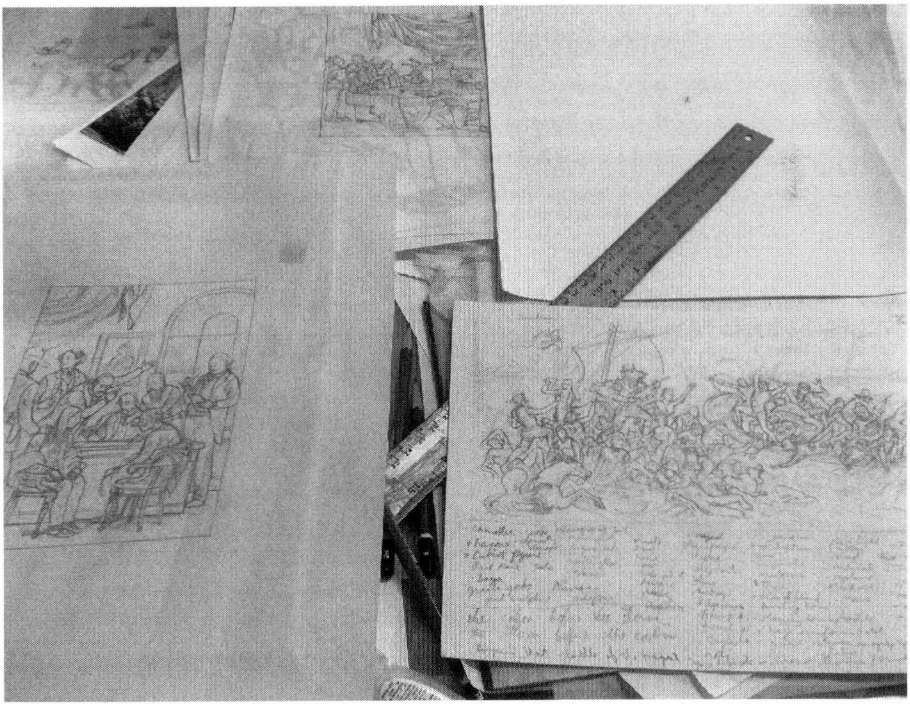

FIGURE 10.9: Kent Monkman's Studio, Toronto, ON, 2015.

> *to do with history from an Indigenous perspective that had essentially been painted out. Then I realized I was tackling not just a deep vast technical challenge, but I was also going into this document of art history and all the museum practice that still supports it. And that was really important for me too, because again as an emerging Indigenous artist, you were instantly categorized and marginalized, because people thought: 'Well, should you be painting this?' So, there were all those preconceived ideas coming at me from all parts of the art world, whether it was museum curators, commercial galleries or wherever. It's less like that now but at the time it was palpable.*

In one area of the studio was the in-progress painting that would be called *The Daddies*, a retelling of Robert Harris' 1884 painting *Meeting of the Delegates of British North America to Settle the Terms of Confederation* which commemorates the 1864 meeting for the Canadian Confederation. In Monkman's version, made for Canada's 150th anniversary, his alter ego, Miss Chief Eagle Testicles sits centre stage inserting an Indigenous queer perspective into the meeting and prompting questions about the history of Canada in relation to Indigenous people.

Monkman's work dissects the fictional lens of history as told through painting, while at the same time proposing how painting can re-tell the story through its capacity to produce fictions. He addressed assumptions about the kind of work he should be doing.

> *Well, people just thought that if you're an Indigenous artist, your work belongs here, so it was more segregated, in terms of audience and, there was not as much room in the contemporary galleries. And then I went through a number of different experiences with public institutions where it was very palpable in terms of how Indigenous people were put in the Indigenous gallery. But for me the most important thing was facing the creative challenge of really wanting to be a better painter and embracing a vocabulary of painting that was as deep and complex as symphonic music, but in the form of painting and that could still be relevant. Could I make it relevant and powerful today with my perspective being Indigenous? They are two ostensibly opposing viewpoints, because there's this Western classical European tradition of painting. But at the same time as I'm critiquing it, I'm also embracing it. So, I think that has been a very interesting position to be in, because it's loaded, that point of contact between cultures is very volatile. There's conflict, there's exchange, so I think my practice was really invigorated by that, by that idea of embracing as opposed to rejecting. And I've heard different Indigenous artists categorically dismiss anything European, any painting tradition, easel painting, or anything. It's like you're going to create work that only comes from one pure pathway of inspiration, and that doesn't make any sense. So of course, European artists were looking at Indigenous artists*

through that period of modernity, and that's what's important in a lot of my recent work, it's how that period of modern art is confused by that outward perspective of Europeans looking at non-Europeans. So, a lot of my work has to do with that reversal of gaze and that reciprocal relationship, that it's never a one-sided thing, of course we're being observed but we were also observing.

11

Threaten to Fall into a Mythological or Fictional Space (Studio as Imaginative)

> *Stories are wondrous in their capacity to reorganize our approaches to our social-material worlds; they are dangerous for their capacity to produce themselves as compelling objects of belief, naturalized, as all too many of us see year in and year out in the classroom, into calcified truths.*
>
> (Loveless, 2019, p. 21)

Create Spaces in Which You Allow Yourself to Imagine

In her book *How to Make Art at the End of the World* about artistic research, Natalie Loveless (2019) examines stories and the possibilities of art to ignite 'our very capacity to speculate, dream and imagine otherwise' (p. 14). Loveless challenges readers to recognize 'the power of stories through which we come to understand the world, and, when necessary, give our all to reorganize them' (p. 22). Art and the stories told through art may prompt us to further understand and examine the worlds in which we live and the worlds in which we may inhabit.

> To say that *stories produce worlds* is not to say that changing stories is an easy practice, nor innocent, nor always possible ... The work of telling new stories, or new versions of stories that need retelling/ recrafting, is propositional; it requires ongoing engagement and a willingness to denaturalize the social, disciplinary, ideological structures within which we are embedded.
>
> (p. 20, original emphasis)

Loveless examines how stories embody and perpetuate worldviews, while also proposing that they have the power to prompt us to imagine differently. She says: 'Curiosity, here, emerges as key to the political capacity of stories to remake worlds' (p. 22). Through this lens, she proposes that artistic research may function through the creation of world-changing fictions that prompt us to review our relationship with the world and imagine new possibilities.

Through her interdisciplinary and participatory practice, Newfoundland-based artist, Philippa Jones (Figures 11.1 and 11.2) examines play, games, and imagination as she explores how we understand our world and construct knowledge. In her studio in St. John's in 2015, we discussed knowledge, exploration, art, imagination, and mythmaking. Jones believes that in society, imagination is pushed aside and even discouraged. Therefore, at the core of her work is a desire to undermine our perception of reality and give people permission to imagine. Jones draws from game theory saying that '*it's much easier to get people to engage with a game than it is to get people to engage with art*'. She observed that when she told people they were playing a game with rules and instructions that they would immediately switch to that role, allowing their realities to shift to the game. Thus,

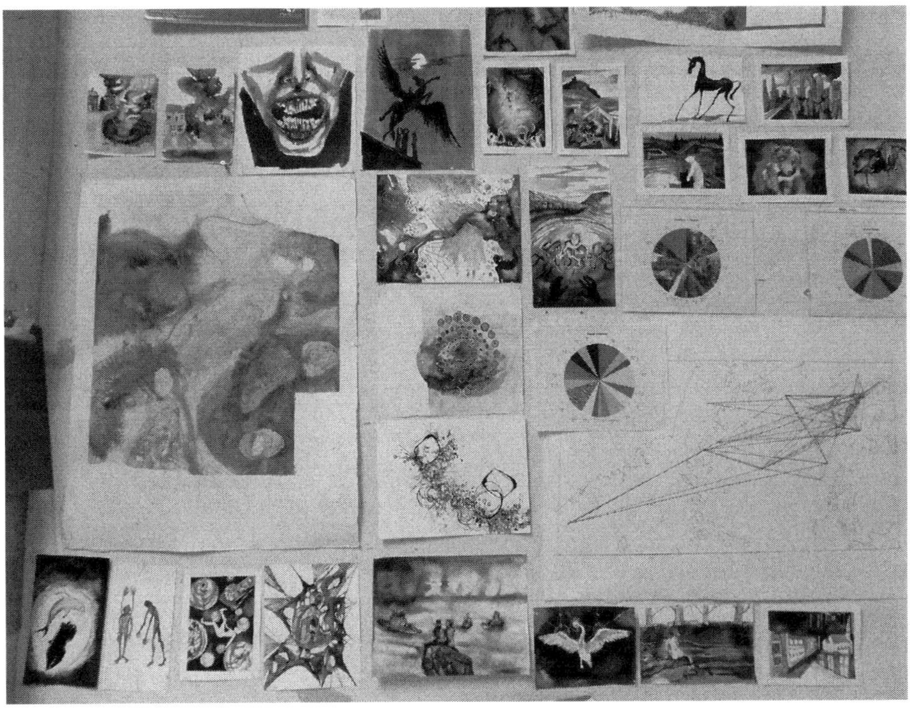

FIGURE 11.1: Philippa Jones' Studio, St. John's, NL, 2014.

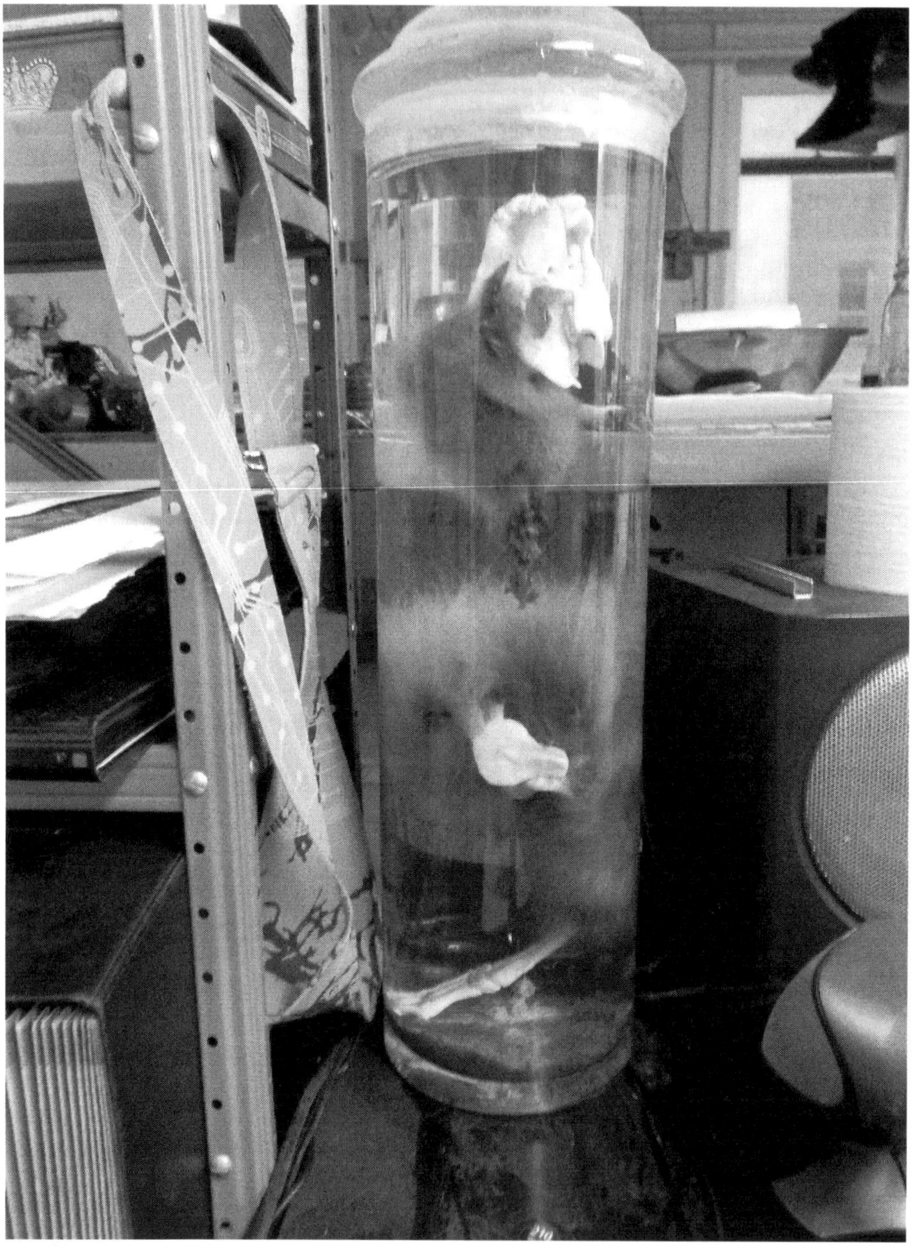

FIGURE 11.2: Philippa Jones' Studio, St. John's, NL, 2014.

a game allowed participants to imagine differently. Through her work, she argues that we must '*create spaces in which we allow ourselves to imagine*'.

To develop her ideas about gaming and imagination, Jones began taking participants on expeditions to an '*undiscovered island*' off the coast of Newfoundland. Participants were each given a different invented job such as geologist, botanist, historian, etc. They had to imagine the island had never been explored, they each had a role, they could bring a kit that supported that role, and they were encouraged to document everything. There weren't rules, but simply a premise through which to enter the imaginary world. They could imagine anything to be true of the place they were exploring, but they needed to have '*evidence*' to back it up. She found that very quickly, participants' individual discoveries began to merge into a collective myth:

> *At first each person's imagination is distinct but what happens is they begin reinforcing each other's. For example, an 'archeologist' discovered the foundations of an ancient temple. And then the 'geologist' said they discovered rocks found in ancient Greece. So maybe this island was a Greek settlement thousands of years ago. And because they are imagining it with 'evidence', it's reinforcing the story. And then someone else explores and it leads back in. And what starts to happen is a narrative is created. It was interesting how people bonded in a specific way. As children you bond because of how you imagine together. In the same way, you could see this other world that they opened up together.*

In the end, Jones merged the myths generated out of four expeditions performed around Newfoundland to create a new myth in an exhibition that featured paintings, drawings, pseudo-scientific displays, and installations. She brought together various strands from the different narratives, including sketches and diagrams drawn from participants' experiences. She used scientific language and aesthetics to mimic a museum exhibition that prompts viewers to examine how they know what they know. For Jones, imagination is a muscle that must be strengthened and practised, otherwise, it will die as we stop creating spaces in which we can imagine. Regarding her belief in imagination and intuition, she exclaimed: '*To comprehend how something works you need to hold it in your imagination.*'

Create a Space for Something to Happen

Simon O'Sullivan (2010) explores the relationship between fact and fiction within art. He develops his theories about myths and stories as a lens through which to engage with histories as a way of reviewing the present. This lens is not an idealization of history nor is it meant to re-state a single narrative, but to recognize how past and present are intertwined. He uses the word *mythopoesis* to describe 'the imaginative transformation of the world through fiction' (p. 203). Through this fictioning, we may produce new myths or stories than the ones in which we don't recognize ourselves. He states: 'When we grasp the world as fiction in this way we begin to "see" the limits of what is seeable/sayable and are thus able to gesture beyond these very limits' (p. 203). Mythopoesis is a form of 'world making', through imagining ways of re-viewing histories, re-shaping the present, and proposing alternative stories and futures. I similarly propose that at its best, most hopeful moments, a studio may also be a 'world-making' place, one that allows for imaginative propositions to prompt viewers to re-engage with the stories they've been told, the stories they've lived, and their hopes for possible futures. Tim Ingold (2021) addresses the binary of imagination and reality and proposes they are intertwined, not separate as he says:

> Imagining for real, in the sense implied here, means setting existence loose amidst the flux of creation. It is a release from confinement which repudiates any separation of mind from body, or of self from world. Here, imagining joins with the real instead of playing off against it.
>
> (p. 4)

Thus, imagination becomes a way of re-engaging with the real and complicating our views of the present through juxtaposing alternative lenses.

Carol Wainio (Figures 11.3 and 11.4) (Ottawa, 2014) connects children's stories with current events as a way of raising questions or generating propositions about the world. She described her painting process as creating a scene and allowing something to happen: '*I'm setting the stage for encounters.*' She will start out with intentions but then something will happen: '*It's part of that play of intent and non-intent.*' There has always been a narrative component to her work, but she asserts that it is not telling a story. Instead, she describes her paintings as propositions. Wainio began being interested in fairy tales when she read them to her young children and observed their first experience with visual images.

> *I was fascinated with that process, interested in how both of my kids' experience of them was almost echoed in and paralleled pre-modern society's apprehension of early images. They were scarce, rare and powerful, as they are for children when they first see them.*

What began within this context snowballed into ten years of Wainio seeking out older versions of fairy tales, seeking out the earliest versions of the stories,

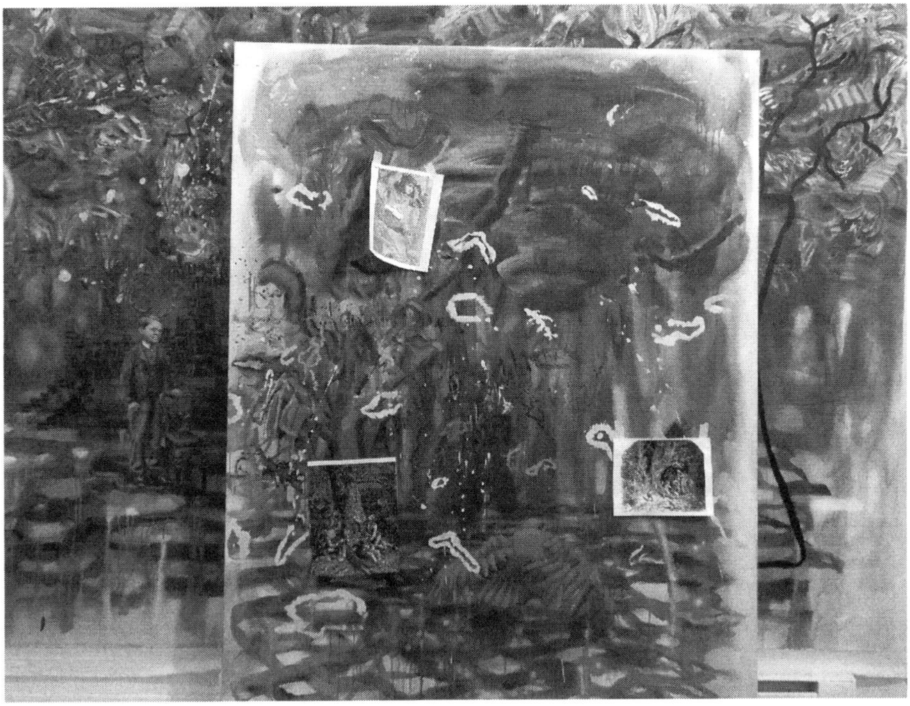

FIGURE 11.3: Carol Wainio's Studio, Ottawa, ON, 2014.

and looking at earlier illustrations, first searching in local libraries and then going to Europe to visit archives with historical illustrations. She told the story of the cat, *Puss and Boots* and how this tale was told and retold. It is a story about an impossible transformation that was set in a time when there was no social mobility. This cat then became a salesman for consumer products in the nineteenth and the twentieth century. Wainio embraced coincidences that would occur as she saw parallels between these stories and contemporary life. For example, she'd been reading about a *Puss and Boots* meeting a seventeenth-century farmer and found parallels in a newspaper article about contemporary farming practices. Through painting, Wainio could bring those connections together in the studio.

> *They start with a place for something to happen. Sometimes I know or think I know what's going to happen, who is going to be meeting who, or what might transpire, or what kind of space I want. I'll have some sense of that, but there will be changes. In a sense, they deal with issues of narrative, but they are not narrative in the sense that you can read them. I don't think there's a possibility for a fixed reading anymore.*

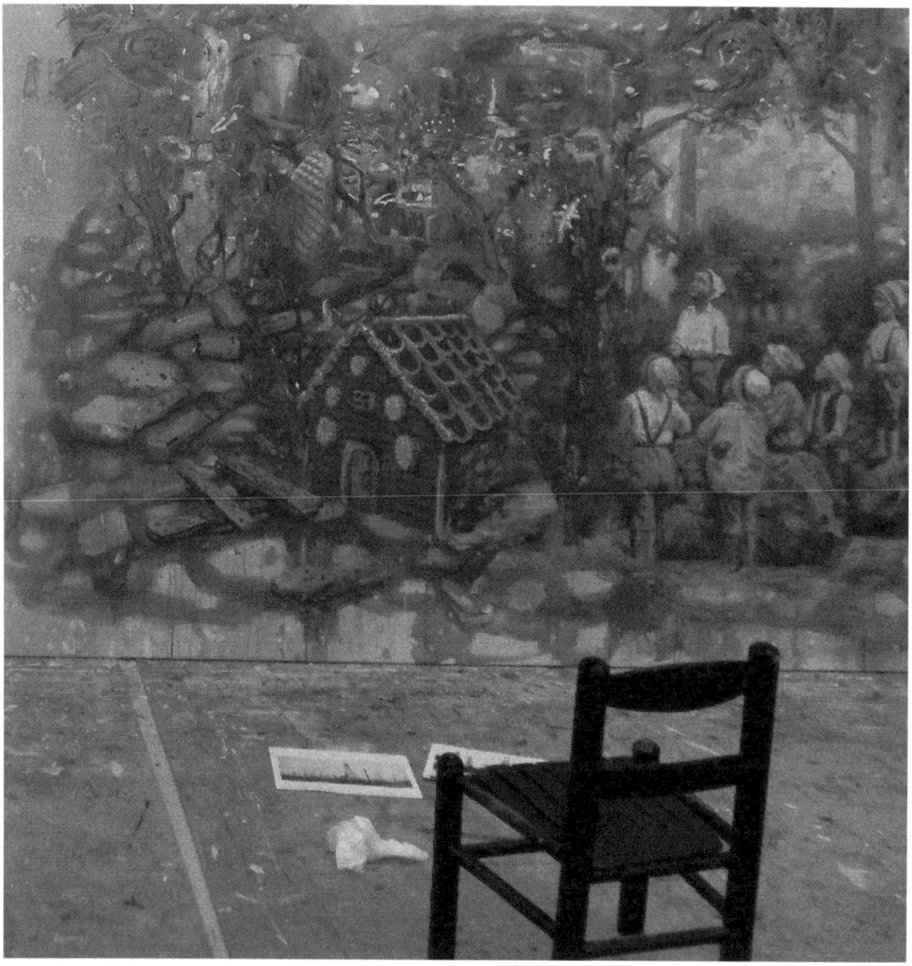

FIGURE 11.4: Carol Wainio's Studio, Ottawa, ON, 2014.

> *So, what happens in them, is that there's a space that gets created, then elements are put into the space to see what they say to each other.*

At the time of our studio visit, there was another painting, with characters that appeared to be *Hansel and Gretel* combined with images of a seventh-grade student's drawing of the greenhouse effect. She explained how she'd combined images from children's books and children's drawings of oil rigs to address climate change, thus merging fact and fiction, past and present.

In her studio in the shed behind her Halifax, Nova Scotia home in 2015, Sara Hartland-Rowe (Figures 11.5 and 11.6) similarly discussed how she draws from

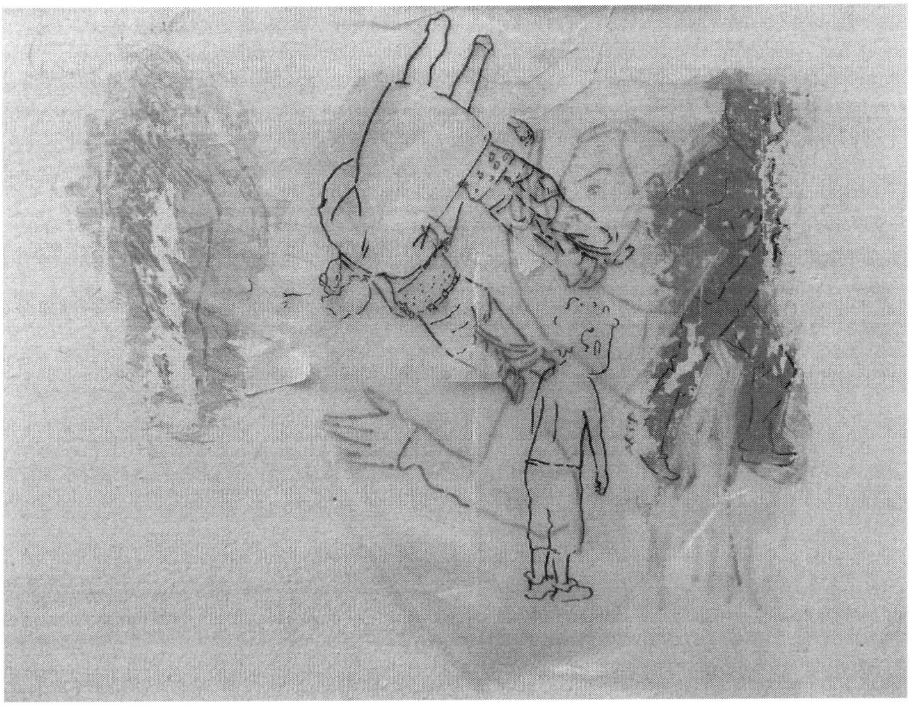

FIGURE 11.5: Sara Hartland-Rowe's Studio, Halifax, NS, 2015.

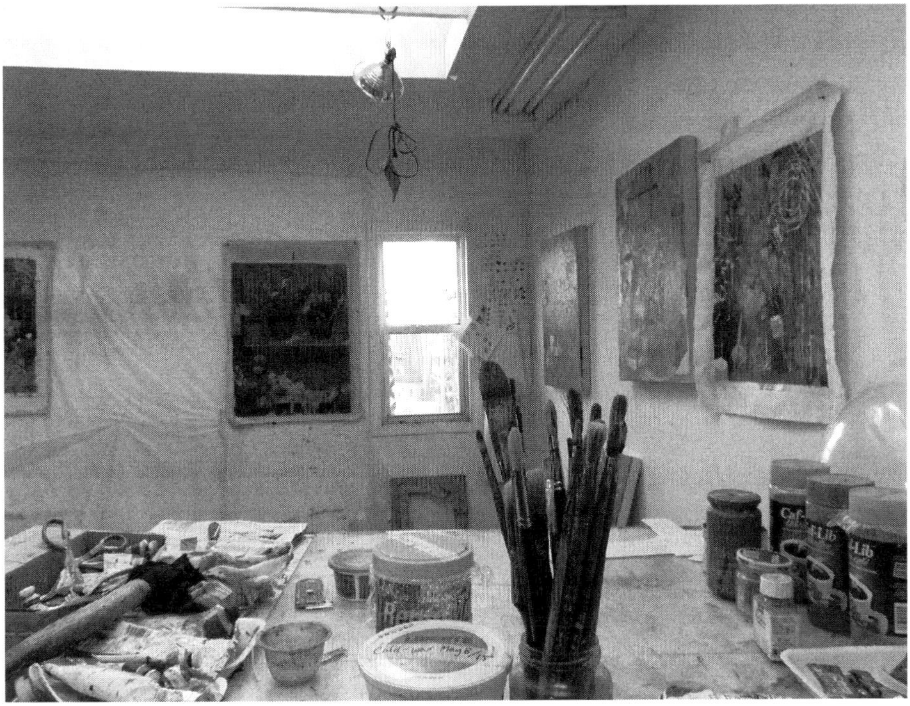

FIGURE 11.6: Sara Hartland-Rowe's Studio, Halifax, NS, 2015.

current events but fictionalizes them to propose multiple narratives and to implicate herself within the story. Her work is characterized by large wall drawings and paintings that contain multiple figures showcasing several small narratives. Along one wall of the studio was a grouping of small drawn figures on transparent paper, cut out and arranged along the wall. Regarding her interest in the figure, she said that as a child she had moved a lot and so as an outsider she would look at people and think '*What do you do?*' and '*How do you do it?*' She would make up narratives as if they were avatars. Rather than seeking out answers or specific directions, Hartland-Rowe said she prefers thinking of her process as following hunches or whims, or curiosities. She became interested in the work of Giotto, a 14th-century Italian artist known for his frescoes, for the stories told within. She was drawn to sub-narratives in a story rather than master narratives, the small interactions that make up people's lives. She described her process:

> *I'd been collecting marginalia from manuscripts, looking at them for little, tiny narrative interactions ... I was told once: 'Your paintings are full of chatter.' And I thought about that. What's chatter? It's the way women talk to each other over the back fence. It's non-consequential, yet it's around us all the time and we all love it. We love those tiny stories. So, I started to look for tiny stories. So, the wall drawing was a whole lot of these tiny moments between one or two figures.*

Hartland-Rowe doesn't believe in overarching narratives but instead believes in tiny narratives, tiny moments. There are common threads between stories but it's the particular way that people are in relationship to those stories that make them interesting. For example, while addressing big themes such as pain and suffering or love and kindness, she is interested in how these themes play out within small interactions. Moreover, her work often addresses ways we implicate ourselves in others' stories. Regarding why she makes art, Hartland-Rowe said:

> *I think it's an interface between me and the rest of the world. I don't think I'm inventing new stuff for the world, but that I can come much closer to the deeper questions I want to answer through art.*

In Winnipeg, Manitoba, Mark Neufeld (Figures 11.7 and 11.8) (2014, 2015) discussed how his paintings address mythologies as he navigates between fact and fiction and prompts viewers to question their relationship to histories. His studio contained objects and paintings related to cowboys and the Wild West. He began this body of work while in Berlin where he learned of a German cowboy novel and delved into fantasies of North America and the Wild West. According to Neufeld, this series is fiction that is also trying to be authentic at the same time.

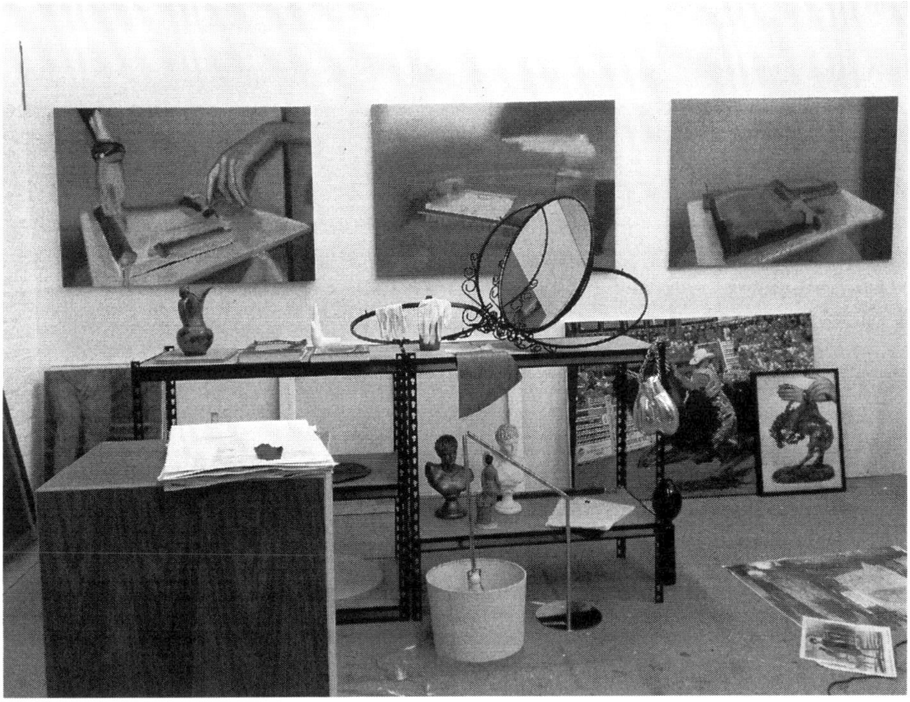

FIGURE 11.7: Mark Neufeld's Studio, Winnipeg, MN, 2014.

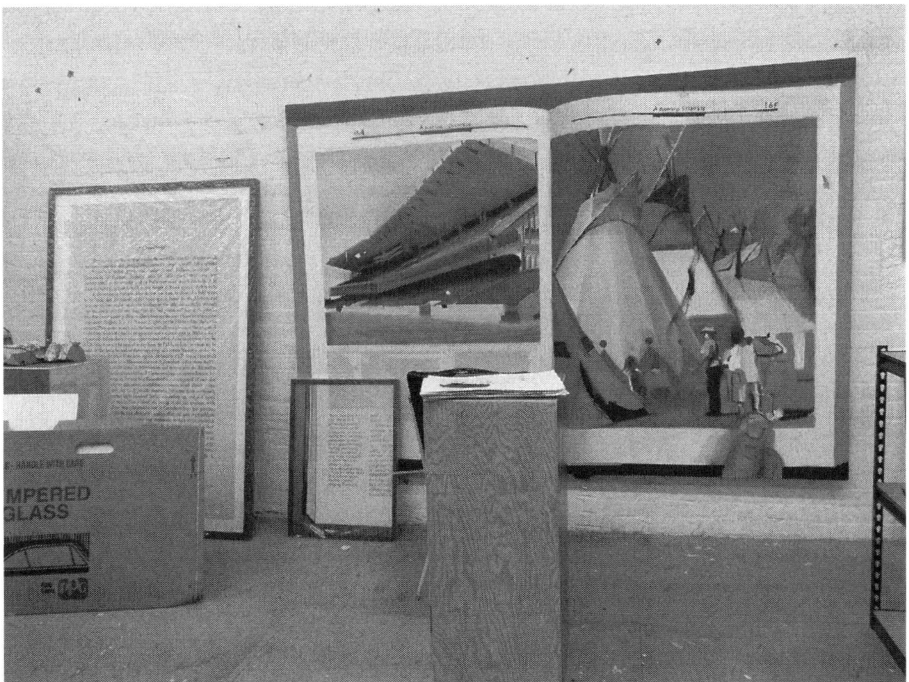

FIGURE 11.8: Mark Neufeld's Studio, Winnipeg, MN, 2014.

Neufeld explores how the history of western America aligned with the invention of photography and film. Thus, he believes that our memory is inscribed with these fictional devices.

> *I think that sets the tone of the work which is infused with fact, factual things, but always threatening to fall into a mythological or fictive space. I read all of the work as 'factual' in some way, as it's rooted in some kind of objective observation. I think it reflects the presence of research in the studio because there is this play with objectivity, but then in the end it doesn't necessarily resolve itself through the usual apparatus.*

Neufeld pointed out a pair of paintings he thought of as history paintings, intentionally made large to capture the original large-scale history painting. He had been looking for pictures of a rodeo and came across a book in the library about the Calgary Stampede. This book that he happened upon told the '*story*' of the Calgary stampede but between the lines of the text was a narrative about First Nations displacement. Neufeld made a series of paintings from a model of a fort near Lethbridge, Alberta, Fort Whoop-up. The paintings became a copy of a copy. They show hands handling sculptures, thus inserting the hand of the curator into the image as they move sculptures. Through the work, he questions the authenticity of representations by revealing the hands of the curator manipulating the objects. Moreover, he shows the translation involved in representations and examines how histories are told and retold through exhibitions of art objects.

Neufeld draws connections between history, art history, contemporary art, and events. Through focusing on a specific topic (in this case, cowboys, the rodeo, and abstract painting) he connects these subjects to other social, political, and philosophical ideas. Neufeld had a recent exhibition that explored the relationship between fact and fiction within film. This work connected the 'Great Train Robbery' depicted in the first western film and a real train robbery that happened in Kamloops, British Columbia.

> *They made a movie about the Kamloops train robbery called* The Gray Fox. *It's the only Canadian western that was made in the early 1980s, and it's based on a train robbery from 1906. The funny thing is that this real train robbery that happened in Kamloops (which was Canada's first train robbery) was inspired by the film* The Great Train Robbery *which was made a few years earlier. So, it was really interesting for me because I was thinking about the relationship between art and life.*

This story reinforced his interest in ways that life mirrors art and art mirrors life. In one painting in the exhibition, he showed the character from *The Gray*

Fox watching *The Great Train Robbery* in an early 20th-century movie theatre. Neufeld described trails of coincidences and tangents that emerged in this work that similarly explore the relationship between representation, fact, and fiction. While working towards this exhibition, he came across an image on the internet of the painting of artist Vincent Van Gogh's boots being handled at an auction, so the photograph showed the hands moving it. He therefore showed a painting of the hands handling Van Gogh's painting alongside the paintings about the train robbery to underscore the relationship between art and life, and the fictional lens of representation. To address the layering and intersection of ideas and influences, Neufeld described intuitive knowledge within studio practice: '*It's like a stack of paper with holes in it, so it's a sculpture and a collage and the holes might burrow from one piece of information to the other.*'

Depict Places that You Could Imaginatively Inhabit

> *It's important that there is art in the world. As a society, and individually, we learn from people who take the time to view the world in a global and sometimes imaginary way.*

This is how artist Eleanor Bond (Figure 11.9) described the importance of art in her studio in Winnipeg, Manitoba in 2015. Bond's large-scale immersive paintings combine an interest in painting, architecture, urbanism, and speculative fiction. She discussed how she developed her early series, *Work Station.*

> *There were eight large paintings and drawings that presented a semi-narrative depiction of an exodus from cities to post-industrial landscapes; forestry, fishing, agriculture and mining. The mid-1980s was a time of employment precarity and changing attitudes and I wanted to address these social and economic changes through speculative fiction. One painting was based on an actual site, Powell River, BC, which was home to the world's largest pulp and paper mill, at the time. The painting presented the mill converted to a recreation and retirement site, an idea that was somewhat prescient. Others presented a fishing village developed as a honeymoon resort, and displaced farmers setting up cappuccino bars and fish farms in Lake of the Woods. So, I was trying to visualize the contemporary shifting economic landscape by using these somewhat plausible propositions.*

At the time, Powell River, British Columbia was already 40% shut down because of massive shifts in mechanization, the beginning of globalization, and increased industrialization of agriculture. Through her work, she considers possible futures.

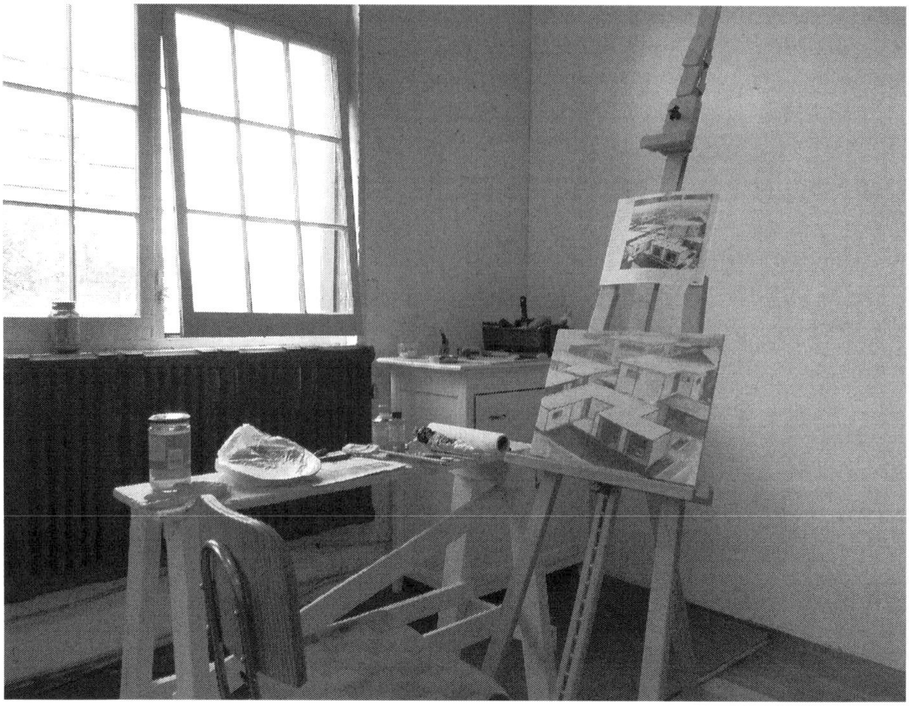

FIGURE 11.9: Eleanor Bond's Studio, Winnipeg, MN, 2015.

For example, she imagined unemployed workers leaving the city to create settlements or communal ways of living. However, in reality, she noted that people weren't leaving cities but were migrating to cities. In turn, her next body of work *Social Centres* depicted places in cities that were re-imagined as temporary housing, educational centres, or parks for people moving to cities. She addressed whether she was proposing pseudo-solutions to problems:

> *I wanted to bring and name concerns that my friends and I were challenged by to painting and to museums where these works were being shown; elder care, health care, housing, community. The first was rock climbers meeting with naturalists on the residential parkade, which was a big spiralling structure based on Brueghel's* Tower of Babel *and the Eaton's parkade in Winnipeg. The second was an offshore barge, a floating city that created service employment and sanctuary. Another was a fertility and reproduction centre, painted during the time of a national commission on reproductive rights. There were multiple issues woven through the series and they were intended to be complex sites for discussion, neither utopian nor dystopian.*

In 1995, Bond was invited to produce and exhibit work about Rotterdam during a residency there, the first of several projects about specific urban sites. She based her four works on the recent history and architecture of the Dutch city which had been heavily bombed during the war and had an '*uncanny need to rebuild itself*'. During her time there, she flew over the city, biked around it, interviewed people, and set up a studio.

> *One of the sites was an area across the river from downtown Rotterdam, an area of constant transformation, of continuous erasures for housing projects and often eccentric architectural interventions. One site was an inner harbour with floating botanical gardens, a glass city made from recycled materials that could provide employment and a sense of home for recent immigrants. Another painting was an underground eco-suburb with fresh air, fresh water and abundant daily sunshine. The works were a way of speaking to chronic re-building, architecture as urban re-branding, and a sturdy belief in engineering and progress.*

The work addresses issues related to social and economic shifts, however often through a personal lens. For example, she made a series of paintings drawn from photographs at a rehabilitation centre that her mother was in, followed by other elder care-related images.

Bond has produced images from research in cities, such as Hamilton, Detroit, and Windsor, whose economies and social structures had drastically changed, particularly in Detroit, due to the loss of industries. She was considering the impact of the global economy and its effect on people in those places as intertwined with various social, economic, and geographical histories. Bond described her work as propositions as she examined why she paints:

> *Painting is an appropriate medium for the depiction of places that you could imaginatively inhabit, sites constructed from imagination and research material and using the tropes of architecture and urbanism. The large-scale immersive images allow visceral and sometimes vertiginous engagement with the image and were sometimes seen as low-tech virtual environments.*
>
> *Making is thinking, so painting is a way of deepening and enlarging my thoughts about whatever subject I'm engaged with. I want to visualize the conversations and debates about a subject.*

12

Long for Something Other Than What Is (Studio as Dialogue)

A performative process generates an image that is an abstraction of the body to assist or to teach the body and other bodies, in their forward movement. Making art images is a way of reminding ourselves of this work already underway in the world.

(Triggs & Irwin, 2019, p. 4)

Learning to Learn

Art educator Rita Irwin (2013) draws a relationship between art and pedagogy as she describes '*becoming pedagogical*' as a process of 'learning to learn' (p. 203). Through this living inquiry, learners learn to recognize 'moments of encounters' that allow them to 'consider other ways of knowing in the world' (p. 201). Irwin addresses the generative qualities of art practice as pedagogy: 'Rather than asking what an art education practice means, the question becomes what does an art education practice set in motion do?' (p. 201). Moreover, Irwin describes the potential of artmaking to continually engage with the unknown and treat learning through making as an ongoing and complicated experiment. Through this lens, artmaking becomes a practice of engaging with learning through continually generating and remaking new pathways for learning. Thus, artmaking is a process of actively creating our own ways of learning.

In a visit with Mark Igloliorte (Figures 12.1 and 12.2) in Montreal, Quebec, in 2022, he connected his experiences on the land to his studio work through the lens of learning. His recent work engages with learning processes, from learning to skateboard, to kayaking, to speaking a language, to painting. An Inuit artist, Igloliorte grew up in Labrador. Following his undergraduate work, he went to the

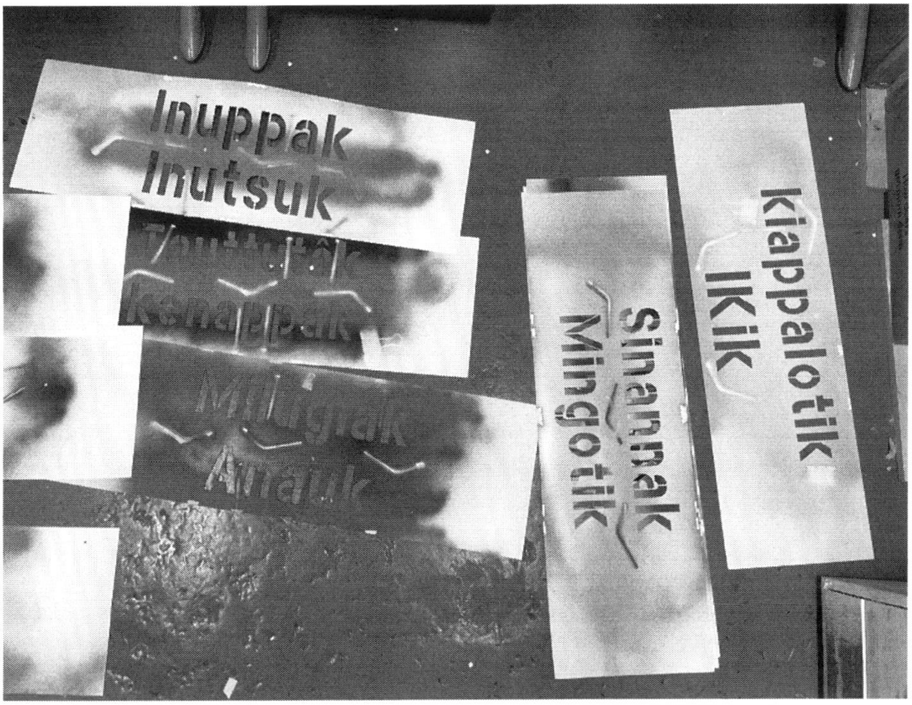

FIGURE 12.1: Mark Igloliorte's Studio, Montreal, QC, 2022.

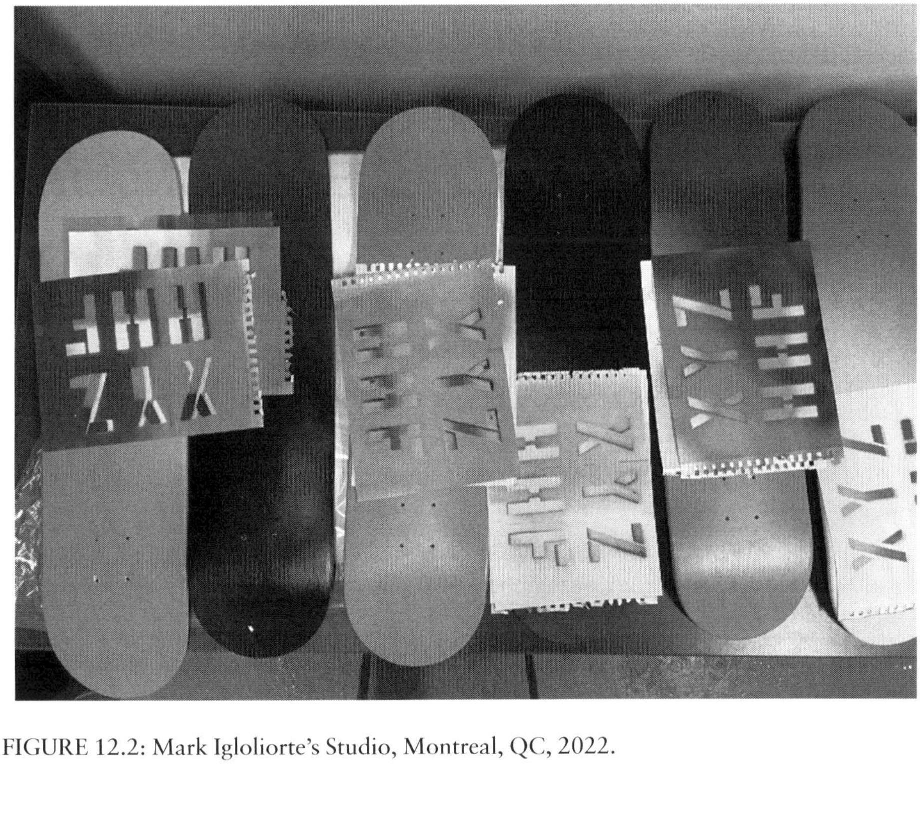

FIGURE 12.2: Mark Igloliorte's Studio, Montreal, QC, 2022.

Banff Centre for the Arts, Alberta in the artist residency program as an Indigenous Work Study Resident supporting the program. There, he was introduced to many practising contemporary Indigenous artists. While at a residency in 2006, he googled 'Labrador kayaking' and came across a collection of early photographs from Okak. '*The images were striking in that I was looking at images of my ancestors and felt a connection to them.*' The kayak is an Inuit innovation, made initially for hunting. He shared an image of the painting of kayaks with a phrase written on it that says: 'KAYAK IS INUKTITUT FOR SEAL HUNTING BOAT.' Igloliorte addressed this work: '*I wanted to think about what is lost in translation and also assert the Indigenous origin of the boat.*' Upon moving to Vancouver, Igloliorte bought a kayak, learned how to do a kayak roll, and visited the Museum of Anthropology where they had old kayak models from over a hundred years ago. He connected to this subject:

> *They were living a precolonial life, hunting, being on the land, speaking the language. Coming back to the 'Eskimo roll', what I like about it is that it's an Inuit maneuver. That felt like connecting to an Indigenous way of doing things.*

More recently, Igloliorte began working with the skateboard as a surface for painting. Within the studio, there lay several skateboards, brightly painted. Growing up in an isolated place, Goose Bay, Labrador, he remembered his amazement at watching someone on a skateboard and went on to learn skateboarding tricks after moving to Corner Brook, Newfoundland where there was an active community of skateboarders.

> *I always knew that once I decided to learn an Eskimo roll that I would learn how to do it because I learned to skateboard. And it influences my feeling toward education. I feel that any of my students could learn to do anything, and I think that's a powerful mindset.*

On the skateboards surrounding the studio, Igloliorte wrote phrases related to the process of artmaking. For Igloliorte, the text was all about his learning process. The first two series of skateboard paintings had phrases related to the creative process. Some of these phrases include: 'Take a good look'; 'Finally do something'; 'Pull himself up'; 'Become better'; 'Begin to grow'; 'Fall on one's face'; and 'Do by trial and error'. He described the intention:

> *All these things speak to learning and process. It's interesting in terms of using language to process your experience. There are all these things embedded in Indigenous language. My father went to residential schools, so I didn't have that*

> *exposure to Inuktitut because of that colonial process. So, for me, not being able to speak it, that's a real barrier to entry in terms of what I'm going to do to engage with Inuktitut and learn things. And being an art educator, you hear so many reasons people haven't completed their project. For me, having barriers to getting started to speak Inuktitut wasn't enough of a reason to not learn it. I can start with single words and use them to start translating my experience whether it's being on the land or being in the studio.*

More recently, the text on the skateboards shifted towards collaboration, highlighting small moments or small stories, from working with his research assistant to thinking about moments with family. Igloliorte reflects on learning as both individual and collective through the lens of learning his Inuktitut language, which also connects him with his family heritage.

Within his work, he addresses the cultures we are born into and those we choose.

> I'm really thinking about what kind of culture you take on in your life and what kind of culture you're born into ... For example, skateboarding is something that I chose to pursue. But my family history, my being Inuit: this wasn't my decision. I think it's interesting to bring those two things together and see where they overlap.
> (Inuit Art Quarterly, n.d.)

During our visit, he expanded on this idea:

> *Skateboarding is an active choice. But I've been thinking about how stuff I do for myself as an Indigenous person is becoming more and more an active choice. It's an active choice to be kayaking, to be engaging with language and make something of it and explore those meanings and make those connections. I think for me, in terms of art, Indigeneity, skateboarding, kayaking, it all comes down to being an active choice for me.*

For Igloliorte, his reason for making art relates directly to his reasons for teaching.

> *I enjoy that satisfaction of doing something well, and having that immediate feedback, 'I finished it', 'I did it well', whether it's a painting or a skateboard trick or language. I've gotten such great feedback about the Inuktitut skateboard work. It was about having an enthusiasm for one's language. I have had a number of students that have said they want to do stuff with their language. So, it's not just about Indigenous language, it's about finding where you come from meaningful. So even*

though it starts with being satisfied and having that achievement with myself, I like the generosity of it. It's for other people to be inspired and see that they can engage with their culture in different ways. I'm interested in students thinking about the community of art, what happens in the visual arts and the conversation going on around it.

Studio as Garden

Biesta (2018) contends that 'art itself appears as the ongoing exploration of what it means to be *in* the world, the ongoing attempt at figuring out what it means to be here, now; to be – here – now' (p. 17, original emphasis). He calls for a world-centred approach to art education as he proposes that artmaking is the creation of a dialogue with the world. Biesta suggests that artmaking is driven by desire but that this desire is in relation to the world. He says:

> Art makes our desires visible, gives them form, and by trying to come into dialogue with what or who offers resistance, we are at the very same time engaged in the exploration of the desirability of our desires and in the rearrangement and transformation.
>
> (p. 18)

Through the dialogue with the world, 'art *is* the exploration and transformation of our desires so that they can become a positive force for the ways we seek to exist in the world' (p. 17, original emphasis). Through this process, he proposes that education is re-embedded within the arts as art is a means through which to examine how we live in the world, and that this is the value of learning through art. Furthermore, Biesta argues that dialogue emerges through encountering the resistance that may come through handling materials:

> Encountering the reality of paint, stone, wood, metal, sound, bodies, including one's own body, encountering resistance, in order to explore possibilities, meet limits and limitations, and out of this create forms, establish forms and find forms that make existing-in-dialogue possible, that is what I see in the 'doing' of art.
>
> (p. 17)

Thus, Biesta calls for an emphasis on being in and with the world through artmaking. Similarly, art educator, Cala Coats (2023) argues for embracing curiosity within learning as an active way of being engaged with the world. For Coats, curiosity emphasizes sensory and affective responses to the world and embraces uncertainty and indetermination as she proposes that a pedagogy driven by curiosity provokes 'active engagements that resist the desire to define what the world is, asking instead what it can do' (p. 13). Through this lens, engaging with the world through art is a form of questioning.

I met Emmanuel Osahor (Figures 12.3–12.5) in his Toronto studio in 2022. He had moved to Canada from Nigeria when he was 17 to study in Alberta. He remembers an instructor in an Art Fundamentals class encouraged him to study fine art, saying: '*You have this curiosity around questioning and materials.*' Years later, upon moving to Guelph, Ontario, Osahor started taking long walks around his neighbourhood. Fascinated by the different colours in Ontario compared to Alberta, from brighter greens to longer Autumn colours, he took hundreds of photographs of gardens surrounding his home and laid them out on the studio floor to start collaging.

> *I was thinking that I don't have my own garden, but if I treat these photographs like seedlings, I can transplant them and then the work I create can be their own garden. So, to take the metaphor further, the studio became a garden. This was my gardening practice; this was a space I cultivated and nurtured.*

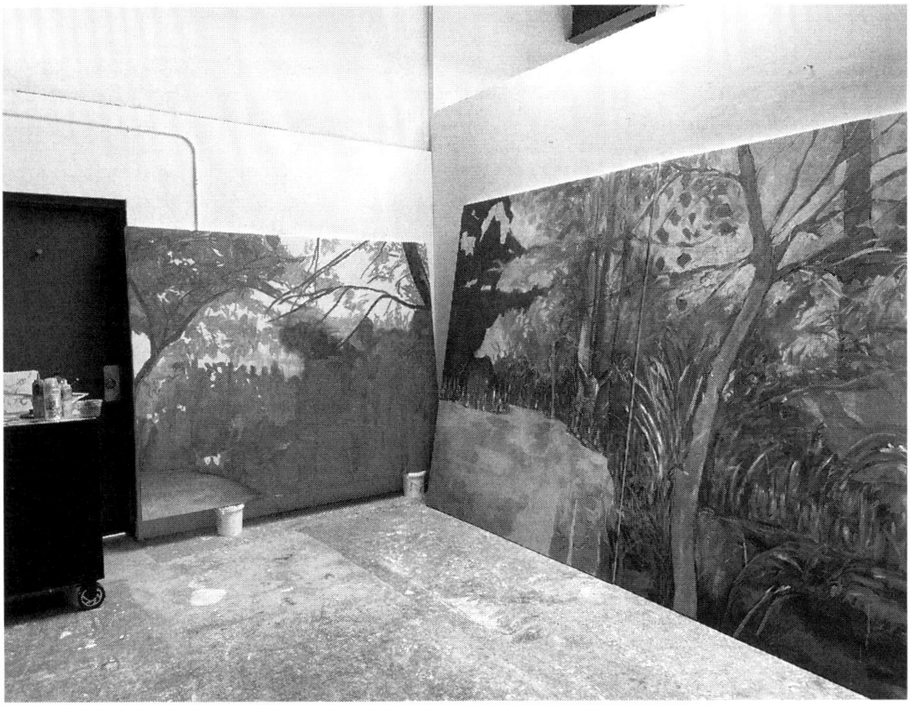

FIGURE 12.3: Emmanuel Osahor's Studio, Toronto, ON, 2022.

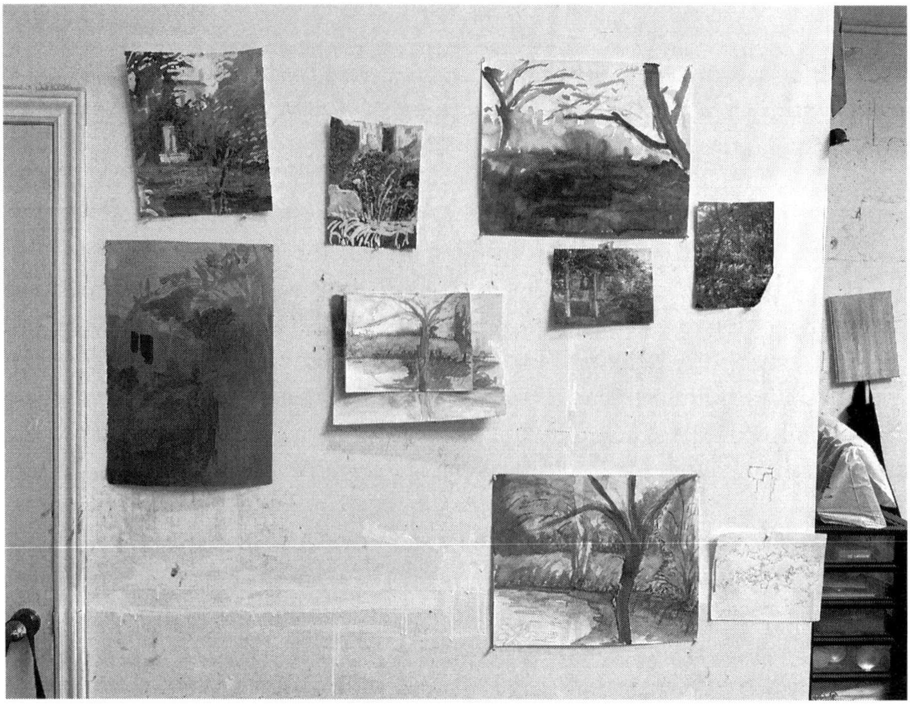

FIGURE 12.4: Emmanuel Osahor's Studio, Toronto, ON, 2022.

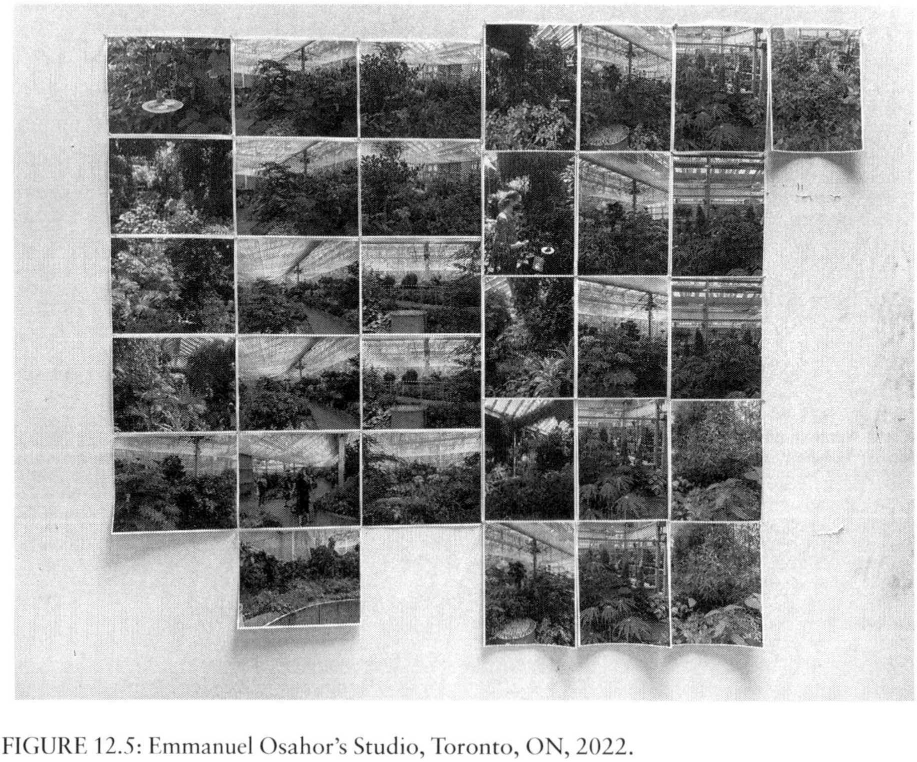

FIGURE 12.5: Emmanuel Osahor's Studio, Toronto, ON, 2022.

For Osahor, gardens were a way to think about the studio, painting, and uncertainties.

> *The landscapes are a way to think about abstraction and the sublime and this sense of not being able to make sense of a really incoherent and overwhelming thing. The past few years, the world makes less and less sense and I'm trying to figure out how to sit with that and be at peace with that. Through painting, there's a sense of acceptance and letting go and allowing things to go and take you where they will.*

We discussed his complicated relationship with the subject as we addressed his interest in gardens rather than natural forest areas. He had a memory of going to a butterfly conservatory in Cambridge with his goddaughter where he had had a conflicting experience being in this controlled space with butterflies shipped from around the world. But then watching a young child run around, he would remind himself to be in that space and let his body feel that space. Regarding working from gardens, he said:

> *I think it has to do with the fact that it is constructed, the same way a painting is constructed. This facsimile of natural order that is actually human designed and human controlled, but when you're in those spaces you actually have an experience that transcends how it was made. If you go to the botanical gardens, it's obvious it's a constructed space, but when you're looking at a plant, you're not thinking about everything else, you're just having this intimate experience with this plant. We make these spaces and there are various reasons why we make these spaces. A lot of these botanical gardens are really colonial products with all these plants we've taken from other places. So, there is a sort of human quagmire because the plants become this record of what we've done to ourselves and the environment. But there is still the personal human experience when you are in these spaces.*

Osahor was partway through his graduate work when the COVID-19 pandemic happened which prompted a deep dive into his studio practice, while also questioning the role of artmaking in society. He was looking at the work of 19th-century French painter, Pierre Bonnard. Through his research, he learned that Bonnard's partner had severe depression which led to creating fictionalized landscapes as he was not able to travel so instead made works based on memories or photographs that he used as collage material. Regarding his own work at the time, Osahor said: '*I realized that's what I was doing. I'm going through a pandemic in a time many people in my life are struggling, I'm really struggling, I need to create these fictions that help me.*' As a constructed space, similar to a garden, the studio allowed Osahor to create a fictional world. While not an answer or solution to the problems in the world, it provides a space to think and rethink, to construct and reconstruct the world in which we exist. Through a conversation with a friend, he had suddenly realized: '*I'm making romantic paintings*.' The paintings are a way of engaging with the world as he would like it to be. '*I've been making up these fictional spaces that could potentially be great places because part of me wonders, where is that?*' He addressed his reasons for artmaking:

> *Painting is a way of thinking. It's a thought out loud. As opposed to the result of a finished thought. A painting is just a part of the sentence, it's not a conclusion, it's just a thing that allows you to keep thinking about it. It's about not knowing. That's why we do this thing because we don't know, and we can't know, but you have to do something in between ... It's about a personal longing and navigating of a desire that never gets fulfilled.*

For Vancouver-based artist Ben Reeves (Figures 12.6 and 12.7), artmaking is a dialogue with the world that prompts an understanding of how to live in the world:

> *Art is probably one of the most, if not the most useful vehicle for me to think about things, and for me to understand my place in the world. So, it's a way of investigating things. It's a speculative way of thinking, theorizing, philosophizing and exploring things. A lot of my work is about how perception functions to generate understandings of things. Often when my work is representational, they take sources that are really close to home, highly regional, local, from my every day and start to pull that experience apart. So, they're about the world in that sense, and about trying to understand it, but they also become really self-conscious about the lens that they offer for understanding. So, they start to pull themselves apart too. The picture starts to become a subject as a device for understanding the world, which is also a subject.*
>
> *I make things and then I think about them and then I make things in order to think about them. But I'm also reflecting on it. I'm thinking about meditation too. Where you're trying to evacuate thought. And that also oddly has a place in studio practice where it is an immersion in a moment and in a place. As I'm saying it, it sounds contradictory, but in the work, it doesn't feel contradictory at all because thinking and being are a part of the same thing ... When I use the word thinking, I use it in an expanded way, where it's not limited to language. There are material ways of thinking, there are pictorial ways of thinking, colour can be a way of thinking. It incorporates the body as well as part of the process. So, for me, the paintings are, or the work is, a moment of intersection between the world, the intellect and the body.*

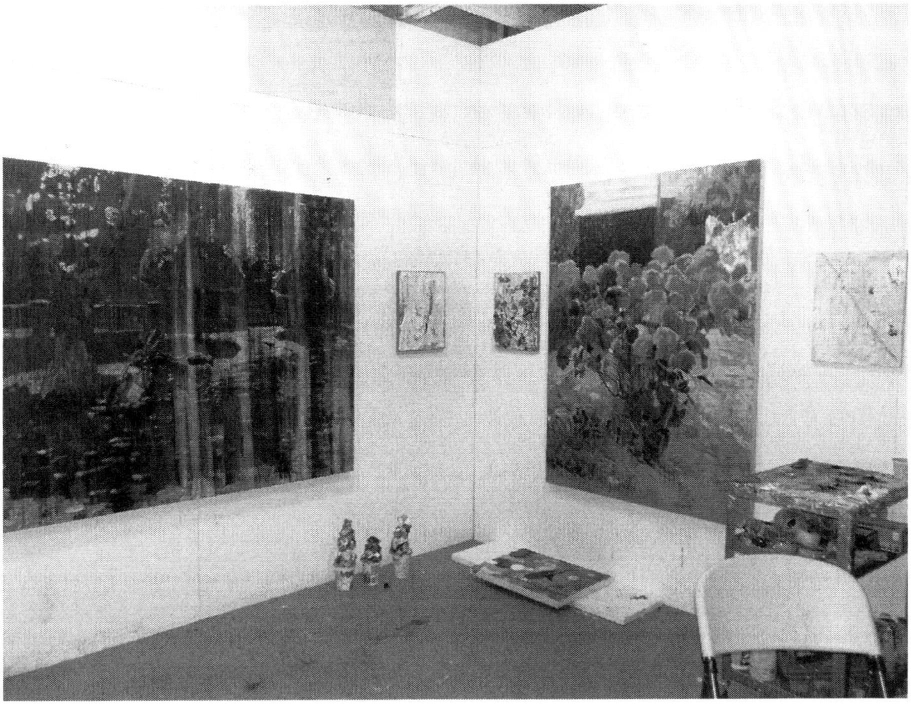

FIGURE 12.6: Ben Reeve's Studio, Vancouver, BC, 2014.

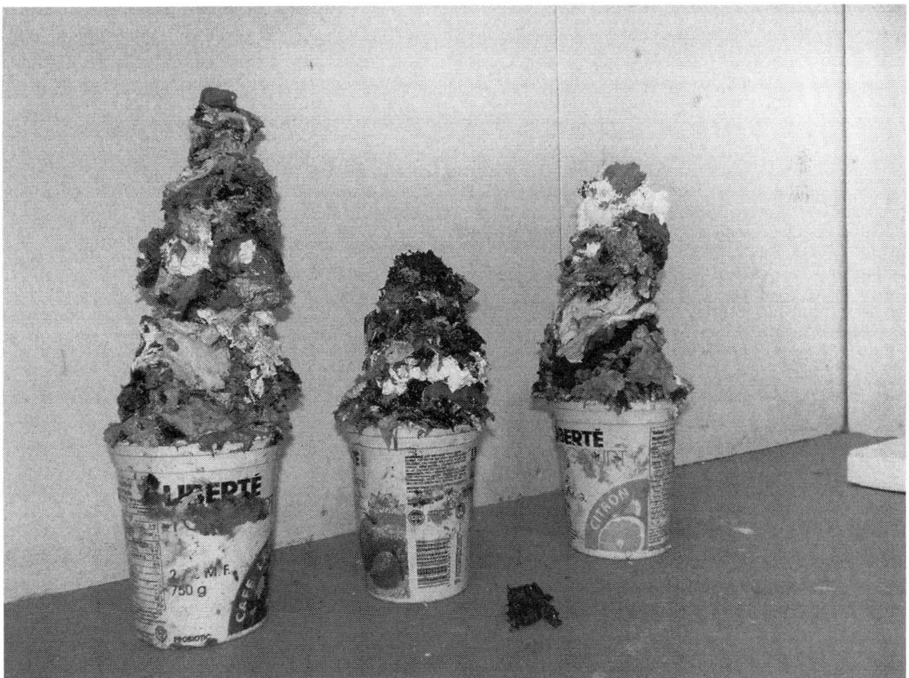

FIGURE 12.7: Ben Reeve's Studio, Vancouver, BC, 2014.

In a visit to Ottawa in 2015, Martin Golland (Figure 12.8) similarly addressed how artmaking is a way of understanding and engaging with the world.

> *I make art because it is a space that goes beyond certain social orders. It is a free space, a space to do things. If you feel compelled to talk about the world and respond to the world, it is a fantastic space to do it. Very little art comes out of contentment and complacency. But art does come out of a condition of adversity, dissonance, dissatisfaction, ennuie and a longing for something other than what is. At the end of the day that is exactly why I make art.*

Throughout the years, Golland sought to find ways to discuss his experiences through painting.

> *I was trying to find a new way of talking about experience. But I was also talking about the notion of fractured experience. I liked the notion of a space being far more about painting rather than about perceived experience. So, I was expressing ideas about fracture, dissociation from the world and about a kind of ordered disorder, playing with ideas of chaos and chaotic convergence of elements together.*

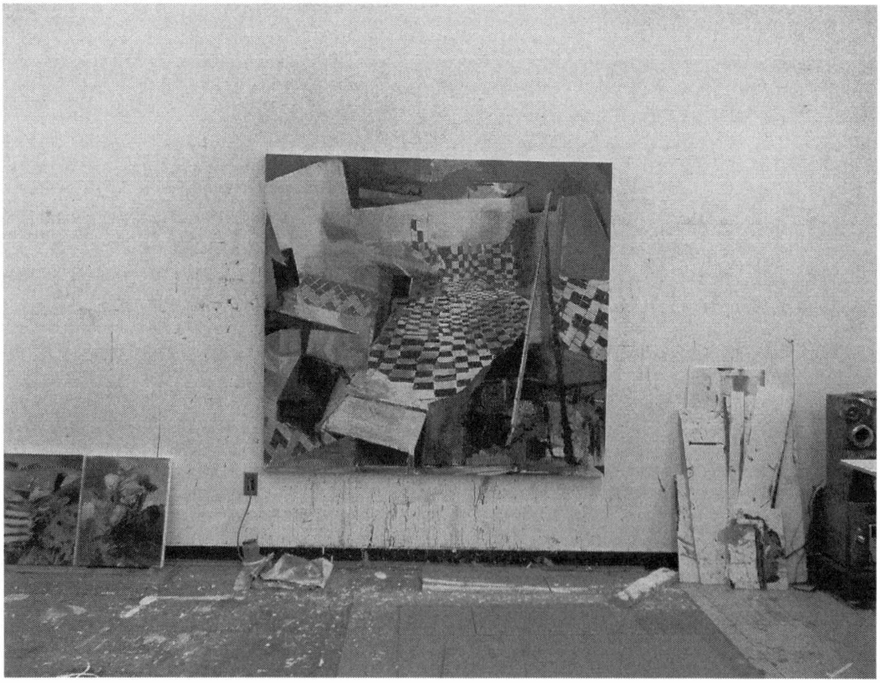

FIGURE 12.8: Martin Golland's Studio, Ottawa, ON, 2015.

For Golland, artmaking is more about creating a dialogue than a fixed narrative and about how that dialogue opens up a relationship with the world:

I'm setting up the conditions for a narrative to take place, but I'm not delivering necessarily the narrative. The narrative is made up of both you and me looking at the work. I like the unfixed, the potentiality for a narrative rather than an explicit delivery. Meaning comes out of an inference that we glean when we're looking at a body of things and looking at interrelationships and deciding what those interrelationships are.

We forget we are part of a lineage and a legacy, a multifarious one, and a conflicted one, but a legacy none-the-less that we have to fight, align ourselves with, separate ourselves from and forge forward with new ideas and new ways of talking about our world ... The notion of knowledge and our understanding and definition of knowledge is changing. But I think the central problem remains that learning is difficult, and learning about art takes time. So, the challenge is, how do we respond to the world and respond to art's current conditions and its histories and still make something that is true to us.

Having a Sense of Belonging Prompts Us to Take Responsibility

Through her art practice, Jinny Yu (Figure 12.9) (Ottawa, 2014, 2022) reflects on her place and relationship to the world. Yu addressed how her work shifted from examining her own identity as she moved through her life towards considering her responsibility to the world. In 2014, I visited her at an exhibition that included ink on mirrors. She pointed at this work to exemplify how it served as a means of understanding her existence. Her work was created by spraying ink on a smooth surface, where the ink should not stick but does.

It makes me think about how I exist in the world. Metaphorically, I am the ink, and the mirror my environment: I should not stick to the world so well, but I do, just the way ink sticks on the mirror in this work. This is an example of the ontology of painting – parallel to our precarious existence in this world.

Yu and I discussed the function or role of art for her:

Art helps me live. To find snippets of answers to big questions. It makes living worthwhile somehow. And with art, we find collective individuality. It is a collective thing, not necessarily just an individualistic activity. We all strive to find answers in this world, and we find our own answers. By making art I manage to find my own answers. I get answers, small answers to different facets of questions, and that's the driving force behind art. We keep asking questions.

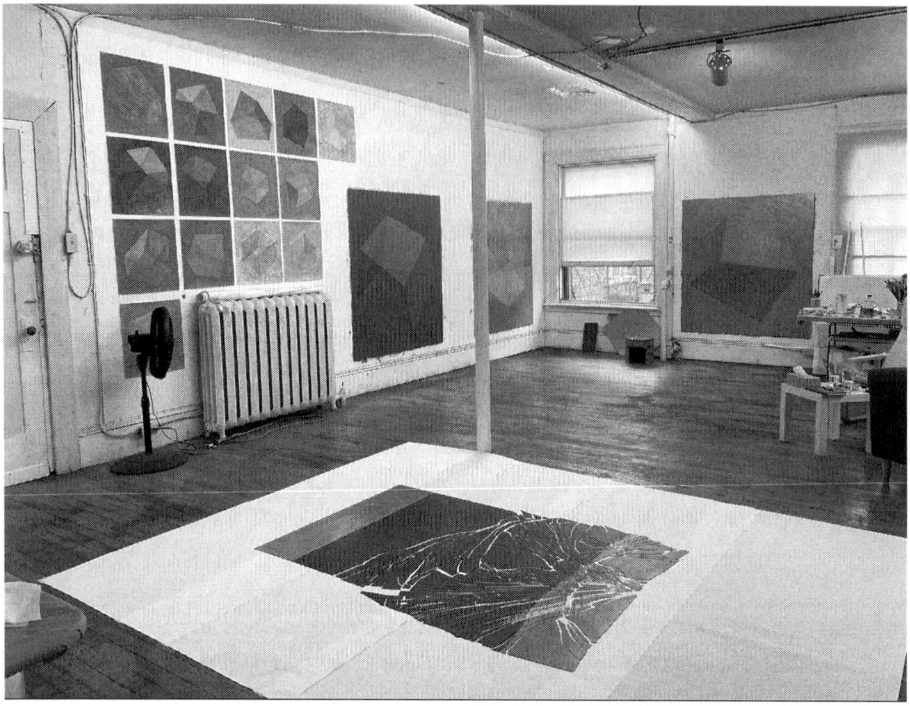

FIGURE 12.9: Jinny Yu's Studio, Ottawa, ON, 2022.

Using aluminum as support was a way of questioning her relationship to the painting as it is semi-reflective. So rather than a more traditional view of painting as a window into the world, it is a reflective space, a moving space, a changing space, one that reflects the world in a literal way, as a changing and moving space. This work also alludes to Yu's changing identity as someone who has moved around a lot through life. Yu had moved to Montreal from South Korea at 12 years old, and she reflected on how the constant moving has changed her:

> *The main effect of all the moving around is my being able to see things in an abstract way. When you're in one place, it's hard to see things around you from distance, but once you start moving around, you start to do so, which is a process of abstraction.*

I met with Jinny Yu in her Ottawa studio again in the summer of 2022. Since our first visit, she had reflected on herself as an artist, trying to situate herself in relation to the land she inhabits. Since our visit, Yu had made work for the Venice Biennale in 2015 called *Don't They Ever Stop Migrating?* (2015). She addressed a transition in her thinking: '*I was now thinking about society as a whole, thinking about how my experience could contribute to different ways of thinking and understanding the world.*' For Yu, the celebration of Canada's 150th anniversary prompted her, as a relatively recent immigrant and settler to Canada, to examine the colonial history of Canada and explore her role within it. While continuing to use painting as a form of self-portrait, she began to examine how her work related to the place in which she lived in Canada, on the traditional lands of the Algonquin Anishinaabe Nation. Creating a body of work called *Perpetual Guest* (2019), she examined her relationship to this place as a guest on the lands.

> *The work* Perpetual Guest *is my expression of how I feel living and working on this land to which I will never be able to fully belong. In this new work, I'm thinking about the relationship of host, guest and the land on the pictorial level.*

On the floor of Yu's studio, there laid another work (*Perpetual Guest*, 2019/2022, *Impossibility of Repair*, 2023) that came out of this series, an oil painting on glass that had been in an exhibition and someone had stepped on it and shattered it because they thought it was meant to be an interactive piece. She pieced it back together. Through this process, she considered what it means to repair, particularly in relation to her relationship with the land on which she lives. Yu reflected on our conversation years earlier, where she claimed that moving around, she could see things from a distance. As she was trying to understand her relationship to moving and to place, she considered a residency that she had participated in in Dawson City, Yukon. While there, she had a chance to visit Moosehide with the members of the Tr'ondëk Hwëch'in First Nation and she was drawn into how intricately they knew the land. It reminded her of her mother in her native village. She reconsidered her previous proposition about seeing the world from a distance as she thought about intricately knowing the lands on which we live.

> *This is sense of belonging. My idea of having distance leading to having an abstracted or 'objective' view of the world as something positive just shattered. So, this whole idea of guesthood and hosthood was not really about my positionality, but about having a sense of belonging prompting everyone to take responsibility.*

Artist and educator, Rachel Payne (2016) describes painting as a process of questioning through material exploration and through examining the ways it functions in the world:

> Painting is about a form of questioning and whether that form of questioning is embedded within the materiality of the medium itself or stretched out from that medium across other spaces, whether of art or not, it is still and maybe more so than

> ever a vitally productive force that has an essential part to play, not just within the confines of art (or the nature of art and for that matter the extensive questioning of it) but also how painting impacts upon the world in a broader social and cultural sense.
> (p. 24)

Thus, artmaking at its best prompts questions about our relationship with the world, and in turn forms a dialogue with the world (Biesta, 2018). Yu similarly described the role of artmaking as a form of questioning.

> *I've been reflecting on the ontology of painting and linking it to the reflection of my existence in this world. I question who I am. An age-old question. And by finding answers to what painting is, I find answers to who I am.*

SECTION 4

CONCLUSION: LEARN TO LEARN

Art educator, Gert Biesta (2018), provokes us to ask what education does: 'Rather than asking what education *produces*, we should be asking what education *means*. And rather than asking what education *makes*, we should be asking what education *makes possible*' (p. 13, original emphasis). Throughout this section, I asked how studio thinking and making promotes a dialogue with the world. This dialogue is generated through the ways that artmaking may prompt an ongoing process of learning to learn. Furthermore, I contend that this process of learning to learn exists within an ecology of practice. Reflecting on the connections between creative processes and a studio classroom, professor at Emily Carr University of Art and Design, Landon Mackenzie refers to the 'wildfire effect' as the way creativity spreads through artmaking within a studio classroom as each individual's learning process is confronted by others' learning processes. As an emergent approach to pedagogy, the 'wildfire effect', allows the creative process to be generated through interactions with others in the studio. While studio practice may be an individual act of making, the communal studio classes and conversations that come from studio visits allow for a community and creative ecosystem to emerge and thrive. Furthermore, through its transdisciplinary nature, artistic research and studio-based learning resist disciplinary tendencies within higher education. Moreover, the subjectivities and storytelling within artistic inquiry push back against the dominance of objectivity in research and invite subjectivity, affect, and personal experience in research through artmaking (Loveless, 2019).

Thus, the studio prompts one to become pedagogical through the ongoing process of learning to learn inherent within studio practice. Triggs and Irwin (2019) examine how becoming pedagogical is a way of engaging with the world and the 'organizing of human experience in relation to other experience' (p. 2). It is not simply about finding the connections between practices of teaching and practices of artmaking. It is rather about understanding a way of being and a way of learning through our everyday encounters. They describe image-making as an embodied experience and a performative practice. Knowing and learning, they argue doesn't happen at a distance but rather through engaging with the world. The creation of images is a way of both recognizing and materializing our embodied experiences in the world.

Rather than focusing on learning to make art, Manning (2016b) argues that art is a way of learning:

> Art as *a way* of learning, acts as a bridge toward new processes, new pathways. To speak of a 'way' is to dwell on the process itself, on its manner of becoming. It is to emphasize that art is before all else a quality, a difference in kind, an operative process that maps the way toward a certain attunement of world and expression.
>
> (p. 47, original emphasis)

Thus, I propose that art is a way of learning with the world and reimagining ways of living in the world. Through the emphasis on individualized learning, the materiality of making, communities of practice, and creative ecosystems, I contend that a studio classroom is a unique learning space. I propose the following propositions for studio-based learning: 'Embrace a process of unlearning through prompting students to question how they know what they know'; 'Create prompts for the imagination and the retelling of the stories that we live'; 'Create a dialogue about why we make art and how it impacts how we live in the world.'

Conclusion: Create a Template for the Imagination of the Next Person (Studio as Never-Ending)

I think about the power of the arts in the world and I think it's a bigger army than any army that's out there. So, in a way, this is the thing I can do to perhaps change the world to make it a little better. Even if it's better just for the moment, then I've done something.

(Wanda Koop, 2016, 0:25, Canada Council for the Arts)

Unfolding Differently Through Time

In Landon Mackenzie's Vancouver studio (Figures C.1 and C.2), 2022, on one wall, there was a painting with flowing colour on it. The previous summer when she went to her studio on Prince Edward Island, she had pulled a piece of linen out of storage; it was dirty and covered in mouse droppings. She took this piece of fabric and washed it in soapy water and then washed it in the ocean. It went through many transformations before going back to her Vancouver studio to be stretched and reworked. Regarding the ongoing change produced on the fabric, Mackenzie said: '*It had collected all this energy.*' Through her long conceptual process of painting, Mackenzie described how her paintings have to live time. The time that is contained within the objects of artmaking embodies the process of the making. In her Montreal studio, Eliza Griffiths discussed the role of time in painting and how the acts of making are embedded within the painting:

Temporality in painting is confusing because it's all distilled into this one surface, so, people don't see it as a temporal thing. Painting unfolds differently through time. I think there is a residue in the membrane of the painting from the time and energy

> *put into a painting. There is some kind of friction or residue of that energy in the layers, and you can feel it.*

In Ottawa, Jennifer Lefort similarly described painting as important for its production of relationships:

> *There is something very direct when you talk about painting. There's a tactile way about it. There is a fundamental human sense to it that is really strong. With the absence of the artist, you still feel the presence of a human being. And at the end of the day the human relationships need to exist and there is something about painting that leaves it there no matter what.*

I propose that a studio similarly holds memory. The traces of experiences, the energy of artmaking, and the relationships forged through the making are embedded within a studio.

Much has changed in education and society since I began this research in 2014. As discussed throughout, shifts in technology, expedited through the COVID-19 pandemic, have led to an increase in online learning platforms. These shifts have led me to believe that there is an urgency in recognizing why studios are unique learning spaces, ones that exist within and in response to a particular time and space. Further, increased online and artificial intelligence platforms and other tools for learning celebrate efficiency in teaching and research. I argue that studio practice resists this desire for efficiency and instead requires a different way of being in time and space. Time spent in the studio allows for experimentation, wandering minds, and curiosity-driven learning that is essential to creative processes. Similarly, while on the one hand, universities have increasingly embraced artistic teaching and research for its transdisciplinary quality (Loveless, 2019) and recognized creative practice for its subjective and open-ended approach, on the other hand, more research is needed on how to create the time and space for artistic learning within the structure of postsecondary institutions. To truly embrace creative practice and the value of studio-based learning, more emphasis needs to focus on the process of learning through artmaking rather than only the product. New materialist theory, which has permeated many fields of research in the past decade and has emphasized process, performativity, materiality, and relationality, opens discussions towards the significance of embodied and affective forms of learning. Thus, I propose that a studio is an ideal place to examine new materialist pedagogies, and in turn to discuss studio-based education and what can be learned from studio pedagogies within broader educational systems and concerns.

Within my own teaching and artistic practices, much has also shifted. Throughout the past five years, one of the greatest influences on my understanding and approach to artistic pedagogy has come from teaching introductory studio art classes, such as painting, to non-visual art majors. Through these courses, I teach students from across the university who are studying subjects such as Psychology, Economics, English, Biology, etc. These students may be introduced to art and studio learning for the first time. What struck me most about teaching these students is that I wasn't simply teaching them how to paint or draw, but instead, I was teaching them how to learn in a different way. For students who were used to taking courses with right/wrong answers, with direct and pre-defined outcomes and prescribed approaches to achieve those outcomes, many were encountering the messiness of art materials for the first time. Further, many students were not only apprehensive but also eager to explore the subjective and personally meaningful quality of learning through making wherein art classes pushed them to understand themselves and their relationship to the world. For many of these students, a 'making' centred class and the messiness of materials confronted their sense of control over their learning. It is through this lens that I have come to this research as a means of recognizing the significance of learning through making in a studio.

Within my art practice, I have similarly developed and changed throughout the past decade. I am deeply indebted to the artists with whom I met, as I constantly hear their voices in my mind while in my studio. This project highlighted the significance of spending time with others, having time to listen to artists' stories, sharing space with their art, and relating their words to myself as an artist. When feeling lost in the process, I am reassured by Janet Werner's metaphor of digging a hole and finding my way out, or Dil Hildebrand's discussion of being lost in the wilderness without a map. I reflect on Laura Millard and Erica Mendritzki's assertion that doubt is an essential quality of learning. I embrace the permission from Charlene Vickers to find healing through making. I welcome artmaking as a prompt for the imagination as described by Philippa Jones. I consider, in the words of Ufuk Gueray, how fertile and generative one small idea may be. And I appreciate Emmanuel Osahor's discussion of finding places of hope, optimism, and a little bit of romance like a garden, in the studio.

One conversation that was particularly meaningful within my practice was with artist Monica Tap (Toronto, 2022) who discussed how leaning into a wondrous experience in a particular place helped her recognize how she exists in the world through the lens of painting. She had a realization that rather than painting the world as she saw it, painting was in fact shaping the way she experienced the world. Within a rhododendron garden in Germany, in a moment of awe and wonder, she recognized that she saw the world through the lens of the artists that came before her:

> *I went for a bike ride one night and it was like being inside a painting! The light, the colour, the design of the plantings, the rhododendron bushes, I had no idea they could be so big and so varied in oranges and violets and lilac. I realized that I see through painting, so I asked, why not construct some paintings according to how I see?*

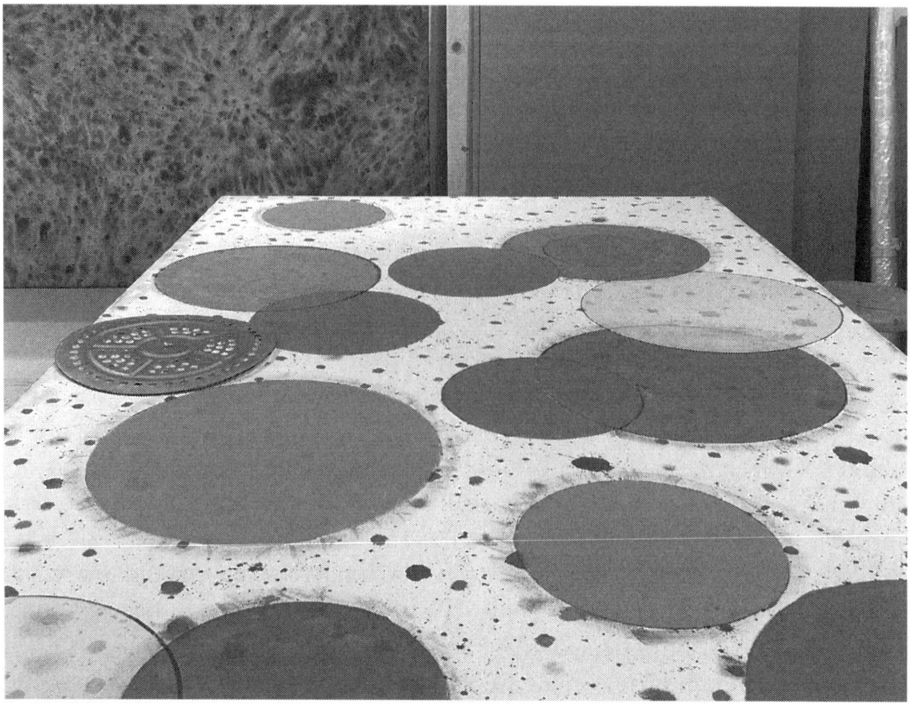

FIGURE C.1: Landon Mackenzie's Studio, Vancouver, BC, 2022.

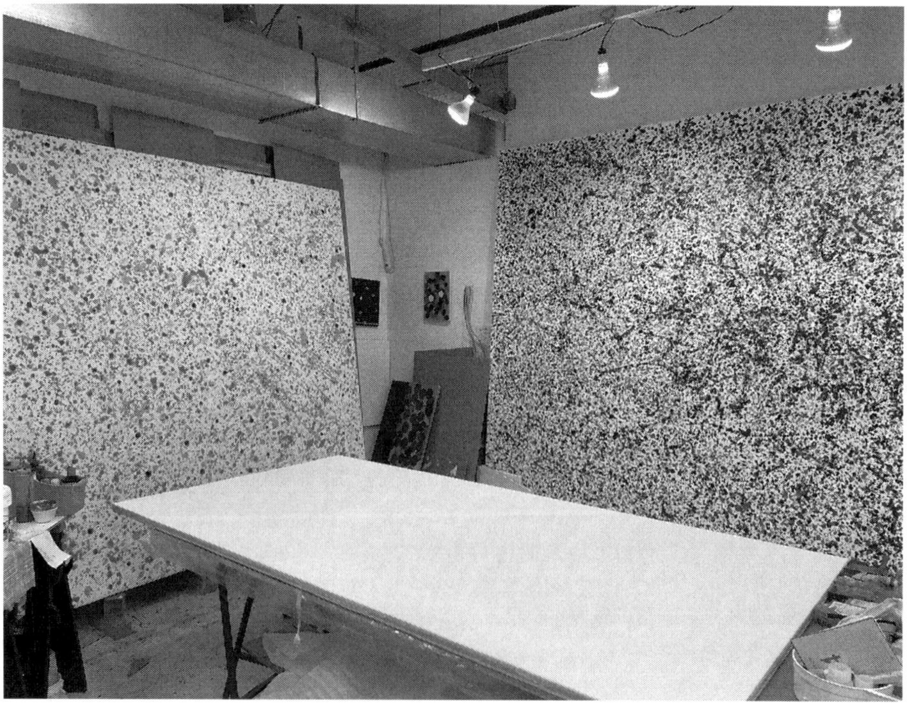

FIGURE C.2: Landon Mackenzie's Studio, Vancouver, BC, 2022.

Tap's words about 'being inside a painting' prompted a new way of viewing my own painting practice. Further, she provoked me to recognize the ways that a studio is a lens, a way of being in the world through curiosity and imagination. I have come to recognize these moments within my local surroundings on Vancouver Island where I become immersed within local tide pools and feel as if I am inside a painting as my body feels interconnected with the moving water and ever-changing ecosystems through the movement of the tides. My recent paintings inspired by local tide pools propose that intertidal zones function like constantly evolving collages and as metaphors for studio practice. These new iterations of never-ending paintings continue to change much like the ebb and flow of the tides that bring with them ever-changing ecosystems. Through this perspective of being inside a painting, I embrace curiosity as a way of engaging with the world for its 'affective capacity, and relational process, drawn to the strangeness of the everyday, and attuning to the invisible, uncanny, silenced and buried' (Coats, 2023, p. 13). I embrace becoming pedagogical (Irwin, 2013) as a way of being in the world as an artist within a never-ending and active ecosystem, constantly changing while grounded within the moment of a particular time and place.

The Liminality of a Studio

Over the past decade, I have moved studios several times, each time immersing myself within a new art ecosystem. I have witnessed how worn-down buildings, old factories, or government buildings have been re-animated through studio practice, while at the same time, witnessing the constant disappearance of studios within cities. A couple of years ago, the building where my studio was as part of the artist collective *Ministry of Casual Living* was sold and we had to move. At the same time, two other studio art collectives in the city had lost their spaces and finding a studio was becoming increasingly unattainable. As a stroke of luck, an old art deco-style building in downtown Victoria became available for temporary use. The building built in 1949 was meant to be a hospital but instead was used for government offices until it was bought in 2019 to be developed. As preparations for development were being made, arts organizations could inhabit this place. For a temporary moment, 85 Victoria-based artists moved into the building, transforming the old institutional building into studios. As I walked through an 'Open Studios' event, paintings and drawings adorned the hallways. An artist-in-residence painted in the gallery. And an old vault was turned into a temporary art gallery creating an immersive exhibition of light and sound.

There is a vibrancy that an active studio life has on a neighbourhood and community. This invisible energy is present. However, as cities are constantly changing, studios by their nature are temporary; they exist in a specific time and place. Even if the place continues as a studio, it is constantly changing as artists come and go, or artworks transform. Thus, as I recognize the temporariness of studios, I propose that a studio is a liminal space (Shields, 2022). I consider liminality as a threshold, or being in a state of in-betweenness. The in-between can refer to a time, a place, or a way of being. The studio remains active through the in-progress artworks that may transport us elsewhere (Sandra Meigs, 2014) and create a parallel universe (David Elliott, 2015) or through the potentials for multiple universes to be generated (Carol Wainio, 2014). Therefore, viewing the studio as a liminal space prompted me to view this state of in-between-ness not as a negative, or something to be overcome, but instead as a space to dwell in, to embrace. Perhaps liminality is the inherent quality of a studio; it is impermanent by nature. A studio is a messy place, a room in an old building. But if we look closer, we can see that it is filled with wormholes and portals that may take us elsewhere (Andrea Kastner, 2014). These portals allow us to embrace liminality, not as a stagnant moment, a space between a before and after, but instead as a moment that allows us to imagine other possibilities. Through this lens, a studio is a temporary and imaginative occupying of space. Similarly, to engage with educational spaces as studios is to recognize their liminality, as places that exist in a particular time and place. This lens of a studio classroom recognizes that classrooms are also, by nature, constantly in flux. As new students inhabit the space and bring their own experiences, perspectives, and artistic approaches into the space, they continuously re-activate and transform it. The liminality of the studio embraces the process of learning, as an ever-changing ecosystem. Further, liminality embraces being present and responsive in a current moment.

Thus, I return to the discussion of speculative pedagogy as described by Ellsworth (2005) in relation to places that act as hinges: 'What places are capable of acting as this moment's "hinge?" What environments and experiences are capable of acting as the pedagogical pivot point between movement/sensation and thought?' (p. 8). Through examining the experience of learning, she asks: 'What is an experience of the learning self?' (p. 8). Ellsworth contends that through examining architectural spaces as places of learning, she is not proposing a model or an example. Instead, she presents an argument for considering them for their potential as 'speculative pedagogy', as places that prompt us to think differently about learning.

> Creating room for speculation enables an educator to explore her understanding of the places in which people encounter enjoyable learning experiences and the means through which she, as an educator, could imagine making and using such places … My intention is to open up such an area of speculation about pedagogy.
>
> (p. 9)

Through 'speculative pedagogy', I invite readers to re-imagine education through the lens of studio inquiry in a way that embraces the materiality, relationality, and messiness of learning. Coats (2023) suggests that curiosity may push back against established structures within education:

> As a pedagogical force, vital curiosity creates a radical tendency to test the pliability and porosity of established boundaries through direct and embodied experimentation (Mitchell, 2013). Learning through curious experimentation creates an intensive drive toward complexity and change.
>
> (p. 22)

For her, curiosity may activate questions rather than answers and move towards uncertainty and 'the creative and emergent energy of curious indeterminacy' (p. 24). Through this curious lens, 'storytelling becomes a creative method of remaking reality in all its actuality, but in such a way that curiosity makes visible what was hiding in plain sight' (p. 26). Through curiosity, the studio as a never-ending painting continues to expand outward. Thus, I end this book by discussing how propositions are a pedagogical positioning of curiosity within a particular moment in time and space that embraces openness rather than closure.

Propositions, Being Present, Resisting Closure, and Inviting Curiosity

Throughout the four sections of the book, I have examined studios as spaces of learning through four lenses: place; time and process; materiality; and dialogue with the world. Throughout these sections, I have gone more into depth into these four categories as I examine the role of not knowing, affect, the body, imagination, relationality, and conversation within studio practices and, in turn, studio classrooms. These four sections are not meant to be read as separate and distinct categories, but instead through how they interact with each other to foster a creative and ever-changing ecosystem. Moreover, I propose that through recognizing and embracing the material quality of the place of making, we may stand in resistance to efficiency and objective-driven education systems, even if for a moment. Thus, I encourage artist-researchers, educators, and students alike to dwell within the studio, and through doing so, dwell within the learning process, within the affect, messiness, and uncertainties that come with it. Further, I propose that propositions provoke us to embrace the particularities of the place and time of artmaking and respond within this current moment. In this way, I view propositional thinking as a connector between artmaking, teaching, and research all of which, for me are grounded in studio inquiry.

For art educators, Lee et al. (2024), propositions are a way of grounding art, teaching, and research within lived experience through generative and open-ended processes that encourage readers to engage with them through their own creative lens. Rather than conclusions or fixed outcomes, propositions are a prompt and curricular invitation for examining our own approaches, cultivating relationships, and engaging with the world differently (Lee et al., 2024). They say: 'Propositions such as these act as "lures for feeling" (Whitehead, 1978, p. 25) that linger in an experience that is in between what is perceived and what is yet-to-be perceived' (p. 7). While they address walking to examine learning within a particular time and place, I propose that a studio similarly be viewed as a 'pedagogical event' (Lee et al., 2024). Through the pedagogical event of artmaking, propositions emphasize sensory, embodied, and affective experiences, as well as connections generated through making. This inquiry-based approach views 'propositions as speculative, event-oriented, and occur in the immediate present context of the inquirer' and as 'imaginings, invitations to be altered and adjusted at the moment, and invite us to build new adventures that are pedagogical despite status quo understandings of how one comes to know' (Irwin et al., 2024, p. 5). Through propositions, the work of Lee et al. (2019) 'investigates what matters to one's life and interrogates questions through a pursuit of personally meaningful, fragmentary, situated and embodied understanding(s)' (p. 682). As such, propositions are active rather than fixed, responsive rather than conclusive. Lee et al. reinforce how propositions are about being present to the unanticipated through three lenses: 'being present to possibility'; 'being present in-between place and relationality'; and 'being present to interiority' (2019, p. 681). I take up their call to 'be present' as an active and generative proposition for studio inquiry.

Drawing from Irwin et al. (2024) and Lee et al.'s (2019) discussion of propositions for walking and learning, I posit that the act of being present within learning spaces may be a form of resistance within education. Through their personal situatedness, propositions resist closure and fixed conclusions and instead promote generative and emergent thinking. To be present within artmaking, learning and researching is to reject pre-planned directions and outcomes. Instead, it promotes being responsive within the place, time, process, and materiality of that moment and generating a dialogue of our lived experience with the world. Through examining the studio through the lens of propositions, we may shift the focus from one of outcomes towards one of process. Furthermore, through my studio visit research methodology, I similarly embraced the particularities and situatedness of artistic inquiry within the materiality of the studio. Thus, I propose that artists and art educators may embrace propositional thinking as a way of resisting closure and conclusion and instead embrace artmaking as a way of being responsive to the time, place, and emergent dialogue within that moment along with all the uncertainties, sensations, and affects that emerge therein. Moreover, I propose that propositional thinking fosters learning for understanding, learning for relationality, learning for dialogue, and most importantly learning for questioning.

Propositions are an invitation for studio inquiry that is drawn from one's own personal lens and approach. Rather than conclusions which offer fixed and directed approaches to thinking and learning, propositions allow for openness. Propositions prompt the generation of more propositions. They highlight the endless possibilities and entanglements of making within the ever-changing ecology of the studio. Within my studio practice and studio teaching, and drawing from the conversations discussed in this book, I engage with the following propositions: Allow the ecologies of the studio to emerge and evolve through making and conversation; Embrace the slowness of time to dwell within wonder, messiness, and curiosity; Re-imagine the world as if being inside studio. I end this book with a final, yet generative proposition drawn from a studio visit with artist, Landon Mackenzie. During our visit, Mackenzie reflected on her artistic ecosystem through the interconnections between artists. Through considering how artists learn from each other within a community, she described how this community allows the work to remain active and in dialogue. '*So, the work goes on to have another life. I've always said that the work is a template for the imagination of the next person.*' This proposition is a powerful way of looking at the relational and ecological quality of studio practice. Through this lens, our practices exist within the past, present, and future and engage with a vast and intertwined ecosystem of making.

References

Ackerman, F. (2012). *Heterotopia: A paper trail to Foucault*. Fiona Ackerman. https://www.fionaackerman.com/heterotopia-2012

Atkinson, D. (2013). Pedagogy of the not known. In E. Fisher & R. Fortnum (Eds.), *On not knowing: How artists think* (pp. 136–145). Black Dog Publishing.

Ayliffe, M., & Mieves, C. (2016). Dirty practice: A painting workshop and the hidden curriculum. In I. Hartshorne, D. Moloney, & M. Quaife (Eds.), *Teaching painting: How can painting be taught in art schools?* (pp. 52–57). Black Dog Publishing.

Bachelard, G. (1957/2014). *Poetics of space*. Beacon Press. (Original work published 1964).

Baldacchino, J. (2018). Weak subjects: On art's art of forgetting – An interview with John Baldacchino by Gert Biesta. In C. Naughton, G. Biesta, & D. Cole (Eds.), *Art, artists and pedagogy: Philosophy and the arts in education* (pp. 137–146). Routledge.

Baldacchino, J. (2019). *Art as unlearning: Towards a mannerist pedagogy*. Routledge.

Barad, K. (2007). *Meeting the university halfway: Quantum physics and the entanglement of matter and meaning*. Duke University Press.

Barrett, E. (2007a). Introduction. In E. Barrett & B. Bolt (Eds.), *Practice as research: Approaches to creative arts enquiry* (pp. 1–13). I.B. Tauris & Co Ltd.

Barrett, E. (2007b). Studio enquiry and the new frontiers of research. *Studies in Material Thinking*, *1*(1), 1–3.

Barrett, E. (2013). Materiality, affect, and the aesthetic image. In E. Barrett & B. Bolt (Eds.), *Carnal knowledge: Towards a 'new materialism' through the arts* (pp. 63–72). I.B. Tauris.

Bennett, J. (2010). *Vibrant matter: A political ecology of things*. Duke University Press.

Biesta, G. (2018). What if?: Art education beyond expression and creativity. In C. Naughton, G. Biesta, & D. Cole (Eds.), *Art, artists and pedagogy: Philosophy and the arts in education* (pp. 11–20). Routledge.

Bolt, B. (2004). *Art beyond representation: The performative power of the image*. I.B. Tauris.

Bolt, B. (2007). The magic is in the handling. In E. Barrett & B. Bolt (Eds.), *Practice as research: Approaches to creative arts enquiry* (pp. 27–34). I.B. Tauris.

Bolt, B. (2013). Toward a new materialism through the arts. In E. Barrett & B. Bolt (Eds.), *Carnal knowledge: Towards a 'new materialism' through the arts* (pp. 1–13). I.B. Tauris.

Bolt, B. (2016). Artistic research: A performative paradigm. *Parse Journal*, *3*, 129–142.

Brennan, G. (2016). Teaching painting at Edinburgh College of Art: An awkward period of self-reflection and identity crisis, work in progress. In I. Hartshorne, D. Moloney, & M. Quaife (Eds), *Teaching painting: How can painting be taught in art schools?* (pp. 17–22). Black Dog Publishing.

Buren, D. (1979). The function of the studio. *October, 10*, 51–58.

Canada Council for the Arts (2016). *Wanda Koop*. https://www.youtube.com/watch?v=RoL2tT5b_jE

Carter, P. (2004). *Material thinking*. Melbourne University Press.

Clay, A., & Warland, B. (2015). Oscar, Part 30. Betsy Warland. http://www.betsywarland.com/oscar-part-30/

Coats, C. (2023). *New materialisms and embodied encounters in education: Curiosity's vital potential*. Bloomsbury.

Cocker, E. (2013). Tactics for not knowing: Preparing for the unexpected. In E. Fisher & R. Fortnum (Eds.), *On not knowing: How artists think* (pp. 126–145). Black Dog Publishing.

Cole, M., & Pardo, M. (2005). *Inventions of the studio, Renaissance to Romanticism*. University of North Carolina Press.

Dunne, E. (2016). Learning to unlearn. In A. Seery & E. Dunne (Eds.), *The pedagogies of unlearning* (pp. 13–24). Punktum Books.

Elkins, J. (1997). *The object stares back: On the nature of seeing*. Harcourt Brace.

Ellsworth, E. (2005). *Places of learning: Media, architecture, pedagogy*. Routledge.

Fisher, E., & Fortnum, R. (2013). *On not knowing: How artists think*. Black Dog Publishing.

Fogle, D. (2001). The trouble with painting. In D. Fogle (Ed.), *Painting at the edge of the world* (pp. 9–25). Walker Art Center.

Fortnum, R. (2008). *Introduction to symposium* On not knowing: How artists think. University of the Arts London.

Fortnum, R. (2013). Creative accounting: Not knowing in talking and making. In E. Fisher & R. Fortnum (Eds.), *On not knowing: How artists think*. Black Dog Publishing.

Garber, E. (2019). Objects and new materialisms: A journey across making and living with objects. *Studies in Art Education, 60*(1), 7–21.

Garoian, C. (2008). Verge of collapse: The pros/thesis of art research. *Studies in Art Education, 49*(3), 218–234.

Garoian, C. (2013). *The prosthetic pedagogy of art*. State University of New York Press.

Garoian, C. (2015). Performing *The Refrain* of art's prosthetic pedagogy. *Qualitative Inquiry, 21*(6), 487–493.

Granat, A. (2010). 1107. In M. Jacob & M. Grabner (Eds.), *The studio reader: On the space of artists* (pp. 259–260). The University of Chicago Press.

Gueray, U. (2017). *Peasants and squares*. Presented at University Art Association of Canada, Annual Conference, Banff, Alberta, Canada.

Hamilton, A. (2009). Making not knowing. In M. J. Jacob & J. Baas (Eds.), *Learning mind: Experience into art* (pp. 67–74). University of California Press.

Hannula, M., Suoranta, J., & Vadén, T. (2014). *Artistic research methodology: Narrative, power and the public*. Peter Lang.

Harris, D. (2021). *Creative agency*. Palgrave Macmillan.

Hickey-Moody, A., & Page, T. (Eds.). (2015). *Arts, pedagogy and cultural resistance*. Rowman & Littlefield.

Hofstadter, D. (2007). *I am a strange loop*. Basic Books.

Ingold, T. (2022). *Imagining for real: Essays on creation, attention and correspondence*. Routledge.

Inuit Art Quarterly (n.d.). https://www.inuitartfoundation.org/profiles/artist/Mark-Igloliorte

Irwin, R. L. (2013). Becoming a/r/tography. *Studies in Art Education*, *54*(3), 198–215.

Irwin, R. L., Lee, N., Baldus, A. Barney, D., Ursino, J., & Valiary Eskandary, Z. (Eds.). (2024). *Pedagogical propositions: Playful walking with a/r/tography, book three: Curriculum*. InSEA Publications.

Jacques, M. (2022). Moving towards loving painting again, or Dear Denyse. In R. van der Avoird, S. Frater, & M. Jacques. *Denyse Thomasos: Just beyond* (pp. 68–84). DelMonico Books/Art Gallery of Ontario/Remai Modern.

Jones, R. (2013). On the value of not knowing: Wonder, beginning again and letting be. In E. Fisher & R. Fortnum (Eds.), *On not knowing: How artists think* (pp. 16–31). Black Dog Publishing.

Kearney, R. (2014). Introduction. In G. Bachelard, *Poetics of space* (pp. xvii–xxiii). Beacon Press.

Kentridge, W. (2016). *No it is*. Walther Konig, Koln; Har/Psc edition.

Kind, S. (2018). Collective improvisations: The emergence of the early childhood studio as an event-full place. In C. Schulte & M. Thompson (Eds.), *Communities of practice: Art, play and aesthetics in early childhood* (pp. 5–21). Springer.

Kleinman, A. (2012). Intra-actions (interview with Karen Barad). *Mousse Magazine*, *34*, 76–81.

Lee, N., Irwin, R. L., Baldus, A., Barney, D., Ursino, J., & Valiary Eskandary, Z. (Eds.). (2024). *Pedagogical propositions: Playful walking with a/r/tography, book one: Encounters*. InSEA Publications.

Lee, N., Morimoto, K., Mosavarzadeh, M., & Irwin, R. L. (2019). Walking propositions: Coming to know a/r/tographically. *International Journal of Art & Design Education*, *38*(3), 681–690.

Lippard, L. (1998). *The lure of the local*. The New Press.

Loveless, N. (2019). *How to make art at the end of the world: A manifesto for research-creation*. Duke University Press.

Manning, E. (2009). Taking the next step: Touch as technique. *Senses and Society*, *4*(2), 211–226.

Manning, E. (2016a). Ten propositions for research-creation. In N. Colin & S. Sachsenmaier (Eds.), *Collaboration in performative practice: Premises, workings and failures* (pp. 133–141). Palgrave Macmillan.

Manning, E. (2016b). *The minor gesture*. Duke University Press.

Mavor, C. (2013). *Blue mythologies: Reflections on a colour*. Reaktion Books.

McClenaghan, J. (2016). Against production. In I. Hartshorne, D. Moloney, & M. Quaife (Eds.), *Teaching painting: How can painting be taught in art schools?* (pp. 32–36). Black Dog Publishing.

Mehretu, J. (2016). Notes on painting. In I. Graw & E. Lajer-Burcharth (Eds.), *Painting beyond itself: The medium in the post-medium condition* (pp. 271–277). Sternberg Press.

Munro, S. (2022). Tracing the minor gesture in painting: A shift from reflection to diffraction. *Journal of Art Practice, 21*(3), 241–257.

Nasgaard, R. (2008). *Abstract painting in Canada*. Douglas and McIntyre.

Nemiroff, D. (2009). *Sandra Meigs: Strange loop*. Carleton University Art Gallery.

O'Donoghue, D. (2015). The turn to experience in contemporary art: A potentiality for thinking art education differently. *Studies in Art Education, 56*(2), 103–113.

O'Sullivan, S. (2001). The aesthetics of affect: Thinking art beyond representation. *Journal of Theoretical Humanities, 6*(3), 125–135.

O'Sullivan, S. (2006). *Art encounters Deleuze and Guattari: Thought beyond representation*. Palgrave MacMillan.

O'Sullivan, S. (2010). From aesthetics to the abstract machine: Deleuze, Guattari and contemporary art practice. In S. Zepke & S. O'Sullivan (Eds.), *Deleuze and contemporary art* (pp. 189–207). Edinburgh University Press.

O'Sullivan, S. (2016). Myth-science and the fictioning to myth-science. *Paragrana, 25*(2), 80–93.

Ontario Heritage Trust (n.d.). Doris McCarthy artist-in-residence program. https://www.heritagetrust.on.ca/dmair

Payne, A. (2016). On painting: The discipline, interdisciplinarity and disciplinarity. In I. Hartshorne, D. Moloney, & M. Quaife (Eds.), *Teaching painting: How can painting be taught in art schools?* (pp. 23–30). Black Dog Publishing.

Perez de Miles, A., & Kalin, N. (2018). Speculative realism(s) objects/matter/entanglements of art and design education. *International Journal of Education Through Art, 14*(1), 3–12.

Rancieres, G. (2016). Un-What? In A. Seery & E. Dunne (Eds.), *The pedagogies of unlearning* (pp. 25–46). Punktum Books.

Relyea, L. (2010). Studio unbound. In J. Hoffmann (Ed.), *The studio* (pp. 218–223). MIT Press.

Richardson, J. (2011). Materiality of space. In P. Bolin & D. Blandy (Eds.), *Matter matters: Art education and material culture studies* (pp. 3–11). The National Art Education Association.

Richardson, J. (2013). Time unhinged. *Visual Arts Research, 39*(1), 90–107.

Roy, K. (2024). *Myth, mystery, and the magic of art education: Beyond the artifact*. Palgrave Macmillan.

Ryden, J. (2014). Painting in the gravitational field. In K. Bength, J. Habib Engqvist, J. Ryden, & S. Sandstrom (Eds.), *Studio talks: Thinking through painting* (pp. 36–49). Arvinius & Orfeus.

Schneemann, C. (2010). The studio, June 22, 2009. In M. Jacob & M. Grabner (Eds.), *The studio reader: On the space of artists* (pp. 154–155). The University of Chicago Press.

Sillman, A. (2016). On colour. In I. Graw & E. Lajer-Burcharth (Eds.), *Painting beyond itself: The medium in the post-medium condition* (pp. 103–118). Sternberg Press.

Sillman, A. (2020). *Faux pas: Selected writings and drawings*. After 8 books.

Sjoholm, J. (2013). *The role of the art studio in contemporary artistic production*. CIND Centre for Research on Innovation and Industrial Dynamics.

Solnit, R. (2006). *A field guide to getting lost*. Penguin Books.

Springgay, S. (2022). *Feltness: Research-creation, socially engaged art, and affective pedagogies*. Duke University Press.

Springgay, S., & Truman, S. (2016). Propositions for walking research. In K. Powell, P. Burnard, & L. Mackinlay (Eds.), *Routledge handbook of intercultural arts* (pp. 259–267). Routledge.

Springgay, S., & Zaliwska, Z. (2015). Diagrams and cuts: A materialist approach to research-creation. *Cultural Studies: Critical Methodologies*, *15*(2), 136–144.

Sturgis, D. (2016). Condensed knowledge. In I. Hartshorne, D. Moloney, & M. Quaife (Eds.), *Teaching painting: How can painting be taught in art schools?* (pp. 10–16). Black Dog Publishing.

Thiel, J. (2018). 'A cool place where we make stuff': Co-curating relational spaces of muchness. In C. Schulte & M. Thompson (Eds.), *Communities of practice: Art, play and aesthetics in early childhood* (pp. 23–37). Springer.

Triggs, V., & Irwin, R. L. (2019). Pedagogy and the a/r/tographic invitation. In R. Hickman, J. Baldacchino, K. Freedman, E. Hall, & N. Meager (Eds.), *The international encyclopedia of art and design education*. John Wiley & Sons.

van den Boogerd, D. (2013). *Mary Heilmann: Good vibrations*. Maastricht: Bonnefantenmuseum.

Verwoert, J. (2005). *Emergence: On the painting of Tomma Abts*. David Zwirner Gallery.

von Heyl, C. (2010). Charline von Heyl. In M. Jacob & M. Grabner (Eds.), *The studio reader: On the space of artists* (pp. 125–126). The University of Chicago Press.

Wainwright, L. (2010). Foreword. In M. J. Jacob & M. Grabner (Eds.), *The studio reader* (p. ix). The University of Chicago Press.

Walker Art Center (producer) (2013). *Jan Verwoert: Painting in the present tense*. https://www.youtube.com/watch?v=scYj-bDEaKI&t=2137

Welish, M. (2010). The studio revisited. In M. Jacob & M. Grabner (Eds.), *The studio reader: On the space of artists* (pp. 181–192). The University of Chicago Press.

West, A. (2011). *Mapping the intelligence of artistic work*. Moth Press. http://www.judithwesterveld.nl/text/FINAL%20VERSION%20THESIS%20(compressed).pdf

Wood, C. (2005). Indoor-outdoor: The studio around 1500. In M. Cole & M. Pardo (Eds.), *Inventions of the studio, renaissance to romanticism* (pp. 36–71). University of North Carolina Press.

Studio Visits

Adam Gunn, Halifax, NS, August 21, 2014.
Alex Livingston, Halifax, NS, November 9, 2015.
Alexis Lavoie, Montreal, QC, August 28, 2014, October 10, 2015.
Allyson Clay, Vancouver, BC, June 12, 2015.
Andrea Kastner, Kamloops, BC, July 10, 2014, Hamilton, March 24, 2016.
Angela Teng, Vancouver, BC, June 9, 2015.
Art Green, Stratford, ON, November 21, 2015.
Ashleigh Bartlett, Calgary, AB, July 14, 2014, Toronto, September 28, 2015.
Ben Reeves, Vancouver, BC, July 9, 2014.
Carly Butler, Halifax, NS, August 22, 2014, November 10, 2015.
Carol Wainio, Ottawa, ON, September 3, 2014.
Chris Cran, Calgary, AB, July 13, 2014.
Chris Millar, Calgary, AB, July 15, 2014.
Christine Major, Montreal, QC, October 18, 2015.
Colin Dorward, Halifax, NS, October 26, 2014, London, October 28, 2015.
Colleen Heslin Montreal, QC, November 21, 2014, Vancouver, June 10, 2015.
Cynthia Girard, Montreal, QC, August 27, 2014.
Daniel Hutchinson, Hamilton, ON, July 25, 2014, November 20, 2015, April 15, 2016.
DaveandJenn, Calgary, AB, July 12, 2014.
David Elliott, Montreal, QC, October 15, 2015.
David Blatherwick, Elora, ON, August 4, 2014, July 21, 2016.
David Kaarsemaker, Ottawa, ON, September 2, 2014.
Dil Hildebrand, Montreal, QC, August 25, 2014, October 19, 2015.
Doug Kirton, Kitchener, ON, August 4, 2014.
Ehryn Torrell, London, UK, April 21, 2016, Toronto, ON, July 7, 2016.
Eleanor Bond, Winnipeg, MN, June 25, 2015.
Eliza Griffiths, Montreal, QC, August 28, 2014, October 19, 2015.
Elizabeth McIntosh, Vancouver, BC, March 2, 2016.
Erica Mendritzki, Winnipeg, MN, July 19, 2014, June 27, 2015.
Fiona Ackerman, Vancouver, BC, June 23, 2014, May 31, 2015.

Gary Evans, Barrie, ON, April 13, 2016.
Gavin Lynch, Ottawa, ON, September 1, 2014.
Gwenessa Lam, Vancouver, BC, May 23, 2015.
Holger Kalberg, Winnipeg, MN, July 18, 2014.
Ian August, Winnipeg, MN, July 21, 2014.
James Gardner, Toronto, ON, October 17, 2014, August 24, 2015.
Janet Werner, Montreal, QC, August 26, 2014, October 13, 2015.
Jennifer Carvahlo, Toronto, ON, August 2, 2014, December 7, 2015.
Jennifer Lefort, Gatineau, QC, September 4, 2014, August 21, 2015.
Jeremy Hof, Vancouver, BC, June 6, 2015.
Jessica Groome, Toronto, ON, September 17, 2014, October 24, 2015, Berlin, June 15, 2016.
Jinny Yu, Ottawa, ON, September 2, 2014.
John Armstrong, Toronto, ON, December 11, 2015.
John Brown, Toronto, ON, August 8, 2014.
John Kissick, Elora, ON, August 5, 2014, July 21, 2016.
John Will, Calgary, AB, July 14, 2014.
Jordy Hamilton, Vancouver, BC, June 25, 2014.
Julie Trudel, Halifax, NS, November 8, 2015.
Katie Lyle, Toronto, ON, September 25, 2015.
Kent Monkman, Toronto, ON, November 24, 2015.
Kim Dorland, Toronto, ON, September 10, 2014.
Kym Greely, St. John's, NL, August 11, 2014, November 14, 2015.
Laura Findlay, Toronto, ON, September 23, 2014.
Laura Millard, Toronto, ON, August 25, 2015.
Linda Martinello, Toronto, ON, August 8, 2014.
Maegan Harbridge, Guelph, ON, September 26, 2014.
Mark Mullin, Calgary, AB, July 12, 2014.
Mark Neufeld, Winnipeg, MN, July 22, 2014, June 23, 2015.
Martin Golland, Ottawa, ON, August 17, 2015.
Mary Pratt, St. John's, NL, November 12, 2015.
Mathew Reischertz, Halifax, NS, August 21, 2014, November 8, 201.
Melanie Authier, Ottawa, ON, August 17, 2015.
Mitchell Wiebe, Halifax, NS, August 17, 2014.
Monica Tap, Toronto, ON, July 30, 2014, September 4, 2015.
Patrick Cruz, Guelph, ON, October 8, 2015.
Patrick Howlett, London, ON, August 7, 2014, November 17, 2015, April 14, 2016.
Pearl Van Geest, Guelph, ON, August 5, 2014.
Philippa Jones, St. John's, NL, August 12, 2014, November 13, 2015.
Rebecca Brewer, Vancouver, BC, June 15, 2015.
Renee Van Halm, Vancouver, BC, June 2, 2015.

Rick Leong, Victoria, BC, July 4, 2014.
Robert Taite, Winnipeg, MN, July 20, 2014.
Ryan Peters, Vancouver, BC, June 25, 2014, June 1, 2015.
Sandra Meigs, Victoria, BC, July 3, 2014, June 18, 2015.
Sara Hartland-Rowe, Halifax, NS, November 10, 2015.
Sarah Cale, Toronto, ON, December 7, 2015.
Suzanne Fennell, Halifax, NS, August 8, 2014.
Ufuk Gueray, Winnipeg, MN, July 19, 2014, June 27, 2015.
Van Maltese, Toronto, ON, August 6, 2014, April 8, 2016.
Will Gill, St. John's, NL, August 12, 2014, November 14, 2015.

Index of Artists